'It's a legal thriller, a murder mystery, a social com... ...ory and a travelogue of the most sensational court case of the past decade. It is exhaustively researched, beautifully written, totally mesmerising and absolutely riveting. My wife is reading it now – I'll have to fix my own dinner for the next few nights.'
Deon Meyer, author of *Blood Safari* and *Thirteen Hours*

'*Fruit of a Poisoned Tree* is an important contribution to understanding the textures and dynamics of important aspects of South African culture as well as of the machinations of the criminal justice system. Altbeker excels in his relentless and meticulous re-arguing of the Lotz murder case, painstakingly picking through evidence and testimonies, like a latter-day Sherlock Holmes, and bringing into play not only an astute judgment of facts and character, but also offering a compelling analysis of the degeneration of the investigative prowess of South Africa's law enforcers. It is a chilling revelation of the rotten state of the administrative capacity and of the professional bankruptcy of policing in South Africa.

'This is obligatory reading for those interested in the current state of the nation. It reads like a thriller and is utterly un-put-down-able. It leaves the reader with serious food for thought. It almost convinces one that fiction has become redundant in this country.'
Marlene van Niekerk, author of *Agaat* and *Triomf*

'Altbeker's account of the Inge Lotz murder trial is both shocking and riveting. It is also beautifully written.'
Peter Harris, author of *In a Different Time*

'South African literature has not seen true crime of this standard for a very long time. Antony Altbeker has married an expert's knowledge of the criminal justice system with a storyteller's flair for narrative and suspense. The result is a book that provides rare insight into the often compromised nature of our courts, yet reads like a high-voltage thriller. If you thought you knew something about the Inge Lotz murder trial, Altbeker has come, like a master decoder, to disabuse you of that notion.'
Kevin Bloom, journalist, editor and author of *Ways of Staying*

'Altbeker has established himself as a genuine authority on our crime pandemic.'
James Mitchell, *The Star*

Fruit of a Poisoned Tree

A true story of murder and the miscarriage of justice

Antony Altbeker

JONATHAN BALL PUBLISHERS
Johannesburg & Cape Town

Published in trade paperback in 2010 by
JONATHAN BALL PUBLISHERS (PTY) LTD
PO Box 33977
Jeppestown
2043

Reprinted once in 2010

ISBN 978-1-86842-333-0

Cover design by Michiel Botha, Cape Town
Text design by Triple M Design, Johannesburg
Set in 11/16 pt Minion Pro
Printed and bound by CTP Book Printers, Cape

FOR JACKIE, MIA, BEN AND GEORGIA
My north and south, my east and west

Likewise every good tree bears good fruit,
but a bad tree bears bad fruit.
A good tree cannot bear bad fruit,
and a bad tree cannot bear good fruit.
Thus, by their fruit you will recognise them.

MATTHEW 7:17–20

PROLOGUE

The video begins with a shot of a doormat and the bottom quarter of a door. A muffled, off-screen voice says in Afrikaans, 'It is March 17, 2005. The video operator is Inspector Desmond Share. I am at Klein Welgevonden Estate, 21 Shiraz, Stellenbosch. The video begins.'

Two shadowed legs move into frame. A hand swings the door open to the right, and a shaft of light falls onto a doormat before the camera bounces into the room. The cameraman steps over a yellow strip of plastic bearing the blue-printed legend 'South African Police Service: Do not cross'.

We are in a small kitchen of plastic-coated, processed wood. As the camera turns to the left, before it pauses on the empty sink and the kitchen counter on which lie a pair of sunglasses, a set of car keys and a cellphone, before it is pointed into a half-opened straw basket in which we see something indistinct (a book or a large envelope, perhaps), before it scans the walls and curtains of the living areas beyond the kitchen, before it does all that, it captures a tangle of hair hanging over the arm of a small sofa. From the doorway, it looks like a young woman, having fallen asleep watching the television set in the corner, is lying on a light-coloured couch, her legs curled up in front of her.

The woman doesn't move as the cameraman goes about his business.

The camera turns to the kitchen, exploring it intrusively, forensically.

A drying rack contains a single plate and mug. An oven glove hangs squarely, inch-perfect in the middle of the oven's horizontal handle. Pressed neatly against the wall are a kettle and two bouquets of plastic kitchen implements sprouting from matching stands. It is a compact space, and the housekeeping is prompt and conscientious.

A waist-high counter separates the kitchen from the lounge. When the camera turns in that direction, we see, once again, the tangled hair of the woman on the couch away to our right. Another couch, dark blue with red cushions, has its back to us. There are also two uncomfortable-looking wooden chairs with high back- and armrests. Between the woman and the TV set in the corner, a small coffee table with a pile of books and magazines stands in its shadow on a carpet. A black DVD cover lies empty and splayed on top of the books and magazines. On the wall to the left hangs a painting that appears at first to be an abstract of a human head but which turns out to be an unremarkable image of a vase and flowers. Below it stands a pot plant, dark and green and healthy-looking.

A decorative bunch of dried grass bristles in a corner on the far side of the couch on which the woman lies. On this side of the couch, between it and the camera, a cloth-covered side table is home to framed photos of family and friends along with a small glass dish of sweets. In a moment, the camera will reveal that the sweets, the carpet, the coffee table and some of the walls are spotted with blood. These spots, a police forensic expert would testify nearly two years later, sprayed from the woman's head 'as if from a fountain' when she was struck by the blows that killed her; they did not fly off from the weapon as it was swung.

An unnecessary detail? Perhaps. But it is one that has its ramifications.

* * *

The flat's rooms are conservative and plain, a little characterless even. They belong to someone of quiet, conventional tastes or to someone whose tastes have not yet developed. And it may be this seemliness, this unquestioning obedience to the conventions of the middle class, that makes so overwhelming the sight of the woman's bloodied body.

She lies on a couch with her head resting in the crook between its puffed-up backrest and its padded arm, her face turned towards the wall to her right. She is wearing a sleeveless yellow vest and satiny sleeping shorts. Her legs are open but the soles of her feet touch each other almost from heel to toe, with the heels tucked into the gap where the two cushions of the couch meet. Her left hand rests lightly on her thigh, the right lies across her stomach. It is a pose that will be described by the pathologist as being typical of someone who has died after massive trauma to the brain. In life, wakeful and dressed in these clothes, her pose would have seemed indecent, incongruous in so conservative a home.

But she is not alive.

The woman's upper body is a picture of suffering. Her face is a black mask of gore. Hair that would have flowed in life is matted by dried blood. Blood has pooled, too, above the hand that rests across her stomach. Her forehead is all but crushed, and its flesh has been torn away, allowing matter, hideous and dark, to seep out. Later, when the police find the hammer they believe caused this wound, they will demonstrate that possibility by burying it deep in the skull of a sheep. In the post-mortem report, the effect of the wounds is conveyed as the pathologist's very first finding: '*Kop pap as gevolg van stompgeweld.*'

Head pulped as a result of blunt-force violence.

Moving away from her head, the camera shows other wounds to the woman's neck and upper torso. Exposed to the camera, these are a mess of caked blood and puncture wounds of varying breadth and depth. Such was the power of the blows, the pathologist will note, that the blade sheared through two ribs. The woman's left ear, on which the camera focuses after pausing again on the wounds to the head, appears to have been ripped in half. Other wounds on her hands and arms, small and innocuous-looking in comparison to the rest, suggest that she may have tried to ward off at least some of the blows that rained down on her.

Cataloguing all of these injuries, the pathologist will speculate that the blunt-force injuries to the woman's head were the first blows struck. She will say that blood in the woman's lungs, the foam on her lips and the defensive wounds to her hands and arms show that she lived through the initial beating and perhaps even some of the stabbing. She will not say, because she will not know, how conscious the woman was of what was happening to her. Nor will she say which was the killing blow: there are too many possibilities.

* * *

The camera moves again.

Now it focuses on blood that has pooled on the floor beneath the hair hanging over the arm of the couch. It focuses on fluids that have soaked into the couch and oozed into the depression caused by the weight of the woman's torso, staining a blanket beneath her thighs. It focuses, too, on splatter marks on and below the coffee table, as well as spots of blood on the wall above the couch. Some of these are metres from their source, the distance a gauge of the violence of the assault.

At last, the camera leaves the woman to follow a trail of dark droplets away from her body and towards a bathroom. Light from that room spills through the door onto the tiled floor.

In the bathroom, our attention is drawn to the window above the bath. It is opened slightly, but – and this is the point – there are security bars and they are intact. Tilting downwards, the camera's next stop is a white towel lying on the floor, crumpled and bloody. As it zooms in, long strands of hair become visible in the blood. Next to the towel is a red mark, small and sharply defined. Shaped like an angry scorpion, the mark is perhaps four centimetres long. When the time comes, debate about its significance will consume days of court time. Before that happens, it will engage the interest of some of the world's leading forensic experts in Cape Town and Pretoria, in England and the United States.

Stepping over and around the towel and the scorpion mark, the camera is pointed into the basin, where it reveals more loose hairs and bloody stains. Then it explores another towel, this one still hanging on its rack. It, too, has been used to clean gore off hands and, perhaps, a weapon.

The cameraman stands on the foot pedal of a small dustbin, and its raised lid reveals its treasure: a crumpled tissue or two. The lid closes with an incongruous clang, the sound loud and hollow on the video's hissing audio track.

Outside the bathroom, we move into a small study, a room that seems less ordered than the lounge and kitchen would have led one to expect. Textbooks and pens and notebooks are piled willy-nilly on a small desk whose drawers are not all properly closed. A laptop computer, on which the camera lingers meaningfully, sits at an angle on the desk, a corner hanging over the open space below. On the floor, a pencil lies next to an ugly knot of wires. Untidy though the room is, its disorder is of a kind that you would associate with a student rather than a burglar.

There is little else in the room on which the camera pauses, and soon we are in a bedroom: white and clean, with teddy bears reclining on a comfortable chair. A cupboard door is open and, reflected in the mirror that hangs within, we see the cameraman for a moment: an alien presence.

This room is neater than the last. The bed – a modest single – is made, its white bedspread pulled evenly across it. A bookshelf is packed as if for military inspection. The cosmetics revealed on the shelves of the open cupboard are neatly stowed. The one anomaly is that the bed is at an angle to the wall, its foot having been pulled away, leaving a space of perhaps 30 or 40 centimetres. It is impossible to guess why this might be so, or whether it is in any way related to the violence that took place in the lounge. Nor is there any way to know if the half-open suitcase on the floor, from which clothes spill, was disturbed by the killer.

Focusing on that bag, the camera zooms onto a label, so that a name and address become visible. INGE LOTZ, it reads, giving also an address and phone number in Welgemoed, Cape Town. Moments later, as the camera focuses on framed photographs on the wall, a pretty face with fair hair, dark eyebrows and a wide smile is put to the name. In one picture, the woman stands alone in an evening dress, a picture of a certain bare-shouldered, girlish sophistication. Other people appear with her in more photos. They are young and happy, all smiles and arms draped over shoulders.

We are nearly done: the final shots of the video are of the body in the lounge.

The cameraman says, 'The time is 1:23.' The screen goes blue.

* * *

It is impossible to see the video and refrain from formulating a story, to search for the meaning of the bare facts it depicts, to read it as one might a text.

What are we supposed to make of the unbroken security bars and the unstolen valuables, to which our attention is continually drawn? What do the woman's position and posture and clothing tell us of her final moments? In the first days of the trial, almost two years later, the neighbour who found Inge's body, one Christo Pretorius, will be recalled to the stand by the judge after having left the court and driven more than an hour across town. The judge will request his return because, when Christo first described the events of that night during his testimony, he had said that the woman he found was 'in a seated position' while the video clearly shows her almost fully reclined. Christo will be made to drive back to court to explain the discrepancy. Then, despite the witness's having specifically requested that he not be shown any pictures of the crime scene, the judge will insist he look at one to confirm that this was, indeed, how he found her.

For my part, I spend the first few days after seeing the video obsessing about incongruous details. The most intriguing of these is a remote control perched on the woman's right hip, where it rests against the cushioned backrest of the couch. It is a precarious position, and even the smallest movement would have caused it to fall into the gap between thigh and cushion. Another remote lies near her feet, within striking distance of a flailing foot. A magazine – a wholesome title, dedicated to healthy lifestyles – lies open across her feet.

I cannot understand how these things can be where they are. She would have kicked, surely. She would have twisted and thrashed around. Why have these things not fallen to the floor? Why have they not been thrown across the room?

The magazine across her feet in particular bothers me. It simply could not be there if she had been aware of the danger: her first movement would have closed it and pushed it to the floor. At most, it may have been dragged marginally closer to her when her feet slipped between the cushions of the couch, in the process pulling a white rug that had been lying across the two cushions into the gap between them.

To my layman's eye, the magazine and the remote control suggest that the dead woman must have been caught entirely unawares. One possibility is that she knew and trusted her killer, and, given her attire, may also have been on close or intimate terms with him. The other possibility is that she was asleep. That she could have been awake and aware of the presence of someone in her home whom she did not know well seems impossible: this is not how a conservative young woman would dress if there were neighbours or workmen in the house. And, indeed, this is something her mother will confirm from the witness stand. Asked by the prosecutor whether her daughter would appear before people in these clothes, she will reply, 'Not before strangers, certainly not. She would appear in those clothes before her parents, maybe her best friend, but definitely not before people who are not part of our immediate circle.'

What about her boyfriend, the judge will ask, would she walk around in her pyjamas in front of him? To this her mother will reply, more ambiguously than she probably intended: '*Nie sommer nie.*' Not just like that.

So, she was asleep or she knew her killer. Or she was asleep *and* she knew her killer. These are the only possibilities suggested by the position of her body, the unbroken security bars, the absence, in fact, of any other signs of forced entry, and the overall neatness of the flat, a neatness accentuated by the presence of valuables left untouched and the cupboards left unransacked.

What happened after the murder reflects the dangerous power of the story implicit in these details, the unstoppable force of its logic.

PART ONE

1

At about 22:30 on the night of 16 March 2005, Christo Pretorius pressed the button of 21 Shiraz. It was a small, two-bedroomed flat in a complex on a wine estate just outside Stellenbosch. Christo had met the resident of number 21, Inge Lotz, only a couple of times in church and at a local Bible-study group; he was not the sort of acquaintance who could call on her at such an hour. He made the visit, though, because he'd received a call fifteen minutes earlier from Marius Botha, a mutual friend of his and Inge's, who had asked him to look in on her. Inge, Christo had been told, had not been answering calls or responding to text messages since three in the afternoon. He was also told that her boyfriend, Marius's flatmate, was concerned enough to have set out on the thirty-minute drive up the motorway to see if she was okay.

In a sense, then, the request to Christo was redundant since Inge's boyfriend, Fred van der Vyver, was already on his way and would get there as soon as he had collected a spare key from her mother. But Fred knew that Inge had once had a nasty fall after fainting, and had struck her head, badly bruising an eye. If she'd knocked herself out this time, some urgency might be called for. If, on the other hand, she was fine and her phone was merely malfunctioning, Christo could get her to call home.

Christo buzzed Inge's flat from the gate. Then he buzzed again. There was no answer. Spotting another resident of the complex, he asked to be let in to check on a friend. The man obliged and opened the gate. Christo climbed a couple of flights of stairs and knocked on Inge's door. Again, he got no response, but, through a window, he could see that the television was on. Testing the door, he found that it was unlocked. He pushed it open and, seeing someone on the couch, he called Inge's name. Again, he got no response. He stepped into the darkened flat, its interior lit only by the electric glow of the television. Then he saw the wound to Inge's neck and the dark mess on the floor beneath her head.

His immediate thought was that Inge had killed herself and, seeing an object he took to be a knife near her hand, he thought she must have cut her own throat.

In a panic, Christo ran from the flat to find the man who'd let him into the complex and ask him to call the police. While the man did that, Christo made three other calls – one to Marius Botha, one to the pastor at the church he and Inge had attended, and, himself in need of comfort, one to his own brother. To each, his first words were that Inge had killed herself.

Having made their respective calls, Christo and the other man returned to Inge's flat to await the police.

The first officer to arrive was Captain Frans September. Entering the flat, the officer saw Inge on the couch and approached her. From the gaping wound to her forehead and the bleeding from her chest, he could see immediately that this was no suicide. He hurried back to his van to call for backup. Soon the flat was swarming with officers from across the

Cape Peninsula. Among them were ordinary cops and student constables from the Cloetesville and Stellenbosch stations, more highly trained and experienced detectives from the Serious and Violent Crimes Unit based in Bishop Lavis, fingerprint experts and photographers from Paarl, and, finally, members of the province's elite team of crime scene investigators based in Cape Town.

* * *

For a country with a murder rate that is amongst the highest in the world and which has, as both cause and consequence of this, amongst the world's lowest ratios of police officers per murder, the initial investigation into the murder of Inge Lotz was well-resourced and thorough. It is true that one of the investigators, Bruce Bartholomew, testified that an electrostatic dust-lift conducted on the carpet around the couch in the lounge had failed to find any usable shoeprints because the policemen on the scene had been 'terribly curious' and had left their own shoeprints around Inge's body. Still, by local standards, the mere fact that a dust-lift was conducted made the handling of this crime scene exceptionally unusual.

Though the dust-lift in the lounge through which his colleagues had trampled revealed nothing useful, Bartholomew had more success in the bathroom. There, beneath the basin in which bloody marks suggested the killer had washed up, his dust-lifter – a device that uses static electricity to lift otherwise invisible patterns in dust and other residues onto a strip of foil – produced the impression of a sports shoe that was clear enough to hope that it might one day be matched to the shoe that left it.

Bartholomew was not the only forensic investigator in Inge's flat that night. One of the province's most senior and most respected forensic analysts, Superintendent Johannes Kock, arrived some time after three in the morning to search the flat for any genetic material that might have been left by Inge's murderer. Trace DNA evidence of the sort Kock was looking for is usually left in one of four ways: blood from an attacker's injuries, semen from sexual contact, naturally lost hair, and spittle left on cigarette *stompies*. In the absence of *stompies*, Kock's search focused on bloodstains that were not obviously Inge's and on any surfaces on which either hair or semen might be found. The result was a sizeable collection of items to be tested in the police labs, including facial tissues from the dustbins, bloody towels from the bathroom and the duvet on Inge's bed.

Kock sealed all of these in evidence bags and sent them to the Forensic Science Laboratory so that they could be screened for blood and semen and hair. After the autopsy was completed on 18 March, the clothes Inge was wearing when she was killed were added to this collection.

In addition to these items, individual hairs found in the flat – especially in the shower – blood found on the basin in the bathroom and clippings of Inge's fingernails were collected. So were swabs from her vagina and combings from her pubic hair. Almost all the genetic material tested would prove to have been Inge's however. The only exceptions were a pair of pubic hairs found in the shower whose owner has never been identified.

Apart from looking for trace DNA evidence, Kock's other role at the crime scene was to conduct an analysis of the shape and patterns of the bloodstains found at the scene. It is a skill in which he was one of the country's leading exponents, and his analysis revealed a number of details about the crime. The pool of blood beneath Inge's head, for instance, and the 'drip-into-drip' pattern of splashes that ran down the side of the couch told Kock that Inge had been murdered where her body was found. He was also certain that Inge was struck from behind her left shoulder, since the absence of drops of blood on three or four tiles in that area suggested that the killer must have been standing there. A corollary of this, Kock would testify, is that the killer was likely to have had bloodstains on his clothes, mostly below his waist.

Kock could not be completely certain about whether the magazine lying across Inge's feet was in that precise position at the time of the murder. There was a small drop of blood on one of the open pages that was probably projected from one of her wounds by the force of the blow, and there were no marks beneath the magazine. Those findings made it quite possible that the magazine was on Inge's feet when she was killed and caused the bloodless shadow beneath it. By the same token, however, there were similar spots of blood on the coffee table, so the magazine could have been moved from there after the murder. Constructing a reason for this is difficult, although one of the faces on the page on which the drop of Inge's blood landed belonged to a friend of hers who'd recently been a finalist in a Miss South Africa competition. Was there a connection? It is impossible to know.

Kock saw significance in the absence of some kinds of bloody stains. There were no 'cast-off marks', for example, of the kind sometimes left when a bloodied object is swung through the air, and which are found on the floors, ceilings and walls in straight lines mirroring the arc of a killer's swing. For Kock, this meant that the implement used in the attack was quite short and its use did not require a 'whippy' action. 'One would usually expect cast-off marks in a blunt-object attack, but they are not always present,' he would testify. 'It depends on the force with which the object is handled, as well as its size: in cases where a golf club is used, one sees cast-off patterns more often. There may not have been cast-off marks in this case, despite the violence, because the deceased's hair may have prevented the blood from getting on the instrument.'

In all likelihood, however, the implement used to kill Inge did get bloodied since Kock also found heavily diluted bloody marks in the basin, suggesting that something – in all probability the murder weapon and the killer's hands – had been washed there. The weapon was also almost certainly dried on the towel that was found on the bathroom floor, since, apart from the blood, it also bore long strands of Inge's hair. That blood took the form of what Kock would classify as a 'butterfly pattern': a stain consisting of two marks that appear to be mirror images of each other, separated by a bloodless gap between them. This, he would testify, is characteristic of a cloth in which a relatively small bloodied object has been wrapped and then wiped.

There was some urgency in conducting the dust-lift and searching the flat for traces of DNA; evidence of this kind can decay quickly and is easily contaminated. Apart from that, the taking of crime scene photos and the recording of the video, however, it was decided that the rest of the work, especially the hunt for fingerprints, was better left for the natural light of the following day. So, after the removal of Inge's remains, Bartholomew and Kock locked up the crime scene, intending to return the next morning.

In the meantime, other detectives, led by the acting commander of the Serious and Violent Crimes Unit, Superintendent Neville de Beer, had opened up another line of inquiry. Having established the identity of both the victim and her boyfriend, at dawn on the day after the murder, barely eight hours after her body had been discovered, Fred van der Vyver was brought in for an initial interview.

* * *

It is important to be clear that, at that very early stage of the investigation, there was no particular piece of evidence that had led the police to think that Fred had killed his girlfriend. He was not, formally speaking, a suspect. Or, to put it more accurately, everyone was a suspect. Still, the police had good reason to think that Inge had been killed by someone close to her. There was the sheer violence of the assault, for instance, something that suggested that the crime was, in some way, personal. A burglar, surprised to find someone home, might shoot or stab or punch his way out, but will seldom take the time, or feel the rage required, to rain dozens of blows down on a lifeless corpse.

Then there was the fact that there were no signs that the killer had broken into the flat or that anything had been stolen. As murder scenes go, Inge's flat was exceptionally tidy. 'Everything,' the lead investigator would later testify, 'was in its place.' Inge's cellphone and laptop and car keys, for example, were found exactly where it might be presumed she had left them, and subsequent inquiries would conclude that the only items missing were a remote control for the complex gate and a kitchen knife. Neither was ever found.

If these were concrete reasons for the police to begin their investigation by looking at people in Inge's immediate circle, another reason, more abstract and sociological, had to do with the character of femicide in South Africa, where female murder victims tend to have been killed by someone close to them. Or, as a policeman of my acquaintance once told me, when a woman has been killed, a detective's first instinct is to smell her husband's firearm.

Purely from the point of view of the character of the crime, then, calling Fred in for a police interview made sense: even if he were not himself the killer, he might have an inkling about other people in Inge's life to whom the police should talk. Little wonder, then, that the notes taken by the officer who interviewed Fred, Superintendent Neville de Beer, show that he spent a large proportion of the interview asking Fred about Inge's friends and family and ex-boyfriends, taking down names, phone numbers and even details about the cars they drove and whether or not they smoked.

De Beer's interview with Fred was less helpful than the policeman might have hoped, however.

Fred, De Beer's notes record, had no visible injuries: none of the scratches to his arms or face that he might have received in a fight with Inge; none of the cuts to his hands and fingers that frequently mark the killer in multiple stabbings. And, despite an attempt to throw Fred off by saying that they had a witness who'd seen him in Stellenbosch the previous afternoon, Fred also provided the police with a full and verifiable account of his movements.

According to the notes, Fred told De Beer that he'd slept at Inge's flat the night before the murder, that they'd breakfasted together before he'd gone to a lecture at the university, and that he'd seen Inge briefly after the lecture at about 10:00. The notes also record Fred saying that after leaving the university he'd stopped at a nearby store to pick up a cupboard for a friend who, like Fred, lived in Cape Town. After that he'd driven to the office, where he remained for the rest of the day, spending much of it in a meeting with his colleagues.

Fred told the police that after work he'd gone home, where he and his flatmate, Marius Botha, had cooked supper and watched the news, before delivering the cupboard Fred had collected that morning. He and Marius had chatted with the cupboard's new owner before returning home. At around 22:00 that night, Fred had become concerned about Inge's failure to return any of the text messages he'd sent or the phone calls he'd made. His anxiety growing, he'd called Inge's mother who agreed that he should collect a key from her so that he might look in on Inge. At that point, Marius had offered to call Christo, and Fred had left the flat. Fred said that he had just left Mrs Lotz's home with the key when Marius called to say that Christo had phoned back, that the news was not good and that he should return to the Lotzes' home. Marius met him there and told him that Inge was dead.

It was as detailed an account of a person's movements as any detective might hope for, and De Beer's notes are extensive. This was because he wanted to be sure to remember all the details, but it was also because the sooner a detective can pin a potential suspect down to one version of events, the better. First, it gives the cops something to test. Second, it makes it hard for the interviewee to change his story if evidence emerges that contradicts it. De Beer, who had three decades of experience in the police, must have known this because his notes suggest that he asked Fred to give him the names and numbers of people who could attest to his story: his professor at the university and the name of the furniture store from which he'd collected the cupboard; his boss and his flatmate.

From the lack of immediate follow-up by the police, it seems that

Fred's story did not immediately arouse any suspicions. Certainly, no one rushed off to test his claims: no one so much as called his boss or his flatmate or the owner of the furniture store, all of whose names were in De Beer's notes. This seems odd, in retrospect, because De Beer would testify later that he felt there was something unconvincing about Fred's emotional disposition that morning. Fred, he would tell the judge, had seemed unnaturally calm, and the tears he'd shed when the policeman had refused to say whether Inge had been raped had seemed forced and insincere. 'It's very hard to explain,' he would testify. 'The one moment he was clinical, saying he was at this time at that place, and the following moment, when I asked if they had had relations, he asked if she'd been raped. I told him it was still too early to share anything with him. I could not say. And that was when he burst into tears.'

To which the judge would ask, as a follow-up, 'When he arrived at the office, was he upset?'

'M'Lord,' De Beer would reply, 'he was not upset.'

'Not upset?'

'On the contrary, he was very calm and relaxed.'

* * *

Although it had been Superintendent De Beer who had interviewed Fred, a task usually reserved for the designated investigating officer, responsibility for the investigation into Inge's murder quickly passed to one of De Beer's more junior colleagues, Inspector Deon de Villiers, when he came to work on the morning of 17 March. According to standard police procedure, De Villiers should have been at the crime scene the night before because his name was next on the duty list. He had, however, been inexplicably uncontactable that night and his colleagues had not been able to reach him.

The same procedures that dictated that Inspector de Villiers should have been at the crime scene the previous night also dictated that he could not be made formally responsible for the investigation without first taking physical control of the scene. So after Superintendent de Beer completed his interview with Fred, he and De Villiers drove out to Stellenbosch to walk through the flat together.

By the time De Villiers and his boss arrived, a team of scene-of-crime investigators, consisting of Captain Bruce Bartholomew and three fingerprint examiners, were wrapping up their morning's work. Together, the four officers had searched the flat for the murder weapon and anything else that might help move the investigation forward. In this they had been largely unsuccessful. They had, however, found a couple of receipts dated the day of the murder, receipts that would later help establish Inge's movements that afternoon.

More significantly, the fingerprint experts had moved through the flat, dusting surfaces and lifting any prints that seemed sufficiently clear to be usable for identification. In addition, later that day, Bartholomew would return to the flat to spray some of the walls with ninhydrin, a chemical that turns purple when in contact with the amino acids left by sweat. It is a substance sometimes used to develop latent fingerprints on porous surfaces, such as paper and plaster, which cannot be dusted effectively with brush and powder.

In all, Bartholomew and the fingerprint team found eleven identifiable palm- and fingerprints, taking them from six surfaces in the flat: the doors at the entrance and the balcony, a security gate at the front door, a drinking glass found on the coffee table, the cover of the DVD on the coffee table and the security phone linked to the buzzer at the main gate.

Eleven was not a very large number of lifts for a flat in which someone lived and through which a number of people had moved in the days leading up to the murder, and, later, international experts would criticise the officers' failure to find more usable prints. That would be many months down the line, however. More immediately, in the days after their lifting, the eleven sets of fingerprints were tested against electronic databases:

one of prints of people previously convicted of crimes, the other of prints that had been lifted at other crime scenes but which had not been linked to particular suspects.

Both tests drew blanks.

* * *

At the flat, De Villiers was briefed on what had been done. He then did what any cop in his position would do: he started knocking on doors, looking for anyone who had seen Inge the day before. These efforts met with some success when he spoke to some builders who'd been working at the complex and who said they'd seen Inge return home at around 16:00. One of them said he had helped her lug a box of tutorial papers up the stairs. Apart from the murderer, he was probably the last person to see her alive.

* * *

The following day, Friday 18 March, De Villiers and Bartholomew attended the autopsy performed by Dr Rachel Adendorff, a local doctor and part-time district surgeon.

During the procedure, Adendorff documented and measured and photographed the nearly fifty individual wounds to Inge's body. Having done so, she noted that, in addition to some marks that appeared to have been made by her assailant's fist, as many as three weapons seemed to have been used. One of these was relatively easy to describe: a knife with a straight-edged blade that had been used to stab Inge in the chest and neck. The source or sources of the other marks was less certain. Some, Adendorff suggested, might have been inflicted with a monkey wrench, the curved edge of which could account for the distinctive shape that repeated in a number of Inge's wounds. Other wounds, however, suggested something smaller and more fully circular than a monkey wrench because the damage was more focused, crushing and compacting bone in sharply defined half-moon depressions.

Adendorff's advice to the detectives was to look for a hammer.

* * *

Precisely how and why police prioritise some cases over others is always and everywhere controversial, and police departments are usually loath to provide any reasons for these decisions. This is particularly true of police departments serving divided societies in which this kind of thing has the potential to become highly politicised. In this case, the closest we will ever come to an explanation of why the police would come to focus so large a proportion of their investigative resources on finding Inge's killer would be offered by one of the officers who testified in the case two years later. 'M'Lord,' he would say, 'it was my opinion that this was not a normal murder case. What I mean by that is that it was not a Saturday-evening knifing where two people fought and one accidentally stabbed the other.'

For anyone seeking to understand police decision-making, it is a sentence that almost deconstructs itself. From a practical point of view, however, the extent of the South African Police Service's commitment to the case fell off rather dramatically after the initial burst of activity.

Having begun on the morning of 17 March with a flurry of energy and a veritable phalanx of experts and investigators, by 19 March, De Villiers, who had other crimes to investigate and to shepherd through court, was left more or less to his own devices.

In his late forties, with salt-and-pepper hair and a moustache to match, De Villiers is a man whose career has been spent in some of the toughest and most violent police stations in the world. Despite that, his dark eyes shine with a vulnerable, sympathetic softness that seems mismatched with his experience and job description. Whether this sheen is a reflection of an innate kindliness or of a life marked by repeated defeat is more difficult to say. What we can say is that about the only work De Villiers appears to have done in the next few weeks was to request Inge's cellphone records and to follow up the receipts found in her bag. Using these, he established that she'd gone to the local shops on the afternoon of her death to buy a magazine and a hamburger, and to rent the DVD – *The Stepford Wives* – she had watched or was watching when she was killed.

During these weeks, De Villiers also made a series of appointments with Fred and with other people in Inge's life in order to take their statements and to get their fingerprints. He needed these so that any prints that had been left by people who'd had legitimate reasons to visit Inge could be excluded from the investigation. Most of these appointments were aborted, however, and by early April the police knew no more than they had two days after the murder, more than two weeks earlier: statements had not yet been taken from Inge's friends and family, none of the exclusion prints had been obtained, and no forensic tests had been done on any of the items taken from the flat. There were no suspects, and, despite the initial interest in him, nothing had yet been done to test Fred's alibi.

The case stood still.

Concern about the lack of progress in a crime that had already attracted a lot of media attention began to filter up the Police Service, and as a consequence pressure started to filter down. One marker of this was a letter written to the province's most senior detective by Commissioner Sharon Schutte, the officer in charge of all the country's Serious and Violent Crimes units, in which she requested a progress report. Another indication of growing pressure came in the form of a stormy meeting between De Villiers and one of his superiors, Superintendent Mike Barkhuizen, on 7 April. That was some three weeks after the murder, and Barkhuizen appears to have been sufficiently upset by the lack of progress as to threaten to have De Villiers relieved of responsibility for the case.

De Villiers's account of the meeting was captured for posterity in the marginalia he wrote on a memo from Barkhuizen that arrived about a week after the meeting. His boss, these notes suggest, was being unfair: De Villiers had had no help and he lacked so basic an investigative aid as a car. His notes also suggest that Barkhuizen was a racist. Why else would he have issued an instruction to treat Inge's friends with tact when asking for their fingerprints and hair samples, but to give the workers at the complex no choice in the matter? De Villiers, who is, in our apartheid-legacy argot, 'coloured', made these feelings clear in two hurried notes in his investigation diary on the day of his meeting with Barkhuizen: 'Racist pig,' he wrote about his boss. 'Believes black and brown people are suspects.'

Whatever the flaws in Barkhuizen's attitude, and however powerful the currents of racial mistrust and enmity flowing through a Police Service that fifteen years before was enforcing apartheid, Barkhuizen did have a point about the investigation's having ground to a halt. New steps would have to be taken. What these steps would be became clear about a week later, on 12 April, when Director Adriaan 'Attie' Trollip was appointed as 'overall coordinator' of the investigation. This was an odd designation for someone involved in an investigation into a single crime, and it was aimed, one suspects, more at managing De Villiers's ego than anything else. De Villiers's job as the investigating officer, after all, was as much to coordinate a collective effort of street and lab cops as it was to conduct inquiries of his own. As 'overall coordinator', Trollip was effectively the investigation's new head.

Trollip is a small man in his fifties. Grey and wizened and gnomish in aspect, all his features are small and tight, save only his ears, which stand out smartly. Described to me by a man who has known him for twenty years as 'the complete professional', Trollip was high enough up the police hierarchy to ensure that things got done. This explains why De Villiers, for whom Trollip's appointment must have been a slap in the face, described the event (with winning, if probably inadvertent, honesty) as 'a blessing in disguise'.

If Trollip's appointment as overall coordinator was a significant moment in the course of the investigation, its bearing on the final outcome paled in comparison to another event that day. For it was also on 12 April that Fred van der Vyver, his flatmate, Marius Botha, and the man who found Inge's body, Christo Pretorius, came to De Villiers's office to swear out statements about their movements on the day of the murder, and to provide the long-delayed fingerprints the police needed to determine whether any of their prints were among the eleven lifted in Inge's flat. That it should have taken so long for this to happen was a gauge of how the investigation had been allowed to drift. Still, the fingerprint-elimination process became much more significant when, later that evening, Bruce Bartholomew phoned Trollip with news that would crack the case wide open: Inge, Bartholomew asserted, had been murdered by her boyfriend.

How did he know? Because when Fred's inked prints had been compared with each of the eleven sets of prints lifted at Inge's flat, three matches had been found. Of these, two were consistent with entirely innocent explanations: his prints on the security gate could have been left when he arrived on the evening of 15 March or when he left the following morning; his prints on the bathroom basin were deposited before the blood had been, so they could have been left when he shaved that morning.

The third match was different. That was with the prints lifted from the cover of the DVD, a DVD which the police knew Inge had rented during the afternoon of the day of the murder. Fred's prints on that surface annihilated his claim to having been at work. The only reasonable conclusion was that he must have lied about this, and, if that were so, it could only mean that he was her murderer.

Suddenly, out of nothing, the police had their man.

2

Immediately after taking the call from Bartholomew on the evening of 12 April, Director Trollip called Inspector de Villiers to tell him the news and to instruct him to go to the video store the next morning. De Villiers had returned the DVD and its cover nearly three weeks earlier, so there was no prospect that these could now be subjected to further tests. But that was also unnecessary since South Africa's laws of evidence prescribe that once a print has been lifted, it is the lifted print itself – physically captured on tape or in a high-resolution photograph – that is to be used as evidence, rather than the object from which it was lifted. Still, Trollip felt the police needed to get whatever evidence they could about the time Inge rented the movie and to see if the clerk might recall if Fred had been with her. He also told De Villiers that they would need to prepare an application for a warrant to search Fred's work and home.

De Villiers went to the video store on 13 April and took a photo of a computer screen showing that the DVD had been checked out by Inge a little after 15:00 on 16 March. No-one remembered if anyone was with her.

Because he had another case in court that day, De Villiers was not able to join the team of detectives who searched Fred's office and home two days later. Instead, he left that responsibility to some of his colleagues.

At about midday on 15 April, six officers arrived at Mutual Park, the headquarters of the insurance giant, Old Mutual, where Fred worked as a junior actuary. They took possession of his laptop and searched his desk and briefcase. Then, taking Fred with them, they went to his home in nearby Pinelands. There they seized a large proportion of his wardrobe, taking the items away so they could be tested for Inge's blood and DNA. They also took his shoes, which, apart from potentially bearing traces of blood, could also be compared to the shoeprint Bartholomew had lifted from the tiles beneath the basin in Inge's bathroom. A search of the flat for possible murder weapons, however, yielded nothing. Fred's interrogation was equally fruitless, with Fred, who had no lawyer, refusing to depart from the account he'd given De Beer on the day after the murder and which he'd repeated when he'd sworn out a statement just two days earlier. Fred refused their demands for a confession even when they offered him a deal: confess to the murder, and he'd be taken to a local clinic for observation by psychologists; refuse to confess and he'd be spending time in the cells in Pollsmoor prison.

He didn't budge.

*　*　*

If the demands for a confession went nowhere, the cops struck gold in Fred's car. In it, behind the driver's seat, they found a hammer. And not just any hammer, but a hammer of an unusual design, with a bottle-opener where a carpenter might expect to find the claw-grip needed to pull a nail from a plank. The peculiar shape meant it might account both for the wounds the pathologist thought had been made by a hammer as well as for those she'd said might have been caused by something with a wider curve – a monkey wrench perhaps. Together with the still-outstanding knife, Fred's hammer reduced the number of weapons that the police needed to locate from three to two.

The discovery of the hammer was also preceded by something else that raised police suspicions: an exchange between Fred and Superintendent Johannes Kock, the officer who'd searched Inge's flat, and who was also on hand to look for similar evidence in Fred's car. It was an exchange that the policeman would later characterise as 'surprising'. Testifying in the court case, he would relate that he'd asked Fred if there was anything valuable in the car. Fred, he would say, told him that there was and, when asked to remove it, returned to his vehicle, pushed the driver's seat forward, and took the hammer out from behind it.

'What was your reaction?' the prosecutor would ask.

'I was a bit surprised. I expected it to be money or jewellery or something like that that he would take out. I didn't regard this as a valuable.'

The officers' suspicions were further aroused when Fred told them that Inge's parents had given the hammer to him for Christmas, nearly four months earlier. If that was so, they wondered, what was it still doing in his car?

The sinister air that had quickly settled over the object would thicken when, a little more than two months later, screening tests located invisible traces of blood on the hammer.

* * *

Nor was the hammer the only piece of incriminating evidence the police found that day: earlier, when they searched Fred's briefcase at work, they'd found a letter written by Inge on the morning of her death, and about which they previously had no inkling.

Written in a girlish hand, the letter fills both sides of an A4 sheet. In it, Inge expresses her love for Fred, but in terms that could be read to suggest that there were serious problems in the relationship. So, while the letter is interspersed with hand-drawn hearts and smiley faces and x-shaped kisses, it begins a little ominously for a lover's letter: 'This is going to be a bit more difficult than an email (can't delete and change sentences again and again ☺ ...), but I must get these things off my chest this morning. I am sorry you left here this morning so con-fused – initially, I was unreasonable and then the whole thing got out of control.'

It is a striking, even startling sentence when one realises that it was written perhaps ten hours before its author was beaten to death, and the effect is not much reduced by the fact that much of the rest of the let-ter is taken up by expressions of Inge's love for Fred and her desire to spend her life with him. Instead, the opening of the letter tends to add weight to later passages that allude to problems in the relationship. At one point, for example, Inge asked God for the wisdom to manage what she calls 'the situation'. Indeed, even when she writes about her love most explicitly, other currents reveal themselves beneath the chocolate-box sentiment in which she sometimes expresses her feelings. 'I feel that I disappoint you if I don't do things right and that you deserve to have a beautiful girl who looks nice and can cook ☺ and who is in all respects as perfect as you, and I struggle to achieve that. Perhaps that is the hardest thing for me.'

Or, elsewhere: 'You must <u>NEVER</u> again doubt for one moment that I am absolutely committed and that I want to be with you forever, with everything that is in me. I want to promise you today that I will no longer be dependent on you for a good self-image and for security, but that I will go to God with this, that I will support you in everything that you do and that I will be absolutely honest with you in all areas of my life.'

Or, even more intriguing, is this: a promise that 'with God's help, I will never go behind your back.' It is a promise that replaced an earlier version which, while crossed out, remains legible, and is, if anything, more arresting still: 'With God's help, I will never betray you.'

Reading the letter a few months after it was obtained, a police psychologist and expert in 'psychological content analysis' would tell the investigators that it was an attempt to soothe Fred, to placate him. It had been written, he would conclude, after a heated argument on the morning of the murder or some time the previous evening, and he would speculate that it had blown up because Fred had discovered that Inge – who says repeatedly she does not want to bother Fred with her 'issues' – had gone elsewhere for emotional support. The crossing-out of the commitment not to betray Fred, the psychologist would suggest, may have been because that was precisely what she had done, and to leave it in the letter would have looked and felt hypocritical. And, although the police psychologist missed it or did not know about it, it is hard not to see a connection between the letter and Inge's taking home a copy of *The Stepford Wives*, of all things, just a few hours later.

A peculiar emotional gravity attaches to a letter that captures someone's last thoughts, and, in the light of the subsequent murder, it was easy to see Inge's words as a link in an all-too-familiar sequence of causation leading from Fred's feeling a sense of betrayal for some slight, real or perceived, to an argument and a mounting rage that culminated in murder. That interpretation seemed to have been made more reasonable by Fred's failure to mention to the detectives that he and Inge had fought the night before her death, as well as by his apparent attempt to mislead Inge's mother about the letter. She had known that Inge had written something for Fred on the morning she died, and had asked to see it sometime that night. Instead of showing her this letter, however, Fred had given her another. That letter – a short, undated note of only a few sentences – was written in a hurried, sloping hand, and, though it mentions Inge's 'problems', it lacks the fraught ambiguities and hesitations of the longer one; it spoke only of Inge's love for Fred and thanked him for listening to her.

If on 11 April the investigation had revealed next to nothing about who might have killed Inge, a mere six days later the case seemed open-and-shut: Fred's fingerprint was on the DVD cover, a hammer that may have killed her had been found in his car, and there was mounting evidence of a lovers' quarrel in the twenty-four hours before her death. If anything, Fred's guilt now seemed over-determined.

And still the evidence against him continued to flood in.

*　*　*

Captain Bruce Bartholomew was the key forensic investigator attached to the investigation into Inge's murder. A dark, broody man with heavy features and a steep widow's peak, he arrived at the crime scene in the early hours of the morning of 17 March and, after kicking out a large number of officials whose presence was compromising the search for evidence, he took control of it. He helped carry Inge's body out of the flat, covering her hands in envelopes in case biological samples could be found under her fingernails. He supervised the search for fingerprints in the flat, and he oversaw a sophisticated, though unsuccessful, attempt to lift prints directly from Inge's body using vaporised superglue. He attended the autopsy and took photographs of Inge's wounds so that these could be compared to any potential weapon the police might find. Bartholomew's true speciality, though, was shoeprints.

As recondite an area of forensic work as any, footwear impression evidence is used to link a suspect to a crime scene by the marks he leaves walking to, in or through it. The basics of this are similar to those of fingerprint identifications: at the appropriate level of magnification, every shoe leaves a unique impression. That means that if a shoeprint is found at a crime scene it can later be compared with shoes found in a suspect's possession, shoes that might then be matched or excluded by the examiner.

Like fingerprints, the biggest challenge for the investigator is to find a shoeprint that has sufficient detail to allow for the making of a match with

31

enough confidence as to exclude all other shoes as its source. Finding and then lifting shoeprints requires dedication, skill and technology, but, because forensic investigators strongly believe in the exchange principle – famously formulated as, 'every contact leaves a trace' – they also believe that every step taken has the potential to leave an impression of the shoe that was worn. All that is required is the appropriate equipment, deployed by an appropriately trained investigator in the period between when the impressions are left and when they either decay or are disturbed. It was for this reason that Bartholomew kicked the other cops out of Inge's flat immediately after he arrived. It is why he broke out his dust-lifter at the first opportunity. And it is also why his efforts were only partially successful: although he found nothing but evidence of police footwear next to Inge's couch, he did find an impression left by a sports shoe in the bathroom.

Bartholomew was a member of the team that searched Fred's flat on 15 April, helping to select and pack the clothes the investigators took for blood tests. That process, though, proved to be disappointing because none of the items revealed blood or other trace material that could be linked to Inge. His interest in the search of Fred's flat, however, was less in Fred's clothes than in his shoes, and it was especially piqued by a pair of squash shoes that appeared to have been recently washed, with their laces having been removed from their holes and then tucked out of sight in the toes.

Suspicious as this appeared, back at the lab, Bartholomew was able to establish very quickly that the shoes had not, in fact, left the shoeprint he'd found in Inge's bathroom: the design elements of the patterns on their outsoles didn't match the lift he'd made. Like the unsuccessful search for blood on Fred's clothes, that was disappointing. But Bartholomew, the province's leading shoeprint impression evidence expert, was not finished.

Deciding to have one last run at the flat, he asked that some colleagues from Pretoria come down to test surfaces in the flat, including the bathroom floor, with a chemical called Amido Black. Reacting with proteins, Amido Black turns a deep black when it comes into contact with blood, even if the surface has been washed and those traces are invisible to the naked eye. The procedures for its use are well known in other jurisdictions, but, since it was relatively new to South Africa, Bartholomew had not yet been trained in its correct application. Hence his need for assistance from Pretoria.

His request approved, Bartholomew and three members of the national crime scene investigation team returned to Inge's flat on 28 April, six weeks after the murder and nearly a month after the keys to the flat had been returned to her family.

With Bartholomew in tow, the investigators worked a number of surfaces in the flat, spraying Amido Black on some of the walls and floors. They concentrated their efforts, however, in the bathroom, focusing most intensively on a small, scorpion-shaped mark near the basin. And they struck it lucky: the mark itself, being blood, turned black under treatment, but, as they processed the area around the original mark, other marks also became visible. The resulting, newly enhanced mark would become another telling piece of evidence for the prosecution when, twelve weeks later, a microscopic comparison of Fred's squash shoes with those elements of the mark newly made visible by the Amido Black, would turn out to match each other precisely.

At some point, it seemed, Fred's shoe had made contact with Inge's blood.

*　*　*

The microscopic measurement and comparison of the bloody mark and Fred's shoes were conducted in July 2005 by Captain Frans Maritz. He was then a member of the ballistics unit of the Forensic Science Laboratory in Cape Town. By the time of Fred's trial, however, he would be a senior officer in the laboratory of the state police in South Dakota.

This was not Maritz's first contribution to the investigation into Inge's death, however.

On 19 May and then again on 2 June, he and his team had conducted a series of tests on the ornamental hammer that had been found in Fred's car during the search on 15 April. Screening tests had identified a substance on the hammer that might have been blood, but had not established from whom it came. Nor were the police trying to establish this any longer, because they knew with complete certainty that the only traces of DNA on the hammer were not Inge's. They couldn't be – they had come from a man. Maritz, who is an expert in ballistics and tool-mark identification, was recruited to see if there was another way to link the hammer to the crime.

After measuring and weighing Fred's hammer and then making clay imprints of both the striking surface and the bottle-opener, Maritz tested Fred's hammer on the carcasses of sheep and pigs to see whether the size, shape and depth of the marks it left in the animals' flesh and skulls would correspond with the dimensions of Inge's injuries. The tests were done at an abattoir and involved smashing the hammer into the heads of the carcasses of pigs and sheep, the officers involved pausing in their endeavours only to photograph and measure the results. And, testifying later, Maritz would say that the hammer caused wounds to the pigs and sheep – half-moons that were driven through the skin and which crushed the underlying bone – that were very similar to the injuries to Inge's head and face.

In addition to the physical testing of the hammer, Maritz also created a set of transparencies on which images of the hammer's striking surface and bottle-opener were printed. Overlaying these on the pictures Bartholomew had taken of Inge's wounds during the autopsy, Maritz showed that most of Inge's wounds were consistent with the size and shape of the hammer and the bottle-opener. There were, he admitted, some differences between the dimensions of the wounds and those of the hammer, but these could all be accounted for by the elasticity of the skin or by the killer's failing to strike his target with the full face of his implement. Glancing blows, for instance, would obviously create wounds of a shape not quite the same as that of the hammer itself.

Maritz could not say that this hammer was definitely the source of Inge's injuries, but only that it could have been. Crucially, though, there were injuries that corresponded with the damage done by *both* sides of the hammer, its striking surface and the bottle-opener. That this shape was exceptionally unusual, and that there did not seem to be injuries that would correspond to the claw-grip of a normal hammer, reinforced the conclusion that Fred's hammer must have been the murder weapon.

*   *   *

By the end of July 2005, all the key elements of the police case against Fred van der Vyver were in place. For motive, they could point to a lovers' quarrel so serious that Inge felt she needed to write a placatory letter to Fred on the morning of her death. For a weapon, they had a hammer, the dimensions of which matched the catastrophic wounds on Inge's head and face, a weapon, not irrelevantly, that had been given to Fred by Inge's parents the previous Christmas, and whose presence in Fred's car in mid-April, suggested either habits that were unconscionably untidy or that it had been used recently. For evidence that Fred had been at the crime scene, the cops were almost spoilt for choice: his fingerprints on the cover of the DVD that Inge had rented at 15:00 obliterated his claim to have been at work all day, while a bloody shoeprint left in Inge's bathroom had been matched to one of his squash shoes.

The only missing element of the story was the issue of opportunity: could Fred have committed this crime in Stellenbosch some time in the late afternoon or early evening of 16 March if he worked and lived about 30 minutes down the road in Cape Town, where he claimed to have been in a meeting with a group of colleagues for much of the day?

As Old Mutual's headquarters and the home of many of its important

assets, the building in which Fred worked boasted a sophisticated security system with security guards and card-readers and cameras at every
entrance. Scouring the records that these systems produced, the police
found video footage proving that Fred had arrived at work a little after
11:00, an hour or so after his class at Stellenbosch University had ended,
and that he had left a little after 18:00. The police knew from Fred's flatmate that he had arrived home too soon after 18:00 to have driven to
and from Stellenbosch in that time, so the question became whether he
might have left the building sometime between 11:00 and 18:00.

Hours spent poring over CCTV footage from each of the building's entrances yielded no direct evidence of Fred's having left at any time during
the day. A blank was also drawn from a review of the records created by
the card-readers at those entrances. The detectives did establish, however, that there were a number of flaws in the building's security system.
These included the possibility that a security guard, distracted or bored,
might not notice if someone used a colleague's card as he entered or left
the building. Another weakness was that at certain times of day the glare
of the sun made it impossible to see people moving through some of the
cameras' fields of vision.

It was possible, the investigators concluded, that someone could have
left the building unobserved and unrecorded. Since all the evidence
in the world showed that Fred had bludgeoned Inge to death with his
hammer, this was what he must have done. Precisely how and when and
where he had done so was uncertain and unimportant. What was key
was that the absence of evidence of Fred's leaving the building need not
be read as proof that he had been there all day.

* * *

It was an open-and-shut case, then, and one that sounds like a
Holmesian fantasy of the perfect investigation: detectives working with
next to nothing piece together an impregnable case against the vicious

killer of a beautiful young woman. And yet, when it came at the end of November 2007, after a marathon trial that produced a 5 000-page transcript and included testimony from a slew of experts, Judge Deon van Zyl's decision was emphatic: not only had the prosecutors failed to prove Fred's guilt beyond a reasonable doubt, but their account of how the murder happened was 'highly improbable, if not impossible'. 'The question arises,' the judge would add, 'whether there were ever sufficient grounds to bring the accused before the court.'

This was not a mere acquittal. It was a vindication.

So what went wrong? The complete answer to that question is a tale of dark deeds and dirty tricks, a tale that demonstrates the enormous difficulty a democratising society confronts when it tries to build a decent criminal justice system on the bones of institutions built in more authoritarian times. But a shorter answer is that the judge, who'd given every indication of being as prosecution-minded a presiding officer as any policeman could hope to meet and who as a consequence of this went out of his way to avoid using the word, was finally persuaded that the police had lied and lied and lied again.

Which, for many, left an important question unanswered: did Fred van der Vyver, whose father spent R10 million on his defence, get away with murder?

PART TWO

3

Everyone said I had to talk to Jannie.

'Gagiano's your man,' Professor Andrienetta Kritzinger, an academic sociologist and long-time resident of Stellenbosch, told me. 'No-one will have more interesting things to say about Stellenbosch. He's like an unofficial mayor.'

It was April 2008, and I'd been interviewing Kritzinger about the way the people of Stellenbosch had reacted to the trial of Fred van der Vyver, who had recently been acquitted for the murder of his girlfriend and fellow student, Inge Lotz. The murder and the subsequent prosecution had captured the local imagination, filling the papers and dividing dinner party conversation for months. Why the obsessive interest, I'd asked her? What explains the fact that nearly everyone I met in town had an explanation for the murder and of the trial and of the trial's outcome to which he or she seemed utterly committed? These contending versions ranged from the banal to the exotic. Some were sure that Fred was a murderer. 'You can see it in his eyes,' I was told perhaps a dozen times. 'The rich get away with murder,' I was told. 'Look at OJ.'

Others said they knew for sure that Fred was secretly gay, by his own lights, a mortal sin the exposure of which would humiliate him and lead to his being cast out of his church. 'He didn't do it himself,' I was told. 'But he knows what happened in that flat. He's protecting someone.'

Still others were resigned to poor policing, and, picking up on hints that had emerged during the trial that the police had investigated the possibility that a drug gang had been involved, had persuaded themselves that the cops had simply dropped the ball. 'What do you expect in the new South Africa,' I was told. 'They go after whoever looks easiest. If a case looks like real work, they drop it.'

Local interest in the case was completely understandable, Professor Kritzinger said, before enumerating the elements that made this the classic soap opera. 'You have a very bright, very beautiful girl who is killed. And in such a horrible way. She's local. She's the only child from a rich family. This is the archetype of the victim in popular consciousness. And then there's the drama of the passion. If her boyfriend did it, he did it because he was jealous. Of whom was he jealous? Why? Well, this is melodrama of the highest order. And the way it's reported in the press … We never knew what was going on. Not everything. It was like a constant tease, as if they were deliberately stimulating our interest.'

'And the church?' I prompted, referring to His People Church, a fast-growing but highly controversial church to whose services Fred had taken Inge. 'Does that explain some of the interest?'

'Of course it does. People in Stellenbosch are very worried about those churches. They're getting a lot of influence among the students, and lots of people are worried that they *smokkel* with the students' heads. They're seen as a kind of cult – very intrusive and interfering. They say that they dictate how their members can conduct their sex lives, who they can date and who they can't, what they can do with each other and what they can't. They tell you what to think and what not to think.'

These were views I'd heard before. I recall one senior academic at the university telling me how his own daughter had lost friends who'd broken off with her after they joined His People Church. Others had spoken of the effect of growing membership of this and similar churches on the mundane business of teaching university classes. 'Members won't answer exam questions about evolution,' one academic told me. 'You get the most aggressive questions in class when you speak about our equality legislation, of gay rights,' another had said, adding that she'd seen an openly gay fellow lecturer hounded into misery. 'I had to stop going to one of my local restaurants,' a third reported. 'I couldn't bear all the God-talk around me.'

There was, then, a sense that these churches represented some measure of excess: an excess of faith, an excess of enthusiasm, an excess of certainty. I had never found anyone who'd studied the phenomenon up close, so instead of talking about the way the churches worked with their members, I asked Kritzinger something I'd asked others: 'What explains the rise of the churches? Why has there been this strong turn to charismatic religion among students here?'

It was then that she said I should talk to Jannie Gagiano. 'He'll have a view. And it will be interesting.'

*　*　*

Every people has its holy ground, places at which the complex unity of its ideals and its delusions and its resentments is so densely compacted, it seems to take on physical form. The Jews have Masada and the Wailing Wall and the ovens of Auschwitz. The Americans have the Lincoln Memorial, the battlefields of their Civil War and the 58 000 names etched into the black granite of the Vietnam Veterans Memorial. The Japanese have Mount Fuji and Hiroshima.

For Afrikanerdom, Stellenbosch is such a place.

It is true that the town is not the site of an historical act of martyr-dom. For that, one must visit the dusty fields in the north of the country, places where, a century ago, 20 000 Boer women and children died of disease and starvation in British concentration camps. But Stellenbosch, first named and settled in 1679, can nevertheless lay claim to being one of Afrikanerdom's spiritual homes.

Just down the road, the first stirrings of the Afrikaans language move-ment began in the 1870s. It was here also, more than a century and a half earlier, before the language even existed, that someone first explicitly de-fined himself as an Afrikaner. That was in 1707, when Hendrik Biebouw, all of sixteen years old and drunk at the news that a hated governor was being recalled to Europe, refused an order by the local magistrate to cease his carousing: 'I am an Afrikaner,' he declared, using a term very different from the words settlers usually used to describe themselves – 'Christian' or 'European' or 'burgher'. Then, initiating a long history in which the self-image of the Afrikaner would be tied up with the idea of resistance to being ruled by others, Biebouw added, 'Even if the Magistrate beats me to death and even if he puts me in jail, I cannot and will not submit.'

It was in Stellenbosch, also, that South Africa's first Dutch Reformed seminary was established in 1859. It was this institution that would one day be transformed into the University of Stellenbosch, through whose doors generations of Afrikaner leaders – spiritual and secular – have passed. In fact, of the last six Afrikaner prime ministers and presidents of the Republic, their combined reigns running from the late 1930s to the mid-1990s, only the last (FW de Klerk) had no formal connection with the institution. Of the others, three were students (JC Smuts, DF Malan and BJ Vorster), one a lecturer (HF Verwoerd) and two (Vorster, again, and PW Botha) were chancellors. And there should be little won-der at the close connection between Afrikaner power and the University of Stellenbosch, for it was here, in the early part of the twentieth century, that the philosophical and theological ideas that were to become apart-heid were developed by young scholars, newly returned from European universities where they had imbibed dangerous enthusiasms for mystical ideas of blood and race and soil.

It is this quasi-spiritual history, forged around ideas about God and Afrikanerdom, that has shaped a pretty town of oak-lined streets and whitewashed, gabled homes, a town whose layout and architecture reflect notions of town and country that are more deeply rooted in Europe than Africa. These are streets and buildings organised around an idea of villagey wholesomeness that, for all its age, still seems artificial and fragile, almost vacuum-packed. And in fact the pastoral image of the town faces multiple threats. One of these is the gentrification that has followed the post-apartheid boom in wine exports, and which has brought in its train a string of boutique hotels and five-star restaurants that are not quite of a piece with the sleepy, country-districts ambience the town seems to cultivate.

More telling than the hotels and restaurants, though, is the atmosphere on the streets in the commercial heart of town. This is more fluid and uncertain and volatile than the rows of filigreed historical buildings would usually allow. The uncertainty and volatility are especially marked at the mall that dominates the town's CBD. It is an ugly, functional structure with doors that are too small, lighting that is too mingy, and shops that are appointed too cheaply. Around this monument to the mass market, people in the streets are poorer and blacker than in the rest of town, and the car guards in their reflective bibs are only the most obvious sign of the sea of poverty and deprivation in which Stellenbosch floats. It is a grim, uneasy space, peopled by wretched men and women who see little point in moving too far from the pavement in front of the bottle store. It's a space in which it is all but impossible to meet a fellow pedestrian's eyes without that reflex being followed by a request for money or food. The effect is to create an entropic sense of one's proximity to a social fault line that cannot be easily mended, a feeling that trouble is not far away.

The ambivalence of the town's aura, its schizophrenic alternation between wholesomeness and meanness, was on full display in the *Eikestad*

Nuus, the local weekly, in late May 2009. On the front page of the same edition in which it was reported that Inge's parents had dropped the lawsuit they had instituted against Fred shortly after his acquittal, the newspaper described the murder of a local traffic policeman. Headlined HE DESERVED BETTER the story told of a 'star of the department', who'd been shot in the back of the head as he returned to his vehicle to get his citation book. The offenders, it was believed, were four men fleeing the scene of an earlier robbery.

Deeper in the same edition, another story concerned the arrest, else-where in the province, of a certain Kiaam Majal, reputedly Stellenbosch's pre-eminent drug lord. The arrest was for the possession of a stolen car, but something else caught my eye. It seems that at the time of his lat-est arrest, Majal was out on bail on other charges, and that one of the conditions of his bail appeared to have been drawn less from the ethos of constitutionalism that supposedly pervades our law, and more from the script of a Hollywood Western: he was prohibited from setting foot in Stellenbosch at any time other than when he was due in court. All of which stood in uncomfortable juxtaposition with a piece on the opinion pages written by a city councillor about the appropriate procedures de-velopers ought to follow when seeking permission to build in town, and which began with a pained nostalgia for a forgotten time. 'It would be lovely if we could keep Stellenbosch as it was before the extensive demo-litions of the sixties,' Councillor Dawid Botha noted, 'but it is no longer possible.'

*   *   *

It was in an ill-lit coffee shop, amidst the car guards and changeable at-mosphere of the Stellenbosch CBD, that I went to meet Jannie Gagiano, whose career in the political studies department at the University of Stellenbosch began in the late 1960s. Gagiano is an intense man filled with conversation and humour, and his dense, sandy hair curled above a deeply lined face. He seemed to know everyone in the room, sharing jokes as freely with a dye-haired, tartan-clad student as with a middle-aged man flipping through the morning paper. A councillor in the municipal government, he was clearly a man about town.

I explained to Gagiano what I was doing and that I was interested in understanding the roots of what I understood to be the relatively recent turn away from mainstream churches by Stellenbosch's students towards more charismatic forms of worship. This, I told him, was because I thought it might shed light on the social milieu from which Fred and Inge came. It was like putting a match to touch paper. 'The religious fervour that has entered Stellenbosch,' he said, rolling the words around his mouth as a connoisseur might a rare vintage. 'A fascinating question.'

Repeated out of context, some of what Gagiano told me might seem banal: religion is often a sanctuary in times of uncertainty and instability, and a growing religiosity among Afrikaans youth was, therefore, no surprise. Indeed, another academic had said pretty much the same thing more pithily a few days before. 'When times are tough, people often find God at the bottom of a maize field,' he'd said. 'Happened to my sister when Rhodesia was falling apart.' But, taken as a whole, Gagiano's thesis was not banal because he wasn't interested only in the eruption of religious fervour, but also in the reasons for the decline of the once-hegemonic Dutch Reformed Church in favour of a more charismatic brand of worship.

'It is a surprise to some,' he said, 'but one of the fundamental premises of Afrikaner thought is that, as a people, its role in history is essentially benign.' It is, he went on, a self-conception that, while not exactly imploding, has lost a great deal of traction in the past few decades. Certainly, it had lost its connection with power, a factor that has been made more destabilising because the whole idea of preserving a unique Afrikaner identity had been actively de-legitimised by government since 1994. By way of example, he told me that Pallo Jordan, one of the ruling party's most senior members and a former Minister of Arts and Culture, regarded these kinds of issues with a great deal of suspicion. 'He thinks that insisting on the preservation of one's own language is in conflict with nation-building, and told the university that its attempts to remain an Afrikaans-medium institution were not the innocent protection of a language but an attempt to exclude black people.'

The ANC's refusal to countenance the preservation of distinct cultural identities had led to a 'Jacobin' programme aimed at de-linking historically Afrikaans institutions from their socio-cultural moorings.

'Historically, most whites have regarded it as self-evident that the basic building block of a society is the cultural or language group, with the corollary being that each group was entitled to its own social and political institutions. For decades, these institutions have conferred meaning and pattern on communal life. They anchored community values and social expectations, and Afrikanerdom's sense of its place in history. But in South Africa now, any group that tries to insist on its identity as a group runs up against the ANC's universalist ideology, which simply rejects ethnic claims. It's something they're very aggressive about. For Afrikaners, this has created both a crisis and a social and political vacuum.'

So what happens? I asked.

'Two things. For a few, there is a morbid withdrawal from the world, a rejection of the new ideologies, a retreat to Orania. Most don't do this, however. Instead they try to come to terms with this new universalist paradigm. For the religiously inclined, their political commitment means they cannot easily continue to embrace a parochial church like the Dutch Reformed Church. Instead, they must embrace a more universalist church. They can't embrace a Christianity that is in conflict with their political commitment. That's why the old church lost so many members so quickly. It was one of the first victims of the disestablishment of Afrikaners.

'That's the underlying story about these new churches: unlike the old Dutch Reformed Church, theirs is a universal god, not one that is attached to any one anointed people to whose historical project he gives meaning. So, when people moved from one to the other, they were entering a whole new universe of commitment. They were embracing a universalistic god and rejecting a commitment to community that was previously part of Afrikaners' theology and religious practice. But – and this is the key thing – they are doing so in ways that avoid a conflict between the political commitments they make to life in the new South Africa.'

* * *

Gagiano's exposition excited me. It helped explain, I thought, a great deal about what I'd heard about the dismay that the emergence of these churches had generated among many of the older-generation Afrikaners. It also helped explain the nature of the challenge to established churches – especially Afrikanerdom's *volkskerk*, the Dutch Reformed Church – that they seemed to represent.

What he didn't say, but what I was to learn later, was that there has always been a conflict within the Afrikaans churches between the universalist claims of Christianity – expressed by one theologian as the Christian proclamation that 'there is neither Jew nor Greek, slave nor free, male nor female, for you are all one in Jesus Christ' – and the more parochial and chauvinist claims of the dominant Dutch Reformed theology. Because this was a conflict that could never be fully resolved, and because apartheid could never be wrapped in scripture with complete security, the universalist ethic in Christianity may have been a foothold that was readily available to those who wanted to use it. It was inevitable, however, that the embrace of this ideal would have devastating consequences for a church that had previously decreed that people of different races must worship in different churches. A church, moreover, that had apologised for getting its theology wrong.

These are serious matters. But murder is more serious, and, after Gagiano had explained why he thought charismatic churches had gained so much traction among young Afrikaners, he wanted to talk about Fred

49

and Inge, and about why I was writing my book. I explained a little about my project and then asked what he thought of Fred's case.

'Well, of course he did it,' replied Gagiano, whose explanation for the appeal of charismatic Christianity to so many young people had seemed so subtle. 'You can see it in his eyes.'

4

I spoke to Jannie Gagiano in April 2008, some four months after Fred had been acquitted, 14 months after his trial had begun in the Cape High Court, and more than three years after Inge Lotz had been bludgeoned and stabbed to death in her flat a few kilometres from where we sat. That had been on 16 March 2005, and to read the headlines of the days and weeks that followed is to be cast into a tragically typical South African nightmare.

The front-page story of *Die Burger*, a Cape-based, Afrikaans broadsheet, on Friday, 18 March was STUDENT MURDERED BARBARICALLY, with the subhead SHE HAD A HEART LIKE JESUS'S, SAYS FRIEND. The next day, the newspaper carried the death notice provided by her parents: 'Our only *liefling*-and-sunshine child has been taken from us forever. She was our angel, as she was for everyone around her.' And, the day after that,

Rapport, the country's largest-circulation Afrikaans broadsheet, carried the story under the headline LIEFLING-INGE'S PARENTS ARE BROKEN, the subhead recording that CRATES OF WHITE ROSES WILL SOFTEN STAR STUDENT'S MEMORIAL SERVICE.

The Inge described in these stories was a daughter of a professor of medicine and a cousin of an Olympic gold medallist. She was 'beautiful' and an 'exceptional student', having achieved the fourth highest aggregate matric marks in her province when she'd graduated from high school a few years earlier. She was a 'Child of God' who sang in the church choir ('voice of a nightingale'). She was 'a *staatmaker* of the community'. She was loved by all who knew her.

Running alongside news of her parents' heartbreak, an account of the murder and the subsequent investigation also began to emerge. At the heart of this was the idea, terrible in its own way, that Inge had been murdered by someone she knew well. Her flat, readers were told repeatedly, had security gates on the doors and bars on the windows, and yet there was no sign of forced entry. Readers were also repeatedly told that nothing appeared to have been stolen. Little wonder, then, that on 27 March, *Rapport*'s front page was dominated by a headline that screamed, 'IT WAS A PASSION KILLING', the words bracketed in quotation marks, attributed to a senior detective, and strung across the page above a picture of Fred standing before a wall of bouquets. It was an account to which the following day's paper added a grim corollary: STUDENT'S KILLER 'WAS PROBABLY AT THE MEMORIAL SERVICE AND KNEW HER'. In the story that followed, a private investigator hired by Inge's parents to assist the police was quoted as saying, 'We are studying closely a recording of the funeral service because we suspect that the person we're looking for was in the church.' He was also quoted as saying, 'She knew her attacker; otherwise she would not have let him into the flat. She was almost paranoid about security, especially after a friend in her matric class was raped.'

Later that week, the same private investigator, Niel van Heerden, who also happened to be a former chief of police in the Western Cape, told

FRUIT OF A POISONED TREE

Die Burger that the police were waiting for the results of certain forensic tests on blood and fingerprints found in Inge's flat. He expected a suspect to be arrested within weeks. 'One must be patient,' he said. 'These things take time.'

These suggestions, repeatedly made, of there having been a relationship between Inge and her killer, were finally consummated in the press about a month after the murder when it was reported that her boyfriend, Fred van der Vyver, had been taken in for questioning and that his home and office had been searched. It was also reported that the process had angered Fred's lawyers, who complained that their client had been denied the right to talk to a lawyer, had been subjected to 'rough' questioning (with the police, it was reported, even resorting to re-creating the sounds they imagined would have accompanied the murder). It was, Fred's lawyer said, an attempt to 'squeeze a confession out of him.'

By early May, Fred was the only suspect, but his lawyers told whomever would listen that their client had cooperated fully with the investigation, that he had what they called a 'watertight' alibi. He had also offered to undergo a lie-detector test. What's more, they would add, the private investigators appointed by Inge's parents had disagreed with the police about Fred and had withdrawn from the investigation.

Then, in early June, a new story broke. On the fourth of the month, half of the front page of *Die Burger* was devoted to a photo of Fred and Inge together, over which had been superimposed a near-life-size image of a combination hammer/bottle-opener. DEATH HAMMER, screamed the inch-high headline, above a story that opened, 'An ornamental hammer, the suspected murder weapon and latest clue in the mysterious murder of the star student, Inge Lotz, is believed to have been a Christmas present from her parents to the suspect.' The hammer had been found in April, the report said, when the police had searched Fred's office and home, with the following day's *Rapport* recording that 'a single drop of blood on the suspected murder weapon is probably the last link in the chain with which Inge Lotz's murderer will be tied to the gruesome deed.'

Although a great many hints about the nature of the forensic evidence the police had found had appeared in the press by this point, with particular emphasis having been put on the possibility that a bloodied finger- or palmprint had been left by the killer in the bathroom, news of the hammer was a clear indication of how Fred was to be linked to the crime. More was to follow in mid-June, when, after Fred handed himself in for arrest, the police presented the outline of a case against him at his bail hearing.

Summarising the evidence they had laid before the magistrate, *Die Burger* recorded, once again on 16 June, that nothing had been stolen from Inge's flat, that there were no signs of forced entry and that she had died from head wounds believed to have been inflicted with an ornamental hammer. 'Streaks of blood,' the article added, 'showed that the murderer had washed his hands in the guest bathroom', and 'reports also suggest that she and another person watched a DVD together on the afternoon of her death', and 'Fred had been linked to the crime scene through a fingerprint of his found on the DVD.'

After the bail hearing, Fred's lawyers went on a charm offensive. By that weekend, the press was reporting more details about the alibi that may or may not have been watertight. This included news about a sequence of SMSs and phone calls made or received by Fred on the day of Inge's murder, and which seemed to show that he and Inge were in love.

'Nice lunch with W!' read one of Inge's messages, sent to Fred at 13:36, 'Tiles already laid! Missing you already. xx.' More importantly, data generated by the cellphone networks was said to show that Fred had not been anywhere near Stellenbosch after 11:00, and that the security systems at Fred's office showed that he'd arrived at work shortly after that time and had stayed there until just after 18:00. The newspapers were also told that he'd spent the day in a meeting with thirteen colleagues, all of whom would vouch for his presence, while his flatmate would swear that Fred arrived home shortly after he left work.

If Fred's lawyers were happy to describe their client's alibi as 'watertight,' police spokesmen were just as happy to indulge in the same metaphor about their case, noting with some irritation that 'the results of technological and forensic investigations will be presented in court. These, rather than word games in the press, would be decisive.'

An unusual development was reported in September, when, at a hearing to set a date for the trial, it emerged that the colleagues whom Fred's lawyers had said would vouch for their client's presence at work on the day of the murder, were now being listed by the prosecution as witnesses for the state. This meant that Fred and his lawyers could no longer speak to them about the case. It implied also that the defence's claims about what these witnesses would say about Fred's presence at work that day must have been misrepresented or exaggerated by his lawyers.

Perhaps to counter the perception that these witnesses would not confirm the alibi, Fred's lawyers made available to the journalists the views of a number of forensic experts with whom they had been in contact. Readers of the front page of *Rapport* on 18 September, for example, were told that these experts believed that the police investigation would prove to be a 'serious embarrassment' and that the evidence they had accumulated was so 'tenuous and bizarre' that the murder trial would go nowhere. The hammer, readers were told, had been examined by Dr David Klatzow, a renowned private forensic investigator, who said he believed it could not be linked to the crime. Other experts, readers were told, had identified numerous 'irregularities' with respect to the fingerprint taken from the DVD which, readers were also told, had been returned to the video store from which it had been rented and was now 'in someone else's house and machine' and could not be examined by the defence.

*   *   *

These were the terms in which the media war over Fred's case was waged through the winter of 2005. Although more evidence would be produced by the police and more counter-arguments would be generated by Fred's lawyers, the clash between the 'watertight' forensic evidence and the 'watertight' alibi would turn out to be the motive force of Fred's trial. However, it was not just the emerging facts that were remarkable, but the tenor of the coverage of the murder and the subsequent investigation.

There was, for example, the repeated emphasis on the fact that Inge had been found 'fully clothed', a detail whose significance would not have been lost on an audience fed a diet of appalling crimes against women. There was, however, also the unattributed claim that semen stains had been found at the crime scene, a claim that was cast in the most prurient of passive voices and buried at the end of an article about something else. 'Semen stains on the couch in Lotz's lounge are also part of the investigation,' *Rapport*'s indefatigable Marlene Malan told her readers on 1 May. 'It is suspected that the semen landed on the couch after her death.'

There was also a marked tendency in the coverage of the investigation to present the story in its most melodramatic terms. Thus, while the presence of semen stains deposited after the murder would seem to be of great significance to the investigation, in fact it accounted for only the last two sentences of a story headlined, MURDERED STUDENT WAS 'CURSED': POLICE TARGET LOTZ'S FRIENDS. 'Shortly before her death,' the story read, 'a close friend of the murdered girl, Inge Lotz, asked for forgiveness for a curse he had uttered about her and her boyfriend. The curse is contained in documents that form an important part of the police investigation into the mysterious murder that, six weeks later, still has detectives scratching their heads.'

'*Rapport*,' the story continued, 'has seen an extract of the document in which the curse is contained. It reads: "Forgive me the curses that I uttered about Fred and Inge."

'In other extracts that *Rapport* has seen, the friend writes that he comes out of a family with a long history of emotional dysfunction. He also says that he fears failure and rejection, feels inferior and is sometimes suspicious and bitter. According to him, it is the result of a curse that has been passed down to him across the generations.'

For legal reasons, *Rapport* did not name the author of these notes, but it did suggest that investigators were concentrating on an exchange of letters between Inge and her friends in order to close in on the killer. 'They hope,' Marlene Malan wrote, 'that certain revelations contained in these, as well as an emotional, possibly homosexual, triangle among some of her male friends, will lead to the offender.'

Some months later, this idea of a 'homosexual triangle' found its way into another story. In April 2006, under the headline GRUESOME MUR-DER GETS NEW TWIST, it was reported that the lead investigator, Director Attie Trollip, had visited the family of another girl who'd died under mysterious circumstances and to whom Fred had been linked. The dead girl, Danicha de Villiers, had drowned in knee-deep water on a freezing Bloemfontein night in 2004, nine months before Inge's death. It was reported that Fred, who had been at school with Danicha's brother, had sometimes visited her home. He was also said to be linked to a man, tellingly described as a 'self-confessed' homosexual, who had been a close friend of Danicha and who had been with her on the night she died.

Trollip, a model of official rectitude, wouldn't be drawn into speculation about a link between the two cases, but Danicha's father was quoted as telling *Rapport* that the detective had visited him to establish whether he knew of links between Fred and Danicha's gay friend. 'What Trollip told me,' he was quoted as saying, 'nearly knocked me over. I can't reveal the contents of our discussion, but when things fit together so well, it says something. It's just amazing how many similarities there are between the deaths of our two families' daughters.' He said that he himself had not seen Fred and Danicha's friend together, but that 'the story is that they met on the internet.'

This note of melodrama also found expression in another article by Marlene Malan in December 2005 in which she informed her readers: INGE LOTZ BELIEVED TO HAVE BEEN MURDERED AFTER BREAKING UP WITH BOYFRIEND. The article culminated in a list of unanswered questions. Who, readers were instructed to ponder, was the mysterious girl whom Inge's smss to Fred indicate had 'verbally abused her' on the morning of her death? Why were Fred and his former flatmate, Marius, no longer on speaking terms? Why were no photos of, or letters from, Fred found among Inge's possessions? Why had Fred been telling people that he'd been going out with Inge for a year when her diary mentions him for the first time only four months before her death?

Then there were other odd little details, many of which seemed to draw their significance from a more biblical register. There were statements from the Lotzes' pastor about Inge and about her parents' loss. There were character references from two pastors that were offered at the very first hearing in order to support Fred's bail application. One of those was from the minister of the Dutch Reformed Church from Fred's home town, who described Fred's family as having been members of the congregation for generations, before offering the seemingly irrelevant view that Fred's parents were 'committed believers [who] do not shy away from applying their principles in everyday life.' Fred, he added, was 'well brought up', and had his 'feet on the ground. People of his calibre are not just thinly sown; they are hand-planted.'

A similar sentiment was expressed by Ben Schoeman, a pastor in His People Church, who said that his relationship with Fred sprang from 'a shared love of God.' He wrote that, 'As spiritual mentor and leader in Fred's life, we have striven together to have a positive influence on the campus of Stellenbosch University and to make a difference, especially in the lives of the men in Eendrag hostel.' Fred, he said, was 'beyond all suspicion', especially in relation to 'drinking alcohol' and 'social interaction with ladies.'

All of which, in the context of a young man's attempt to show that he was no danger to society, might have been predictable. Less predictable, and therefore more noteworthy, was Fred's comment, in an article devoted to how 'isolated' and 'abandoned' he felt, and offered, readers were told, to someone shortly after his arrest: 'If I get hold of the man who killed Inge, I will go to *Tannie* Juanita [Inge's mother] and I will forgive her unconditionally. I will go on as if nothing has happened. Seventy times seven.'

Another comment that seemed to operate at a spiritual pitch somewhat higher than an outsider might be expected to hear was the curious note on which a story about Inge's funeral began: 'A congregation divided over the sacrament was yesterday united in its grief at the funeral of a student who was murdered last week.'

5

Febrile as was all the coverage of Inge's murder and the developments leading up to the trial, living in Johannesburg and reading English-language newspapers exclusively, I was utterly unaware of them. My ignorance ended in December 2006, a little more than two months before the trial was to begin, when I received a call from a number that my cellphone did not recognise.

'Mr Altbeker,' a voice said. 'My name is Alfons van der Vyver. I wonder if you've heard about the Inge Lotz murder trial?'

I confessed that I hadn't and Alfons said he wanted to talk to me about it, explaining that a gross injustice was being done and that his brother was being framed. He said he wanted my advice on how to approach police management to persuade them to take seriously his family's repeated requests that they investigate the fabrication of fingerprint evidence. 'Our lawyers have been sending them letters and faxes for over a year but we seldom even get an acknowledgement of receipt.'

Naturally, I was intrigued. But I was also suspicious. Why, I wondered, would the cops bother to frame anyone? South Africans had become accustomed to their murders going unsolved, and the concoction of fingerprint evidence seemed like too much effort to credit. Certainly, I couldn't see why they'd do so unless they were utterly convinced of their suspect's guilt. Police officers may lie, I reasoned, but that didn't mean a suspect was innocent. Besides, if the case had been set down for the High Court, as Alfons told me, senior prosecutors must have looked at it. Since the law says that they can take cases to court only when they believe they have a reasonable chance of obtaining a conviction, and since prosecutors were widely thought to tend towards the overly cautious in their decision-making, I assumed immediately that there must be more evidence against his brother than Alfons had let on.

Still, the story was too interesting to ignore, and I agreed to meet him for an after-work drink. The place we chose, at my suggestion, was completely inappropriate for the discussion he had in mind: a hippy-ish bar happily close both to my home and to the accounting firm where Alfons worked. I mention this detail because the venue obviously bothered Alfons, something I realised when, fifteen minutes before the appointed time, he called me to ask if I were still coming.

'I'm on the way,' I assured him. 'I'll be there in ten minutes.'

'OK,' he replied. 'I'm easy to spot. I'm the only one dressed for work.'

When I arrived, I found that what Alfons had said was true: he was, in fact, easy to spot. Trim and neatly dressed in shirt and tie, he was far younger in person than he'd seemed on the phone. His compact features, rimless glasses and careful grooming made him seem the very model of the modern auditor he was; he seemed the kind of man who would seem most at his ease when in a business suit. He was entirely out of place in this crowd. Besides, the room was also too noisy to talk. 'Could we find somewhere else?' he asked.

When we sat down at a restaurant down the street, he laid out the problem.

His brother was on trial for killing his girlfriend. The evidence against him was a fingerprint which the police said was lifted off a DVD cover, but which experts working for the defence – including a prominent international expert from the USA, whose report he handed me – had concluded must have been lifted from a glass. The difference, he said, was crucial because the DVD had been hired by the victim on the afternoon on which she was killed and it was being used to place his brother at the crime scene at the time of the murder. Then there was a second piece of evidence: a bloody mark on the bathroom floor had been matched to a shoe belonging to Fred. 'But,' he said, 'we've got photos that prove that they manipulated the mark. There's a series of pictures of it, and you can see that the later photos have an extra mark like a little tongue. On the court chart the police prepared, the new mark is being matched to a groove on the sole of Fred's shoe.'

It's hard to overstate how implausible this seemed to me. It is true that most cops I know don't think much of the maxim about it's being better that ten guilty men go free than one innocent man go to jail. It is also true that not all cops are honest and that even the best will sometimes focus their energies on the wrong person. But to think that they would lie about a fingerprint and then manipulate a bloody mark in order to match it to a suspect's shoe seemed ridiculous. I felt angry at being sold such a silly story.

'Why would they frame your brother?' I asked.

'That's the question we all ask,' he said. 'We think that they were just responding to pressure from above.'

'But they must really believe that he did it. What other evidence have they got?'

'That's it. If you read the summary of material facts, that's all that's mentioned: the fingerprint and the bloody mark.'

I was sceptical and listed reasons why. 'That's not how these things work. Our cops aren't that diligent. They don't go the extra mile just to manufacture evidence against someone who's innocent – especially when he's rich and white.'

'Well, they've looked for anything and everything that they could use. They even sent a detective to Queenstown to sniff around and to see what they could dig up about my father and our family.'

'What did they find?'

'They found that Queenstown is a small place and that not everyone has nice things to say about my dad.'

'That wouldn't be what they'd have been looking for,' I replied. 'They'd have been looking to find out if your brother has a history of violence, if he's known for getting angry and chasing people down the street with a hockey stick.'

Alfons's response to this surprised me: he didn't deny it. He didn't say that such a thing was inconceivable. He didn't say that Fred would never hurt a fly or that he was as pure as the driven snow. What he did say was that his brother was an intense man with strong Christian beliefs, beliefs he could sometimes press on others in ways that might grate. He said that he and his other brother – a man Alfons habitually calls 'my middle brother' – had had what he called 'a tiff' with Fred the last time they'd all been together before the murder because Fred had been judgmental about their having a few drinks: 'I mean, it was my middle brother's wedding …'

At the time, Alfons didn't explain the extent of the 'tiff', and I was left with the impression that fists had flown. It was an impression reinforced when Alfons told me that Fred was a big man and that he had played schoolboy rugby at Grey College.

All in all, it was an odd picture to paint under the circumstances. Here he was, seeking to persuade me that his brother had been falsely accused of murder, and yet the image of Fred he was building was of a farmer's son who combined religious fervour and physical strength. For a secular, city-born, English-speaking liberal like me, it was a combination that stirred prejudices as fixed as they are ancient. This guy's just got to be guilty, I thought.

Even as he spoke, I wondered at the unconscious motivations that might have led Alfons down this path, but I now think that there was probably more calculation in what he'd said. And more challenge. He would have read all the stories that the media had carried about the case and which had frequently emphasised Fred's religiosity and his size. These were stories I'd missed, but could have downloaded since he'd first called me. What he was saying was akin to a dare: 'You believe what you want to believe. I know my brother, and I know he didn't do it.'

In fact, those were virtually his last words to me that night. 'Mr Altbeker,' he said, 'I have never even asked my brother if he's guilty. It never crossed my mind.'

6

At that first meeting at the end of 2006, Alfons and I must have spoken for about an hour. When we parted, though, I wasn't at all sure what he expected me to do for him. I had already suggested the names of a number of people in the senior ranks of the Police Service to whom his brother's lawyers might write to ask for an investigation into their claims. But every name I'd mentioned elicited only a shrugged response: each had already received a letter at some point; none had responded positively. Handing me the report of an American fingerprint expert, Alfons said that I should look at it. Once I understood the extent of the fraud being perpetrated, I might come up with other ideas about what could be done.

Dated three months earlier and consisting of twenty-three single-spaced pages, the report was written by Pat Wertheim, an American fingerprint expert whose CV said he'd begun his career thirty-five years earlier in a small town in Texas, and which went on to document a career spent in fingerprint analysis and training for a variety of law enforcement agencies across the American South. The CV also explains why the defence had approached him, because it set out to show that Wertheim's peculiar expertise was with fingerprint evidence of doubtful provenance. 'I have studied all of the available literature on fingerprint forgery and fabrication,' the statement reads, 'and have conducted numerous experiments on those topics since February 1992. I have published numerous articles, given numerous talks, and taught numerous classes on the topic. I am recognised as an expert in the detection of forged and fabricated fingerprint evidence.' As evidence for that last claim, attached to his statement was a copy of a peer-reviewed article that had appeared in the *Journal of Forensic Identification* in 1994, and which was entitled 'Detection of forged and fabricated latent prints: Historical review and ethical implications of the falsification of latent fingerprint evidence'.

Having dispensed with the formalities needed to persuade a court that he had the expertise needed o reach the conclusions to which he had come, Wertheim's report turned to his examination of the evidence that had been sent to him by Fred's lawyers. This, it says, consisted of copies of the eleven fingerprints the police had found in Inge's flat, as well as photographs of the crime scene. For anyone concerned about the quality of police investigation in South Africa, his first observation about the evidence is arresting: 'It seems,' he writes, 'highly likely there would have been more than eleven identifiable fingerprints on surfaces inside the flat. The fact that only eleven lifts were taken indicates either that the flat and all contents were phenomenally clean or that only a superficial effort was made to locate fingerprints.'

This was a point to which he returned a little later, when, after noting that the eleven prints had come from only six surfaces (the DVD cover, a drinking glass, a washbasin, the intercom for the security gate and the security gates at the front and back doors of the flat), he writes,

'It is hardly conceivable that these were the only six surfaces in the flat that would have yielded latent fingerprints.' What about the kitchen? he asked. What about the bedroom? What about the doors and doorframes within the flat? What about the toilets and the dustbins? That no other prints were found, he said, suggested that the search for them must have been perfunctory.

Wertheim's principal concerns, however, were not with the overall quality of the investigation, but with what would be called throughout the trial 'Folien One' – the lift that may or may not have come off the cover of the DVD that Inge had rented.

*   *   *

Folien One (*see* PLATE 1) is about the size and shape of a postcard. It is stiffer than paper but a little more flexible than a photograph. To the layperson's eye, it consists of a series of foggy white shapes of different sizes and consistency that appear white against a black background. For the most part, the shapes – the residue of aluminium powder that clung to a surface after the rest was dusted off – lie between two bright parallel lines that seem to curve a little. Each shape seems the shadow of something different: some are longer than they are wide, others are wider than they are long; some are bright, some are faint; two seem like nothing so much as splash marks, while others are thin lines running north to south, as a child might draw rain. This is the layperson's description of what the folien reveals. Here, with only minor editing, is how Wertheim described its nine principal features:

A Two distinct apparent edges of the substrate, parallel approximately 80mm apart and slightly curved.
B The side of a fingerprint, identified as the left index finger of Fred van der Vyver, showing a degree of curvature.
C Two adjacent latent prints lacking sufficient detail for comparison.

D   A latent fingerprint that has the characteristics of a right
    thumb located 'below' Van der Vyver's left index finger,
    pointing in the same general direction as the other prints,
    and identified as Van der Vyver's right thumb.
E   An elongated semi-elliptical latent mark that was deposited
    while wet or damp but which had dried before it was
    powdered, and which is consistent in size, shape and
    location with a lip print.
F   Assorted other fragments of ridge detail lacking sufficient
    quantity and quality to be of value for comparison.
G   At least two areas, one of which overlaps the print of Van
    der Vyver's left index finger, which appear to have been
    wet at the time the surface was powdered, leaving the areas
    completely occluded with powder and showing striations
    that probably represent brushing by the fibres of the brush
    used to apply the fingerprint powder. This suggests that
    there were at least two drops of liquid on the substrate at
    the time it was powdered.
H   A number of shapes that seem to reflect completely dried
    droplets on the surface at the time it was powdered.
I   Apart from the areas of specific development, little powder
    appeared to have adhered to the substrate, suggesting a
    clean surface with no propensity to attract or hold powder
    on its own.

Having set out his description of the key elements present in Folien One,
Wertheim tries to make sense of these marks, going about his work in
much the same way as an archaeologist might seek to read from a shard
of pottery the shape of the pot from which it came and its place in the
daily life of the civilisation that produced it.

Several aspects of Folien One struck him as noteworthy. The first of
these was the pair of parallel lines which, because they are 'heavily de-

veloped', must have been caused by something on the substrate itself. Separated by a distance of about 80mm, however, they do not conform to the dimensions of any of the standard design elements of a DVD holder. Besides, they are slightly curved rather than straight, as they should be if they'd been caused by the edge of a DVD cover. Finally, the edges of a DVD cover tend to have a groove where the transparent plastic overlay has been bonded to the hard, opaque plastic of the holder itself. Any lift from these edges ought to show a dark line running through the centre of the edge-line where the folien would not have been in contact with the plastic in the depths of the groove. The lines on Folien One show no such strip.

After the parallel lines, Wertheim's report moves to the fingerprints themselves. He notes that Fred's index finger made contact with the substrate along three joints, but did so with the side of the finger rather than with its centre. The finger was also curved at the time that the print was deposited. Because it is more natural to hold flat surfaces with straight fingers rather than curved ones, Wertheim writes, all of this is usually indicative of the print's having been left on a curved surface (such as a coffee mug).

Finally, the report turns to the lift itself. Why, he asks, would a folien have been used on a flat, smooth surface like a DVD? Foliens, he writes, are better suited to 'curved surfaces, convoluted surfaces, or textured surfaces.' In fact, the only other folien lift in the eleven taken from Inge's flat had been taken from a drinking glass, a substrate much more suited to folien lifts than a DVD cover would be and on which Inge's prints had been found.

Having noted all these concerns with Folien One, Wertheim's report describes a series of experiments he conducted in order to test whether the elements of this lift could be consistent with a lift from a DVD cover.

After dusting a set of DVD covers sent to him from South Africa, Wertheim writes that he lifted whatever prints had been developed using both foliens and ordinary Scotch tape. It was a process, his report suggests, that reinforced his doubts that Folien One had been lifted from a DVD cover. One reason for this is that in each test lift, the only parallel lines that appeared were of the DVD cover's edges. In none of these were the lines curved or, indeed, 80mm apart. In addition, all his test lifts exhibited significant 'background development' – clouds of powder in areas in which there were no prints to which it could cling, but where it had adhered directly to the plastic. He ascribed this to the chemical make-up of the plastic, which contained elements that are close enough to the oily organic matter deposited by human contact that the powder would adhere to it as easily as it would to latent fingerprints. Crucially, this kind of 'background noise' was not a feature of Folien One, making its appearance inconsistent with a powdered print lifted from that kind of surface.

All of which also raised another question, one that Wertheim didn't actually ask: if Folien One had really been lifted from the cover of a rented DVD, why did it contain only Fred's prints? Where were the prints of previous customers? What about the prints left by the clerk at the video store when he handed Inge the DVD? Where, come to think of it, were Inge's?

*   *   *

Wertheim's report doesn't end with his experiments on the DVD boxes. Instead, it goes on to describe his efforts to identify a more likely candidate as the true substrate from which Folien One was lifted. In this endeavour, the folien itself offered a number of clues.

Looking at the curved parallel lines, for example, Wertheim notes that these could be associated with an object that was 80mm tall and which was also a truncated cone. Something, he says, like a drinking glass. The key question, however, is whether the ordinary handling of a drinking glass could account for the pattern of prints that appear on the folien. After a series of experiments, it is a question Wertheim felt he could answer in the affirmative.

Thus, one of the effects of the way a glass is usually gripped is that the index finger and thumb will curve to accommodate its shape. In addition, because of the pressure on the friction ridges of the index finger caused by the weight of the glass when it is lifted, a certain amount of distortion will usually run through the middle of the print. Precisely that kind of distortion, the report notes, is visible through the middle of Fred's fingerprint on Folien One.

In addition, if Folien One came from a glass, it would explain why both wet and dry droplets appear to have been developed when it was dusted. If the print was lifted from a glass, it would also help explain why one of the marks in the upper left corner of Folien One looks so much like it had been deposited by a wet lip.

Wertheim's experiments with the glass, the report says, could also help to account for the surprising observation that Fred's *right* thumbprint appears just to the left of a print of his *left* index finger, both of which lie just below the lip print, and both of which are pointing in the same direction. This, it turns out, is the pattern that sometimes appears when a glass is held in the left hand while liquid is poured into it from a bottle or pitcher held in the right, if, after being filled, the glass is then set down before being raised to the drinker's mouth with the right hand.

* * *

Wertheim's report concludes by asking a disturbing question: if Folien One was not lifted off a DVD cover but came, instead, off a glass, was this an honest mistake or a deliberate attempt to mislead?

To answer this question, Wertheim lays out what his research into problematic fingerprint evidence has suggested are the three most characteristic features of the most common form of fabricated fingerprint evidence – the deliberately mislabelled lift. The first characteristic is that these tend to be lifts with background noise that is inconsistent with the surface from which the print is said to have been lifted. The second is that the prints themselves are of a shape and disposition that is not quite what one would expect of prints found on the object from where they were supposed to have come. The third is that supporting documentation that could corroborate police claims about the origin of the print is either absent or deficient.

In relation to all three of these characteristics, Folien One failed Wertheim's test for authenticity. There was none of the background cloudiness that would be the inevitable result of using aluminium powder and a folien to lift prints from a DVD cover. The fingerprints were curved and distorted in ways that are not consistent with the normal handling of a DVD box (though they are consistent with the normal handling of a drinking glass). Finally, there is no corroborating documentation, such as photographs of a dusted DVD cover or, indeed, of the DVD cover before it was dusted.

Then the report goes a step further. Not only did the lift come from a glass rather than the DVD cover, but, Wertheim says, this could not be a mere mistake: it is, he wrote, deliberate, conscious fraud. 'If there were a latent print lift in this case that was consistent with having come from a DVD case but which had been mislabelled as having come from a drinking glass, we might accept that the two lifts were simply mixed up and cross-labelled. But, in the absence of any such lift, we can only conclude that the presentation of lift #1 as having come from a DVD case is an intentional fabrication of evidence.'

'In summary,' he writes, 'it is my conclusion that lift #1 was taken from a drinking glass and was intentionally mislabelled as having come from a DVD case. Lift #1 has all of the characteristics of fabricated fingerprint evidence and, in my opinion, is intentionally fabricated fingerprint evidence.'

* * *

Let me confess it immediately: I was seduced by Wertheim's report.

This wasn't a question of style and language, though there was a certain Gilbert and Sullivan quality to his intermittent declaration, often in the midst of a highly technical discussion of one of the finer points of fingerprint analysis, that some or other claim being made by the police was 'preposterous'. Nor was it because I necessarily believed that his interpretation of the folien was all that might be said about it and that there were no counter-arguments, which, as a layperson, I could neither anticipate nor weigh. For all I knew, Wertheim was no more than a hired gun with a long career spent trashing police claims for huge fees.

Fundamentally, the aspect of the report that most fired my interest was its method, the archaeological rigour with which the lifted print had been read; the way Wertheim, armed with nothing more than a magnifying glass and his mind, had chipped away at the folien until it was forced to disclose its secrets.

As a form of investigation, this exercise, with its reliance on minute observation and careful argument, was as close as I'd ever been exposed to the ideal of justice and policing that dominates the liberal tradition. Here, science had been invoked, reason had been exercised and logical deductions had been made, and, as a consequence, a wrong might be put right. It is an ideal of justice in which the detectives and prosecutors and judges combine to restore coherence to the world after it has been disturbed by the commission of a crime. It is an ideal of justice in which this is done using only the very best elements of our civilisation – its reason, its science and its intelligence. I have strong doubts about whether justice really is best understood in this way, and I have even greater doubts about the degree to which the police and the courts have ever approached this ideal. But to see how close the promise of this ideal had been approached in Wertheim's report was both potent and tantalising: I was swept off my feet. If this were how the trial would be conducted, I wanted to be there.

PART THREE

7

The history of police abuses of power in South Africa is deep and rich. And it is for this reason that I am often surprised at how controversial is the right to a fair trial. An instructive example of the suspicion with which this right is viewed can be found in the widely publicised comments by Susan Shabangu, then South Africa's deputy minister of policing, in April 2008. Addressing a public meeting in Pretoria about the state's role in improving public safety, Shabangu said she wanted to assure police officers 'that they have permission to kill these criminals. I won't tolerate any pathetic excuses for you not being able to deal with crime. You have been given guns, now use them.'

Warming to her theme, she said that the police should 'shoot the bastards' and went on to offer the wisdom of the battlefield: 'I want no warning shots. You have one shot and it must be a kill shot. If you miss, the criminals will go for the kill. They don't miss. We can't take this chance. Criminals are hell-bent on undermining the law and they must now be dealt with. If criminals dare to threaten the police or the livelihood or lives of innocent men, women and children, they must be killed. End of story. There are to be no negotiations with criminals.'

'No negotiations with criminals.'

It is a startling thought: for the deputy minister of police, the alternative to gunning suspects down is 'negotiation'. Not arrest, prosecution, conviction and incarceration, but 'negotiation'.

It would be one thing if all of this were an anomaly, but, in South Africa in the early years of the twenty-first century, it isn't: Shabangu received a standing ovation, and, a few days later, some ninety percent of respondents to a snap survey run by one of the country's newspaper houses said she was right. Nor was there any sign of a Clintonesque apology for 'misspeaking'. Quite the reverse: Shabangu's spokesperson was quoted as wondering why critics of her speech were so exercised by it. 'What,' he asked, 'should she apologise for?'

When he was asked to comment on the fuss, Jacob Zuma, then the newly elected president of the ANC, gave a qualified, if not entirely comprehensible, endorsement of what she had said, 'If you have a deputy minister saying the kind of things that Shabangu said, that is what we need to happen. What the deputy minister said is what we should be doing in dealing with criminals rather than talking about it.' Zuma, who would give Shabangu a promotion after he became the country's president, was clearly making a point. Precisely what that point was, was not initially clear. It became clearer, however, in the second half of 2009 when, by now the country's president, he told a meeting of the commanders of South Africa's thousand-plus police stations that the days of warning shots were over.

It was fashionable, in the days and weeks after Shabangu's speech, to argue that it was inevitable that people would take the law into their own hands as a consequence of the unconscionable level of crime and the apparent inability of the state to do anything about it. Thus, Fred Khumalo, the lead columnist for the country's largest newspaper, wrote a column titled MAKE NO MISTAKE: THERE WILL BE BLOOD in which he sympathised with the experience of a man who had chased down and then shot to death a twelve-year-old boy who had smashed his car window and grabbed his cellphone. Having killed the child and retrieved his phone, the man got back into his car and drove off into the sunset, never to be identified or charged. South Africans, Khumalo wrote, were 'at the mercy of these pieces of cow dung who have more rights than tax-paying, law-abiding citizens.'

This was heady stuff and, when one adds to it the arresting view expressed some months later by Nathi Mthethwa, the new minister of police in Zuma's government, that the 117 police officers who had been killed during the previous year had died because 'they hesitated to defend themselves as they feared the media and some human rights practitioners', it suggests that the idea had taken hold that the full and effective use of the state's power to control crime was being held back by overly fastidious legal protocols.

Reading the comments made by Shabangu and Zuma and Mthethwa, one is immediately struck by two things. The first is the obvious – that a state which advocates extrajudicial execution is playing with fire. The second is not obvious and stands in some contradiction with the first. This is that the statements seem to have their roots in a fantasy about how things work that was at least as expressive of the real limits of a state's power as was the resort to vigilantism in the first place. After all, if the police knew enough about who the criminals were to gun them down, then it might be wondered why they didn't simply use that knowledge to make more arrests. Seen in this light, the politicians' statements come to seem a form of performance art, a ritual expression of outraged machismo. Still, if it is a ritual, its effects are not exclusively symbolic, and one of those effects is to obscure the obvious point that, whatever they may say, the police simply do not know who the criminals are. Whether this fact was being obscured from the audience alone or from the audience and the speaker himself was less certain.

The truth, however, is this: that it is police ignorance about the identity of criminals, not any excess of fear police officers may feel for the 'the media and some human rights practitioners', that explains the inability of the state's law enforcement machinery to deal with crime. And it is also why the idea that the basic problem in the criminal justice system is that criminals 'have more rights than tax-paying, law-abiding citizens' is so badly off the mark. The protections afforded by the law are not intended to protect criminals, but to protect the fundamental right every person has not to be convicted of a crime he has not committed. These protections exist because convicting the innocent (to say nothing of seeing them die in a hail of police bullets) is not widely regarded as being in the interests either of justice or of the community.

This is a point that appears to be in surprising need of being made in South Africa, sixteen years after the death of apartheid.

Still, if the community has no interest in seeing innocent people going to jail, that does not mean that such things are in no-one's individual interest: in fact, poorly framed managerial techniques, together with pressure and an excess of zeal can lead police officers to pursue the wrong man. In this regard, an exchange as instructive as Shabangu's comments is to be found in the transcript of the twentieth day of Fred's trial.

On the stand that day was Captain Jannie Bester, a police fingerprint expert who had been called by the prosecution to testify about the matching of Fred's prints to those found on Folien One (something he had done on 12 April 2005). As an expert in fingerprint identification, Bester was also asked whether he thought Folien One looked like it came from a drinking glass or a DVD cover.

Under cross-examination, Bester had acknowledged that there were many aspects of the lift that suggested a drinking glass, including, as he had readily agreed, a mark that looked to him to have been left by a wet lip. At that point, Fred's lawyer, Advocate Petrus de Bruyn SC, asked a seemingly unrelated question: 'Are you aware of irregularities that happen with fingerprints?'

A: Not 'that happen'. That have happened.

Q: Excuse me. You are completely correct. Irregularities that have happened in this division, here in the Western Cape.

A: Yes, irregularities have happened. I can't remember the dates or years. It is a few years ago.

Q: And a number of police officers were dismissed and are now being criminally charged, not so?

A: Yes. I believe they were all charged and that there have been some convictions.

Q: There have been convictions already?

A: That's correct.

Q: So, it's not a fairy tale to say that fingerprints might be tampered with. It happens? Or has happened?

A: It is possible.

That's as far as De Bruyn took the issue, but, once he had finished with Bester, the prosecutor who called the policeman to the stand rose from his bench and, ignoring the advice given to generations of litigators, chose to ask a question whose answer he did not know. 'About the irregularities to which you referred, that ones that occurred here in the Western Cape,' the prosecutor asked. 'I assume that with your years of experience, these must have been some of your colleagues?'

A: That's correct.

Q: Do you know what the alleged irregularities were? We have heard this morning about the planting of fingerprints and about fabrication. What were the irregularities that these people committed?

A: Fabrication, M'Lord.

ANTONY ALTBEKER

The answer was so astonishing, the judge, who rarely needs much of an invitation to ask a question, leapt into the fray. 'Fabrication?' he asked in some disbelief.

    A: Fabrication.

JUDGE: To what end?

    A: M'Lord, I don't know. But in my opinion, it was in pursuit of targets. Every person had a number he had to reach every month, and I think it was an effort to hit that target. I can't think of any other reason.

JUDGE: For personal gain, then?

    A: For personal gain.

8

Shortly before lunch on 12 February 2007, after the formalities of Fred's pleading 'not guilty' to the charge of murdering Inge Lotz by 'unlawfully and deliberately striking her head with an unknown blunt object and/or an ornamental hammer/bottle-opener, and stabbing her repeatedly in her neck and chest', the prosecution calls its first witness. It is Juanita Lotz, Inge's mother.

Mrs Lotz is a small woman, delicate and attractive. She is dressed in a black shirt and a green trouser suit highlighted by pearl earrings and large gold crucifix. She climbs the stairs to the witness stand and, as she settles into it, offers a flickering smile to her family and friends. She has a sad composure about her, making unnecessary the first words of both the prosecutor and the judge, which are a request that she speak loudly. 'The presiding judge,' the judge says of himself, 'is busy becoming a bit hard of hearing.' Then, dropping the officious third person and smiling, he adds, 'If I ask you occasionally to repeat yourself, please don't think badly of me.'

Mrs Lotz offers the gentle smile of someone recognising another's kindness and turns, bird-like and alert, to look at the prosecutor, Carien Teunissen.

Teunissen is a senior prosecutor who is said to have had just one loss on her record in over a decade's service in South Africa's courts. She is a bosomy woman with blood-black hair and sharply drawn eyebrows, and she takes her witness slowly through her evidence. Her questions, however, are not always consecutive, and there are frequent reversals and revisitings, creating a somewhat broken narrative that is not always easy to follow or recount. She begins, however, by asking questions about Inge.

*   *   *

When she was murdered, Inge Lotz was twenty-two years old and studying for her master's in mathematical statistics at the University of Stellenbosch. The daughter of Juanita Lotz and her husband Jan, a medical school professor, Inge had previously earned a bachelor degree in actuarial science and a postgraduate degree in statistics.

Inge, Mrs Lotz says, was an only child, born after ten years of marriage. She had no major health problems. She sang solo at a conservatory in Stellenbosch, in the choir of her parents' church, as well as in a variety of other choirs and quartets. A dedicated student who worked to a strict routine, her mother describes how she would often get into her pyjamas in the late afternoon or early evening so that she could not be tempted to leave the house. When she studied like this, it was her habit to put her cellphone on silent and to avoid all interruptions.

Given Inge's routine and her dedication, Mrs Lotz says she was surprised when she learnt that her daughter had rented a DVD on the afternoon of her death. It is something that strikes her as exceptional. Inge did, however, enjoy her pop culture, and was addicted to the local soapies, *Egoli* and *7de Laan*, watching them every evening.

When Inge became a student in 2001, she moved to Stellenbosch, thirty minutes down the highway from her parents' home. Until a few weeks before her death, when she'd moved to an apartment in a new security complex on the outskirts of town, she'd lived in a house her parents owned in town. The combination of modern communications and the short distance between her parents' home in Welgemoed and her digs in Stellenbosch meant that mother and daughter had remained in close contact, phoning each other as many as five times a day. In addition Wednesdays were washing days and Mrs Lotz, together with her maid, would drive to Stellenbosch to clean Inge's home and deliver the laundry. Inge, for her part, came home every weekend, and would accompany her parents to church on Sunday mornings.

More often than not, a group of Inge's friends and classmates would follow her home on the weekends. There they would spend long hours together in the house and garden. The Lotz household, more comfortable than the student digs and hostels, emerges as a kind of weekend retreat for Inge and her friends; and the image one gets is of a home with an atmosphere of unfeigned and unaffected hospitality. It is easy to imagine long, sunny afternoons, lots of earnest and not-so-earnest conversation, bottles of wine drunk around a braai or in front of a television tuned to whatever cricket match was on; *Tannie* Juanita and her maid fussing over snacks and dishes.

It was on one of these weekends that Mrs Lotz met Fred.

Although he'd been in Inge's class since 2001, Fred was not originally a member of the group of friends who visited the Lotzes' home. Appearing on the scene in the second half of 2003, Mrs Lotz met him only when he and one of Inge's more established friends picked her up to go to a classmate's twenty-first birthday party. Some months later, in April 2004, Fred took Inge to a movie for the first time, and it took another seven months of getting to know each other before they declared themselves a couple. During that time, though, Fred came to the Lotzes' home more and more often, occasionally spending the night in the guest room.

* * *

Having established some of the basic facts about Inge's life and about her relationship with Fred, Advocate Teunissen turns to some of the elements the prosecution wanted to establish in order to obtain a conviction. One of these is Inge's high level of security consciousness, a fact that reinforces questions about how the killer gained access to her flat.

Inge, Mrs Lotz testifies, refused to move into her new flat until it was made 'totally secure'. The flat itself was in a security complex with high walls and remote-controlled gates. Even so, Inge insisted that a security gate be installed on the door. And, despite the flat's being on the first floor, Inge also insisted that all its windows have bars. Inge, Mrs Lotz says, would never leave the door of her flat unlocked; she wouldn't even drive in her parents' car if the doors were unlocked.

At one point, the judge asks what Inge's security concerns might be ascribed to. 'We don't know,' Mrs Lotz replies. 'She was always like that.'

'But did something happen in her younger years?' he prompts, having read, perhaps, the media reports that had spoken of one of Inge's school friends' having been raped. 'A break-in or something like that, the sort of thing that could make you more security conscious?'

'We had a burglary in 1998. But even as a small child, she insisted that car doors be locked. There was no incident.'

'Just very careful …,' the judge muses, making a note to himself.

* * *

By this point, the morning session has come to its scheduled end and the judge closes proceedings for the lunch break. He and his assessors rise, bow shallowly to everyone in the courtroom and receive their bows in turn. Then they file through a door behind them. Along with the crowd of journalists, I shuffle into the corridor where I greet Alfons, Fred's brother, and the only person in the room I've ever met before. He is tense and surprisingly angry. 'Mrs Lotz is misleading the court,' he says, when I ask how he thinks the day has gone so far. 'There are sworn statements from the tilers in Inge's flat that say she was not security conscious. One of them says he had told her that morning that she mustn't just open the door for anyone who knocks.'

His words and emotion strike me as insensitive. It is true that, unlike him, I have nothing at stake here: my brother is not on trial for murder. At the same time, it had been impossible to listen to Mrs Lotz's quiet, steady voice and not be stirred. Her only daughter – a beautiful, talented, supremely intelligent young woman – had been bludgeoned to death by a hammer-wielding monster whom the police believed to be a young man who'd slept under Mrs Lotz's own roof, a young man who'd eaten breakfast at her table, a young man who now sat in the same room as she, breathing the same air. It must have been an impossible burden, and, as I'd listened to her, I'd been conscious of nothing but the immensity of her loss. In context, Alfons's anger jars. And it's not just me who's bothered by it: almost before Alfons has finished making the point about the tiler's statement, Fred, his face set, hustles over to instruct us to keep our voices down. '*Tannie* Lotz will hear you,' he admonishes. 'You'll make her upset.'

Feeling a little embarrassed, I say to Alfons that the defence will have a chance to cross-examine.

'Maybe not,' he replies with some frustration. 'Fred has instructed the lawyers that they mustn't cross-examine Inge's mother: they mustn't upset her.'

* * *

After lunch, Teunissen turns Mrs Lotz's attention to the day of the murder.

After establishing that she and her maid, who would normally have gone to clean Inge's flat that Wednesday, had not done so because they'd come twice the previous week, Teunissen leads her witness through testimony that establishes that Mrs Lotz had a remote control for the gate to Inge's complex and a set of keys for her flat. The keys would have been useless that Wednesday, however, because the day before Inge's murder the lock of every front door in the complex had been changed: some accident of subcontracting had meant that many of the first set of locks and keys that had been installed were identical to each other, undermining the vaunted security of the complex. Then Teunissen asks a question that comes like a punch to the heart: 'When was the last time you saw your daughter alive?'

'On Sunday afternoon on 13 March. At five o'clock.'

* * *

The last weekend of Inge's life began like most others. Friday night was family night, and Mrs Lotz, whose husband was in Bloemfontein, had Inge to herself. Fred arrived on Saturday afternoon, but had to spend some hours alone because Inge was at choir practice. Fred slept in the guest room that night, and, after the three of them went to church the next morning, they spent the afternoon at home. Late on Sunday afternoon, Fred and Inge went their separate ways: he to his flat close to his office in Pinelands, a suburb in the north of Cape Town; she to her home in Stellenbosch. As Mrs Lotz remembers it, though, there was a disagreement between the two just as they were getting into their cars, when Fred asked Inge if he should pick her up for church that evening or if she would be getting there by herself. 'What was Inge's reaction to the invitation to join him at his church?' Teunissen asks.

A: She said that she would not be going to church that

evening because she had been in our church in the
morning. Then she started her car and said, 'In fact, I
am not going to that church again.'
JUDGE: You heard that conversation with your own ears?
A: Yes.
Q: Was there any reaction from the accused?
A: He looked unhappy.

The following day, when Mrs Lotz is asked by the defence about the conversation she says she overheard but which Fred's lawyers say Fred would deny happened, Mrs Lotz will add that Inge had extended her neck as she spoke of never again attending Fred's church. She doesn't say so, but Inge's lengthened neck is probably intended to suggest a note of defiance in her daughter's attitude.

Mrs Lotz says there was no further discussion after Inge's words, however, because Fred's phone rang just then. The call was from someone in England, and he asked the caller to phone him on the Lotzes' land line before hurrying inside.

* * *

Inge, Mrs Lotz testifies, phoned her mother at ten minutes before eight on the morning of the day she died.

Mrs Lotz says that she couldn't take the call because she was driving, but Inge called again at 9:15, by which point Mrs Lotz was home. She says that Inge was in high spirits – 'her usual cheerful self' – and that the call was to wish her dog a happy birthday. Having sung to the pooch ('I hope the dog appreciated it,' the judge comments), Inge told her mother that she had to ring off because she had to go to the university to give Fred something. Mrs Lotz didn't ask her daughter what that 'something' was, but says that she assumed it was a letter because Inge was a habitual letter-writer and frequently wrote notes to people for whom she cared.

Inge called her mother again at around 13:20, shortly after returning from lunch with a friend. She told her mother that a workman was fixing a tile on the patio and Mrs Lotz asked if she should come to see if the tile was in order. Inge said no, that it wasn't necessary, that she could see that it was in order. Laughing, she pointed out that she was almost twenty-three years old. Mrs Lotz heard Inge thank the tiler and then heard the sound of the lock as Inge closed the security gate behind him. Inge told her mother that she was tired from having to give a class that morning, and that she would rest in the afternoon before hitting her books again at five. Then she hung up.

It was an unmemorable conversation about a stupid, insignificant detail of modern living, a conversation whose only emotional content – apart from the fact of the call itself – was Inge's laughing reminder to her mother that she was growing up.

Insignificant as the conversation was, it would be the last time Mrs Lotz would ever hear her daughter's voice.

*   *   *

At ten that evening, Fred phoned Mrs Lotz to say he hadn't been able to reach Inge and was growing concerned. He'd already sent her an SMS inquiring if she had spoken with her daughter, but Mrs Lotz says she hadn't seen it. This direct communication was unusual, she says, because Fred seldom made independent contact with her or her husband. She also says that she wasn't immediately worried about Inge, believing that she was studying and had simply switched her phone to silent. Worried or not, she did try to contact Inge. The phone went straight to voicemail.

Mrs Lotz cannot say conclusively who called whom next, but a second conversation between Fred and Mrs Lotz took place some minutes later, when she told Fred of her own failure to reach Inge. At that point, she heard as Fred turned to his flatmate, Marius Botha, to tell him that he was now seriously worried. She also heard Marius's response to the effect

FRUIT OF A POISONED TREE

that he knew someone who lived close to Inge, and that he could ask him to look in on her.

Something about this arrangement was unsatisfactory to Mrs Lotz, though, and she says she told Fred that 'if you are so worried, you should rather go yourself.' Because the question is never put to her, it is unclear whether her dissatisfaction was the result of an irritated sense that Fred was being melodramatic or because, by now concerned herself, she wanted Fred to take responsibility for checking on her daughter. Whatever the reason for Mrs Lotz's suggestion that Fred go himself, a difficulty arose: if Inge was not answering her phone, she might also fail to answer if he buzzed her from the gate. Fred, who had no remote control for the complex gate, would not be able to get in. It was agreed that he would come past Mrs Lotz's house to fetch her remote control.

Mrs Lotz says she was still not overly concerned when Fred arrived some time later, but says that Fred seemed anxious to her. So much so, she says, that she sought to calm him. He asked her if she wanted to accompany him to the flat, but she declined saying that he should tell Inge to call, and that she ought to know better than to switch off her phone when she was alone.

Fred then left the house and Mrs Lotz went to sit in the lounge to wait for a call from Marius, whose friend had already been sent to look in on Inge and whose report should arrive well before Fred would get to Stellenbosch. The call didn't come. A short time later, after she had become convinced that she ought to have heard from him, she called Marius and asked what his friend had had to say. Marius told her that he didn't have good news for her and that he was already on his way to her house. Marius also told her that he'd already called Fred and told him to return, too.

Immediately on hanging up, Mrs Lotz tried to call Fred. There was no answer.

By now, waiting in the silence of her home, Mrs Lotz had become very concerned. Marius was some way away still and, as the clock ticked away, her fears mounted. Where was her daughter? Had something happened? An accident? Something worse? A parent's imagination – especially a South African parent's – can quickly turn dark. Eventually, needing air perhaps, or trying to cut short the agonies of the delay by getting physically closer to Marius, she went into the street to wait. There, she saw something unexpected: Fred's car. In it, she saw Fred hunched in his seat, his eyes closed.

'Fred,' she demanded through the open window, 'what are you doing here?'

He didn't answer immediately, though he did begin to get out of the car. Before he could speak, however, Marius arrived from the other direction, parking in the driveway. Mrs Lotz turned and, with Fred following a few steps behind, went over to him. Marius got out of his car and walked towards her. Fred joined them. Marius said something to her or to Fred or to both of them. She didn't hear it completely, catching only two words, the worst two: 'Inge' and 'murdered'.

'Where is my child?' she cried.

'*Tannie*,' Fred answered, 'Inge was murdered in her flat this afternoon.'

Mrs Lotz screamed.

And Fred's response in the face of her anguish? He turned to her and said, '*Toe maar, Tannie*, everything is going to be okay. I will move into the back room. I'll study at her desk. I will be the child in the house.'

* * *

This testimony – about Fred's presence at the Lotzes' house when Mrs Lotz received the news of her daughter's death – is delivered more slowly and with more deliberation than the rest of the evidence Mrs Lotz offers. As she recounts these events, the silence in the courtroom deepens and the pressure ratchets upwards. As if to heighten the drama, as she begins to answer these questions, Advocate Teunissen cautions her to move especially slowly. 'Take it step by step,' she says, 'and tell the Court sentence by sentence.' Moments later, when she feels Mrs Lotz is speaking too quickly, she renews her plea: 'Slowly. Just watch His Lordship.'

Sensing the significance the prosecution attaches to this, the judge leans in a little closer and asks questions of his own. When Mrs Lotz says she heard the words 'Inge' and 'murdered', it is the judge who asks whether Marius was talking to Fred or to her. When she says that Fred told her that Inge was murdered in her flat that afternoon, it is the judge who asks, 'Did the accused say that?' When she reports Fred's assertion that everything would be okay and that he would become the child in the house, it is the judge who repeats the words, '"Everything will be …"?' and who elicits her reiterated response, '"Everything will be okay."'

*　*　*

After going back into her home, Mrs Lotz called a friend who arrived a short while later. Neighbours arrived, too, concerned by the scream they'd heard in the street. She tried to call someone in Bloemfontein who might break the news to Inge's father. When that failed, she called him herself. Once she'd spoken with him, she found that she could no longer stand and handed the phone to Fred, who repeated the news.

Another friend was called. So was her doctor. She took a tranquilliser, dulling her pain and her memory of events.

Throughout the evening, she says, Fred told her how good things had been between himself and Inge, adding odd details like the great break-fast Inge had made that morning. He also repeated the phrase he'd offered as condolence in the street, but which was really no condolence at all: 'Everything will be okay.' At one point she shouted him down, saying, 'Nothing will ever be okay again.'

Mrs Lotz cannot be certain about when Fred left her home, whether it was that night or the next morning. What she is certain of is that Fred did, in fact, move into Inge's room, making a bed on the floor, installing his computer on the desk and lighting a candle. If Fred asked her permission to do this, Mrs Lotz has no memory of it and recalls realising that he'd moved in only when she saw his clothes in the room. He stayed there, she says, until the following Tuesday, the day of the funeral. By that point, Mrs Lotz's brother had noted that there were even more of Fred's clothes in the house, and that they'd been laid out in cupboards and drawers in the guest room. When her brother told her about these clothes, Mrs Lotz asked him to get rid of them. He did this by putting them in garbage bags and leaving them in the kitchen.

Fred took the hint and left that day.

*　*　*

Towards the end of the day, Advocate Teunissen turns to the issue of the letter Inge gave Fred on the day she died. It becomes clear immediately that there will be much said about this letter and that its significance will be heavily contested. So contested, in fact, that the prosecution and the defence do not agree whether the documents found by the police constitute a single letter or two separate letters. As a result, when the clerk is handed two sheets of paper, she is asked to mark them respectively as exhibits D and E. The first of these is a white A4 sheet with the standard blue lines and red margin of a student's notepad. Both sides are covered from top to bottom with Inge's neat script. The second is a blue sheet of flimsy letter paper, much smaller than the first, with only a few sentences written on it. These are written in a much hastier hand, the lines sloping drunkenly away from each other.

Mrs Lotz tells the judge that, sometime during the night, she asked Fred about the letter Inge had given him earlier that morning. The letter he gave her the next morning was the shorter of the two. It is undated, and reads:

Hi skat!
I just want to say also how much I appreciate you and how special
you are!
Thank you for your love, understanding and soft heart and that
you are ALWAYS prepared to listen to my little problems!
I love you VERY, VERY, VERY much!
All the best for your day and week and know that Jesus is with
you every moment!
Love and XX
Inge.

'What was your reaction to the letter?' Teunissen asks.

    A: I read the letter through and I immediately thought that it was strange that Inge says 'All the best for your day and week' when it was Wednesday already. And, for a moment, I thought that I had seen the letter before.

    Q: Why do you say so?

    A: On a previous occasion when I was walking through the house on a Sunday, I saw that she set down a small letter like this for the accused in order to say, 'Enjoy your week.'

    Q: If she says 'enjoy your week', would this usually be on a Sunday before the week began?

    A: Yes.

Teunissen then shows Mrs Lotz the second, much longer letter, a letter which it had been agreed would not be read into the record in order to protect Inge's parents from some embarrassment: 'Have you ever seen this letter?'

    A: I was shown it by Director Trollip. I think it was a copy.

    Q: Do you remember how long that was after the incident?

A: It was much later. I can't remember how much later. Weeks perhaps.

Q: Have you ever spoken to the accused about this letter?

A: Never.

Q: Have you read it?

A: Yes. I am completely familiar with its contents.

Q: What was your reaction to this letter from Inge to the accused?

A   My reaction was that it is definitely not entirely in Inge's nature to write this kind of letter. My eventual interpretation of the letter was that it was intended to placate him.

It is an opinion with which the judge quickly concurs. 'I can see clearly,' he says, 'that there had been a quarrel, that she got a reaction from the accused that she did not expect and that she tried to placate him. "Sorry," for example, appears many times in the letter.'

9

The first day of the trial closes with some evidentiary housekeeping and the confirmation by Mrs Lotz of certain facts that were not in dispute. It was established, for instance, that the ornamental hammer had been a Christmas present from the Lotzes, and that it was she who arranged to have the legend FRED 2004 engraved into its shaft. Having established minor points of this sort, Teunissen turns to the judge, smiling in a manner that suggests exhaustion and which is also a nonverbal plea for some recognition of the emotional strain of her efforts. 'M'Lord,' she says, 'I am almost finished. I think that this is an appropriate time to adjourn. I would just like to go through our notes to make sure that we have covered everything.'

Reasonable as this sounds, the preference of lawyers not to end their questioning of a witness at the end of a session, much less the end of the day, is an old trick of court-craft intended to delay the start of cross-examination, after which it is no longer permissible for them to speak to the witness about the case. Leaving open the possibility that a few more questions might be asked, then, usually has less to do with the professed desire to be thorough than with allowing more time to prepare the witness for cross-examination. In this instance, however, the prosecution has a surprise up its sleeve. The next morning, bright and clear as only Cape Town can be, Teunissen addresses her witness for a final time. 'Mrs Lotz, to round off: the last weekend that Inge was home, the weekend before the fifteenth of March, did you notice anything strange?'

'Inge came home her cheerful self,' Mrs Lotz responds to this most open of open-ended questions, before adding a qualification that is a specific as it is shocking: 'But after lunch I asked her why she was covered in blue marks.'

> Q: Can you tell the judge where the blue marks were?
> A: They were reasonably symmetrical on her legs and arms. I don't know why, but I asked her, 'Don't tell me that Fred hit you.' She answered, 'What are you talking about, mom?' Then she turned around immediately and went to her room to put on other clothes which covered the marks.
> Q: Did Inge play any sports actively?
> A: No, she did not participate in sport.
> Q: What could have caused the marks?
> A: That was the only question I asked about this. And all she said was, 'What are you talking about, mom?'

On that dramatic and surprisingly note, after a series of questions and answers that fill less than a page of transcript, Teunissen announces she has no further questions and hands the witness over for cross-examination.

*   *   *

Rising from his bench, Fred's lawyer, Advocate Petrus de Bruyn SC, has the bearing of a man who is angry and confused. Shell-shocked, even. 'Mrs Lotz,' he says, 'I want you to understand that it is very difficult to cross-examine you. Indeed, originally I had instructions not to question you at all. But, painful as it is, it is my duty to put certain questions to you. Especially after this morning's bit of testimony, you will surely understand this.'

The duty to ask questions of this witness to which De Bruyn refers arises from the way courts will treat as undisputed any evidence offered by a witness that is not challenged by the opposing side while that witness is on the stand. Obviously, judges are not fools and if a witness says that up is down or black is white, they will treat this as no more than a working hypothesis. If, however, a witness says that the pants an accused wore on a particular day were black, but the accused believes they were grey, he is best advised to get his lawyers to put this difference to the witness. If he doesn't, the prosecution will be entitled to argue that the failure to put the evidence in dispute while the original witness was on the stand means that the point must now be regarded as settled. The defence, in other words, must serve notice that it will dispute a piece of testimony, and must do so while the witness who offers that evidence is still on the stand. To do otherwise is to accept that evidence as established fact, and failing to do this risks having subsequent evidence on this point disallowed. It is essential, then, that when a lawyer hears a witness say something about which he may wish to lead contradictory evidence, that he raise it with the witness. 'If the accused says that the pants he was wearing that morning were grey,' he might ask, 'would you have any comment on that?'

All of which is to say that there are sound technical reasons why any competent defence lawyer would have had to contest some parts of Mrs Lotz's testimony if any of his own witnesses, the accused included, were likely to dispute it. Whatever reservations Fred may or may not have expressed about upsetting Inge's mother, his lawyer had to cross-examine her. This duty to cross-examine Mrs Lotz – a duty she acknowledges with a somewhat-reluctant-but-nevertheless-understanding nod of the head – cannot explain, however, why De Bruyn seems so angry and surprised and frustrated when he rises to begin.

Universally known as 'Dup', De Bruyn is a short, stocky man nearing his sixtieth birthday. As he speaks, he adjusts his glasses, settling them higher up on his nose. This is a tic that will become familiar in the months to come, as is his habit of glancing at his notes and then, in the tight confines of his bench, rocking back on his heels to look heavenward. When especially agitated, he will also sometimes raise his index finger to emphasise a point. His age and his black robes, his rocking, the upward glances: all put me in mind of an ageing man at prayer.

'Mrs Lotz,' he says of the blue marks, 'the evidence you gave His Lordship and the Learned Assessors this morning: when was the first time you told anyone about it?'

    A: About a week later.

    Q: To whom did you mention it?

    A: My domestic.

    Q: Your domestic?

    A: Yes.

    Q: Anyone else?

    A: Later I told the legal people – Advocate Teunissen.

    Q: When is 'later', Madam?

    A: October last year.

    Q: Were you asked to make a further statement, Madam?

    A: No.

    Q: Is it correct to say that you made a long statement in May 2005 and that there is not a single word about this mentioned in that statement?

    A: Yes, I said nothing about this.

    Q: Was there a reason for this, Madam?

A: I didn't think it was important.

Q: How can that be? How could it not be important?

A: Because my daughter and I didn't discuss it any further.

Q: But, Madam, your daughter was killed in one of the
most vicious murders that people have seen. When you
made your statement in May 2005, the police would
have already told you that the accused's fingerprint had
been found on the DVD, not so?

A: Correct.

Q: 'Correct.' So there could not have been any doubt in
your mind that the accused was the murderer, not so?

A: I wasn't certain yet.

Q: What did you think?

A: I didn't think about it again.

Q: You didn't wonder if he was the murderer?

A: No.

Q: Did you think about the blue marks again?

A: Never again.

Q: 'Never again.' Until in October two years later – or
a year and a half later – you mentioned it to the
prosecutors?

A: Yes.

Q: What made you think about them again suddenly in
October?

A: In the time that my daughter had been dead, many
pictures came to my mind, which was, in the
beginning, blank.

De Bruyn's incredulity explodes: 'But, Madam, with the greatest respect, do you expect His Lordship and the Learned Assessors to believe that you, as a mother whose child was viciously murdered, that
you didn't think about the exceptional blue marks she had the weekend

before, when everyone is debating wildly about who the murderer is? Is that the evidence you expect His Lordship and the Learned Assessors to believe?'

At this outburst, the judge, who's been looking restive for some time, almost rises out of his chair. 'What the judge and the bench will believe,' he admonishes, pronouncing the words more quickly than usual and in a tight voice that verges on the menacing, 'is a question of the Court's own attitudes to the evidence. I don't think you must ask that kind of question. I don't think it is a fair one.'

* * *

Let us pause for a moment and consider this exchange.

De Bruyn had clearly been taken by surprise by the evidence led that morning. Later in the day, on one of the many occasions on which he would return to the blue marks (the number of these occasions being its own mute testimony to his surprise and lack of preparation), De Bruyn would note that he had been under the impression that Mrs Lotz had completed her testimony the day before. Why, he would ask then, hadn't she offered this testimony when she'd described Inge's last weekend at home, a point at which it would have fitted more naturally into the chronology of events? In response, Mrs Lotz would say that the prosecution simply hadn't asked the question. On rereading the transcripts, however, that answer seems a less than completely transparent explanation because, as a matter of literal fact, Mrs Lotz wasn't asked about the blue marks on the second morning either. The question Teunissen asked then and which had elicited the description of the blue marks and her unsatisfactory conversation with Inge, was: 'Mrs Lotz, to round off: the last weekend that Inge was home, the weekend before the fifteenth of March, did you notice anything strange?'

But De Bruyn was not surprised merely because he had not expected Mrs Lotz to continue testifying, but because, until that morning, he had never heard mention of any blue marks for the simple reason there was nothing in the docket about them. De Bruyn's surprise, then, was understandable and it left him with no option but to cast doubt on the veracity of Mrs Lotz's testimony.

Obviously, he could not refute her testimony that she saw blue marks on Inge's arms and legs. What he could do was to try to show that Mrs Lotz's own attitude to those marks over the previous twenty-three months suggested that the judge might not want to attach too much weight to this testimony.

It is implausible, De Bruyn's questions implied, that the mother of a murdered girl would tell no-one involved in the investigation – no-one at all, in fact, apart from her maid – that just days before the murder she had seen marks of a nature that had led her to wonder whether Fred had a violent streak. This, she'd said, was because she'd forgotten about them, but if that were true, she would also have had to have forgotten about her own response to the marks (the curiously framed question, 'Don't tell me that Fred hit you?') as well as Inge's non-answer ('What are you talking about, mom?'). Mrs Lotz would have had to have forgotten the subsequent conversation with her maid as well, one that, by her account, must have taken place a few days after the murder. Is this chain of forgotten events credible, De Bruyn was asking? Could she really have forgotten both seeing the marks and the subsequent speech acts, acts that would have reinforced the memory of the marks itself? The question went unasked, but one might also wonder about the police and the private investigators: did none of them think to ask Inge's parents if any of their daughter's boyfriends had had a violent temper? And in fact there is evidence in the docket that at least one officer did think to do this. This evidence comes in the form of the memorandum Superintendent Barkhuizen wrote after his conversation with Inspector de Villiers in early April 2005 about the poor state of the investigation, and in which the more junior man had received instructions that he regarded as racist. There, as point 23 out of 43, Barkhuizen instructed De Villiers to go to

Mrs Lotz with a woman police officer and to ask her about Inge's relationship with her boyfriend.

All of which makes the sequence of actions and omissions that must have occurred for Mrs Lotz to have failed to report the blue marks to the police seem implausible. How implausible can be gauged by a single metric: the blue marks were mentioned in court only once more during the whole of the next ten months. And, when they were brought up again, it was for one of the prosecutors to himself pooh-pooh them. This occurred at the close of the state's case, when the defence asked that the charges against Fred be dismissed, and referred in written heads of argument to the marks as an example of 'trial by ambush'. In response, Teunissen's colleague, Christénus van der Vijver, told the judge that 'It was never the prosecution's intention to make a big thing of the marks. We simply offered an opportunity to a mother to share with the Court certain things that came back to her in retrospect, when things were calmer. More than that, we never intended.'

With that single exception, it is as if a blanket of embarrassed silence fell over the whole business.

* * *

And what of the other key elements of Mrs Lotz's testimony? What about the strange words she attributed to Fred – his offer to become 'the child in the house' and the incriminating knowledge that Inge had been murdered that afternoon (a detail about which even the pathologist could not be sure)?

Like the blue marks, these details about his behaviour did not appear in either of Mrs Lotz's two sworn statements.

This is curious, especially since the statements Mrs Lotz gave were taken after Fred had been arrested, when the police ought to have pressed her to remember anything incriminating about their suspect's actions and words. But the omissions would be less curious if these new details simply filled a void. Instead, at least one appears to be directly contradicted by evidence that Mrs Lotz did include in her sworn statements from May 2005.

Given to the police about a month after they had matched Fred's fingerprints to those on Folien One and had subsequently searched his home and office, Mrs Lotz's statement makes no mention of Fred's telling her that Inge had been murdered in her flat in the afternoon. Instead, it says that after she came out of the house and saw Fred in his bakkie, he climbed out of the vehicle to approach her. As they were walking towards the house, Marius drove up. So far, so good. What is recorded next is more troubling: 'I wanted Fred to tell me what was going on,' the statement reads. 'He said I must stay calm and hear from Marius. Marius, Fred and I walked towards my front door, to just inside the security gate. I wanted to know what was going on. Marius said we must go inside. I can't remember Marius's precise words, but at that point he said that Inge had been murdered. At that point I was very upset and I went into the house. Fred and Marius followed me.'

So, in contrast to her testimony on the stand, Fred did talk to her before Marius arrived, telling her to stay calm and to wait to hear from Marius. What he is not reported as having said is that Inge had been murdered that afternoon. By this version, only Marius spoke of Inge having been murdered, though even he is not recorded as having said that the crime had been committed in the afternoon.

This version of events, De Bruyn pointed out when he cross-examined Mrs Lotz, was also supported by Marius's statement to the police in which he described arriving at the Lotz house and meeting Fred and *Tannie* Juanita. 'While Fred and I stood outside the front door,' Marius's statement reads, 'I gave him the news. As I spoke to him, he leaned against the wall. I could see he was very emotional. I thought he might collapse and I supported him physically. Fred said nothing and began to cry. While I spoke with him, *Tannie* Juanita came outside. I could see that she expected the worst and I shared the news with her. *Tannie* Juanita was very badly upset and ran into the house.'

In neither Mrs Lotz's statement nor Marius's is there any mention of Fred's conveying the news to her. Until Mrs Lotz's testimony, then, there had never been any suggestion other than that Marius was the messenger.

The discrepancies are curious. And they would become even more so later when it would emerge that, by the time Marius arrived at the Lotzes', the only information he had been given had come from Christo Pretorius, the friend he'd asked to check on Inge. Christo would testify that in the first call he made to Marius, and, indeed, the first calls he made to two other people, he had said that Inge had committed suicide. He had also said as much to Inge's neighbour, who called the police and reported that to them. How Christo could have thought this if he'd seen Inge's mutilated body is a mystery no-one can explain. It is, nevertheless, a fact that the police records of the emergency call they received indicate that they were called out to an apparent suicide. It is odd, then, that Mrs Lotz's statements and testimony agree that when the news was conveyed to her, the words used, the words that stuck in her mind and which she will never forget, were 'Inge' and 'murdered'. How could either Fred or Marius – whomever it was who conveyed the news to Mrs Lotz that fateful night – know that Inge had been murdered?

It is a question that would nag the judge throughout the trial.

10

Journalistic convention dictates that those who cover public spectacles must assume either an air of cynical, hard-boiled detachment or of the kind of scholarly calm that is thought to attach to the well-informed and objective observer. If you project the latter, you are marked as wise; if you project the former, you are not just wise, you are wise to the ways of the world. The great difficulty with either of these approaches to writing about a criminal trial is that they inevitably misrepresent the experience of the spectacle itself, which is, above all, one of excitement.

A trial, writes Janet Malcolm, feels like a duel before dawn; to follow one closely is to feel that one has 'been brought to the clearing and can smell the wet grass; at the end, as the sky begins to show more light and the doctor is stanching a wound, one takes away a sense of having attended a momentous, if brutal and inconclusive, occasion.'

The main reason trials are so exciting is that so much is at stake. Will the truth come out? Will justice be done? Will the dead be avenged? Will the guilty be punished? Will the innocent go free? These are amongst the weightiest questions any human, process must ever answer. But

Malcolm's most important insight, I have come to understand, is that a court case is always in some way 'inconclusive'.

Nor is it hard to see why this is so: a trial is always about something that happened in the past, and has become, for that reason, inaccessible to mortal man. Whatever it is that may or may not have happened when the crime was committed, because it is shrouded by the veils of time, no judge, jury or Grand Inquisitor can ever observe the event for himself. The result is that a trial is only indirectly about what really happened. Instead, it is much more concerned about weighing what the evidence suggests about what really happened. Whether that evidence consists of memories lodged in the minds of those who were present or of a pair of hairs that might easily have gone unnoticed but for the hard work of the forensic investigators, it is hard to overstate the significance of the distinction between the crime itself and the evidence of that crime.

While it might be said that what really happened in Inge's flat exists in some way that is independent of all inquiries into it, and that what happened is independent also of the physical and mental traces it left behind, the same is not true of evidence. Evidence is a human artefact, something that is found and produced and interpreted by investigators, whether they are street cops interviewing the victim's neighbours or lab-coated scientists testing swabs of blood. Each and every piece of evidence in a trial owes something to the application of conscious thought and deliberate action. And, because each piece of evidence is at least as much a human artefact as it is a fact of nature, its relationship to 'what really happened' is, to that extent, attenuated.

There is, in other words, a gap between 'the crime' and 'what we know about the crime', the extent of which is determined by how much evidence is gathered, how well it is interpreted and how honestly it is presented to a judge. Some witnesses will forget things – sometimes, important things. Some witnesses will tell the judge what they think the prosecutor or the defence wants them to say. Some will condense complex events into simple chronologies of 'and then ... and then ... and then'. Some will say things that contradict what they have said previously. Some will express themselves imprecisely or ambiguously. There is not much point in berating witnesses for all of this. This is, after all, how the mind works, and we are usually comfortable living with the fuzziness and equivocation and contradiction that it entails. That is how we are, and judicial processes would never produce justice if their procedures did not evolve to deal with this.

And yet the consequences of all of this remain incredibly important because, however small it seems, the gap between 'what really happened' and what the evidence is understood to show is always, finally, unbridgeable. We can never really, really know what happened because we can only access the past through the flotsam and jetsam that is left behind. We must try to establish the cause by careful examination and interrogation of its effects.

But that is not all.

Evidence is required to establish the facts, but, having been established, most facts must themselves morph into evidence, a process that requires divining their meaning through inference and interpretation. A court may establish as a fact, for example, that my fingerprints were found at the scene of a bank robbery, but that may only mean that I am a client of the bank. The interpretation of a particular fact, in other words, is at least as important as the fact itself.

It is confusingly, maddeningly circular: evidence must be interpreted to establish the facts; the facts, after they are interpreted, become evidence.

An instructive example of the problem relates to how the police reacted to the detailed account Fred provided to them, less than twelve hours after the murder, of his movements on that day. This was in the early hours of the morning after Inge's body had been found, when detectives collected Fred from Inge's parents' home. At their offices, he was interviewed by Superintendent Neville de Beer, whose notes record that Fred told him that he had slept at Inge's flat the night before the murder, that he had gone to a lecture in the morning, that he had seen Inge briefly after the lecture, that he had collected something from a furniture dealer in town, that he had gone to his office where he spent the day in a meeting, and that he had gone home shortly after six.

Fast-forward from Fred's interview with Superintendent de Beer on 17 March to the middle of the following month. By this point, Fred's home and office had been searched by the police and he knew he was their prime suspect. At that point, his lawyers wrote a series of letters to the man now heading the investigation, Director Attie Trollip. One of these letters pointed out that their client had an alibi which the police had not yet properly investigated, and listed, once again, the names of Fred's boss and colleagues.

Nothing happened.

None of Fred's colleagues were interviewed. No statements were taken.

Then, towards the end of May, rumours were heard that the police had sought a warrant for Fred's arrest, the development even making it into the newspapers.

And yet Fred's alibi witnesses were still not interviewed by the police.

Then, on 28 May, Fred's father stepped in, employing private investigators, former members of the police and the Scorpions, to take statements from people Fred claimed to have been meeting with on 16 March. It was an unusual step, and, because these were agents of Fred's father, a controversial one. Still, the statements were taken – six of them – and a not unrepresentative sample of the relevant portion of one of these reads: 'As far as I can recall, Fred gave a presentation on 16 March 2005 and also joined the discussion that followed. I knew he had a lecture that morning and he had arrived late for the session. Fred sat between Shahana and Mkuseni on the days he attended. He never left the session for a prolonged period. We all left the session at the same time.' That statement was signed on 13 June 2005 by Moneira Francis, a 43-year-old systems engineer who'd worked for Old Mutual for 23 years.

Fred was arrested two days later, on 15 June, and, in the days after his arrest, his lawyers made the statements taken from Fred's colleagues available to the police. It was only then that any effort was made to follow up his claim to having been at work.

The defence, when they got their opportunity to cross-examine Director Trollip, made a big deal about all of this. Fred, they said, had given the police detailed, specific information about his movements on the day of the murder, information that amounted to a complete alibi. A guilty man, they said, would not have proffered all this information because, for all he knew, it would be followed up immediately. Doesn't the fact that he gave that information so early help prove that it was true? they asked.

Director Trollip had two answers to this, one of which takes us down a logical rabbit hole. 'Reference was made yesterday to an alibi that was set out as early as 17 March,' he offered about halfway through his second day on the stand. 'I find this strange, in the sense that here is a person who is simply being interviewed by the police, and already he is beginning to set out an alibi for something he was not charged with and for which he has not even been told that he is a suspect. All those statements look as if he has already begun to carefully consider how he will account for his time. M'Lord, this was just a person whom the police approached for general information.'

It's a peculiar claim, suggesting, as it does, that the earlier a suspect is able to set out his movements on the day of the murder, the more suspicious it will be. Later that night, next to the notes I had taken as I listened to Trollip testify, I scrawled, 'Usually it takes them three or four months to come up with an alibi.' Peculiar though this claim seemed to be, it was not peculiar enough to prevent Advocate Teunissen from repeating it twice during her closing arguments. It was strange, she would say then, that Fred, who was not a suspect at the time, had a complete alibi ready when Superintendent de Beer interviewed him on 17 March.

The argument, I thought, got no stronger through repetition.

The second explanation Trollip offered for the lack of urgency the investigators showed in following up Fred's alibi was in some ways less logically alarming, and revolved around the fact that it had been private detectives employed by Fred's father who had taken these statements. Because they were employed by the accused's father, Trollip implied, they might not have been objective in their work. It was a claim he spiced up with an insinuation that Fred and his father may have also sought to influence the content of the witnesses' statements by talking to them before they were interviewed by the investigators.

'I delayed dealing with those statements for a while for very specific reasons,' Trollip said to De Bruyn. 'It was strange, firstly, that private people were going to take statements from people who were potential state's witnesses. My information was that they were first brought together, and that a discussion was had with them before statements were taken. This really influenced me: to go there at that point, and to take statements from such people worried me. I wanted first to get as much information as possible before I would then approach the right people.'

Later, he added a further cause for suspicion: that arrangements for the interviews between Fred's colleagues and the private detectives had been facilitated by one of the personnel officers at Old Mutual.

Trollip was on thin ice with this testimony because he knew that he could present no evidence at all that there was ever an attempt made by Fred or Louis to influence the contents of the alibi statements. The only information he had was from Marius Botha, Fred's by-now former flatmate, who'd told Trollip that he had seen Fred and his father having coffee with two staffers at the Old Mutual headquarters in one of the on-site coffee shops. Trollip had no knowledge of what transpired in this conversation and certainly had no evidence that a deal was being struck to lie on Fred's behalf.

But maybe Trollip didn't need evidence; maybe all he needed to do was to insinuate a conspiracy, since the judge seemed quite happy to join the dots himself. Certainly, this was my impression when the judge interrupted De Bruyn as the lawyer was putting to the detective his thesis that throughout the investigation, the police had proceeded from the assumption of Fred's guilt, and that it was this prejudice that had led them to see a conversation over coffee with some of Fred's colleagues as evidence of a conspiracy. 'Innocent matters,' De Bruyn complained, 'became the subject of suspicion.'

Before Trollip could respond to this, however, the judge stepped in: 'Well, we don't know yet that it was innocent.'

'"Seemingly innocent?"' De Bruyn suggested as an alternative.

'That is something different,' the judge agreed. 'They could perhaps have been busy with some or other conspiracy. We don't know until we hear testimony about what was said and what happened.'

Whatever the constitutional niceties about whether the defence has to prove that a 'seemingly innocent' conversation was, in fact, innocent, it is clear that the possibility of a plot to influence witnesses' testimony had been planted in the judge's mind, as Trollip had clearly hinted. It is, however, a proposition so extraordinary that one really must pause to consider the contours of the imagination in which this idea could take root.

Fred's alibi witnesses were not his friends or family or fellow congregants at his church. They were his colleagues and superiors at an office at which he had worked for less than three months. They came from different generations and they moved in different social circles. In this context, it is hard to conceive how Trollip, who had 35 years' worth of experience in the police when Inge was murdered and who spent 14 years in the security branch and four post-apartheid years as the head of the Western Cape's crime intelligence division, could have come to believe that they would all lie for Fred. To what end? For what reason?

Nor is it easy to think that, if Fred were guilty, either he or his father would have taken the unnecessary risk of asking these people to lie on his behalf. This, after all, was something they might very easily report to the police.

It is possible, of course, that the witnesses were mistaken about Fred's whereabouts at the time of the murder. But to profess a concern that they might have come under the influence of Fred and his father's plotting suggests a paranoid's gift for finding explanations for unwanted facts in the machinations of one's enemies. There is another, darker question that might be asked, too: where could Trollip, with all his experience as a policeman, have come to the conclusion that people in some institutions will reflexively lie for their colleagues? Could it be that his suspicions about the organisational culture in Old Mutual reflect something of the organisational culture in the police?

But perhaps his suspicions were not directed at Old Mutual's organisational culture, however. Perhaps they were directed at Fred as an individual. I say this because it is not just his colleagues whom Trollip appears to believe came under Fred's baleful influence. The same is also true of the private investigators hired by the Lotzes to help the police investigate the death of their daughter.

It is public knowledge that these investigators – themselves former police officers, one of whom was Trollip's boss before retiring – withdrew from the case or were fired from it (depending on whom one asks) because they did not agree with the police's focus on Fred. So, when De Bruyn raised their report in court, Trollip said that he had been concerned that the private detectives seemed to be trying 'to protect' Fred and that the report they wrote to Inge's parents 'was written from the accused's perspective'. Fred, he complained, was the source of all the investigators' information and they had completely excluded him as a suspect.

It is tempting to suggest that, in the context of Fred's demonic powers of persuasion, it is almost a miracle that Trollip himself was able to stay so focused, but it is important not to be too judgmental of the policeman. Indeed, one might even feel a little sorry for an officer so close to retirement who is reduced to suggesting that it is suspicious when suspects provide verifiable alibis too swiftly or that they can turn the heads of their colleagues, their bosses and even the former cops employed by the victim's parents. The truth is that, given the weight of forensic evidence that had accumulated against Fred by the middle of 2005, Trollip was probably right to question the contents of the alibi witnesses' statements and of the private investigators' report.

At that point, Fred stank of guilt.

PART FOUR

11

The High Court in Cape Town sits a few blocks from Parliament. Before I found more convenient parking on the opposite side of the court building, I would hurry past the legislature's ornate buildings, with their air of self-importance and the anachronistic statue of a long-dead English queen, past the anonymous building that houses much of the provincial government, and turn into the bohemian atmosphere of Long Street. If I had the time – and I usually did – I would stop for a coffee and watch tourists and backpackers wander the streets. I'd check my email and read the paper. My coffee done, I'd gather my things together and head to court, passing, inevitably, the police vans arriving with their loads of awaiting-trial prisoners whose day in court had come at last and who were being offloaded, amidst shouted laughs reminiscent of a school outing, at the secure back entrance of the building. I, of course, used the public entrance. This was fronted by a pair of heavy wooden doors at the top of a short flight of steps that rose unexpectedly and with very little grandeur out of the pavement. Usually, the court's smokers and reporters would congregate here before we began. The exceptions to this rule were those mornings when crowds of particularly rowdy activists or supporters of some or other cause claimed the steps as their own. When that happened, the smokers and the journalists stood across the street.

Immediately beyond the heavy wooden doors that led into the building was a steeper, narrower flight of stairs at the top of which one entered a high-ceilinged lobby with a marbled floor that was cool and grey. It was a space that would have felt open and airy were it not for the thick sheets of security glass that channelled the public into narrow, impatient queues and which made the room feel cramped and ill-planned. The surly guards, the clunky metal detectors and the x-ray machines created a sense that the outside world was a threat, something to be kept out.

Beyond the metal detectors, things were different. There, the building took on a certain otherworldliness, and inverted the apparent purpose of the security measures: now it seemed that these had less to do with keeping the armed and dangerous out of the building, and more with the preservation of a world somewhat removed from the quotidian realities outside. This otherworldliness was not just a matter of the dress code, which had lawyers bedecked in the traditional garb of their tribe, scurrying through ill-lit corridors, the swirls of their black robes making them look like great birds of prey. Nor was it just a consequence of the language of court, where those to whom the right to speak was granted would address each other as 'My Lord' or 'my learned friend'. These had their effect, defamiliarising the world and reconfiguring social interaction, but, over the months of the trial, I came to see that these elements were like the dress of the woman from Lhassa described in a poem by Wallace Stevens: 'an invisible element of that place made visible.'

The 'invisible element' that animated all of this strange attire and behaviour was nothing less than the law's idea of itself, and, in particular, its sense of itself as separate from and elevated above the common run. The sense of antiquity and majesty and formality were all aspects of this self-presentation, but so too were the law's preciousness and rigidity and even its eccentricity. The result was the courtroom in which Fred's trial was heard seemed a space densely packed with rituals, a space in which it seemed only fitting that, when the afternoon sun shone through the room's glass-domed ceiling, it would illuminate only the judge, leaving the rest of the court to bathe in his reflected light.

The judge so eloquently lit by the afternoon sun was Deon van Zyl, a middle-aged man with thinning hair swept over his skull from left to right, a man thickening beneath his red robe, a man who was hearing his last case before he would be retiring. On either side him sat two assessors. One was a purse-lipped woman, a lawyer with decades of experience and an expensive hairdo. She had a sharp, penetrating look, and, as she listened to the evidence, she would lean forward as if to reach out and catch the testimony. The other assessor was a dapper, elegant man – a former magistrate, neatly pressed and utterly inscrutable. He whispered occasionally to the judge, but his face gave nothing away. Over the weeks and months of the trial, piles of annotated, well-thumbed paper, some collected in files, others bound and stapled willy-nilly, would accumulate before these three. But at the start of the trial, the long desk behind which they sat was bare, a blank slate.

Behind the three people who would decide Fred's case, the court's walls were panelled. The wood was old, well oiled and beautifully worn, and it created an ambience as stiff, as impractical and as pleasing to the eye as a dress uniform. In the centre of the wall behind the judge's head was mounted a carving of the national coat of arms, which had been designed and adopted in 2000. Its wood was redder, newer and coarser-grained than the rest of the wall, and the contrast with the older panelling made it seem what it was – a recent addition, not yet comfortably integrated into the cultural and institutional whole.

Beneath the platform on which the judge sat in his high-backed chair, three court officials, whose duty it was to keep the record straight, faced into the court. The first of these was the stenographer, an earnest, mousy woman who sat behind her computer and fussed about the cellphone signals that interfered with her microphones. In the centre, the judge's secretary, glittering in jewellery and blond dye, kept track of the documents being entered into evidence. She was flanked by the court usher, a man who slouched habitually in his seat, his attention permanently but surreptitiously drawn to a newspaper folded before him until the defence or prosecution required his services. When that happened, he would rise to collect multiple copies of papers and distribute them: one each for the judge and the two assessors, one for whichever witness was in the stand, and one for the opposing counsel. His every movement was tired and reluctant, his bearing that of a man of small ambition and little energy. But how he and the documents he bore travelled! From a lawyer to his opposite number to the judge to the witness and then back, each poring over the text or photo or object before handing it back to the usher. Just mapping the Brownian motion of this evidence through the overly air-conditioned, occasionally sunlit space would tell one a great deal about how truth was being uncovered and how contested it was.

Across from the officials and beneath the dock in which Fred would spend his days, was a series of pews so small and cramped they seemed to have been built for the more diminutive people of an earlier time. In these sat the lawyers, both for the defence and for the prosecution, as well as the occasional expert witness drafted in to assist one or other side to ask questions of a witness. The benches were reserved for participants in the trial, a category that did not include either Inge's family or Fred's, all of whom were consigned to chairs and stools and unbacked benches pressed against the walls, or to a public gallery that projected over the dock.

Fred sat elevated and alone behind his lawyers and the prosecutors. The dock had been built for security – it could be entered, for example, by a steep flight of stairs that rose from the cells beneath the floor – but there was also a psychological element to its design and placement. From where he sat, it was impossible to avoid the judge's eye or to fail to look his accusers in the face.

Alone in a structure built to hold as many as a dozen accused, Fred looked small and abandoned.

*   *   *

There was about this room a sense of faded grandeur. It was something that was imparted by the warmth of the wood on walls and floor. It was something that oozed from the lawyers' cramped benches, with their scuffed leather and the old-fashioned gold-and-black notices stencilled on the ends. It was something that rose from the ancient bags in which the lawyers carried their briefs but which seemed like nothing so much as old, faithful pets. Basset hounds, I thought. Here, the room seemed to proclaim, is the glory and dignity of another age.

There was a sadness about this, a sense that one was witness to something passing into history, and my first impression was that something of immense importance was being lost. Later, though, after I had wandered around the building more and after I had spent some time in the annexe in which more modern courts had been built, I came to understand that the whole point about the grandeur of this courtroom was that it was fading. It was precisely the sense of its belonging to another age that made the law seem both majestic and durable, and it reflected, I thought, not so much the effect of the passage of time, but the core of the law's idea of itself. It was an idea whose most romantic expression comes from an American judge quoted by VS Naipaul: 'The common law is a majestic thing,' he said. 'It has a remarkable capacity to resolve disputes in a way that not only preserves civilisation, but enhances it. It is not unusual for me to find myself guided in a decision by a decision which a judge made a thousand years ago. I am aware I'm serving a larger civilisation. And I know I am serving it.'

It was, in other words, not just nostalgia or sentimentality that shaped the ambience of the court, but something more strategic. It was an assertion of age-old wisdom and decency, the staking of a claim to a rich and ancient history whose age and richness were some of the reasons why people would choose to subject themselves to its authority.

All these signs of a fading world were, in other words, entirely, if perhaps unconsciously, functional. They were gestures to what might be called a symbolic dimension, one which operated to present the law as a manifestation of an ancient wisdom and an old-world sense of fairness. It was, however, a symbolism that seemed more plausible in the abstract than it was on the scene itself. There it would be confronted at every turn with the dangerous question of whether the law could truly lay claim to the dignity and majesty of a different age if its agents and officers seemed so often to depart from the standards of wisdom and honesty and fairness that were essential components of that dignity and majesty. An instructive example of the gap between the expectation one might have of how the agents of the law ought to behave and the manner in which they actually did behave arose almost before the trial began. It revolved around the duty of the prosecution to disclose information to the defence about the evidence the police had accumulated so that a proper defence could be mounted.

The incident in question related to a visit one of the investigators – Bruce Bartholomew – had paid to a world authority on shoeprint evidence in the middle of 2006, about eight months before the trial began, and which had been reported in the press in October 2006 under the headline FBI MAN HELPS IN LOTZ MURDER.

'The testimony of a former special agent of the FBI who was involved in the cases against OJ Simpson and Timothy McVeigh, who was responsible for the Oklahoma City bombing,' *Rapport*'s story began, 'will be used in the Inge Lotz murder trial.' It went on to record that Bartholomew had visited that former agent, a certain William Bodziak, in the United States, and that the American had supported Bartholomew's finding that a bloody mark found on the bathroom floor in Inge's flat matched the sole of one of Fred's shoes. The report also noted that Fred's lawyers had objected strongly to the fact that the state had refused to hand over Bodziak's report to them. It was an objection to which Fred's lawyers returned on the first morning of the trial when they complained of the failure of the prosecution to respond to their repeated requests for documentation relating to Bartholomew's visit to Bodziak. The complaint was included as a single paragraph in a forty-page statement from the defence that was entered into the record immediately after the prosecutors had read out the charges against Fred. Given that much of the rest of the forty pages were given over to alleging that the evidence against Fred had been fabricated, even at the time it seemed curious that the only issue to which the prosecutors responded after the document had been read was the question of their alleged failure to hand over this documentation. It was this alone that provoked a response from one of the prosecutors, Advocate Christénus van der Vijver.

Van der Vijver, a greying man in his forties, has features so small and sharp they suggest a man who operates on a tight rein. It is an effect heightened by a sharp, pugnacious chin, which might be described by some as strong, but which I thought of as brittle. It creates an impression of a man with a tendency to anger, but one who has sought to master himself, in the process transforming innate anger into sharp prickliness. But there is also an unexpected twinkle in Van der Vijver's eye, a suggestion, perhaps, that his courtroom persona is not all there is to say about this man. It is an impression that would be cemented some months later when I caught sight of him walking in the street with a friend. Out of his robes and the stiff formality of the court, with its 'my learned friends' and its bowing to the judge and the polite laughing at his jokes, Van der Vijver seemed quite different: engaging and happy.

I would see that later. On the first morning of the trial, however, Van der Vijver felt compelled to defend the unbruised integrity of the police and prosecutors. He rose from his pew, his brittle, pointed chin thrusting forward. 'The impression has been created,' he said, 'that there is certain information about Mr Bartholomew's visit to the USA that the state is withholding. We wish to place on record – and these are our instructions – that there is no report of this kind.'

It was as categorical a statement as might be imagined, and it came months after the first requests for documentation, along with the lack of response, had become a matter of public record. And yet, when Bartholomew was on the stand six weeks later, it turned out that there was, in fact, a report. And it turned out that that report had been signed by Director Attie Trollip – the same Attie Trollip who was sitting on a bench immediately in front of Christénus van der Vijver when the prosecutor had stood up to insist that his advice was that 'there is no report of this kind.'

Some dignity. Some majesty.

*　*　*

There will be a time to return to the bloody mark on Inge's bathroom floor and to the report Bartholomew produced about his visit to the USA, but let us leave that for a moment and consider something else that happened on the first morning of the trial. This had to do with the fingerprint that the police said had been found on the DVD cover and which, having been matched with Fred's prints, had been said to annihilate his alibi. This is what Christénus van der Vijver had to say about the fingerprint that morning: 'M'Lord, the summary of material facts that is before you refers, naturally, to the alleged fingerprints of the accused that were found on the rented DVD. The state is not, in fact, going to proceed with this evidence. This is a decision the prosecution has made for a number of reasons. However, if it appears in the course of the trial that it will play a role, it will be necessary for the state to lead evidence about the taking of the fingerprints on the night of 16 March or the morning of 17 March, in order to place the Court in a position to judge for itself the *bone fides* or the *male fides* of the people involved.'

This verbal commitment not to rely on the fingerprint evidence was backed up by a letter to Fred's lawyers signed by Van der Vijver's boss, the head of the prosecution service in the Western Cape. Dated two months earlier, the letter consisted of only two sentences, the operative one being: 'This serves to confirm that the state no longer intends to proceed with the evidence concerning your client's alleged fingerprints on the DVD cover.' To this letter were attached the reports of two forensic investigators at the police laboratories in Pretoria, both of whom raised serious doubts about whether Folien One could have come from a DVD cover.

Given Van der Vijver's words and the letter from his boss, it is impossible not to think that on 12 February the prosecution believed that the fingerprint evidence did not support their case. Nothing else can explain why Van der Vijver would say that the prosecution would not be presenting the evidence except to show that any problems there may have been were not the result of any malice on the part of police officers involved, but were, instead, mistakes made in good faith.

This was not a trivial issue, for it makes a very, very big difference to one's attitudes to the case and to the whole criminal justice system if one thinks that evidence like this was deliberately fabricated or if one believes an honest mistake was made. Still, if the only question was the character of the *fides* of the officers involved, then the question of the fingerprint evidence proving what it was initially said to prove must have been off the table. And yet, some six months later, when arguing against a defence application to have the charges dismissed on the grounds that there was no case to answer, Van der Vijver would take the opposite view. By that point, he was prepared to argue that Folien One was precisely what it had originally been held out to be: an image of Fred's fingerprint lifted from the only item in Inge's flat that could place him there at a time he had claimed to have been at work. At that point, and after reviewing some of the evidence offered by the police officers called to the stand, Van der Vijver would say, 'In all honesty, M'Lord, after hearing all the evidence, after hearing the evidence of Botha and Swartz even on the question about the powder that was used, the state is no longer convinced that a mistake crept in here.'

Those were Van der Vijver's words at the beginning of August 2007. By the beginning of October, during closing arguments, he was prepared to go even further. All but daring the judge to find that Folien One was not what the police said it was, he would list the names of six officers whose sworn testimony would have to be rejected as consisting of nothing more than lies and distortions offered in pursuit of a grand conspiracy. 'With the best will in the world,' he would say then, 'we cannot see any reasons why that should be done.'

In other words, whatever the express attitude of the prosecution to Folien One on the day the trial began, it was clear that Fred's fingerprints were intended to be taken as evidence of his guilt.

Some dignity. Some majesty.

12

There is no subject so settled in the public mind the close examination of which will fail to reveal deep fault lines. An instructive example is dactylography, the formal name for the science of fingerprint identification, a science that is thought to be premised on the assertion that no two fingerprints in the world are identical. Surprisingly, it is an assertion that is as yet unproved.

Perhaps just as surprising as the fact that this is unproved is another fact: that it doesn't much matter whether it is literally true that every fingerprint is unique. Even if this is not the case, it is well established that the likelihood of two prints being exactly alike is so infinitesimally small – the only calculation I've seen put it at about one chance in sixty-four billion – as to be irrelevant for practical purposes. As a consequence, the chances of two people implicated in a single investigation having duplicate prints is vanishingly small.

There is, however, a genuine problem. This is that, in practice, the latent prints that investigators find at crime scenes are always partial and distorted and blurred and broken. It is these imperfect fragments that they must match against the full prints taken from suspects or found in their databases. This is done through the careful examination for what are variously called 'Galton points' or 'minutiae', and which consist of tiny breaks and imperfections in the ridges and furrows that create the basic pattern of a print. If a match is to be made, it is on the basis that there is a precise correspondence between the minutiae found in a print left at a crime scene and those found in the suspect's inked prints taken at a police station or found on the database.

South African law accepts that a match has been made if a fingerprint examiner finds a minimum of seven common and corresponding points. But here's the thing: no-one knows whether seven is the 'right' number. The calculation that produced the one-in-sixty-four-billion-against odds of a false positive was based on a full set of up to fifty Galton points on a fingerprint. Using fewer common points reduces those very long odds, but no-one knows by how much. Bizarrely, there are no universal standards, and different jurisdictions respond to this problem in different ways, with examiners in some having to find more common points than examiners in others.

As far as I can tell, for those justice systems that count points in this manner, South Africa's minimum number of matches (seven) is the lowest accepted. Others require as many as fourteen common points, and would, one assumes, be that much less likely to convict someone based on a mistaken match.

An example of the problem, and one that pains fingerprint examiners no end, is the Mayfield case of 2004, in which the FBI was eventually forced to acknowledge that three of its fingerprint examiners (along with one independent expert) each made their own conclusive match between a fingerprint of Brandon Mayfield, an American lawyer, and one lifted by the Spanish police off a detonator used in the Madrid bombings in 2004.

Mayfield, who happened to have converted to Islam, was detained and interrogated for two weeks by American authorities, and was eventually paid $2 million in compensation after the Spanish police found the Algerian man who had really planted the bombs, and whose prints really matched those found on the detonator.

Mistakes of this kind, however rare, raise questions about the status of fingerprint identification as a science. Another kind of problem is that, while fingerprints – as physical objects – cannot lie, the officers who lift them can. Take the case of Herman Wiggins, a police officer working in San Diego in the early 1970s whose practice it was to stop homeless people in the street, have them stand with their hands on his car, and frisk them. It's not the most edifying of policing practices, but what happened next was worse: after the frisking, Wiggins would drive around the corner, dust the bonnet of his car and pocket the homeless men's prints. Later, when called to a burglary, he would mix these pre-existing lifts into the pile of prints that were lifted at the crime scene. Then, a few days after that part of the investigation was complete, he'd phone the detective who was handling the case to say that he had information from a confidential source to the effect that a certain homeless man living on a certain street may have committed the crime. The detective would arrest the man Wiggins had identified and fingerprint him. Naturally, these prints would match some of the prints lifted at the burglary, and an innocent man would go to jail.

Patrolman Wiggins was caught after forty instances of fabricating evidence in this manner. And it was some version of this that Pat Wertheim's report had said had probably happened to Fred.

* * *

Wertheim's is a Texan personality. His ties are loud. His belt buckles are loud. His voice is not soft. The tone he uses tends to the urgent and his choice of language is not always moderate. Even in the witness box, where a certain restraint is usually thought to be in order, he gesticulates wildly as he speaks; in a coffee shop he poses a significant risk to innocent passers-by. He has grey hair and glasses. He has gold cuff links which sport an impression of a grandchild's fingerprint. He has a persistent case of prostate cancer and a career in fingerprinting that dates back to the 1970s, during the course of which he has devoted a significant proportion of his considerable energies to inquiries into problematic fingerprints and fingerprint identifications.

His motives for this are complex. Undoubtedly there is something appealing to the showman in him about the iconoclasm that this interest entails. Undoubtedly, also, there is something about the pleasures of defending the underdog and the innocent. His official answer when asked this question, however, is that if forensic investigators want to claim to be using science, they cannot be concerned exclusively with pursuing convictions. To do so implies a loss of objectivity. Like their academic and theoretical counterparts, as practical scientists they must be prepared to subject their own practices and, more importantly, fellow practitioners to scrutiny. Not everyone is competent. Not everyone is honest. Not everyone is brave enough to stand up to hard-gunning detectives and prosecutors. And every time a forensic investigator fails to do his professional duty, the whole community suffers. For Wertheim, then, his interest in questionable fingerprint evidence is not just because he is interested in righting wrongs, but because addressing poor practice is an essential check on a craft that, unwatched, might be abused.

* * *

It was Wertheim's report that first attracted me to Fred's case. As will be recalled, the report had sought to show that Fred's prints had not been lifted off the DVD cover (as the police claimed) but had probably come from a glass. Wertheim had come to this conclusion on the basis of a close examination of how the fingerprint and the rest of the folien looked: the orientation and angle of the prints themselves, the apparent presence of a lip print, the evidence that there had been droplets of water on the surface from which the print was lifted (some of which were still wet when it had been dusted), and the absence of the kind of background noise one might expect to find on a dust-and-folien lift taken from a plastic DVD cover.

Wertheim's method, in other words, was to look at the lift and try to determine whether it looked like the sort of thing that might have come from the substrate the police said it had. He said it didn't. He said that because there was no other lift in the docket that might have come from a DVD holder and which might have been accidentally mislabelled, the police must knowingly be lying about the fingerprint, that their evidence, in short, had been fabricated.

But Wertheim wasn't the only person to look at the print, and he wasn't the only one to write a report about it or to offer testimony in court, and the prosecution offered its own experts to try to refute Wertheim's claims. These we will return to. For the moment, however, it is important to focus on the core of the prosecution's argument, which was that the process of lifting the print, documenting it and then storing it safely in police registries meant that, whatever Fred's well-paid experts might say, the continuity of the chain of evidence proved that Folien One must have been lifted from the DVD cover. To prove this, the prosecutors offered the evidence of a wide array of witnesses.

There was Inspector Mariaan Booysens, who was a member of the three-person fingerprinting team in Inge's flat, and who testified that she had dusted the DVD cover and that she had found an identifiable print. Having found this print, she testified, she handed the DVD cover to her colleague, Constable Swartz, who was responsible for lifting all prints found in the flat.

There was Inspector Heinrich Coetzee, the second member of the fingerprinting team, who testified that he had been aware that Inspector

Booysens had found a print on the DVD cover and that she had handed it to Swartz for lifting.

There was Constable Elton John Swartz, the third and most important member of the fingerprinting team, who testified to lifting Folien One from the DVD cover after it had been handed to him by Inspector Booysens. Swartz also testified that he took Folien One, along with the other ten lifts he made, to his offices in Paarl, and that he had had the officers manning the digital fingerprint machines run the newly lifted prints against police databases.

There was Bruce Bartholomew, the shoeprint expert, who was in the flat when the fingerprinting team was going about its business, and who testified that he had been aware of the discovery of a fingerprint on the DVD cover and Booysens's handing of the DVD cover to Swartz. Unlike Booysens and Coetzee, Bartholomew was also prepared to swear that he had seen the results of Swartz's lift while still in the flat, and that Folien One was that lift.

There was Captain Andries Matheus, Constable Swartz's boss, who said he had inspected Swartz's work within the prescribed twenty-four hours and that Folien One was among the lifts he checked. He also testified that he too took Folien One and the other lifts to be scanned into the police database on the morning of 18 March, and that after that he gave orders that the initial work on the fingerprints be completed by having the eleven sets of latent prints photographed. These would then be compiled into a file to be used in the investigation while the originals were stored safely at the Criminal Record Centre in Paarl. He testified that he checked the file again on 6 April.

There was Captain Jannie Bester, who testified that on 12 April, about a month after the murder, his colleague, Bruce Bartholomew, asked him to compare the prints lifted in Inge's flat against the prints of a number of people from her social circle, as well as those of some of the police officers who'd been at the crime scene. Bartholomew, Bester testified, was particularly interested to see whether the palmprint found on the

bloodied basin belonged to Marius Botha, Fred's flatmate. Bester testified that Bartholomew was disappointed to hear that this was not the
case. Bester also said that after having excluded Marius as the source of
the print from the basin, he'd established that the print was Fred's when
he compared it with a set of prints taken from him that morning. Only
after looking at the palmprint from the basin did he look at Folien One,
the prints on which he was also able to identify as Fred's.

13

The great danger with the story of how the fingerprint was found on 18 March, and how the folien onto which it was lifted travelled through the hands of police officers and evidence-room clerks, is that it might be misunderstood as a trivial matter of bureaucratic norms and procedures. In fact, it is the crux of the case against Fred, for what the story is intended to demonstrate is that there is an unbroken paper trail linking Folien One to the DVD box found on Inge's coffee table, a metre and a half from her bloodied body. If that were true, then no matter what Fred's experts might say about whether or not Folien One looked like it was consistent with a lift from a DVD cover, the fact that the path of the folien through time and space could be conclusively proved would imply that it must have been lifted where Swartz said he lifted it. By carefully documenting all of the steps in that process, the police could create a record which would support their version of events. It is precisely because of the importance of this that police procedures mandate the use of a bewildering range of registers and reports in order to maintain the chain of evidence for every exhibit they collect and examine.

In the case of fingerprints, the standard paper trail is made up of five documents. The first is the lifted print itself, which is sealed at the crime scene and on the back of which are recorded details about when and where it was found. The second document is the envelope in which all the lifts found at the scene are stored, on the cover of which information about each of those prints is recorded along with details about what is done with them after they are taken back to the Criminal Record Centre. The third document is a standardised, four-page crime scene report, which is used to note details about when and where every lift was found, what surface it was on and how it was lifted. This document also includes details about the subsequent handling and storage of the prints. The fourth document is a register at the offices of the Criminal Record Centre into which details are recorded relating to the handing-in of the original lifts to the evidence clerk for safekeeping, something that happens after photographs have been taken. At that point, investigators almost never have to see the originals again until they are handed in to court as evidence. The final document is a register of the automated fingerprint identification system, on which is recorded the details of prints taken to that system for comparison against existing police databases.

That the police recognise the importance of maintaining the chain of evidence in this way was made explicit when Fred's lawyer, Advocate Dup de Bruyn, introduced the subject during his cross-examination of Constable Elton Swartz, the man who testified to having lifted Folien One off the DVD cover found in Inge's flat.

> Q: So, the objective of these documents is to create a true and correct reflection of the history of that exhibit. Where it came from, where it went, etc. Not so?
>
> A: That is correct.

Q: So that if there is a dispute, there is that history. Its
  purpose is to protect you, the officer. Not so?
A: That is correct.
Q: It should support the officer's account. And the
  importance of the continuity of evidence, of the chain
  of evidence, of the need for it to be correct, is drilled
  into every police officer?
A: That is correct.

And yet, in spite of the importance of all of this being 'drilled into every
police officer', maintaining an unbroken chain of evidence is not a talent for which the members of the South African Police Service are renowned. An instructive example of the looseness that creeps into police
practice can be found in the records relating to the testing of the eleven
lifts against the Police Service's digital databases. Or, to be more precise,
the example can be found in the complete absence of any record that this
was done. This arises first when Swartz's boss, Captain Andries Matheus,
is testifying and the prosecutor asks him about what he did immediately
after inspecting Swartz's work on the morning of 18 March.

Q: Now, we have heard of the AFIS system. Do you know
  about it, and did you play any role in this regard in this
  specific case?
A: M'Lord, AFIS is our Automated Fingerprint
  Identification System. Because this was a case that
  demanded quality attention, I personally took the
  exhibits to AFIS for scanning. At that point, I didn't
  know if this had already happened. As the officer
  doing the twenty-four-hour inspection, it was my
  responsibility to see that this was done.
Q: Is it not your task just to make sure that someone does
  it?
A: No, M'Lord. In this case, I took it to the AFIS office and

I gave it to the personnel to scan. Then I waited for the results.

That is as far as the prosecutor takes his witness, but when it is De Bruyn's turn, he comes back to this task that Matheus says he performed on 18 March, and establishes that it is unusual for the original lifts to be taken to AFIS at all. The procedure used in most cases is that the originals are first taken to a photographer who takes two photos of each. These are then returned to the officer who lifted the prints so that the photos can be compiled in a file, and it is those photos and that file that are taken to AFIS. So it was unusual for Matheus to bring the original lifts for scanning before all of this was done.

Q: Now the departure here is that, in the first place, original exhibits are not supposed to be taken to AFIS. It's supposed to be the photos that go. It is usually that file, not so?

A: M'Lord, it is not a 'departure'. It is prioritisation. What I mean is that it takes time to print photos and then to take these to AFIS. So it was prioritised in the sense that these could be taken to AFIS, scanned in and then the investigation could begin immediately.

Q: Did you hear anything from AFIS?

A: M'Lord, at that point no. There were no results.

As Matheus finishes his answer, the prosecutor intervenes to make clear that 'no results' is also a result in the sense that it excludes the possibility that any of the prints found in Inge's flat had been left by someone with a criminal record. De Bruyn acknowledges this in his next question: 'No *positive* results?'

A: That is correct.

Q: Can you show us a single piece of paper or any evidence at all that these exhibits were taken to AFIS?

A: M'Lord, I can only testify that I took them to AFIS for scanning and that I got them back.

Q: You didn't answer my question. Are you aware of any register or entry or piece of paper which you, as a police officer, as you stand there today, can show that these exhibits went to AFIS?

A: M'Lord, I didn't make an entry.

Q: And if one takes exhibits such as these to AFIS, then there is a register that must be filled in. There are signatures that must be left. You must sign when you get the exhibits back, etc., etc. Not so?

A: That is correct. But that is when normal procedures are followed. What I mean, M'Lord, is that usually we wait until there are ten cases in a batch. That batch then goes through a standard procedure, and that is what the advocate is talking about. When I get a priority case, then I don't go that route. I go with the specific case and scan it in.

Q: If I understand you correctly, then, if normal procedures apply, then a record would be kept. There is a register that would be filled in. There are people who would sign documents. Is that correct?

A: That is correct.

Q: If abnormal procedures or priority procedures are followed, then no evidence is kept, and no paper trail and no register is signed. Is that your evidence?

A: M'Lord, again, when it is a priority case, it is the officer's responsibility to ensure that the exhibits are scanned in. When this is done normally, I would have taken them to the photographer. He would have printed photos. He would have given them to the member. The member would have made up a batch.

And it would have followed the normal route. In
this instance, it was not the normal circumstances. It
demanded priority, and that is what happened.

JUDGE: Can you remember who you gave it to for scanning?

A: M'Lord, I must admit that I can't remember to whom I
gave it.

JUDGE: How many people are there to whom you might have
given it?

A: M'Lord, there are three people who work on AFIS, but
it is not always the same people. There are three offices
that service that section.

JUDGE: Surely it would be easy enough to establish who was on
duty on the day?

A: It is possible.

JUDGE: It would be easy to establish who was then on duty and
who would have done it.

A: Yes. It is possible, M'Lord.

JUDGE: Perhaps we must establish who the person was. It may
be of use. I don't know if it is important, but it may be
of use.

These last questions – about the identity of the officer manning the AFIS
machine to whom Matheus gave the prints for scanning – were asked by
the judge, and, though they passed me by more or less completely at the
time, there are good reasons to think that these might have been among
the most important questions asked during the whole trial.

It is a pity, then, that no-one seems ever to have followed them up.

14

The failure to enter details of the eleven prints into the register for the AFIS system is but one of a number of instances of the detectives' inability to maintain a continuous record of what happened to Folien One after it was lifted off what may or may not have been the cover of the DVD that Inge rented on the day she was murdered. Other examples abound.

There was the fact that the DVD cover had been returned to the video store a few weeks after the murder, something that spoke to an unusual, but nevertheless woefully misplaced, conscientiousness on the part of the investigating officers. If the cover – a generic rental-store item probably costing less than R10 – had been retained by the police, as they said it had been for the first two weeks of the investigation, there would have been indisputable evidence that it had been dusted and that a print had been lifted from it. In all likelihood, the pattern of residues left by any powder that had not come off the surface after that lift would also have proved or disproved whether Folien One had been that lift.

When asked in court about the returning of the DVD box and whether this had been a mistake, police officers would line up to say that it would have been better to keep it, but that it was not the usual practice to keep the items from which fingerprint examiners had lifted prints. Standard operating procedure, these officers would say, was to treat the lift itself, rather than the item from which it was lifted, as the court exhibit. To do otherwise, they would say, was not usually possible because prints were often found on walls or cars or windows. Embarrassingly, as Fred's lawyer would point out, the policy guidelines issued to fingerprint investigators did in fact suggest that they keep some items from which lifts were taken, and that, when the guidelines made this point, the example they offered was of a video cassette cover.

Still, the DVD cover was not kept.

Another relatively straightforward way in which the police might have been able to prove conclusively that Folien One came from where they said it had would have been to take a photograph or two of the DVD cover. Ideally, one photograph would have shown it as having been dusted, and another might have shown it together with the lifted print. If either photo showed dust that looked something like the pattern on Folien One, the police account of its provenance would have been beyond dispute. Again, this was not done, and, when police experts testified about the reasons for this, they said it was only in 2007 that fingerprint examiners were issued with digital cameras. Until then there had been officers who took these kinds of pictures, but these were the exception to the rule.

So the DVD holder was not retained and no photo was taken of it before, during or after the supposed lifting of a print from it. According to the testimony offered by a number of police officers, it is wrong to expect them to have done so, since that is not what police procedure required. But then it's not clear that if the procedures had dictated that these steps be taken, that the officers would have complied with them. After all, it's not as if those clearly established procedures that did exist were followed.

It is, for example, established procedure that the officer who lifts a print must immediately make a note in his crime scene report about where it was found and the time it was lifted. He must also seal the lift by covering it with plastic, which is fixed to the card by stickers attached to opposite corners. He must sign and date these stickers. Then, on the back of the lift, he must again fill in the same details about the time and location of the lift as appear in his crime scene report, along with details that will help orient the print in relation to the object from which it was taken: in particular, which sides are up and down and which are left and right. Thus, the inscription on Folien One reads, 'F/P 1 lifted from DVD disc holder which was found on a coffee table in the lounge and shows sideways to the left.' Below that, another notation records the address of the crime scene and the precise time and date of the lift.

It appears, then, that Constable Swartz fulfilled his duties and followed procedure.

But he didn't. Or not entirely.

Swartz testifies that while he was on the scene, he sealed Folien One and numbered it. He says he also noted the location of the lift in his crime scene report. He did not, however, make the same notes on the back of the folien. He offers no explanation for why he failed to do this, saying only that he filled in the backs of the foliens only once he'd returned to his office, and that, in doing so, he had relied on the information contained in his crime scene report.

That may be, but, as De Bruyn delights in pointing out, Swartz must have also relied in part on his memory or his imagination for some of what he wrote on the back of the folien because one detail that appears there does not appear in the crime scene report – the precise time of the lift. This was recorded at as being 10:15, barely a quarter of an hour after

Swartz and his colleagues say they arrived at Inge's complex. Worsening his problem is that the times listed on the backs of the other foliens – all of which must have been drawn from memory because none appears in his report – were equally precise. They were times like '10:22' and '10:48' and '11:32', and it is hard not to think that their precision owed more to a calculated attempt to disguise the failure to follow procedure properly than to the capaciousness of Swartz's memory

In the broad scheme of things, copying notes taken at the crime scene onto cards that should have been filled in at the same time may not be a big deal. But, in a tightly fought contest, it is precisely the sort of thing that affects a witness's credibility.

In another departure from procedure, Swartz also admits that he didn't sign the folien or its stickers while still at the crime scene. He had, he says, numbered all of them, but he signed the stickers only when back at the office. Again, it's not a big deal. But, when he failed to sign the foliens, he failed also to ask any of his colleagues to sign them, too. If someone else had signed the lifts at the scene, it would have ensured at least one other voice in support of his claim about how and where it had been lifted. Swartz's failure to get any of his colleagues to sign the folien – and there were three other officers in the flat – means that his testimony has to stand without support that would have been readily to hand. His explanation for this omission is contained in a sworn statement. Deposed by Swartz's boss and the investigation's leader, Director Attie Trollip, his affidavit generously has him take full responsibility for the oversight: 'Although this was not discussed on that day, I decided not to take the exhibit to the other fingerprint investigators for signatures. In my judgment, we were all involved in the investigation to the same extent.'

It is an odd point of view, either wildly hubristic or utterly defeated, since it suggests that Swartz, with all of 18 months' experience at the time of Inge's murder, had come to the conclusion that if a court did not believe one police officer, it wasn't going to believe two. Courts, he seems to have concluded, would take an officer at his word or would treat all officers as a pack of scheming liars. There was no point, therefore, in getting one officer to testify in support of another.

*   *   *

If Swartz's oversights at the crime scene and immediately after meant that a problem with the continuity of evidence existed right from the start, it was greatly worsened by what followed.

Had this been a normal case – rather than a priority case – Swartz would have returned to the office after leaving Inge's flat in order to complete his paperwork. He would have presented this to his boss, Captain Matheus. Matheus would have asked him to correct any problems with that paperwork. The lifts would then have gone to the photographer, a certain Mr Williams, who would have taken two high-resolution photos of each print. These would have been sent back to Swartz almost immediately, and Swartz would have compiled a file. The original prints would have been deposited with the evidence clerk, a certain Ms Kearns, and the file, together with some others, would have gone to the (never identified) AFIS operator, who would have recorded his receipt of the file, his scanning of the prints and the return of the file to Swartz. In the absence of positive 'hits' from AFIS, Swartz would have kept the file until one of the investigating officers had collected sets of exclusion prints from Inge, her friends and from some of the officers who'd been on the scene.

We know already that the delivery of the prints to AFIS didn't follow procedure and is not recorded in the register kept for that purpose. But there was more in question than just that procedural flaw.

Take, for instance, the handing of the originals of the prints to the photographer and the compilation of the photos into a file. This was supposed to follow the twenty-four-hour inspection Matheus conducted on 18 March, and which is reflected as having been conducted on that date both on the envelope in which the originals were placed at the scene and in Swartz's crime scene report. On the latter, Matheus also wrote an instruction to send the prints to the photographer. All of this is signed and dated 18 March.

But Swartz didn't take the prints to the photographer after his boss, Captain Matheus, had endorsed his work, though he did claim to have done so before the twenty-four-hour inspection. Instead, according to Matheus's own testimony, he decided to take the prints to AFIS himself rather than return them to the junior officer. Then, after they were returned to him by the AFIS operator, he still didn't take them to the photographer. Instead, Matheus put them in a drawer of his desk, where they sat for five days.

Asked by the prosecutor to explain why he did this, Matheus offers the following: 'In important cases like this one, one expects that senior officers will call to ask if there are any results. In this case, a number of officers did call about results. My reason for keeping them was that I would be able to give them correct information when they called if, for example, they asked about a particular exhibit, where it was lifted, etc. Then I'd have these exhibits with me and I would be able to give them precise answers.'

It is an explanation he persists with for a time under cross-examination by Dup de Bruyn.

Q: Where did you keep the exhibits?

A: Locked in a drawer in my desk.

Q: For how long?

A: It was for a few days.

Q: Five days?

A: It's possible.

Q: Can't you remember?

A: We can look at the record. If it says five days, then I'll accept that.

Q: And nothing was done with the exhibits in those five days?

A: M'Lord, on the fifth day, I took them to the photographer.

147

Q: For the five days in which they lay in your drawer, nothing was done with them?

A: M'Lord, I don't understand 'nothing was done'. What does that mean?

JUDGE: Did you do something with it? That's what the advocate wants to know.

A: They were locked in my drawer.

JUDGE: Yes. And did you take them out at any point during those five days to do something with them?

A: M'Lord, I handled them when there were questions asked for which I might have needed to be able to read what was on them, after which they were locked up again.

JUDGE: At which point you would take them out of the drawer, look at them, and then lock them up?

A: Correct, M'Lord.

JUDGE: Was it for safekeeping?

A: It was for safekeeping.

Matheus's was an odd story and an unbelievable one.

It is, of course, quite possible that senior officers would have taken an interest in this case and even that they might have called Matheus to ask if there were any results from AFIS. They may even have asked how many prints had been found and whether these included prints from open windows or the balcony. But this was just a few days after the murder, so no-one would have expected an answer of more than something like, 'Yes, Commissioner. We found eleven latents. There were some on some household items. Glasses and a DVD cover, I think. There was one in the bathroom, including one in the basin where the killer washed up. There were a few from the doors and security gates.' The idea that anyone calling from provincial or national headquarters would have wanted or needed or expected more detail than that is strikingly implausible. And if they had, they would surely have happily waited a day or so for details. Besides, Matheus could have simply made a note in his diary about each of the lifts.

There really was no need for him to keep them in his safe.

Interestingly, the idea that his story stretched to the very limits of credibility seems also to have occurred to Matheus because, after lunch, he returns to this question of why he kept the prints in his desk for five days. And this time he offers a much more plausible story.

> Q: Captain, I want to put it to you that, although we don't
> know what happened, we will argue later that your
> explanation about the alleged locking up in the drawer
> cannot be true and correct. Do you want to comment?
>
> A: M'Lord, my response to the question of what I did
> with the exhibits stuck in my head a little because I
> didn't really understand it. During the break, I thought
> about it a bit, and when I came back into court, I
> looked again at the evidence register. It confirmed my
> suspicion. The reasons the specific items were in my
> possession for so long was that it was a long weekend.
> I took them for scanning on Friday. Then there is
> Saturday and Sunday. The Monday was a holiday. I
> can't remember the reasons why, but the official who
> prints the photos was not in on that Tuesday. What I
> wanted to check and what I looked for was when he
> received it. Not just these exhibits, but all the exhibits
> from the whole weekend. He should have received
> them for photographing on Tuesday. He got them only
> on Wednesday. The first day I could give them to him,
> then, was that Wednesday.

The relief in this answer is obvious. But, as any lawyer will tell you, it is a dangerous business to change your story on the stand, even if it is to provide a more plausible account of what you did.

> Q: Do I understand you correctly? You are now saying that the real reason you locked the exhibits up was that it was a long weekend?
>
> A: No, M'Lord. My answer is still that they were held originally to provide information. So that I would have it with me if I needed to get information. But the reason I kept them in my possession for so long was that because of the long weekend. Wednesday was the first time that the photos could be printed.
>
> Q: So you were expecting that officers would call over the long weekend?
>
> A: Yes.
>
> Q: Did any officers call you?
>
> A: M'Lord, Superintendent Dreyer called me. I can't tell you on which dates, but he definitely called me more than once. So did other officers. I can't remember now the dates and the times.

It's another skirmish of uncertain value. Does it really matter that the fingerprints did not go to the photographer on 18 March but on 23 March? And what if the delay was because of a long weekend or the need to appease any of Matheus's more punctilious superiors? What difference would that make?

The obvious answer is that these are minor questions, and, to the extent that De Bruyn hammers on about them, it has little to do with any allegation that something untoward was done with the fingerprints as early as 23 March. The point he is really making is a larger one: that the records about what happened to the fingerprints are not to be trusted. Why so? Because although Captain Matheus's sworn statement says that the original lifts went to the photographer on 23 March, and the same date is recorded on the envelope in which those originals were stored,

Constable Swartz's statement says he received the prints back from the photographer on 22 March, a day before Matheus says he took them for photographing. Worse still, the register that records when the originals were received by the evidence clerk – something that should have happened immediately after the return of the photos – says that this happened on 29 March. It is Matheus's signature that appears in the register on that date even though he swears that it happened on 23 March. It gets worse: two other entries – one signed by the photographer, Mr Williams, and one signed by the clerk, Ms Kearns – say that the prints were photographed two days later, on 31 March. Confusingly, Ms Kearns also signed an entry on the envelope which said that the prints were photographed on 23 March.

How does Matheus explain this? In a sworn statement taken down by his boss, Director Attie Trollip, about a year after these events, he says that he realised on 29 March 2005 that he'd failed to sign the register properly when he gave the originals to Ms Kearns six days earlier, and decided simply to sign those exhibits in with others from another case that he happened to be handing in that day. He then told Mr Williams what he'd done and that the prints had already been photographed, and that he should sign the register accordingly. Matheus has no explanation for why the photographer only did this on 31 March.

All of which is curious enough, but it is made more so by the fact that it is not the last of the anomalies.

*   *   *

Throughout the trial, the police maintained that there were eleven prints lifted at the crime scene, two by folien and nine by ordinary Scotch tape. On Swartz's envelope, however, the initial, handwritten marking-up noted two foliens and ten tape lifts, for a total of twelve lifts. The zero of the ten had subsequently been crossed out, however, and the one had been converted to a nine. The change was not initialled, but Matheus says that that was probably just an honest mistake by Swartz, and that the correction had been made before the twenty-four-hour inspection he'd done on 18 March. That's quite possible; mistakes happen. By an odd coincidence, however, in the column of the register in which the number of photographs received by the clerk was recorded, instead of reflecting that twenty-two individual photos had been handed in (as would be the norm for eleven individual lifts), the entry actually suggests that Mr Williams produced twenty-four pictures, as would usually happen if there had been twelve lifts.

Q: How did that happen, Captain?

A: M'Lord, I could hand in one piece of folien and print twenty-four photos. The reason is that one might print a photo and find that it's not good enough. Then you'd print it again and again until it's perfect.

Q: Captain, if you look at the exhibit register, there are departures every now and then, but in the overwhelming majority of cases – more than ninety percent – there are two photos for each piece of tape or folien. You also just testified that two photos were taken of the lifts in this case. If twenty-four photos were taken, than I'd suggest that Mr Williams photographed twelve items rather than eleven.

A: M'Lord, the question was about how many photos are normally taken. And I said that normally two were taken.

Q: Are you aware of any abnormal reasons why more than two were taken?

A: No.

Q: Do you know of which item more than two photos were taken?

A: I couldn't say. I'm not the photographer.

And it is here that answers to the judge's questions about the identity of the AFIS operator are important. This is not because it is remotely likely that he or she would remember whether there were eleven or twelve prints scanned into the computer on the morning of 18 March, but because, if you follow the logic of the judge's questions, you might ask another question: isn't it likely that the AFIS system, like any other advanced database, would automatically produce transactional data that would reflect how many images were scanned in? More than that, AFIS systems, including the one used by the South African Police Service, can be set up so that they automatically capture images of the prints they scan, rather than just details about the time, date and number of scans. Now this is not something that all systems are set up to do, and my inquiries with police officers in the SAPS have produced divergent answers about whether their system is set up in this way. But if it were, it would be possible to answer this question: was there a twelfth lift, and if there was, did *it* look like it might have come off a DVD cover?

Ordinarily, of course, there'd be no need to ask this question because, once the original lifts were photographed, they would have been stored securely in the appropriate files at the Criminal Record Centre until the court trial, and, in the meantime, all investigations would be done using the photographs. If twelve originals went in, twelve would have come out. In this case, however, the register records something unusual: that on 16 May 2005, the original exhibits were collected by one of Captain Bartholomew's colleagues in the provincial crime scene investigation unit in Cape Town, that they were returned to Paarl on 31 May and that, on the same day, they were re-photographed.

These prints, in other words, had not been kept securely in the evidence register throughout the course of the investigation. And, if there had been a twelfth lift, one that looked as if it really had been lifted off a DVD cover and which also looked different to Folien One, there was more than enough opportunity for it to have been 'disappeared'.

15

The details! The details!

A criminal trial in an accusatorial system is a welter of conflicting details, with the opposing lawyers conducting themselves like a pair of crazed pointillists painting the same canvas, each trying to construct his own image of the vista before him by adding his own spots and erasing the other's. Later in the trial, for example, when Bruce Bartholomew is on the stand and De Bruyn is cross-examining him, the policeman will testify about how he had to break the police seals that had been applied the night before, when he got to Inge's flat on the morning of 17 March.

> Q: You said yesterday that when you got there you had to unlock the doors. You had the keys with you, of course?
>
> A: That's correct.

Q: When you arrived, you unlocked the door; you can specifically recall that the door was still sealed?

A: That's correct.

Q: Who sealed it?

A: Superintendent Kock.

Q: Earlier that morning when you left the scene?

A; That is correct.

Q: You left with Mr Kock?

A: That is correct.

Q: How was the door sealed?

A; With two red stickers.

Q: And you had to break the seals to open the door?

A: That is correct.

Q: So you had to take them off?

A: I just physically opened the door.

Q: Oh. Excuse me. I understand now. You just physically opened it?

A: Yes.

Q: You were satisfied that the seals on the door were still intact?

A: That's correct.

This exchange was the first business De Bruyn raised on the morning of Thursday, 8 March 2007, the fifteenth day of the trial and Bartholomew's second on the stand. On Tuesday, 13 March, the fourth day of Bartholomew's testimony, De Bruyn would return to this question by reading to Bartholomew an extract from his own statement signed on 8 September 2005: 'On 2005-03-17 at about 10:00 I returned to the Shiraz flat. I found Constable Swartz, Inspector Heinie Coetzee, Inspector Share and Inspector Booysens there, where they were in the process of investigating the scene for finger- and palmprints.'

Confronted by the contradiction, Bartholomew stands by the testimony he'd given in court. 'They could not have gotten into the flat,' he says. About his statement, he adds, 'I must concede that I made a mistake.' Can you explain the mistake? De Bruyn asks. 'I can't explain it.'

Like many other minor scuffles, on its own, the stakes here are trivial: in relation to the bigger issues of the trial, it doesn't much matter if Bartholomew found the other cops waiting outside the flat or powdering the inside walls. Nor does it matter that Bartholomew says that Inspector Share was in the flat when no-one else remembers him as being part of the crime scene team that morning. What does matter, however, is a witness's credibility, and lawyers make their money by playing up the tricks of memory and the infelicities of expression that, along with outright lies, lead to the inconsistencies and contradictions that arise when someone is subjected to four or five or six days of intense questioning about events dating back to two years earlier. So De Bruyn wasn't really trying to establish if Bartholomew broke the seals or not. What he was trying to do was signal something about Bartholomew's memory and his consistency and his credibility.

This is a game the prosecution must play, too. So when Bartholomew offered his evidence-in-chief, for example, they had him spend a great deal of time describing his efforts to find latent impressions of shoeprints using a dust-lifter, his having had the walls of Inge's flat sprayed with ninhydrin in an effort to find fingerprints on that surface, as well as his attempt to find any fingerprints on Inge herself by having her remains sealed in a body bag into which superglue fumes were pumped. None of these efforts produced any evidence of any relevance to Fred's trial. They were presented to the judge solely to demonstrate Bartholomew's thoroughness and professionalism. To demonstrate, in a word, his credibility.

* * *

In relation to the fingerprint, it is hard to overstate how much the prosecution depended on the credibility of the wonderfully, whimsically named Constable Elton John Swartz, the officer who had lifted Folien One and all the other latent prints found in Inge's flat.

Although Bartholomew, who admitted to a mistake in his affidavit about arriving after Swartz was already in the flat, says he saw Folien One at the crime scene, and although Captain Matheus says he saw Folien One when he checked Swartz's work on 18 March, no-one other than Swartz saw the lift come off a DVD cover. Not even Inspector Booysens, who says she found the print before handing it to Swartz for lifting.

Swartz, then, with all of 18 months' experience at the time he worked Inge's flat, stood alone.

This is important because a great many experts say that the print on Folien One could not have come off a DVD cover and is much more likely have come off a glass. There was Daan Bekker, a former policeman and fingerprint expert, who produced a report to this effect for the defence in November 2005. There was also Pat Wertheim, the American expert, whose report, also for the defence, built on and extended that of Bekker, and was prepared in August 2006. There was Arie Zeelenberg, a Dutch fingerprint expert who was also drafted in by the defence and who prepared a 210-slide PowerPoint presentation about Folien One in which every single particle of dust on it was examined in microscopic detail, and whose slightly ungrammatical conclusion on slide 202 is: 'It is my firm opinion that, based upon the overwhelming amount of evidence, Folien One is coming from a drinking glass and that at the same time a DVD cover is excluded.'

These were defence witnesses, to be sure, so it is possible that they said what they were paid to say. But there were also police forensic experts who said the same thing.

There was a sworn statement by a Superintendent Rance of the Forensic Science Laboratory in Pretoria, written in December 2006, which concluded that it was not possible to reproduce the patterns of prints and marks on Folien One when using a DVD cover as the substrate. There was another sworn statement by a Senior Superintendent Roger Dixon, also from the Forensic Science Laboratory, who, having run his own tests to try to replicate Folien One, concluded in December 2006 that, 'The features observed on the folien match test lifts made from glasses, and not those made from DVD covers.'

Neither Rance nor Dixon was called to testify. However, because both had taken advantage of a section in the Criminal Procedure Act that permits forensic and fingerprint experts to write reports that may be treated by a court as being *prima facie* proof of what they purport to describe, the evidentiary value of these reports was the subject of endless debate during Fred's trial. The standard rule is that the court will treat as evidence only that which has been subjected to cross-examination in open court, so could these reports count in Fred's favour even without their authors being called as witnesses? The prosecution said no. The defence said yes. For the most part, the judge tended to agree with the prosecution, but eventually reversed himself in his judgment, citing the two officers' reports repeatedly. Whatever the legal merits of that debate about the admissibility of these statements, there is no question that the substance of Rance and Dixon's reports supported the views of Fred's experts.

The common thread running through these experts' work is that none cared about whether the chain of evidence could be shown to have been broken. Theirs was an examination of the substance of the folien: the curved, parallel lines that run across its surface and frame Fred's prints; the water marks; the smudge some said was a lip print; the shape and location and orientation of the fingerprints; the absence of background noise. These, they all said in their various ways, were characteristic of a lift from a glass. While any one of the marks might be found on some lifts from a DVD cover, they said, the possibility that all would be present in such a lift was vanishingly small.

This evidence was so extensive that the prosecution could not simply rely on Constable Swartz's word and the dubious administrative records relating to the storage of the folien to support the argument that the print must have come from a DVD cover; they also had to confront the defence experts on the substance of Folien One. Although there were contributions on this question from Matheus and Swartz, the most important witnesses the prosecutors presented on the question of whether Folien One looked like it could have come off a DVD holder were Captain Jannie Bester (the officer who acknowledged during his testimony that, yes, he was aware that some members of the Western Cape's fingerprinting units had recently been prosecuted for fabricating evidence) and Director Ruben Botha.

Bester, a solidly built man with a bristling moustache, had spent twenty-five years conducting fingerprint examinations, and testified that, in fact, his first impression was that the folien had been lifted off a glass. This, he said, was because of the apparent lip mark, the water droplets and the like. At the same time, however, he said that he thought the print could also have come off a DVD box, as Swartz said it had.

It was true, he testified, that the two bright lines above and below Fred's fingerprints were slightly curved, as one would expect of a glass but not of a DVD holder, but it was possible the curvature was the result of excessive pressure being applied to the soft plastic of the cover.

It was possible, he testified, that there had been other fingerprints on the DVD holder, as one might expect of a rental, but that these had all been insufficiently clear to be usable and had not been lifted by Swartz.

It was true, he testified, that the absence of background noise was characteristic of a glass, but it was possible that the reason there was no background noise on Folien One was that the police sometimes had to use poor-quality aluminium powder, and that this powder would not adhere to some surfaces as readily as better-quality powder.

It was possible, he testified, that the DVD cover was new and had not been much handled.

Ultimately, though, Bester was happy to concede that Folien One looked to him to have come off a glass, but, as a fingerprint expert with a great many years of experience, he also thought it possible that it came from a DVD cover. 'M'Lord,' he concluded, 'if someone were to ask me where this was lifted from, I would not be able to exclude either.' The only person who would know for sure, he said, was Constable Swartz.

In relation to the substance of Folien One and its consistency or otherwise with having been lifted from a DVD holder, Bester's testimony – most of which was offered because it was he who matched Folien One with Fred's exclusion prints – was a sideshow. Besides, because he happily conceded that the mark on the upper left corner looked like a lip print and that the parallel lines were curved and that much of Folien One was consistent with a glass, he was not really all that helpful to the prosecution. In order to make the case that the print had come off a DVD cover, the prosecutors needed someone whose opinion was held with more conviction. This came in the red-headed, garrulous form of Director Ruben Botha, whose written report on Folien One concluded, 'Very possible that the fingerprints lifted by Constable Swartz originate from open DVD holder as found on coffee table on top of magazines.'

On the stand, he happily shortened those odds from 'very possible' to 'very likely'.

*   *   *

Director Ruben Botha is the very definition of the old hand, something he would advertise repeatedly by noting his thirty-two years of experience. It was, perhaps, for this reason that he would repeatedly demonstrate a marked indignation at having his views and methods questioned. These were questioned, however, with the questions arising out of his original report, dated December 2005. It is a report that had been drafted after an agreement between Fred's lawyers and the prosecutors to have the police ask a senior fingerprint expert from their own ranks, but who was not involved in the investigation into Inge's death, to examine Folien One in light of a report written for the defence by Daan Bekker, an ex-policeman who was then working as a private forensic investigator. Two days after concluding that agreement, Bruce Bartholomew and Jannie Bester took the original print, along with Bekker's report, on the thousand-kilometre drive to Ruben Botha's office in Port Elizabeth.

Botha's project, as it emerges in his report and his testimony, is to challenge the idea that there was no way that a print with the characteristics of Folien One could have been lifted from a DVD cover. Partly because Botha's report is in continuous dialogue with Bekker's, however, it is not easy to summarise. It is filled with paragraphs like the following, which, introduced only by the heading DVD HOLDER WITH PLASTIC COVERING, states: 'Static electricity is discharged when the disk holder is handled by a person. It will be further discharged when aluminium powder is applied as it will act as a conductor. It has been found that the powder will adhere to the plastic when a number of persons with a high concentrate of substrate have handled a disk holder. Clean or new plastic disk holders give the folien a clean background, very similar to a glass surface.'

These sentences in Botha's report, in which it may or may not be worth pointing out that he badly misused the technical word 'substrate', are offered in direct response to a point made in Bekker's report to the effect that static electricity on a DVD cover means that aluminium powder clings to it whether or not fingerprints are present. The consequence of this, Bekker had argued, is that one would expect that there would be much more background noise on Folien One than there is. Botha, who says on the stand that he consulted with an electrical engineer about this before putting pen to paper, rejects this argument as part of a case he is making to the effect that it is 'very possible' – or, as he preferred on the stand, 'very likely' – that Folien One was, in fact, lifted from a DVD holder.

To make this argument, Botha has to account for all the elements of Folien One that Bekker identified as being indicative of its having been lifted from a glass rather than a DVD holder, and to reinterpret them as being the plausible characteristics of a folien lift from a DVD cover. These elements included the absence of background noise; the curved, parallel lines; the water marks; the slight bend in the print of Fred's left index finger; the absence of the fingerprints of anyone else; and the presence, next to the print of his left index finger of a print of Fred's right thumb pointing in the same direction.

For the absence of background noise, Botha's explanation is that Bekker is just wrong about the electromagnetics of plastic DVD boxes. It is a point he supplements with another about the quality of the powder that Inspector Booysens may have used when she dusted the cover. 'My Lord,' he says on the stand, his report having failed to mention this, 'my own research has shown that aluminium powder loses its effectiveness as it gets older and becomes more contaminated.' This, he explains, is the effect of what comedian Jerry Seinfeld once called 'double-dipping': the horrifying practice of cocktail party guests who dip a chip into the guacamole, take a bite and then dip again. For a fingerprint examiner, double-dipping is an inherent part of the job, which requires applying powder to a dirty surface with a fine-haired brush, which picks up dirt and dust before being dipped back into the officer's powder. As the powder becomes contaminated, Botha says, it loses its effectiveness and begins to adhere less readily to surfaces.

In addition to the possibility that Inspector Booysens was using old and contaminated powder (a possibility that Botha admits is speculative since he had not spoken with her), Botha also offers another, more surprising, factor that might explain why Booysens's powder failed to stick to the DVD cover: al-Qaeda.

'The powder we should be using,' he says, 'is supposed to be finer than one millimicron (sic). I'm not a chemical analyst, but the word they use in English is "pyro-powder". What seems to have happened is that after the 9/11 disaster in Manhattan, it became apparent that the use of this powder in explosives was dangerous, and its use had to be limited as far as possible. By 2004 and 2005, we did not have enough of the finer powder available to the Criminal Record Centre, and I was informed – and I have confirmed it again – that they obtained powder from the mines that had a much rougher texture than the powder we normally used.'

If problems relating to the adherence properties of Booysens's powder explain the absence of background noise, Botha's account of the manner in which the other features emerged on the print includes the following elements. First, Fred must have handled the DVD cover twice so that his right thumb and left index finger would appear next to each other. Second, on one of those occasions, he handled the cover in a manner that involved a slightly bent index finger. Disagreeing with Bekker, Botha says that this is not 'unusual' or 'unnatural' because there is no usual or natural way to handle a DVD holder. Because the finger was turned a little on its side, Botha suggests that this handling may have involved opening the DVD cover, the process of which might have required the application of pressure and which could bend the finger and distort the fingerprint. On the stand, he demonstrates what he means by using the DVD box, since retrieved from the video store to which it had been returned in March 2005. The effort to get his fingers into the right kind of positions looks strained, but he says it may be that Fred did not open the DVD cover, and may just have held it using a bent finger, the pressure of which was greater on one side than on the other. He also says his own hands are unusually small, and a man with bigger hands might not look so ungainly.

The next elements of Botha's account of what happened to the DVD cover and how it may have been handled so as to produce Folien One also tend towards the speculative. To explain the wet spots in the lift, he suggests that the glass on which Inge's fingerprints were found, and which was also on the coffee table in the lounge, may have been put down on a magazine on the table, and that the DVD cover may have then been placed in close proximity to it. If condensation had formed on the glass, and if this had rolled down its side, and if it had pooled under the glass, that may have wet the cover of the magazine, which may, in turn, have wet the DVD box. That the DVD cover might have been lying on wet spots might also explain why the water had not evaporated in the sixteen or eighteen hours between Inge's drinking from the glass and the DVD cover's being dusted. Another possibility, Botha offers, is that Booysens might have dusted the glass first, in the process transferring droplets from it to the surface on which she had placed it, and that she may then have put the DVD holder on those droplets.

The curved, parallel lines, Botha says, are not really curved. He seems to concede that the bottom one is curved, but he says that, in his view, only the outer edge of the top line is curved while its inner edge, something he calls its 'baseline', is actually straight. This, he says, may be the result of the folien's hanging a little over the top edge of the DVD cover when Swartz lifted the print, so that it wrapped itself around the edge when pressure was applied.

Botha says that the lower line may have been caused by Constable Swartz rather than reflecting any part of the underlying substrate. He says he consulted with Swartz and concluded that the bottom line is a result of a prior lift that had been made in more or less the same place as Folien One. When Folien One was applied to the same area moments later, it overlapped the edge of the first lift, in the process creating the bottom line. Without a double lift of this kind, he says, 'it would be impossible to get a second line on this cover. There is nothing on the front of the DVD cover that would give one these curves.'

Overall, Botha's conclusion is that a straightforward visual examination of Folien One could create the impression that it had been lifted from a glass rather than a DVD cover. But, after a series of experiments in which he had sought to obtain results similar to those as appear in Folien One, he is now convinced that it could have been from a DVD cover. He says, 'Personally, I would say that the only person who can testify to the question of where the fingerprint was lifted is Constable Swartz.'

In response to this, the judge says, 'Well, in his testimony he had no doubt that it did, in fact, come from a DVD holder.' To which Botha replies, 'I think, then, that one must take account of his evidence, My Lord.'

16

Just how reliable is Constable Swartz's testimony?

We know that in December 2006, when they wrote to the defence to say that the fingerprint evidence would not be led, the prosecution had doubts about the provenance of Folien One. We know also that when the trial started in February 2007, those doubts were reaffirmed by Christénus van der Vijver, who said that the fingerprint evidence was not going to be held out as establishing Fred's guilt, but would be led only to show the *bona fides* of the officers involved. We know also that six months after this the prosecutors had come to a quite different view. Then, in the course of trying to persuade the judge to reject the defence request that charges be dismissed, Van der Vijver would say, that, in his view, the fingerprint evidence should stand. 'In all honesty, M'Lord,' he would say, 'after hearing all the evidence, after hearing the evidence of

Botha and Swartz even on the question about the powder that was used, the state is no longer convinced that a mistake crept in here.'

As we know, there is not as much independent evidence of Swartz's account of the origins of Folien One as there might have been. No-one saw him make the lift (though Bartholomew says he saw Folien One at the crime scene and Matheus says he saw it the next day). Apart from Swartz, no-one else signed the lift. No-one photographed the DVD cover or Folien One while it was still in the flat. And, a few weeks later, the DVD cover itself was returned to the store. The records that should have proved the continuity of the chain of evidence – Swartz's envelope and crime scene report, the AFIS register and the separate register managed by the evidence clerk – were a mess. They didn't show that fabrication had occurred (how could they?), but nor did they suggest an administrative process sufficiently rigorous and auditable as to ensure that every print produced in court could be unambiguously traced back to its source. In fact, if anything, they showed the opposite: that the original prints had left the registry for two weeks, during which time they were kept in the offices of the unit in which Captain Bartholomew worked and that they were re-photographed on their return.

In the absence of any independent corroboration, then Swartz's testimony had to stand nakedly before the court. Since the police expert tasked with persuading the judge that Folien One came from a DVD cover, Director Ruben Botha, had concluded that the lower of the two parallel lines could be explained only by Swartz's using two foliens when he examined the DVD cover, it is this part of Swartz's testimony that is probably most important.

* * *

Swartz and Coetzee and Booysens – the three officers tasked with finding fingerprints in Inge's flat – all agree that it was Booysens who dusted the objects on the coffee table in the lounge on which Inge died. They also all agree that it was she who dusted the DVD cover and that she found prints that were clear enough for identification. Since it was Swartz's job to lift all identifiable prints, Booysens handed the cover to him and he took it to the counter in the kitchen. The prosecutor takes up the story

Q: How did you lift them?

A: With the folien. I had the DVD holder in front of me with the open side to the right. I took the folien and cut a corner to show which side was up. I placed the folien on the fingerprint and lifted it from the cover.

Q: How many foliens did you use on the cover?

A: I used two.

Q: Why?

A: We didn't have pieces of folien that could cover the whole holder. I used one at the bottom. I lifted it and could see that there were no identifiable prints. I put that one in my bag. I put the other one at the top, where I could see there were identifiable prints and I lifted it from the DVD cover.

Q: With what you had with you, could you lift the DVD all at once?

A: No.

Q: That's why you used two foliens?

A: That's correct.

Q: You said you took the first one away. You put it in your bag?

A: That's correct.

Q: What did you do with it?

A: We destroy all foliens on which there are no identifiable prints.

Q: What was the result of the lift with the second one that you used, the second folien?

A: There were identifiable fingerprints on the folien.

Q: When you saw identifiable fingerprints, what did you
do?

A: Stickers were put on opposite corners and sealed with
glue. I numbered the fingerprint on these. I decided it
would be the first exhibit. So, on the front of the sticker,
I wrote the number one.

Q: I want to show the original exhibit. Can you look at it
and tell me precisely what it is?

A: That is the folien that was used when the fingerprints
were lifted off the DVD cover.

Q: This is Folien One?

A: It is marked Folien One, yes.

After leading this evidence, prosecutor Christénus van der Vijver takes
his witness through a series of questions designed to show that, having
been sealed, a folien cannot be unsealed without leaving clear signs of
tampering. He also has Swartz read into the record what he wrote on the
back of the folien when he returned to his office and consulted his notes:
that the print was found on a DVD cover in the lounge of the crime scene
on 17 March at 10:15.

When it's the defence's turn, De Bruyn returns to the question of how
the prints were lifted. In order to get as much clarity as possible, he hands
Swartz a DVD cover that Swartz agrees is similar to the one found in
Inge's flat.

Q: I would like you to take Folien One for us and just show
us again how these foliens were placed on this DVD
cover. Now, for the record, that cover has a definite
front and back?

A: That is correct.

Q: You spoke in your testimony about an 'open side'. What
did you mean by that?

A: For me, the open side is the front of the DVD.

Q: I understand. Then, in the way you are holding the
DVD cover, on the right-hand side there is a groove into
which one can put one's fingers to open it?

A: That is correct.

Q: Good. Now, the first lift – the folien that no longer
exists – was it as big as Folien One?

A: That is correct.

Q: Using Folien One, could you show us how you placed
that first folien.

A: That folien was clipped at the top corner. I took off the
protective plastic cover.

Q: Yes?

A: Good.

Q: And where did you put it? There on the bottom?

A: Yes.

Q: The bottom half of the front?

A: That is correct.

Q: Now the second lift. Can you show us that?

A: It was the same-sized folien.

Q: Yes?

A: It was clipped the same way. And stuck down.

Q: Excuse me. I see that it sticks a little out over the top
edge. Did Folien One stick out over the top edge?

A: It stuck over a little, yes.

Q: And the bottom edge of the second lift, where was it in
relation to the top edge of the first lift?

A: It's possible that the first lifter was in the same area that
I put the second lifter.

Q: So you can't say specifically?

A: No. The first lifter was in the same area.

Q: So the bottom edge of the second lift was in the same
area as the top edge of the first lift?

A: Yes, so the second lifter might have …

Q: There could have been an overlap?

A: Yes, there could have been an overlap.

Q: Are you not sure or are you saying there was an overlap?

A: There was an overlap.

It's painstaking stuff, made harder to follow by the inadequacies of some of Swartz's answers and his tendency to mumble, but De Bruyn has a clear purpose in all of this. This emerges a few hours later when, having covered other ground, the lawyer takes Swartz through the sworn statement he had signed in July 2005 at the request of his boss, Director Attie Trollip. In it, Swartz goes through his involvement in the case, his being called out on the night of 16 March, his return to the scene with two colleagues on 17 March, and the events in the flat. In relation to Folien One, this is what that statement says: 'I remember that I handled a DVD cover. When I investigated the cover, the DVD disk was not in it. There was silver powder on both sides of the cover. On the front of the cover (the front is the side that is visible when the opening points to the right) were a number of stickers. The stickers were under a transparent plastic cover that was stuck in place. I don't recall the words on the stickers. Marks/fingerprints were apparent on both sides of the DVD cover. I used only one folien to lift the prints. I was satisfied that the other marks were not identifiable.'

Reading the statement to Swartz, De Bruyn pauses to point out that one of the key sentences – 'I used only one folien to lift the prints' – is not really capable of being interpreted to mean anything other than what it says.

A: That is correct.

Q: Excuse me?

A: That is correct, yes.

Q: The 'other marks' includes both those on the front and the back of the cover: 'I was satisfied that the other

marks were not identifiable.' I put it to you that, as that
sentence reads, there were no other foliens used.

A: The actual meaning is that I used one folien to lift the
identifiable prints that were on it.

Q: You agree that you said nothing about another folien?

A: I agree.

But if this redefinition of the phrase 'I used only one folien to lift the
prints' seems a little forced, it gets worse because, later in the statement,
Swartz has this to say: 'On 18-07-2005, Director Trollip asked me to
demonstrate to him how I placed the folien on the DVD cover to lift the
fingerprint. I put a similar DVD cover down in front of me with the side
that opens to the top.'

De Bruyn again interrupts his reading of Swartz's statement into the
record at this point.

Q: 'The side that opens': which side is that? Are you
referring to the side with the groove or some other
side?

A: The groove is to the right of the DVD cover and the top
side is straight up.

Q: Yes, but which is 'the side that opens'?

A: On the right.

Q: On the right?

A: Yes.

That suddenly seems an awkward answer when De Bruyn continues
reading from Swartz's statement, the following sentences of which read:
'I placed the folien on it, and saw that I used the side that opens as the
top. The side that opens has a groove into which one puts one's fingers
when it is being opened. The demonstration to Director Trollip agrees
with the notes about the position of the fingerprints that I made on the
scene.'

Q: In other words, what you told Mr Trollip there is that you used the side with the groove at the top.

A: No.

Q: No?

A: No.

Q: Explain then what that sentence means: 'I placed the folien on it, and saw that I used the side that opens as the top.'

A: No. That isn't the top.

Q: Can you show His Lordship. You have a DVD cover in front of you. Pick it up.

A: These are the grooves to the right side. That for me is the top of the DVD cover.

Q: You are showing His Lordship the DVD cover with the groove for thumbs on the right-hand side, and then when you point to the top of the DVD holder you say that is the top.

A: That is correct.

*　*　*

From Swartz, then, we have two apparently conflicting accounts of how he lifted the folien. On the stand, he has spoken of two lifts, the first from the bottom half of the front of the DVD cover and the second from the top half with the results reconstructed in PLATE 2. In his statement, prepared after a careful demonstration to his boss of how he lifted the print, he says there was only one folien used. On the stand, he insists that, in terms anyone who uses a desktop printer might recognise, that the DVD cover was oriented like a portrait; in the statement, he seems to say it was laid out in landscape mode.

One almost wishes that was all. But, in fact, Swartz also seems to have given a different account to Director Botha, whose report on Folien

One was supposed to address the initial concerns raised by the defence about the provenance of the lift. That Swartz offered a third account of his works seems an all but inescapable interpretation of the paragraph headed, TWO PARALLEL LINES ON BACKGROUND OF FOLIEN ONE, and which relates to the two bright lines that Botha testified can only be explained by there having been two lifts. It reads, 'Top mark is caused by the top of the DVD cover while the bottom mark was caused by the first lift. The distance 78–80mm was the distance from the top of the cover to the bottom of the first piece of folien used for the first lift.'

Those sentences suggest that Botha understood Swartz's method to have included two lifts taken from the DVD cover oriented, when he held it, like a portrait. That's consistent with what Swartz said on the stand, though it is reconciled with his earlier statement only by doing some violence to the language he'd used there. What is not consistent with either version is the implication of Botha's account of Swartz's method, which is that the two foliens were both applied and lifted from the top half of the DVD cover so that the lower of the bright lines present on Folien One is explained by the bottom edge of the first folien having been about 80mm from the top of the DVD cover. On the stand, he had said that it was caused by the top edge of that first, unrecorded, folien lift.

I'm not sure why both the defence and the prosecutors choose to press neither Botha nor Swartz about the apparent conflict between Swartz's on-stand account of what happened and the account he appears to have given Botha, but I suspect that the considerations of the defence may have been strategic: there would have been no profit for their client in providing the police officers with the chance to clear up that conflict, and they could then allow it to stand for itself during closing arguments. Rather than clarify matters, then, they may have preferred to deal with the question cursorily while Swartz was on the stand so that all the contradictions could be exposed later, long after there'd be any chance of explaining them.

The question of the prosecutors' failure to address this issue is more interesting since so much rested on this aspect of Swartz's testimony: three mutually contradictory accounts had been given of perhaps the most important aspect of his testimony, and yet they did nothing to address the threat this posed to his credibility. Why?

It is possible, I think, that they took the view that they were better off not calling attention to the conflicts – even if they did so only to clarify it – in the hope that the judge might not notice it. It is a possibility that some might see as a little insulting to the judge, and it would have worked only if the defence also failed to pick up on these problems.

On the other hand, it is also possible that the prosecutors simply failed to appreciate the gravity of the problem until it was too late.

PART FIVE

17

If you live in Cape Town and associate with a certain group of journalists and other media types, you may have heard or may yet hear that I am not to be trusted. In particular, you may have heard or may yet hear that I have been seduced by a charismatic psychopath and have, as a consequence, failed in my duty to report the case against Fred fairly and honestly. In fact, you may even have heard it said that Fred's father was paying me.

It is a serious business, this kind of rumour, one that is both personally and professionally insulting, and, in response, I am tempted to point out that some of those who have said this sort of thing are themselves professionally invested in insisting that Fred got away with murder. I am tempted to point out, in other words, that they, too, are not to be trusted. I could say that, or I could say that the market for unfounded and scurrilous rumours during and after Fred's trial was exceptionally deep, and that nasty stories were spread about practically everyone who spent any significant time in Courtroom Four of the Cape High Court.

I've heard it said, for example, that the reason Fred got off was that his father, Louis, bribed the prosecutors to do a bad job. I've also heard that Louis beat his wife when Fred and his brothers were children. I've even heard that in a fit of rage, he chopped one of his wife's fingers off with an axe. I've heard that he did this in front of his sons.

I've heard it said that Fred was shocked and angry when he learnt from the autopsy report that Inge's hymen was not intact. I've heard that a forensic analysis of his computer found notes towards a plan for murdering Inge, along with files full of pornography. I've heard that Fred is secretly gay and that he is scorched by the shame of what he regards as an abomination before God. I've heard that he has killed before and will, presumably, kill again.

I've heard it said that Fred's brother Dawie was expelled from Grey College because he smoked grass, though the relevance of this to the trial is obscure, especially since the source of this rumour also told me that the family was angry with Fred for allowing this to happen to his younger brother. This was an obvious mistake, however: Fred is the youngest of the three boys.

I've heard it said that Alfons had had an angry encounter with Inge's father in court, telling the older man that he was not aware of what he and his wife were doing. I've also heard that at some other point Inge's uncle put his shoulder into Alfons's chest in a manner intended to hurt.

I've heard it said that one of Inge's relatives seduced one of the more senior journalists covering the trial, in the process securing better coverage of the prosecution's case. I've also heard that when the affair ended, he slashed the tyres of cars parked in front of that journalist's house. I've heard that Alfons also seduced a journalist, though he was not said to have proceeded to slash any tyres, whether in front of the journalist's home or anywhere else. (Perhaps the affair ended more happily.)

Not even Inge was spared a grinding through the rumour mill: I have heard that Inge was a virgin. I've heard that she was a terrible tease and may have teased the wrong man. I've heard that she was not a virgin, but had not slept with Fred who suffered the torments of reluctant chastity. I've heard that she was a party girl. I've heard that she was abused as a child. I've heard that she was unfaithful. I've heard that she had an abortion. I've heard that she was into s&m.

Most of these stories I know to be false. Some, I suspect, may be true, or at least true enough. Each, though, is in its own way vicious, and, as such, a measure of the poison introduced into this community by Inge's murder. It is the drawing of this poison – to the extent that that is ever possible – that is one of the most compelling functions of the criminal justice system, the officers of which are tasked with finding, prosecuting and punishing those who murder the innocent.

In the broad scheme of things, then, being said to be naïve and dim and easily swayed by a charming psychopath is small beer. Certainly, it was not as bad as many of the things said of others.

Besides, I may have brought some of this on myself.

*　*　*

Throughout my research I have suffered from a handicap I incurred before I even began and which arose from the manner in which I came to this story: because I was asked by Alfons to advise him about approaching someone in the senior ranks of the Police Service to investigate his family's claims that evidence was being fabricated, and because I actually gave him some advice, I was told by lawyers to whom I spoke that it would be inappropriate for me to make any contact with anyone listed as a state's witness until after the prosecutors had closed their case.

I was told that because I'd given Alfons some advice and the names of people he might contact to discuss the case, it was possible that the prosecutors might regard any contact I might make with their witnesses as being an attempt by the defence to interfere with their case. Although

I had neither asked for nor received any payment for the advice I gave Alfons, I was told that if I made contact with state's witnesses and if the allegation were made that I was part of the defence team, my actions could disrupt and derail the trial. Since that was in no-one's interest, it meant that for the bulk of the trial, the only people to whom I could speak were those who were not on the prosecution's list of witnesses. That meant I could not talk to the police officers, obviously. Nor could I talk to Inge's family and many of her friends. I couldn't even talk to Fred's alibi witnesses. The result was that I was the only journalist in the room who did not develop a relationship with any of these people, and who made no effort to do so.

Little wonder, then, that they thought I was in Fred's pocket. Little wonder also that when I did make contact with the Lotzes after the prosecution closed their case, they ignored my request for an interview.

If this was one problem I faced during the trial, for a long time I also faced its polar opposite: a lack of access to Fred himself.

While my lawyers had told me not to talk to state witnesses, Fred's lawyers had told him not to speak to me. Their concern, of course, was to protect Fred from hostile coverage and to ensure that nothing he might say in an interview would become an issue in the trial.

At the time, I thought that this would become a problem, that I would have little to say about Fred and that he would, for that reason, become no more than a cipher. Books without characters don't work, I thought, and I worried that I would have none to people my pages. After a few weeks in court, however, I was much less worried about this. One reason for this was that the sheer number of people who would make it into my pages. Another, more important reason was that the accused in a trial at law really is a cipher: the trial is about what he did or did not do (or, more precisely, what the evidence suggests he did or did not do); it is not about who he is. As a result, the accused can sit in the dock, silent and unmoved; he can remain a blank slate for the course of the proceedings.

My lack of access to Fred, then, was not dissimilar to the judge's.

Except that, unlike the judge, I had quite a lot of indirect access to Fred through his brother, his father, his lawyer and a number of other people who'd speak to me once they heard what I was doing. This was immensely useful, of course, but it served primarily as an object lesson in why talking to Fred probably wouldn't have produced very much that was novel: it turns out that when people are in the public eye and when the stakes are high, they quickly become adept at managing how they present themselves. Usually, this is not a question of lying. It is, however, a question of choosing which parts of the truth to reveal and how. In digital animation, they call this 'self-shadowing' – the process through which the image of an object or character, itself composed of nothing more than beams of light, must both illuminate and obscure itself as it is made to appear to move through space. On the screen, it is this that creates the effect of depth and dimensionality.

Throughout the trial, all the principal role-players – Fred, the police, the lawyers, the families, the journalists, the judge – were engaged in this kind of self-shadowing, actively seeking to produce impressions of themselves that they thought were most flattering. That this would happen was apparent almost from the start, and it meant that it would have been impossible to get under Fred's skin simply by asking him questions: why on earth would he have told me anything that could hurt him? Why would anyone?

The best I could hope for was that, in the clash of rival narratives during the trial itself, something approximating Fred would emerge.

*　*　*

I met Fred for the first time on the morning his trial began. Before that, I had met with Alfons twice and I had spoken to Fred himself once on the phone – a courtesy call after deciding that I would come to Cape Town for the opening of the trial to tell him that I was considering writing a book. It was during that conversation that he informed me of his lawyers' advice not to grant interviews until after the trial.

The news reports I'd read about the case had spoken of a highly intelligent, deeply religious man. The pictures they'd published most often were of a big, clean-shaven man with brown hair that tended to the spiky, large features and steel in his eyes. These were images that stood in some contrast to pictures of him taken at Inge's funeral and published shortly after. In one of these, Fred had been captured weeping in his mother's arms. In it, he seems utterly bereft and unbelievably young. Because Fred was not a suspect then, those pictures were not intended as portraits of him. Instead they were intended to record the extent of the suffering caused by Inge's death. In effect, these were really images of Inge, portraits of a woman whose profile could be seen in the pain of those left behind.

My first impression of Fred was that he was smaller than expected. Part of that may have been because he'd lost a quarter of his body weight in the previous year, and the collar of his shirt now hung from his neck. I saw him when I walked into court. He was sitting in the dock, looking straight out at the court, his mind on something else. He didn't seem tense or nervous. Instead, he seemed exceptionally self-contained, and my interaction with him was brief and to the point: Alfons introduced us, he greeted me and thanked me for coming. I said, 'Good luck'. For what? I wasn't sure.

What did I think of him?

For a religious freak, a psychopath and a murder accused, I found him surprisingly unintimidating. He was smaller and younger than I'd expected. I thought also that he was less self-pitying than one might expect of someone claiming to have been falsely accused of murder. About the only thing I found disturbing at all was that he seemed entirely lacking in any interest in me, much less in any need to explain or justify himself to me. In fact, his only concession to my existence was the handshake and the greeting. Beyond that, he sat alone in the dock, quietly disengaging himself from what was going on around him, the jacket of his suit ballooning from his shrunken chest.

* * *

Family legend has it that Fred was doing fraction sums in his head before he started school. He would drive around the family farm with his father, so the story goes, adding six tenths to four fifths and subtracting three sevenths from thirteen fourteenths. It is an unusual talent, but it is not, I was told, the main reason why he became an actuary. That, it seems, was the result of a decision he'd made about his future immediately after asking his father which profession made the most money.

Fred's intelligence is something anyone who knows him remarks on. It's not all they say about him. They say he was a sweet, sensitive boy who never gave his parents any trouble. They say that he was the smartest kid in his class (never, I was told with what I hope was some poetic licence, dropping a mark in a school maths test). They say that he was also the hardest-working pupil in his class. They say that he was honest and thoughtful, trusting and caring. In fact, the best I could do in getting anyone to say anything bad about him was the odd comment about the dangers of virtues that are over-developed: he was, I was told, 'too trusting' or 'too innocent' or 'too soft'. 'The police,' someone told me once, 'couldn't have picked on anyone who was more innocent.'

As they say: there's no such thing as poison, only poisonous doses.

An instructive example of this tendency to innocence is a story Fred told me about an incident some weeks after the trial had ended. He was, he told me, driving through Cape Town one day when he was waved down by a pedestrian. He picked the man up and asked him where he wanted to go. 'To the nearest cliff,' the man said. 'I want to jump off.'

Well, it turned out that this man was going through a rough patch in his life: he had a wife and kids to feed, but no job and no prospects, and he wanted to end it all.

Fred told me that he listened to the man and then said that he too had recently been through a rough time. '*Is dit jy?*' the man responded, recognition dawning. 'I thought I'd seen your face before.'

To cut a short story shorter, Fred talked the man out of suicide and bought him and his family a McDonald's meal.

Fred related his story with complete sincerity, but from the moment he began – I'd asked about how people he'd met since the end of the trial had been reacting to him – I was thinking, 'You have got to be kidding! It's a scam. Open your eyes, man.' Then, when he was done, I said something to that effect.

Fred was genuinely shocked to be in the presence of so much heartless cynicism.

* * *

One of Fred's verbal tics is the throat-clearing phrase, 'To be very honest with you.' It is a phrase he might use to kick off even the most innocuous of comments. I don't know if this habit predates the trial or if it is something that comes of spending three years having his protestations of innocence being publicly disbelieved. I do know that, like anyone else, my natural instinct is to distrust anyone who over-uses expressions of this kind because they call attention to the speaker's unconscious doubts about whether he will be believed. Why the doubts, I always wonder?

And yet, in the three years I've worked on this project, I have yet to catch Fred in a lie. Not even once.

That might mean that I'm the credulous naïf of the rumours you might or might not have heard. It might mean that I have succumbed to the charms of one of the world's psychopaths. It's a possibility that I must recognise. Still, I prefer to think of myself as a little more worldly than that (but who doesn't?), and I don't think that I ever took Fred at his word. I always tried to maintain a degree of detachment, waiting and watching for him to slip up. But, as I said, he never did.

An example: Director Trollip testified that one of the key triggers for the heightened investigative focus on Fred after 15 April 2005 was the discovery of the letter Inge wrote on the morning of her death. In it she had alluded to a recent argument with Fred and had used language that

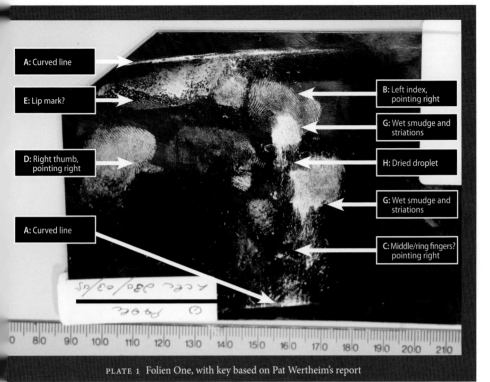

A: Curved line

E: Lip mark?

D: Right thumb, pointing right

A: Curved line

B: Left index, pointing right

G: Wet smudge and striations

H: Dried droplet

G: Wet smudge and striations

C: Middle/ring fingers? pointing right

PLATE 1 Folien One, with key based on Pat Wertheim's report

2 LIFT 10-8-2007
NEW DVD COVER
USED. ±30MIN.
TOP DVD

1 LIFT 10-8-2007
NEW DVD COVER
USED ± 30 MIN
TOP DVD

PLATE 2
Arie Zeelenberg's reconstruction of Constable Swartz's testimony about the two lifts, August 2007

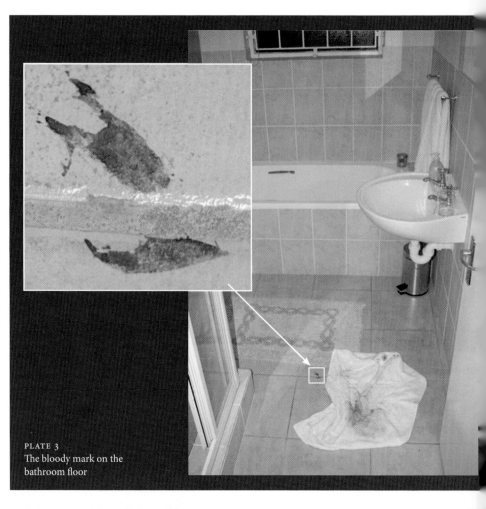

PLATE 3
The bloody mark on the
bathroom floor

PLATE 4 The bloody mark, before and after treatment with Amido Black

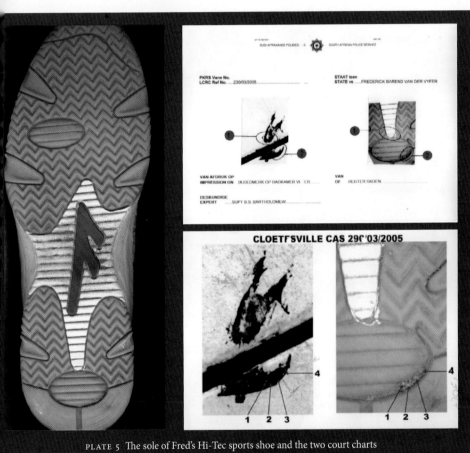

PLATE 5 The sole of Fred's Hi-Tec sports shoe and the two court charts

First step: Oval shape in heel

Second step: V-shape in middle

PLATE 6 The bloody mark, reversed and matched, to the sole of Fred's Hi-Tec sports shoe

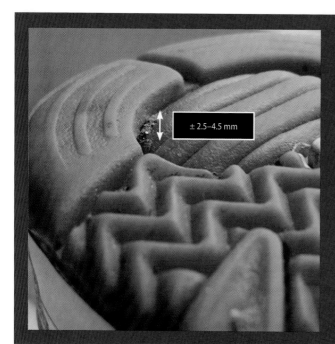
± 2.5–4.5 mm

PLATE 7
The depth of the sand grains in the groove of Fred's shoe

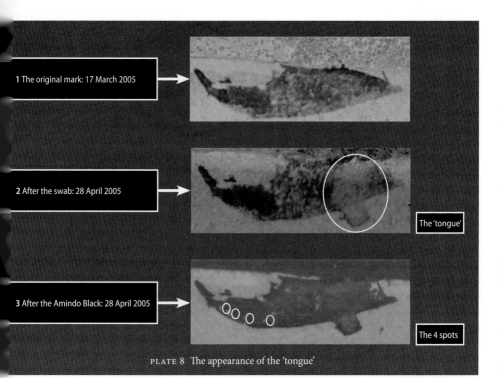

1 The original mark: 17 March 2005

2 After the swab: 28 April 2005

The 'tongue'

3 After the Amindo Black: 28 April 2005

The 4 spots

PLATE 8 The appearance of the 'tongue'

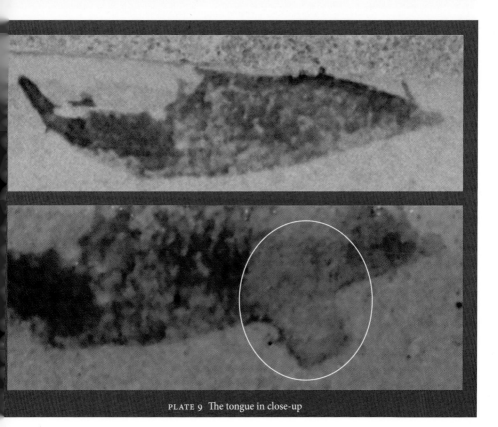

PLATE 9 The tongue in close-up

Location of sand

PLATE 10
The test impression done
with the left shoe

PLATE 11 The grains of sand, close-up

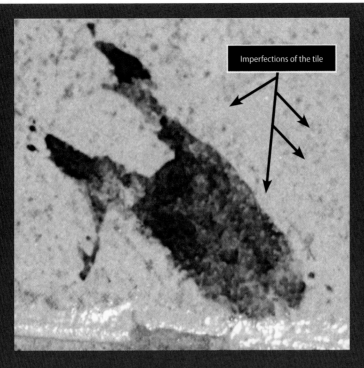

Imperfections of the tile

Swipe marks

PLATE 12 Imperfections in the grain of the bathroom tile,
and evidence that excess Amido Black was wiped away

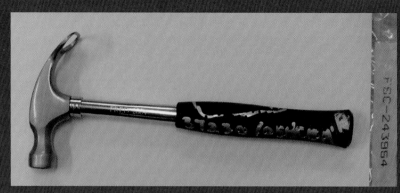

PLATE 13
Fred's hammer
bottle-opener

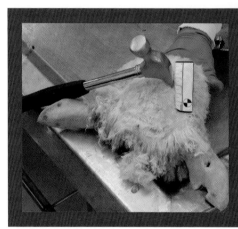

PLATE 14
The ornamental hammer
buried in a sheep's skull

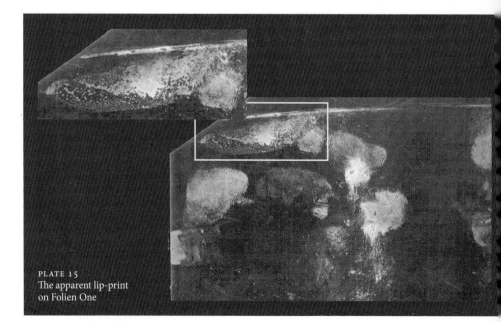

PLATE 15
The apparent lip-print
on Folien One

suggested she felt inadequate in relation to him. She had also promised never to 'betray' him, before crossing that out and replacing it with the softer promise never to 'go behind your back'.

For a suspicious cop who was convinced that Inge had been killed by someone close to her, a letter that was so placatory and eager-to-please must have suggested that all was not well between Inge and Fred. It would have been hard not to suspect that the letter or the fight to which it referred might have been the cause of her death no more than seven or eight hours later. And, as Trollip insisted, he thought the letter was all the more incriminating because Fred had failed to mention its existence – much less that there had been a quarrel – to any of the police officers involved in the case. In fact, Trollip said, Fred had even sought to deceive Mrs Lotz by giving her the shorter, undated letter, the hastily written blue sheet that might have been written on a Sunday.

Fred's response to the claim that he had withheld Inge's letter was put to both Mrs Lotz and to Director Trollip by his lawyer. And it came in two parts. The first was that Fred did not, in fact, withhold the letter. It emerged – and this was undisputed – that two weeks after the murder, Fred had given a copy of it to the private investigators whom the Lotzes had employed. It was, Fred's lawyer insisted, impossible for Fred to know that they would not pass that on to Inge's parents or the police. Certainly, there was nothing he could do to prevent them from doing so.

I thought this argument was sufficient to dispel most of the clouds of suspicion. It didn't entirely explain why Fred hadn't given the letter to Mrs Lotz on the morning after the murder, but it certainly undermined Trollip's claim that he had withheld it. Strong as I thought this argument was, though, Fred and his lawyer insisted on a second argument, one that I thought was altogether too pat to be credible: Fred, they claimed, had initially withheld the long letter from the Lotzes out of a concern for the effect its contents might have on them. The offending passage, they said, consisted of a few sentences in which Inge mentioned that her father sometimes drank too much. 'I am unbelievably afraid about the Easter weekend,' she'd written, 'and that you will see my father after he's had too much to drink. I do not want to lose you because of that and I don't want you to see that side of our family. It probably sounds stupid, but it is a real worry for me.'

It is an intriguing passage, and the Fred that emerges from it is a young man with more than his share of sanctimony. It is also a passage, however, that would not have been easy for Inge's father to read; from it, he would learn that, on the day she died, his daughter's thoughts of him were touched by shame. Little wonder, then, that when the letter was introduced at the trial, Inge's parents initially sought to keep those words out of the record and the newspapers. The result was that, until the very end of the trial, an agreement between the prosecutors and the defence ensured that the full letter was not read into the record, and that this passage could be referred to in only the most oblique of terms. It seemed, then, that if Fred really did withhold the letter out of consideration for the Lotzes' feelings, his concern about the pain it would cause was not misplaced.

Even so, I didn't believe that that was the real reason he hadn't given the letter to Inge's mother.

It seemed to me that De Bruyn's claims that Fred had withheld the letter out of sensitivity implied a degree of awareness and thoughtfulness that was hard to imagine a young man possessing immediately after his girlfriend is horribly murdered. If Fred really was innocent of the crime, I thought, he would have been in a state of shock and trauma when Mrs Lotz asked to see the letter. That was a few short hours after they learnt of the murder, and, under the circumstances, it seemed unlikely that he'd have been sufficiently alive to the pain that the letter might cause Inge's mother. It is true that he didn't have the letter with him, and that he had to ask his flatmate, Marius, to collect it for him the next day. It is true, in other words, that he had some time to consider the issue. But even so, it struck me as a little immodest to claim that he'd withheld the letter out of his own sensitivity. Much more likely, I thought, was that Fred was simply embarrassed about the argument he'd had with Inge.

And yet Fred's lawyers persisted with this claim, putting it to state witnesses and repeating it when they argued for the dismissal of charges after the close of the state's case. I couldn't understand why they attached so much importance to an argument that I thought was unnecessary and which I didn't believe.

Then, out of nowhere, evidence emerged that strongly suggested that what De Bruyn and Fred had said was true – that Fred really had withheld the letter out of concern for the Lotzes. That proof was contained in the file of the Lotzes' private investigator to whom Fred had given a copy of the letter. It was a file that Fred's lawyers had not seen before the start of the trial because the private investigators were listed as state's witnesses. Like many other state's witnesses, they were never called, however, so De Bruyn could speak to them for the first time only after the close of the prosecution's case. As they spoke, he flipped through their case file. In it, he found a copy of Inge's letter together with a covering letter that Fred had completely forgotten he'd written. Addressed to Boet Claasen, the private detective, and framed in the tortured third person of a respectful Afrikaans boy addressing his seniors, it read:

Hello, oom.

Here is the letter I spoke about. Oom can read it to see if it is of any value. I doubt it, but I don't want to withhold anything.

The letter is very personal, and I'd appreciate it if it didn't get into too many people's hands. But do whatever you have to for the investigation. Call me if oom has any questions about the letter or anything else.

Best with everything. I am praying for you,
Fred.

PS: the most important thing for is that the paragraph about her father on the first page must please not get to oom Jan, if at all possible.
Thank you.

Does this handwritten note, dated 29 March 2005, prove definitively that Fred was aware of the dismay Inge's letter might cause her parents on the night of 16 March? It doesn't. But it does show that he was aware of this possibility at most two weeks later. Significantly, that was also two weeks before he became a suspect, at a time when he could very easily have burnt the letter and scattered its ashes.

*   *   *

The only time I thought Fred's answers to questions put to him in the trial struck a genuinely false note was when he was asked about the video that Inge had rented on the day she died, and about his own visit to the store at which she'd rented it a few days after the police searched his home and office. It was a visit during which he hired the same DVD Inge had taken out – *The Stepford Wives*.

The incident in question happened on 18 April, three days after Fred's interrogation by the police and six days after his fingerprint had been matched to a lift the police had told him had come from the DVD cover. On that day, Fred went to the video store that Inge had used and asked the clerk, an Anna-Marie Thomas, about renting the DVD. On the stand, she'd said that she explained the procedures to him, that he filled in the relevant form, and that before he took the DVD home, he'd looked at the synopsis of the film printed on the cover. She said that, having done so, he commented, 'It's strange that she would take home a movie like this.'

There were a number of questions that arose from Fred's renting of the DVD on 18 April. One was the suggestion, briefly made by the prosecution, that Fred had rented the DVD in order to create an explanation for why his fingerprints might be on the cover. It may have been this, the prosecution maintained, that explained why Fred had gone so far out of his way to rent the DVD from the store Inge had used. This was obvious nonsense since he rented the DVD three days after the police confronted him with the claim about his prints. Fred's explanation for his action was more plausible: that he'd gone to the store to find out if there was any way that his prints might be on the box of a film he'd never seen. Was it possible, he might have wondered, that the store used the same DVD covers on more than one movie?

If going to the store seemed odd, his account of his actions was not entirely implausible. However, he did offer some evidence about this incident that jarred. This was in the course of Carien Teunissen's cross-examination of him, when she asked him what the film was about. He replied that he didn't know because he had never brought himself to watch it. 'I couldn't find it in my heart to watch it,' he said. 'I would be wondering all the time whether this was the moment she was murdered.'

That much is plausible. Less plausible is that Fred tried to maintain an air of innocent ignorance about the movie, saying only that he had done a little internet research about it, knowing, for example, that there was an original and a remake and that there were differences between the two. But beyond that, he professed ignorance, remembering only vaguely that he'd read that the wives in Stepford are 'programmed', and making that concession only after it was put to him by the judge.

For an exceptionally smart young man, the vagueness of his memory was surprising, and I could only believe that he really didn't want to answer any questions about what Inge's renting of the movie might have said about her state of mind. Or, for that matter, about the state of her relationship with Fred.

18

The most striking thing about Fred is his self-possession. Uncommonly calm and clear and focused, he comes across as almost too self-possessed. It's as if the whole spectrum of human experience that runs from the silly mistake through the regrettable *faux pas* to the unconscionable error is closed off to him. His speaks quietly, choosing his words and sentences with care and precision. Had he not been on trial for murder, his picture splashed on the front pages next to banner headlines of blood and hammers, one would have found it hard to imagine a person who would seem straighter and more respectable. All of which makes it extraordinarily difficult to picture him among the worshippers attending a Sunday night service of His People Church.

When I was in town in July 2009, the Stellenbosch chapter of His People Church held its services in the hall of one of the local high schools.

It was an anonymous space on the affluent edge of town, its presence advertised by purple banners of a kind more commonly seen at service stations and at product launches for carbonated sports drinks. Inside the hall, the stage, on which a band played enthusiastic rock'n'roll, was dominated by two large screens. On these were projected words and images to accompany the music. The production values were extraordinarily high, suggesting that these videos had been sourced from the church's headquarters in the United States. All of which created an impression of commercial modernity and, consequently, of a certain weightlessness, an absence of social and cultural roots. It was an impression that had been given symbolic reinforcement by the recent rebranding of His People Church as Every Nation Church, a name that reflects a strategy aimed at planting a church in every country in the world by 2010. It is a strategy best described as 'corporate', a franchising model in which church services are treated in the same way as burgers at McDonald's.

On the night I attended its service – as chilly and dark and damp as any in the middle of a Winelands winter – the auditorium was about two-thirds full, and the congregation, composed almost exclusively of students, must have been among the prettiest in all of creation. This was the flowering bloom of South Africa's middle-class youth, and I found the passion they exhibited in their worship deeply troubling: a kind of mass, auto-hypnosis, the effect produced by an hour's worth of singing songs whose riffs were so repetitive as to verge into rock'n'roll chanting. It was heady stuff: people danced in the aisles; young women held each other in mutual support; young men, bearded and strongly built, wept while raising arms and face to the heavens.

'I can feel the spirit of Jesus in the hall tonight,' the band's leader shouted to rapturous acclaim.

The message of the sermon, delivered for something like an hour by a woman dressed all in red, was that no love can come before one's love of Christ. 'Christ is madly in love with you,' she said. 'You must be madly in love with Him. The Bible is the most romantic story ever told, and you are its heroes.'

'Ours is a joyful God,' she proclaimed in a powerful voice. 'Joy is not from the devil,' she said. 'God made the mountains around Stellenbosch so that the mountain bikers can feel joy. God makes the flowers grow.'

In this seething mass of devotion, I felt, a person might quickly lose his grip on himself. To me, the fervour on display felt like a form of enslavement, but for those around me, I had no doubt that they experienced it as the opposite – as a kind of liberation. Which raised the question: liberation from what? When I asked a local psychologist this, her answer was striking: 'It's an enabling faith, not a repressive one. Some of them think they can do anything because when they go back to church, God will forgive them their sins.'

I heard a not unrelated view from a member of a Johannesburg congregation of Every Nation Church. We were speaking about the occasional problematic pastor the church had had: one in Cape Town, he informed me, had engaged in 'revolting' behaviour – an affair with a congregant. The trouble was, he explained, that some of these pastors developed a 'God complex', and, in the course of a conversation in which he'd emphasised that, while His People Church was 'enthusiastic' and 'alive', it was not 'cultish' or in any other way peculiar, he said this of those repugnant pastors: 'Because they are being used by God, they think they are on higher, supernatural plane. They are like Jacob Zuma – they think that the rules don't apply to them.'

It is a sentence to launch a thousand dissertations.

* * *

If I found the church service alien, it was because I am by nature, by conviction and by force of habit an atheist. There is not, I think, a single grain of faith anywhere in me: not for a god or for any supernatural force. It is an absence about which I became exquisitely aware as I witnessed the rapture of the three or four hundred worshippers. I felt nothing so much as a yawning, unbridgeable distance between myself and them. Worse, it was a distance I could not begin to reduce by the usual ways of reading books and talking to experts, because every time I did so, and no matter how satisfied I felt at the end of my immersion, my essential ignorance would quickly reassert itself. It was as if whatever knowledge I gathered could find no traction in my psyche, and would slide friction-lessly out of my head.

Such was the depth of my alienation from what I saw.

But even as I watched and listened, I wondered also how the parents of these kids must feel.

Almost but not quite exclusively white and Afrikaans, a large ma-jority of worshippers in the congregation of Every Nation Church in Stellenbosch must come from families with deep roots in the Dutch Reformed Church. Strict and austere in everything it did and thought and said, it is a church premised on the teachings of John Calvin and his dire view of fallen man's nature as ignorant, slothful and fickle. It was for this reason that Calvin enjoined believers to foster the virtues of 'abstinence, sobriety, frugality and moderation … [and to abominate] excess, pride, ostentation and vanity.' The result was a severity of mind and a suspicion of joy so strict as to sometimes seem a parody of itself. It was a view of the world that was, in every way, a thousand miles from the exuberant display at Every Nation Church.

Nor was the style of worship the only or most important difference between this church and the Dutch Reformed Church of its congregants' parents. Theologically, for example, the Dutch Reformed Church is com-mitted to Calvin's doctrine of predestination, which holds that every individual's salvation or otherwise is predestined by God, and that His judgment cannot be changed by any actions of mortal man. It is a doc-trine that promises the faithful nothing: God has already decided. Every Nation, by contrast, holds that nothing is predestined, that everything depends on the kind of relationship one chooses to have with God. This is not just a belief that one's salvation depends on the conscious decision to embrace Christ, but also that one's destiny in this world can be altered if one believes strongly enough, embraces God closely enough, and prays hard enough.

But if the manner of worship at Every Nation and its underlying theology would have alienated the parents of those singing and dancing and weeping in the aisles, even more troubling for them might be the lack of any organic connection between this church and the idea of Afrikanerdom.

The Calvinism of the Dutch Reformed Church is heavily influenced by that of Abraham Kuyper, a Dutch theologian and prime minister, whose interpretation of Calvin included ideas about the way in which God shaped the character and destiny of nations. This led to a quasi-religious nationalism in which God and the church figured in the destiny of an Afrikanerdom that was seen and understood as a real entity, something organic whose existence was willed by God.

'The church has a special calling with respect to the Dutch-speaking population with whose existence it is bound up in such an intimate manner,' a participant at a 1915 meeting of ministers reported on the resolutions taken. 'It is its duty, in brief, to be nationalist, to watch over our particular national concerns, to teach the people to see the hand of God in their history and to keep alive in the Afrikaner people the awareness of national calling and destiny, on which is laid the spiritual, moral and material progress and strength of a people.'

How wrapped up the idea of Afrikanerdom was in religious garb can be seen in a quotation from DF Malan, apartheid's first prime minister, offered some 37 years before he won power: 'We are Afrikaners and so ought we always to be because any nationality, formed by God through history and environment, has in itself the right to exist. God wills differences between nation and nation. And he wills these because he has placed before each People a unique destiny, a unique calling, like that of any individual. And if I read the history of my own people, a history that shows me the birth and growth of a people despite itself, a people that became a people without its own cooperation, then I cannot free myself of the impression that God desires our people's continued existence. And He desires this because He has a unique calling for our people. My feeling of nationality thus rests finally on a religious foundation.'

Little wonder, then, that the Dutch Reformed Church's aspiration was always to be Afrikanerdom's *volkskerk*: anything else was, quite literally, unthinkable. And, the reality was that, for a few generations at least, the aspiration was achieved and something like ninety percent of Afrikaners who went to church (and most went to church) were Dutch Reformed.

All of which is to say that, for a time at least, the political idea of Afrikanerdom was the same as the religious idea and the nationalist idea. They formed a seamlessly coherent, mutually reinforcing worldview that spoke of a people whose past and present and future could be seen and understood as part of God's plan.

That coherence was always a fantasy, of course. It was fantastic in the usual sense of the word, in that it was never really true. And it was also fantastic in a Freudian sense, in that it represented an unconscious wish. But, for as long as it held its people in thrall, this fantasy about Afrikanerdom meant that, as a people, Afrikaners could avoid asking themselves at least some kinds of existential questions.

As a consequence of any number of stresses and stressors, all of this unravelled quickly and painfully in the last quarter of the twentieth century as individuals cut themselves free from established thinking, in the process unweaving the fabric of social relations and shattering any claim for the existence of a unity of language, culture, nation and faith. And the process has only accelerated since 1994. It is a process that has opened up new categories and ideas, but it is also one that must have produced in many a sense of vertigo as foundations have shifted and shattered, and as established thinking has unwound. And it must feel to some members of older generations to be the work of extremists, of lunatics, of people who have lost their bearings.

These are thoughts to which we will return. For the moment, though, all that really matters is that Every Nation Church differed from the more established church along every dimension. Even its name – Every Nation – seems a deliberate taunting of the defining aspiration of the Dutch Reformed Church to be a *volkskerk*. More important for my present purposes, however, was that I simply couldn't picture Fred, as intelligent and self-contained and undemonstrative a person as I've ever met, singing and dancing and worshipping with the exuberance I'd seen at his church.

* * *

Fred's intelligence and the depth of his faith have always seemed to me to stand in some contradiction.

How is it, I have wondered again and again, that a man might be an actuary – a career in which a facility for finding and analysing empirical evidence is pretty much the only thing that matters – and yet believe in the literal truth of the Bible? Perhaps part of the answer to that question lies in the story of the purely financial reasons that Fred had when he chose this career. Still, it is hard to be good at something without having some commitment to its mechanics and its underlying logic. And Fred, I understand, is a very good actuary, achieving the highest-ever marks for an Old Mutual-supported student. Another part of the solution to this puzzle might be one offered by a friend of mine to whom I'd mentioned this conundrum and whose immediate response was something like, 'Numbers people are the biggest fundamentalists of all.'

It's an interesting thought: that to identify an incompatibility between quantitative empiricism and religious faith is to make a category mistake. Perhaps a conviction about the power of numbers and formulae to shape and explain the world has more in common with religious faith than is usually credited; perhaps each is a sign of a mind in need of order and certainty.

Whether or not this is true, there is an important similarity between

Fred's intelligence and his religious faith: they were both held against him during his trial.

From the very first morning, when Mrs Lotz testified that Inge had refused to attend church with Fred on the Sunday evening before her death, Fred's membership of His People Church was interpreted as evidence of some imbalance in his personality. His intelligence, by contrast, raised an unstated question: was he clever enough to get away with murder?

19

It has never been established with any certainty just when Inge died, with the pathologist concluding only that she'd been dead at least twelve hours. Since the autopsy took place some thirty-six hours after her body had been found, that was not helpful information.

We know for certain that Inge was alive at about 13:00 on 16 March, when she finished lunch with a friend. We know also that she was alive at 13:20, when she spoke to her mother, and at 15:07, when computer records at the store say she checked out *The Stepford Wives*. Inge was also alive at about 16:00, when workers in the complex say they saw her arrive. Beyond that, no-one is certain of anything except that she did not respond to any of the text messages or calls to her phone sent from about 20:00. We know also that her body was found shortly after 22:00.

We know a few things about Fred's movements on that day, too.

There are security camera images of his arriving at work at 11:09 and of his leaving the office at 18:06. There is Marius's statement, which says he arrived at the flat at about 18:15. There are records from his service provider that say Fred received a phone call on his cellphone at 19:10 and that he was in or near his flat in Pinelands at the time. There are statements from both Marius and from Jean Minnaar, to the effect that at about 19:20, Fred and Marius delivered the cupboard he'd collected in Stellenbosch earlier that day to Jean's flat, which was in the same complex as theirs. There are records that show that the wheel of Fred's bakkie was clamped by a security guard at the complex at about 19:30 and was unclamped again between 19:45 and 20:00. There are also cellphone records that show he sent an SMS and made a call to Inge between 20:00 and 21:00. Both the call and the SMS, the records reflect, originated in or near his flat.

Fred's movements after he left work at 18:06, then, are too well documented for him to have killed Inge after that: there simply wasn't the time for him to travel the thirty or forty minutes each way.

That leaves the afternoon.

We know from the usage records of Old Mutual's computer system that Fred logged on to his computer at 13:08 in the afternoon, used it to send an SMS to Inge at 13:10 and logged off at 13:24. Those same records also reflect that someone logged on at 17:14, sent an email to a colleague at 17:17 and logged off at 17:33. Fred's cellphone records for the afternoon show that he received an SMS from Inge at 13:36; that he failed to answer a call from Jean Minnaar at 14:51, and that the call was diverted to voicemail; that he retrieved Jean's message at 15:29; and that he received another SMS at 16:20, this time from a source that did not produce an identifying number.

All of the activity on his phone was registered to a cellphone mast physically located on the grounds of Mutual Park.

It hardly needs to be said that the mere fact that Fred's cellphone was registered as being at a particular place at a particular time does not mean that he was there. It may be that his phone was securely locked away in his office drawer when the sms arrived at 16:20. It is also conceivable that someone else retrieved his voicemail at 15:29. But this, at least, seems unlikely. Unless one imagines the involvement of a co-conspirator, it is hard to see how anyone with whom Fred had left his phone on the afternoon of 16 March, and who had been good enough to download a voicemail for him at 15:29, would have failed to come forward with that information. Absent an accomplice who was also at Old Mutual, one has to conclude that Fred was in Pinelands at 15:29, at least thirty minutes away from Inge's flat.

The same logic applies to the logging-on at his computer at 17:14 and the sending of an email: unless there were another person involved in the murder, whomever it was that did this on Fred's behalf would surely have come forward long ago. Besides, Fred's office is open-plan, so there would have been witnesses to his computer being used by someone else. And, as it happens, the man who uses the neighbouring workstation swears blind that he did see someone at Fred's desk at about that time: Fred.

That witness, Stefanus de Wet van der Spuy, testified during the trial that Fred came to his desk at about 17:10 and that the two of them chatted for a time about the plans Stefanus had for the long weekend.

Conscientiously doing their duty, the prosecutors pronounced themselves suspicious of the accuracy of Van der Spuy's memory. How, they asked him, could he be certain that Fred was there at 17:10 or 17:15? Couldn't it have been later? Given the computer records which confirmed that Fred's computer had been used at the time, this seemed a pointless line of questioning, but again and again Carien Teunissen challenged Van der Spuy about the accuracy of his memory. Why was it that he could remember the time he spoke to Fred, but not what Fred was wearing? How was it that he could remember details of the conversation they'd had, but could not remember anything else about what he'd done at work that day?

Van der Spuy's answer to these questions was that he remembered the incident so well because he had been asked to think about it almost immediately after it occurred. He said that he'd been sent an email the day after the murder, in which he was told of Inge's death and was asked to make contact with Marius Botha. 'The police,' the email said, 'just want to confirm Fred's whereabouts yesterday afternoon.'

Van der Spuy was in Johannesburg on the day after the murder – why? he couldn't remember – so he read the email only upon his return to the office on Friday 18 March. He testified that when he read it, however, he immediately thought about whether he'd seen or spoken to Fred two days earlier. That, he said, is why he remembered so clearly when they spoke, and why it had been relatively easy to provide a high level of detail when, in June 2005, he gave a statement to the private investigators hired by Fred's father.

Subjected to a sour and suspicious cross-examination, Van der Spuy conceded nothing about the timing of his conversation with Fred. And, because his testimony is supported by the computer records, it is hard to doubt that Fred really was at his desk at about 17:15. Nor, in the absence of any evidence to the contrary, is it easy to believe that anyone but Fred used his phone at 15:29 to retrieve his voicemail, a call that his cellphone records indicate was made from the office park.

That leaves 105 minutes of what one of the prosecutors at one point called 'deafening silence'. It is an hour and three-quarters in which he would have had to have driven to Inge's flat in Stellenbosch (something that could not have been done in much less than thirty minutes, and which the police themselves timed as taking closer to forty minutes), gained access to her flat, chatted with her for long enough for her to lie down on the couch, bludgeoned and stabbed her to death, washed up in the bathroom, exited the flat and returned to his office in Pinelands.

Is it doable?

Maybe. Just.

But it would have been an ungodly rush, something that makes significant Van der Spuy's answer to a question about how Fred had seemed that afternoon. 'M'Lord,' he testified, 'I noticed nothing about Fred that was different from any other day. He was normal, relaxed.'

If Fred killed Inge, overcoming the difficulties of doing so between 15:29 and 17:15 was not the least of his problems. In fact, there are two other problems which would have taxed all of his considerable intelligence: how did he get out of the highly secure Mutual Park (and then re-enter it!) without leaving any trace of his movements, and how was it that no-one at the meeting at which Fred was supposed to be present that day remembers that he was absent for any length of time?

* * *

The meeting on 16 March was part of a series of meetings held every day for the best part of three weeks, during which staff at Old Mutual briefed a group of American IT consultants on the insurance products they sold in order to establish how the Americans' system would need to be reconfigured if Old Mutual were to buy it.

According to the people who were there, Old Mutual was represented by ten staff members of whom Fred was one. Not all of these people were available when the investigators hired by Fred's father were conducting their interviews – some were overseas, some were based in Johannesburg – so statements were not taken from every person at the meeting before they were all listed as state's witnesses at the end of June 2005. Despite listing all of these people as potential witnesses against Fred, however, in the end only one was called by the prosecution: the facilitator of the meeting that day, an external consultant called Janine von Stein.

As it happens, Von Stein was one of the six who had given statements to the private investigators. Hers was signed on 13 June, and the nub of it was that Fred had not been at the meeting on the morning of 16 March because he had had a lecture, and that for this reason the agenda had to be shuffled a little. Fred, her statement says, had been asked to introduce the specifications of a particular product that would be under discussion that day, and, because of his lectures that morning, this had been done the previous afternoon. Von Stein's statement also says that Fred's immediate boss, Shahana Toefy, had asked that the discussion of Fred's presentation begin only after Fred was expected to arrive at 11:00 the next day. 'It was important,' Von Stein's statement reads, 'that Fred attend the sessions as he was learning from Shahana.' Still, it concludes, in slightly strained grammar, by saying that Von Stein had no independent memory of whether Fred stayed there all day or not: 'I do not recall that Fred was not in attendance for any part of the remainder of the day. I do not recall noticing anything different about Fred's behaviour during that day.'

This conclusion was reframed and reworded in a second affidavit given a few weeks later, this time to Director Trollip. There, we read this: 'I do not recall Fred's absence or presence for any particular part of the day.'

It is not an especially powerful statement, but it is one Von Stein confirms under oath when the prosecutor asks her if Fred could have left the room unnoticed: 'You would not have noticed that? Or he could have stayed and you would not have noticed either?'

'Exactly,' Von Stein answers.

Whether or not Von Stein's inability to remember Fred's 'absence or presence' with any clarity suggests that Fred was not in the room depends a great deal on how important she would have believed his presence to be. And it is precisely this that De Bruyn raises with her when it is his turn to ask questions. 'I think,' she says in reply to one of these thrusts, 'that as far as 16 March goes, the accused was only expected to be a participant and no more. He was not required to give input to the discussion. I knew Shahana Toefy wanted him there and that was so that he could learn and hear all the discussions, so that he could be a support for her in her role. From my perspective, it was important that Shahana and the systems developers were there. It was not important if Fred – and quite a few other people – were there or not.'

* * *

Von Stein, then, didn't remember Fred's movements. He might have stayed. He might have left. She didn't know which. But perhaps that is not all that surprising: Von Stein was the meeting's facilitator, not Fred's boss or colleague. What, then, did Fred's boss, Shahana Toefy, have to say? Because she was never called to testify, it is a question that haunts aficionados of Fred's trial and her failure to be called is taken by many to suggest that there were problems with Fred's alibi which, in spite of the efforts of the police and prosecutors, went unexplored.

'All Fred had to do was call Toefy,' I was told by a journalist who'd covered the trial and who believes that the prosecutors did such a poor job that she has no way of knowing if Fred was guilty. 'But he didn't call her. Why?' It was a point she emphasised by noting something others had noted, too: that Fred's father had spent the first half of the trial suggesting that when it was their turn, the defence might call only one witness: Toefy. 'You've got to admit, that's pretty strange,' she said.

And the failure of the defence to call Toefy is made more strange by the contents of the statement she gave to the private investigators on 13 June: 'Fred came to the session at about 11:15 on 16 March 2005 as he had morning lectures in Stellenbosch on Wednesdays.' Then, after listing the names of other people she recalls being at the meeting, the statement continues, 'Fred stayed in attendance at the session until we broke for the day between 17:00 and 17:30. He never left the session for prolonged periods except for the mutual tea breaks and at lunch. I cannot recall Fred making any calls or sending SMS messages. He was seated next to me. During tea breaks everyone was together and tea was brought to us. Fred gave presentations the whole week and also participated in the discussions that followed.' Then, later, it reads: 'After the session, I saw Fred again between 18:00 and 18:10 when he left. He walked past my office and greeted me. Fred acted as normal and was not tense.'

This is good stuff, and, especially after all the pre-release publicity that Fred's father had issued relating to the decisiveness of her testimony, it is not unreasonable to ask why Toefy was not called by Fred's lawyers.

The answer, according to courtroom scuttlebutt, was that the police could prove that Toefy had herself not been in the meeting at which she claimed to have sat next to Fred all day. Proof of this, it was said, came in the form of a credit card slip which put her in a shopping mall on the afternoon of 16 March, and it rendered her sworn statement about her knowledge of Fred's movements that day a pack of lies.

So was Toefy not called because the defence suspected that the police and prosecutors were able to undermine Toefy's testimony by producing a damning credit card slip? Was she going to crumble under cross-examination and confess that she had lied to protect Fred?

In truth, I doubt it. I think that what really happened is that the prosecutors made an important tactical mistake.

*   *   *

One of the prosecution's problems with Toefy was that they had signalled early on that they were intent on attacking her. They did this immediately after the close of their case when the defence applied for the judge to dismiss charges. The judge rejected this request, but, in the course of making their arguments, the defence had asked the judge to consider why the prosecution had presented the testimony of only one of Fred's alibi witnesses, Janine von Stein. Her testimony, they pointed out, did not prove that Fred had left the meeting. In fact, she hadn't even asserted that, saying only that she couldn't remember his presence or absence. If that was the best the prosecutors could do, the defence argued, surely it implied that the evidence of the other witnesses was at best no stronger than Von Stein's, and, at worst, that it would undercut the prosecution's case. Indeed, De Bruyn pointed out, Von Stein had indicated that Toefy was better placed to remember Fred's movements. In failing to call Toefy, De Bruyn suggested, the prosecutors had implicitly conceded that her evidence would support the defence's case.

The prosecution denied this. They hadn't called Toefy, they said, because what they really wanted to do was cross-examine her. She was, Christénus van der Vijver said, the kind of witness that a prosecutor would 'love to get his teeth into'. Since courtroom etiquette and the rules of evidence dictate that this kind of thing is not permitted with respect to one's own witnesses, they implied that they would prefer that the defence call Toefy.

Nor was this the first time that it had emerged that the police and prosecutors had had their differences with Toefy: something similar had emerged when Director Trollip had been on the stand a few weeks earlier. Then, he'd been asked by Advocate van der Vijver to talk about Toefy and his experience of her.

'M'Lord,' Trollip had replied, 'It's difficult to say whether it was a result of antagonism or of fear. She was not a pleasant person to speak to. She was not helpful. The best indication I can give is that at the end of the conversation, I suggested to her that if we needed to talk to her again, perhaps she should get some kind of assistance. Even if it is just a legal advisor to support her. So I wasn't comfortable in her presence and I didn't think she was terribly helpful.' As objective evidence of this apparent lack of cooperation, Trollip pointed to Toefy's refusal to sign a receipt for a formal notice to her that she was to be a state's witness that he had tried to serve her on 22 June 2005.

Why would Toefy have been so uncooperative? The prosecution doesn't quite say so, but, it seems they suspected that there may have been an overly close relationship between Fred and his boss. This can be inferred from the framing of a question they put to Trollip about Toefy's demeanour and which had elicited the answer about her possible 'antagonism' or 'fear'. That question had related to evidence that Fred had phoned Toefy just before midnight on the night Inge died. 'Did Toefy ever mention this conversation?' Van der Vijver had asked.

'No, M'Lord. I became aware of this only at a later stage. I found it strange that, in the time I spent with her, she didn't provide information about what occurred between herself and the accused that night.'

Later, when it was De Bruyn's turn to put questions to Trollip, he returned to the subject of the detective's interactions with Toefy. Although the prosecution had recently released Toefy to the defence, De Bruyn said that he had not yet had time to consult with her properly. He said that he had spoken to her on the phone, however, after he had heard Trollip's testimony of the day before. 'Ms Toefy,' he continued, 'told me that it was absolutely untrue that she had been resistant or had been unhelpful. She confirms that it was an exceptionally unpleasant conversation because, she says, you sat in front of her and insinuated continuously that she was lying in order to protect the accused and that you said that her two sworn statements were not true.'

On the stand and under oath, Trollip denied the allegation.

De Bruyn's next subject was the late-night call Fred had made to Toefy, and he asked the policeman whether there was anything suspicious about the fact that Fred had made it. Initially, Trollip ducked the question, insisting only that he found Toefy's failure to mention the call peculiar. De Bruyn refused to accept that answer, however, and kept plugging away until Trollip offered this reason for his doubts: 'I found it suspicious that she didn't mention it because, in the nature of the work I do, I am on the lookout for signs that the accused may be trying to make arrangements about what someone must say if the police come around to ask questions.'

Wasn't it possible, De Bruyn asked, that Fred was simply informing his boss that he would not be able to come in to work the next day, even though she wanted him to be at the meeting? This was possible, Trollip agreed. But he added that if that had been the purpose of the call, it was all the more important that Toefy should have told him about it. If she had, he said, he would not have found it suspicious. It was a characteristic twist in Trollip's logic: failing to report an innocent conversation to the police immediately renders the conversation suspicious, and nothing that happens subsequently, including two years of further investigation, can redeem the initial fall.

'Did you take the trouble to look at how long the conversation was?' De Bruyn asked, referring the witness to the report from the cellphone company.

'No, I didn't.'

'Perhaps you should. It lasted 58 seconds.'

* * *

What really happened between Trollip and Toefy? Because she never testified, it is not possible to be sure. But even without her testimony, it is quite possible to believe that Trollip accused her of lying to protect Fred. Evidence that that may have happened comes from the testimony of Stefanus de Wet van der Spuy. He was the occupant of the workstation next to Fred's, and it was he who testified that he'd seen Fred at around 17:10 or 17:15 on the afternoon of 16 March 2005. But he also testified to something else: that Trollip had threatened to have him charged as an accomplice.

Recall that Van der Spuy, like Toefy, was one of the people who'd given a statement to the private investigators in early June 2005, just before Fred was arrested. Those statements were handed to the police soon after Fred's arrest on 15 June. On the stand, he was asked about what happened next and says that on 20 June 2005, Trollip arrived at Old Mutual in order to interview some of the people whose statements he had just received. De Bruyn takes Van der Spuy through what happened:

> A: Initially, I was with my boss, and Director Trollip spoke to both of us, M'Lord. Then he asked if I'd mind if we spoke alone. I had no objection.
>
> Q: And what did Director Trollip say to you? How did the rest of the conversation go?
>
> A: M'Lord, he said that he had a problem with my statement because of the times in it, and that he had proof that Fred was in Stellenbosch at that time.

Q: Did he give you an example of that evidence that he
   said he had?
A: He said he could prove that Fred van der Vyver's phone
   had registered in Stellenbosch between 17:00 and 18:00.
Q: Did he request anything from you?
A: At that point, he asked me if I would be prepared to
   change my statement.
Q: And your answer was?
A: My answer was 'No.'
Q: So you refused?
A: That's correct. I was certain of my facts.
Q: What was Director Trollip's reaction?
A: At that point we spoke a little more about the case.
   Then he asked if I knew that he could charge me as an
   accomplice to murder if he could prove that Fred was
   guilty. He asked me again if I was prepared to change
   my statement. I refused again.
Q: What was the feeling you had? Were you comfortable
   with that part of the conversation?
A: On the contrary. I felt intimidated.

This testimony generated a rather bitter cross-examination by Teunissen, who sought desperately to discredit it.

Had Van der Spuy told anyone about his feeling intimidated? she asks. Yes, some of his friends and family.

Had he told anyone at work? No.

Had he told his boss, who was present for the first part of the meeting? No.

Had he told the private investigator who'd taken his statement? No.

Had he been intimidated by Trollip's words or just by the mere fact of being in an unfamiliar situation? It's possible that he was intimidated by the situation, Van der Spuy concedes, but he stands firm that he was also intimidated by Trollip's words and the 'insinuation' that he made.

Throughout, Van der Spuy plays this with some finesse. No, he keeps saying in response to Teunissen's challenges, I really, really felt intimidated. It was a genuinely unpleasant experience. At the same time, he softens the implicit complaint about Trollip's methods by saying that he had never been interrogated by a police officer before, and that he thought it possible that Trollip was trying to frighten him in order to test how committed he was to the facts he'd put in his statement. He says that he thought this might be a standard investigative technique.

Why Teunissen doesn't accept this gesture is a mystery. Instead, she complains that the allegation that Trollip intimidated Van der Spuy was never put to him when he was on the stand. De Bruyn quickly rises to object, however, that this is an unreasonable complaint because Van der Spuy was still on the list of state's witnesses when Trollip testified, and the defence had not spoken to him yet; they heard of his experience only after Trollip testified. Accepting defeat on this question, Teunissen says that Trollip denies the allegation that he threatened to have Van der Spuy charged as an accomplice, adding that, if necessary, Trollip would be recalled to the stand to formalise his denial. It is something that never happens, however, so, purely as a technical matter, one might say that the evidence was not disputed.

It's a somewhat amateurish mistake, but it is not the one that led the defence to decide that there was no need to call Toefy to the stand. That arose during Christénus van der Vijver's cross-examination of Toefy's boss, Mkuseni 'MK' Mbomvu, whose testimony was supposed to have been followed by that of Shahana Toefy.

20

Although Shahana Toefy was not called to testify, she did come to court expecting to be asked to do so, presenting herself on the same day as her boss, Mkuseni 'MK' Mbomvu. He was to be called first, and, while I didn't see it myself, I am told that Toefy spent the time MK was on the stand in a coffee shop across the road. I was also told that she looked incredibly nervous: that her hands shook and that there were tears in her eyes. Was she frightened because she had something to hide? Or was she frightened because, if she were called, she would have to stand up in open court and say a senior police officer had lied when he denied accusing her of lying to protect Fred? It is impossible to be sure. What we do know is that by the time MK had finished testifying, the defence no longer felt they needed to put her on the stand.

* * *

Questioned initially by De Bruyn, MK, who was bald and spectacled, said that he was the head of operations of investment services at Old Mutual. He said that he had met Fred in January 2005 when the latter started at the company. He said that during the week of 16 March 2005, he and a number of officials from Old Mutual were involved in a workshop with American IT consultants. He said that the meeting was part of a continuing series that had begun three weeks earlier, and that it was held in the Smooth Room at the Pinelands offices of Old Mutual. He said that at some point in that week Shahana told the meeting that Fred would not be coming in that day because his girlfriend had been murdered. He said that the news shocked those present and that there was then some discussion about what had transpired at the meeting the previous day.

About the day of the murder, MK said that Fred had arrived after 11:00, after which he made a presentation about one of Old Mutual's products. He said that Fred sat to his immediate right after he arrived. He said that there was a break for lunch and that Fred was still at the meeting after lunch. He said that Fred was at the meeting until it closed at around 17:00.

There is an important problem with this testimony, and it is one that the prosecution seized on: by the time MK testified, it had already been established that Fred had made his presentation on the afternoon of 15 March, and that the meeting on 16 March was devoted to a discussion of that presentation. MK, then, must have been mistaken when he said that the presentation was on 16 March. And, if he was mistaken on the stand, it was a mistake that he had also made in the statement he signed in June 2005, which reads, 'As far as I can remember, Fred gave a presentation on the Guaranteed Fund on 16 March 2005, after which it was discussed. I was in attendance the whole day. I cannot recall if Fred was at the session the whole day, but he stayed in attendance once there.'

This suggests, as the prosecutor, Christénus van der Vijver, pointed out, that MK was linking his memory of Fred's presence or otherwise to the presentation he made. Since it was agreed that that had been on 15 March, MK's testimony about Fred's presence on 16 March and his sitting to MK's right must be regarded as 'a huge mistake'.

Everything here turns on the definition of the word 'presentation': did it mean the slideshow and nothing more than that, or did it mean the slideshow and the subsequent discussion? Depending on the context, and depending on the role of the person who presents a particular slideshow in any subsequent discussion, the word could, in principle at least, mean either. It was important, then, for MK to clarify what precisely he meant when he used the word. Unfortunately, he offered contradictory testimony about this.

Asked directly by the prosecutor whether the presentation was the slideshow, he said, 'Correct, so.' This seemed to suggest that the word 'presentation' is to be understood to mean no more than a slideshow. But elsewhere MK offered other definitions. He said, for example, that 'Fred did make his presentation on 16 March, continuing what he had started on 15 March.' He said that during the discussion phase, the presenter of the slideshow 'is supposed to lead the discussions and explain.' He said, 'A person who was not there won't understand how we went about, you know, running this programme.'

The result is far from satisfactory, with the problem, though originating in the ambiguity of the word 'presentation', being greatly magnified by the fact that MK had chosen to testify in isiXhosa. The result was that every question and every answer had to go through a court interpreter, who may or may not have been sufficiently alive to the subtleties of the questions and answers to provide translations with any high degree of precision. Whatever the competence and accuracy of the interpreter, another problem was that words like 'presentation' and 'slideshow' are not easily translated from English into isiXhosa and then back into English. Consider my dictionary's rendering of the noun 'slide (photography)' in isiXhosa: *ifoto efakwa kumatshini eboniswa eludongeni njengakwibhanyabhanya* – literally, 'a photo that is projected onto a screen by a machine that uses light'. It is a construction that introduces an ironic note to the judge's somewhat pouty comment to MK, who, he complained, was using too many words: 'You are giving very long answers. I don't know whether you need all those words to say what you want to say, but you must give the interpreter an opportunity to translate what you are saying.'

Whatever the source of the ambiguity about what MK meant when he spoke of Fred's presentation – whether it was MK's faulty memory or the difficulties and ambiguities of the language – the prosecution sought to go one step further. Not only did MK not really remember whether Fred was at the meeting on 16 March, Van der Vijver suggested, but it was quite possible that MK was also not at the meeting. It was pointed out, for instance, that when Janine von Stein testified, she had been unable to confirm whether MK was at all the sessions on 16 March. Much as she had done in relation to Fred, she didn't say MK wasn't at the meeting, just that she could not confirm that he was.

MK's response, offered through the interpreter whose command of the diction of the workplace seemed increasingly strained, was that, 'Everything that I do is controlled by my diary. Everything that I do, I dot it on my diary, so it is impossible that I was not there on 16 March.' Challenged by Van der Vijver again, he said categorically, 'I am definitely sure that I was there the whole day.'

It was an answer that the prosecution probably didn't want to stand unchallenged on the record, and it led Van der Vijver to ask the question that allowed the defence to get away with not calling Toefy. 'We have an affidavit from Shahana Toefy,' he said. 'We don't know whether she is go-ing to give evidence, but she also doesn't mention you by name as one of the persons at the meeting. She says she can recall some people being at the session, and your name is absent.'

MK offered the only reaction he could – that he couldn't answer for Shahana or explain why she said that – but De Bruyn immediately seized on the mention of Toefy's statement to have it entered into evidence. Ordinarily, he would not be able to do this without putting her on the stand where she would be subject to cross-examination, but the rules of evidence have it that if one side refers to a portion of an affidavit, the other side is entitled to ask that it be entered into evidence in its entirety. Since Van der Vijver had put part of Toefy's statement to MK, De Bruyn could now present the rest of her statement to the judge, who would now see that it contained the express assertion that Fred had sat beside her all day.

It goes without saying that an untested statement does not have the same evidentiary weight as testimony that has survived cross-examination and which has, as importantly, been offered by a witness into whose soul the judge can peer. It is also true, however, that when De Bruyn asked MK and Toefy to come to court, he wasn't necessarily trying to prove beyond the shadow of any doubt and to absolutely everyone's complete satisfaction that Fred had been at the meeting all day. That was not his burden. Technically, all he needed to do was show that Fred's claim to have been at the meeting was reasonably possibly true, a logical corollary of which would be that there must be a reasonable doubt about his having committed the crime. Since the best the prosecution had been able to do was present the evidence of Janine von Stein, who couldn't remember whether Fred was there or not, and who was happy to say that she wouldn't have been paying attention to that, and who had also said that Shahana Toefy would be better placed to testify on that score, Toefy's sworn statement was probably all that the defence needed to achieve this.

On its own, in other words, the statement without Toefy's testimony probably wouldn't have carried enough weight to prove that Fred had spent the day beside Shahana and MK. Certainly, it would not have been sufficient to refute a witness who said that she definitely remembered that Fred had left the room for two hours and remembered wondering where he had gone. But, unless Toefy's statement was decisively contradicted by some other evidence of Fred's guilt, it might very well have been enough to get the defence across an important evidentiary threshold.

Perhaps it was for this reason that Carien Teunissen seemed eager to get her colleague, Christénus van der Vijver, to object to Toefy's statement's being entered into evidence. Recognising the futility of such a request, it was something Van der Vijver quietly talked her out of.

In confronting MK with a portion of Toefy's statement in which the latter had failed to mention the presence of the former at the meeting, then, Van der Vijver had made a significant blunder. A more accurate accounting of the incident, however, would reveal that embedded within it was another blunder that, while less significant to the trajectory of their case, was just as revealing of the prosecution's lack of tactical nous.

Recall that the mention of Toefy's statement was made in order to point out that she had failed to mention MK's name in the list of people who were at the meeting on 16 March. This was offered by Van der Vijver in order to create some doubt about MK's presence at the meeting and about the reliability of his evidence. That's all well and good, but there is another name absent from Toefy's list: Janine von Stein's. Since the prosecutors had themselves represented Von Stein as someone who'd been at the meeting all day, and since she had her contemporaneous notes to prove that she had been there, the defence might easily have shown that the absence of MK's name from Toefy's list did little to prove that he wasn't there.

* * *

It is important to record at this point that the prosecutors never intended to rely on the evidence of Fred's colleagues to show that he had left the meeting to kill Inge. They clearly expected that the burden of showing that he'd been in Inge's flat at the time of the murder would be borne by the three pieces of forensic evidence the police had produced. On their own, any one of these would have been enough to refute anything Toefy might or might not say in a statement or on the stand about Fred's presence at the meeting. MK's evidence and Toefy's statement might be enough to ensure an acquittal if none of the physical evidence stood. Both would prove to be hopelessly too little if any of that evidence was accepted by the judge.

The first leg of the forensic evidence was Folien One, the problems of which have already been described, and which had led the prosecution initially to withdraw the evidence. The others were the bloody mark on the bathroom floor, the one that Bruce Bartholomew had matched to one of Fred's shoes, and the ornamental hammer that the police had found in Fred's car. We will return to this evidence in time. For the moment, however, let us consider the dog that didn't bark: the absence of any statement from any of those who were at the meeting on 16 March to the effect that they explicitly recall Fred's being absent for some portion of the afternoon's proceedings, as he would have had to have been if he killed Inge.

If a silence could scream, this one would scream for some explanation.

* * *

Imagine you are part of a team of ten engaged in a long series of meetings held around a single table in a small, intimate room. The meetings take place over a period of weeks. There is a core team that comes most of the time, but the group changes a little from day to day: sometimes some of the core are absent; sometimes other people are roped in to provide particular information or advice.

Perhaps you are the kind of person who enjoys this kind of thing. Maybe you like sitting with your colleagues for an extended period, getting to know them and learning something about the work for which they are responsible, the challenges they face, the money they make. Maybe someone in the group has a good sense of humour and it is a pleasure to listen to him tell his stories. Maybe sitting in these extended meetings is easier than your day job.

ANTONY ALTBEKER

Perhaps, on the other hand, you hate the experience. Maybe you're shy, a back-room operator unwilling to be dragged into the daylight. Maybe you find some or more of your colleagues annoying. Maybe their meeting etiquette is not what it should be. Maybe they have a tendency to pull discussion back to issues you feel have already been covered. Maybe they always point out problems, never solutions. Maybe they never raise their hand when responsibility must be taken to do some actual work.

Whatever your own personal attitude, over the days and weeks over which the work proceeds, a certain esprit de corps develops: you've all been pulled out of your day-to-day responsibilities, responsibilities that, however important this gathering might be, continue to mount up in your in-tray; you have a shared task to fulfil; you are in it together.

Then, in the middle of all this, you hear that one of your number will not be coming in because his girlfriend had been brutally murdered the day before.

What would happen?

Undoubtedly, there would be some discussion: 'Shame,' you might say. 'The poor man.'

'The poor girl,' someone else might correct you.

'I hope he's okay. We should send flowers.'

'Do you think they were in love? Do you know if they were getting married?'

'This fucking country is going to the dogs.'

'I hope they catch the bastard. It's just a pity that there's no death penalty.'

'He was a quiet kid. I didn't even know he had a girlfriend.'

'Is. He is such a quiet kid. He's not the one who's dead.'

'It's the drugs. They're tearing communities apart.'

'The same thing happened to a cousin of mine.'

'It's the unemployment. The poverty.'

'No-one in this fucking place respects the value of life. Excuse my French.'

'When do you think Fred will be back at work?'

'Well, he's only got a few days' compassionate leave. Maybe he'll take some unpaid time.'

'I suppose we'd better get on with it. Maybe we should pray for him. Or maybe just a moment's silence.'

It's the kind of exchange that must happen thousands of times a year in South Africa's workplaces: whenever someone is raped or hijacked or murdered, friends and colleagues will gather to commiserate, to compare notes, and to count their blessings that today, at least, the conversation is not about them.

Perhaps one consequence of the sheer number of such conversations is that each will shade into the others, losing its individuality and vividness, becoming difficult to distinguish from any another. Maybe you will forget where you were and what you thought when you heard this particular news. Maybe you won't think about it again, and if someone asks you two years later whether the victim's boyfriend really was with you at the time of the murder, you wouldn't be able to remember.

But something is different about this case: it's on the front pages of the newspapers. And not just the next day, but for days and then weeks afterwards. And in just about every report you read, you see that the police suspect someone close to the victim. 'I wonder,' you sometimes catch yourself thinking. 'Perhaps he did it.' Then, barely a month later, the police raid your colleague's office, a raid which the papers confirm the next day was conducted because he is the prime suspect.

Isn't it likely that you would say to yourself, 'It's funny, but now that I think about it, I seem to remember wondering where he was that day'? Wouldn't someone have thought it odd if he wasn't there?

Well, let us admit it: the colleague concerned is junior, the youngest, freshest, greenest person in the room. He's got no authority. Nobody was looking to impress him with their wit or their knowledge or their professionalism; no-one was sucking up to him. So maybe most of the people in the room wouldn't have noticed if he had skived off. But is it likely that no-one at all would have noticed? Not his boss who was sitting next to him and who had given him responsibility for doing the presentation and who had asked that the agenda be shuffled around so that he could be there for the discussion? Not his boss's boss, who was also sitting next to him? Not the guy who found him irritating? Not the guy who liked his sense of humour?

If he had been absent, what are the odds that no-one, but no-one, would remember it?

No wonder Trollip thought that Fred and his father had spread some pixie dust.

* * *

If the police are to be believed, the failure of Fred's colleagues to remember his departure from the meeting is made more striking by a peculiar circumstance: that someone who had never met Fred before that morning remembered seeing him a second time that day, sometime in the afternoon. That witness was Jacobus Nicolaas Swart, the clerk at the furniture store at which Fred bought a cupboard on 16 March.

Swart testified that Fred came into the store shortly after 10:00 in the morning. That much was consistent with what Fred had told Superintendent de Beer in the interview on 17 March. Where Swart's account differed from Fred's is that he also said Fred was accompanied by someone else, that the two young men had done no more than browse, and that at some point in the afternoon both had returned to buy a cupboard.

Asked for details about his account, Swart says that all he can recall about the second man was that he was young and white and that he looked like a student. He says that he doesn't remember what time it was when Fred returned that afternoon, but knows that it was 'a reasonable time' after his boss had eaten his lunch, something the man was in the habit of doing at about 13:00. Unfortunately, he cannot be more precise than that.

Now, there is nothing in the record that directly refutes Swart's testimony. It is, nevertheless, an account that fits poorly with what else is known about that day. For example, it is not disputed that, whenever Fred bought the cupboard, it was bought from Merriman Furniture, the store at which Swart worked. It is also not disputed that, whenever it was bought, the cupboard was intended for Fred's neighbour, Jean Minnaar. The significance of this point is that there is evidence that Fred sent Jean an SMS at 08:37 that morning, and that Jean phoned back ten minutes later. There is also evidence that just after 9:00, during a break in his class, Fred drew R500 from an ATM on campus.

All of which is important because, although there is no time printed on the invoice issued for the cupboard, it was made out for the sum of R499. Fred, in other words, drew exactly the right money to buy the cupboard at 9:00 and must have had it in his wallet when he went to the store at 10:00. That tends to support Fred's account, which is that Jean phoned him to tell him how much the cupboard would cost, that he then drew the money and went to the store to pick it up on Jean's behalf. It is an account that is also confirmed by Jean's statement, which says that he had been in the store some time before, and had reserved the cupboard in question.

If that tends to support Fred's account, some of the aspects of Swart's story seem inconsistent with the rest of the evidence about what happened that day. It is, for example, hard to see how Fred could have added a visit to the furniture store in the one and three-quarter hours he had to get from work to Inge's flat, murder her, clean up and return to the office. Nor is it clear why he'd have visited the store on his return to Stellenbosch since all that would achieve is produce an eyewitness who could confirm that he was in town that afternoon. Certainly, it would then have made very little sense to do what Fred actually did – tell the police on the morning after the murder that he'd gone to Merriman Furniture in the morning. For all he knew, they would have got on the phone immediately to check the records of the store and the memory of the clerk, fatally undermining the gist of his alibi. As it was, the police interviewed Swart only at the end of April, six weeks after the murder and long after Fred's face had been on the front pages of all the local papers and he was known to be the prime suspect.

Finally, there is the small matter of the mysterious second person who apparently accompanied Fred to the store during both his visits that day. Locating him in the logic of the prosecution's case is no easy task. Since it's hard to see how an innocent man, unwittingly accompanying Fred on a murderous trip to Stellenbosch, would have remained quiet so long, one must assume that if such a person existed, he could only have been a co-conspirator. Or that Fred has killed him and dumped the body.

This, then, is what happens if we take Swart seriously: Fred acquires an unnamed, unidentified accomplice for whose existence there is not a single shred of evidence other than Swart's memory.

*　　*　　*

There is something else to say about Fred's alibi: not only was there very little time in which to commit the crime, and not only is it passing strange that no-one appears to remember his absence from a meeting at which he was one of the people with at least some responsibility for providing insight and information, but to get to Stellenbosch and back also meant that he had to leave and then re-enter the office park in which he worked. That office park is the headquarters of one of the largest insurance companies in the southern hemisphere, the seat of its chief executives and of all its proprietary data about clients and their products, so getting in and out unobserved and unrecorded would not have been as easy as it might have sounded to police officers and prosecutors more familiar with the dubious security systems at government buildings.

In theory at least, Mutual Park's security system is good. Working flaw-lessly, every time an employee enters or leaves the facility, he has to swipe his electronic pass at a turnstile at one of the facility's entrances. As he does so, his staff photo appears on a monitor in front of a security guard at that entrance. The guard's task is to ensure that whomever it is who has 'badged' the turnstile is the same person to whom the card has been issued. Each movement through the turnstiles is also captured and recorded by CCTV cameras.

At the time of the murder, Mutual Park had fourteen entrances and exits, four of which Fred could not have used. One, for instance, was reserved for people with disabilities, and would not open for other employees; another two were in a secure delivery bay. So clear was it that these entrances could not have been used by Fred that the police didn't even ask Old Mutual to preserve the CCTV footage from them.

In order to show that security at the other ten entrances was not as certain, however, the prosecution brought in Herman Louw, a senior official in the Mutual Park security division, to explain the system's deficiencies.

It was possible, Louw testified, that a security guard might be distracted when someone 'badged' a turnstile and would not, therefore, check the image that appeared on his screen against the face of the person walking through the turnstile. This, he suggested, wasn't just a matter of the guard's boredom or fecklessness, but a consequence of his also being responsible for issuing temporary cards to visitors and for recording the details of any laptop computers that might be brought into the building. It was possible, therefore, for an employee to use someone else's card and to slip through a turnstile without the abuse being picked up by the guard. It was also possible that someone might crawl under a turnstile or climb over one without ever swiping his card through the reader. In fact, Louw said he'd done so himself once to test his guards, and had left the building without their picking it up.

Nor were the CCTV cameras without their problems, Louw said. Some were placed in positions which made it difficult or impossible to see the facial features of people entering or leaving the building. Others were affected by the sun's glare at certain times of day, over-exposing the image and rendering it all but useless. Finally, at an exit used by delivery trucks, the cameras would not be able to pick up any movement behind a sufficiently large truck, making it possible for someone to slip out unobserved.

Each of these individual difficulties was illustrated by clips from the CCTV footage from the day Inge died. What the prosecution did not show, because they were unable to show it, was footage of Fred himself leaving from or returning to the building at any time between 11:00 and 18:00. Though the police had looked for this, they had not been able to find it. So, in the absence of proof that Fred had left, they pursued the second prize: proof that Fred could have left. This, they seemed to think, couldn't be terribly controversial, and the prosecutors seemed a little bemused by the obsessiveness with which the defence pursued an effort to show that it would have been impossible for Fred to leave the building without leaving any trace of his passing.

Take the question of the delivery trucks that might have obscured someone sneaking out. The defence reviewed the tapes and, under cross-examination, had Louw confirm that only two trucks large enough to obscure anyone used that gate all day. They had him confirm, too, that both trucks had left too early to have been of any use to Fred.

The defence also insisted that the poorly placed cameras and the sun glare were not so serious a set of problems as had been made out. This was partly because any glare would be relevant if, and only if, the security guard manning the computer monitor was distracted and if Fred knew enough about this weakness to exploit it. More importantly, complete records existed of whose cards were used at which turnstile, and these could be checked against images of the people passing through those entrances. If Fred had used a colleague's card, his image would still appear in the CCTV footage. And if that image were unclear, you could trace the passage of that card through the building to see if the person using it appeared more clearly in footage from any other camera. If you did that, you might very well confirm the identity of every single person who used the turnstiles on 16 March, no matter how obscure the images.

So confident was the defence that each person who left the building could be positively identified, they laid down a simple challenge to the police and prosecution: they would hold Louw's cross-examination over to give the police and Old Mutual's security staff the opportunity to go over every single tape from 16 March 2005 and to find every single image of any person whose features were so unclear as to leave open the possibility that he was Fred. If you do that, the defence said, we'll prove the identity of every one of those people and, in the process, prove definitively that Fred never left the building.

This was duly arranged, and, over the weekend of 21 and 22 April 2007, Louw and five police officers reviewed all the relevant tapes. But, during his testimony the following Thursday, it became clear that the instructions to the officers had been, shall we say, 'misunderstood'. Instead of producing every suspect image, as the defence had believed the officers would do, they produced a show reel of a great many clips reinforcing the idea that there were problems with the system. This was hugely frustrating for the defence, because, using every scrap of the formidable meticulousness of a family that had produced an actuary and an auditor, they had done what they set out to prove they could do: they had positively identified every single young, white man whose image appeared – however unclearly – in the clips presented to the judge: none was Fred.

PART SIX

21

From the start of the trial, I have struggled with the figures of Inge's bereaved parents, Jan and Juanita Lotz. With only one or two exceptions – when pathologists testified about the mechanics of Inge's death and the nature of her wounds, for example – they attended every session of the case. I have wondered about the permanence of their presence in court. Was it healthy? Was it something I would do? Was it something I could avoid doing?

In the Jewish tradition, the loss of a child is regarded as so great and so unnatural a tragedy that it grants to the parents immediate passage to heaven: all one's sins are forgiven. But if the death of a child is always shattering no matter what its cause, a murder must be that much worse. Compared with a drowning or a car accident, say, or with a death from illness, in each of which mourning can begin immediately, when a child is murdered the investigation and trial must feel inseparable from the death itself, leaving it open and delaying the point at which mourning can properly begin.

Dominick Dunne, who wrote about celebrity murder trials for *Vanity Fair* and whose own daughter was murdered – strangled to death for perhaps six agonising minutes by an ex-boyfriend – used to insist that parents should be at the trials of their children's killers. Apart from the nakedly strategic fact that their attendance reminds the judge and the jury about the victim and about the sufferings of those whose lives have been ripped apart, the trial of their killer, Dunne wrote, is the last business of a murdered child's life. The parents' attendance was a moral and emotional imperative. And yet, a veteran court watcher has told me that the presence of parents at these cases in South Africa is a phenomenon of comparatively recent vintage. 'In the past,' she said, 'people seemed to think that it was better to leave this process to the justice system and to try to get on with their lives.'

Whatever was true in the past, though, was no longer true by 2007. It was a year that saw a number of cases in which the families of murdered children committed themselves to every minute they could bear of the resultant murder trials. One of the most sensational of these was the trial of the self-confessed paedophile-murderer and self-diagnosed schizophrenic known variously as Theuns Olivier and as 'Theo' and as 'Ruuss', who had raped and strangled to death six-year-old Steven Siebert in 2005. Steven's parents, their pain and their hatred for their son's killer blazing from them like an emotional supernova, spoke of Olivier in ways that suggested they would happily tear him apart with their own hands.

Olivier's trial was in the same building as Fred's, as was the trial of the killers of Richard Bloom and Brett Goldin, two young men whose naked bodies had been dumped in Cape Town in mid-2006, having been shot to death by a group of drugged-up gangsters. Goldin's mother, whose story was captured in a documentary by Shakespearean actor and former

Capetonian Antony Sher, became a figure of impossible, inconsolable loss.

The winter of 2007, then, was a season of devastated parents. But, in a country of fifty-plus murders a day, their experience was terribly mundane, a horror the country has learnt to accommodate and, with only a few unrepresentative exceptions, to observe more or less unremarked.

*   *   *

In court, Professor and Mrs Lotz would sit next to each other, close to the prosecutors with whom they were obviously on friendly terms, but they seemed to interact with each other only infrequently. Of the two, Mrs Lotz seemed more consistently and keenly interested in the cut and thrust of the trial. She would follow testimony with rapt attention, nodding in agreement or shaking her head in disbelief as the occasion dictated, while her husband stared out into the middle distance.

Small and delicate, with fine blonde hair cut in a full fringe, Mrs Lotz had obvious grace and breeding. She wore trouser suits and a gold crucifix, and when she spoke to members of the press she would adopt a smile of implausible sunniness. She must be, I thought more than once, the perfect hostess: animated and interested and charming and able to put aside personal distress in deference to her guests' needs. I saw no evidence of overt hostility to Fred, but Mrs Lotz plainly believed him to be guilty. She would huddle with the police and prosecutors during the day. She would nod encouragingly when the judge criticised the defence or questioned the conclusions of their experts. She had testified against Fred at the start of the trial.

Sometimes, after a day in court, I would sit in the benches the Lotzes had vacated and read through my notes of the day's proceedings. What were they thinking when the defence pointed out inconsistencies in police testimony? Were they angered by the investigative inefficiencies and inaccuracies of the police evidence, and by a defence that drew attention to these technical deficiencies? What about the evidence of outright lies? Did the Lotzes see these as transgressions committed in a just cause, or did they create doubts about Fred's guilt?

Believing that Fred had bludgeoned her daughter to death with a hammer, Mrs Lotz must have thought that his defence was a ragbag of lies and misdirection concocted by an expensive team of lawyers who had built an edifice of falsehoods on imagined ambiguities in the evidence and the not infrequent missteps of the police.

If she allowed herself the consolations of hatred, how she must hate Fred's lawyers!

My impression of Jan Lotz, Inge's father and a professor of radiology, was a little different. He seldom spoke to people in court, and, while he appeared to exchange pleasantries with the police and prosecutors in the hallways, he was the one participant in this trial whom I would never see lunching at any of the nearby coffee shops, whether alone or in company. Where he went during all the breaks and stoppages, I cannot say.

Professor Lotz was a large man, and he seemed weighed down by a grief he could not or would not conceal. He seemed asphyxiated by his loss. He also seemed to have invested less emotional energy in seeing Fred convicted. This last impression was cemented in my mind in the second month of the trial, shortly after the testimony of Ian Myburgh, Mrs Lotz's brother.

A feisty, aggressive man, with a stocky build and grey hair, Myburgh's testimony about Fred's behaviour immediately after the murder had painted a picture of a young man with something to hide. He told the court, for example, that when Fred had arrived at the Lotzes' home after his interview with the police on the morning of 17 March, he'd muttered something about how the police believed that he was the killer. He said that Fred 'tried to appear grief-stricken', that his behaviour was 'affected' and 'overdone' and 'insincere'. He also said that Fred had moved into the Lotzes' home, where he became a nuisance. As examples of his nuisance value, Myburgh cited Fred's screening of the Lotzes' calls and his efforts at preventing Inge's parents from seeing the newspapers. Later, when challenged on this last point by De Bruyn, Myburgh admitted that the withholding of the papers had not actually happened, that it had been, instead, an idea that Fred had discussed with him after Mrs Lotz had been overcome one morning by something she'd read in one of the dailies. In court, Myburgh said he disagreed with Fred about this, and said that he could not remember precisely what his response had been to Fred's suggestion. De Bruyn, perhaps keen to paint a picture of a witness a little unhinged, read the words Myburgh had attributed to himself in a sworn statement in which he'd mentioned this incident: '"Fuck you,"' De Bruyn quoted Myburgh's words back to him, '"It's a reality."'

In the course of this increasingly fraught testimony, Myburgh suggested that Fred's parents, Louis and Carien, had also made nuisances of themselves in the Lotz home. 'They were there almost every day from seven in the morning until ten at night', he said, adding that his impression was that people from outside the family were causing the Lotzes a great deal of stress and tension. 'How two complete strangers could intrude into a home – this was the first time the Lotz family met them – is something I don't understand.'

After the lunch break a few hours later, however, Professor Lotz, through the person of Christénus van der Vijver, repudiated the idea that any enmity had developed between the parents of the two families, and apologised if that idea had been created by his brother-in-law. 'Professor Lotz has asked me to tell the court,' the prosecutor said, 'that Mr van der Vyver senior called him shortly after hearing about Inge's death to sympathise with him, that he cried with him, and that he came through early on the morning of the seventeenth and gave him wonderful support.'

It was an extraordinary gesture that spoke of a proud and generous dignity, and it suggested that Professor Lotz was not prepared to throw any and every conceivable insinuation at Fred and his family. It was also a gesture that, in disavowing the testimony of his brother-in-law, may have cost Professor Lotz something.

Or maybe not.

Maybe it was a reflection of his opinion of Myburgh; perhaps theirs was a relationship filled with squabbles and grievances, and, for Professor Lotz, this was just another instance of his brother-in-law's blustery tendency to overshoot himself.

Still, for the most part, Professor Lotz sat in court lost in his own thoughts, appearing to take little interest in the cut and thrust of lawyerly argument and technical detail. There was, it seemed, less at stake here for him than for others. That, I thought, might simply mean that, having lost so much already, he felt he had nothing left to lose. Something about the sadness of his bearing put me in mind of a passage from Graham Greene's *The Heart of the Matter*. At a dinner party, Scobie, a deeply religious colonial policeman who is contemplating the unforgivable sin of suicide, is asked by someone whether he believes in Hell. He replies that he does and is asked by his questioner if it consists, as she has been taught, of 'flames and torment'.

'Perhaps not quite that,' he replies. 'They tell us it is more like a permanent sense of loss.'

Another guest, hearing his answer, says, 'That sort of Hell wouldn't worry me.'

'Perhaps,' Scobie replies, 'you have never lost anything of any importance.'

22

What do we expect of our detectives?

It is a question that may be better answered by looking at their depiction in popular culture than by examining the legal requirements and institutional arrangements that govern policing. It is in the pages of our best-selling books and in the scripts of our most-watched television dramas that we will find the most fully developed and carefully nurtured conceptions of what it is that detectives can and should and must do. And if we examine these sources, we will see that the fictional construction of the good detective is built on one thing: his single-minded devotion to the details of empirical reality.

The detectives that people the popular imagination are not interested in ideas. They don't deal in abstractions and theories. They have no patience for academic debate and scholarly nitpicking. And yet, despite their dismissal of what South African cops call 'book learning', fictional detectives are among the world's most astute readers. They read the street. They read situations. They read people. They read crime scenes. They are arch-empiricists, taking insignificant, almost invisible details and using them to unwind spools of effect after effect after effect until they find an ultimate cause. Perhaps they do this using their intellect alone or perhaps they supplement the power of their brains with that of their fists and guns. But, however they solve their crimes, the focus of a good detective is always on the details. These they squeeze and squeeze until something cracks and the case opens up to reveal a crime's hidden mastermind.

It is an awesome construction, one of the most potent in all of popular culture. But it is also one that must be a terrible burden for real-life cops. Or so I thought again and again as I listened to the testimony of Superintendent Bruce Stuart Bartholomew, the principal forensic investigator of Inge's murder.

*   *   *

Bartholomew, who was a captain when Inge was murdered and who was promoted to the rank of superintendent shortly afterwards and who has subsequently left the Police Service, is a compact, powerful man. His hair, receding from a forehead that rises above a pair of small, dark eyes, is black and closely cropped. Around his hard-edged mouth is a small, dark beard. His dark clothes complete the almost completely monochromatic image: his suit is black, his shirt is black, his tie is black with white spots. As a rare point of contrast, he wears a thick silver wedding band.

His is a cultivated look, and, together with his voice, which has the gravelly roughness of the chain smoker who first lit up behind the woodshed at school, he seems the kind of hard-nosed cop all too many precincts cry out for. Here is a man filled with determination and certainty, his appearance proclaims, a man who will seldom take a backward step.

Given this persona, Bartholomew's role in the police at the time of

Inge's murder is perhaps surprising: as the province's leading expert on shoeprint evidence, it was his job to attend scores of crime scenes every year, at each of which he would bury his nose in the carpet in the hope of finding the impression of a shoe with which he might one day link a suspect to a murder or a robbery or a rape. It is fine, precise work, demanding meticulous attention to detail, and, when he first begins to testify, the prosecution worked hard to build the idea that Bartholomew was as good at this as his appearance suggested he may be at the blunter, more direct work that policing sometimes entails. It was important that they do this because it is Bartholomew who had claimed to have matched a bloody stain on the bathroom floor with the sole of one of Fred's shoes, concluding his report on this by saying, 'Concerning the type, size, place, position and relationship of the unique characteristics to one another, the class of the shoeprint agrees with the right shoe belonging to one Fredrick Barend van der Vyver.'

Before we get to this report, however, Bartholomew is taken through a series of questions posed by Carien Teunissen, the purpose of which was to offer an account of his involvement in the investigation of Inge's death.

* * *

Bartholomew says that he arrived at Inge's flat just a few hours after her body had been found, and that, as the duty officer of the province's elite crime scene investigation unit, he helped define the investigation's immediate priorities. Police officers with no business in the flat were kicked out. The local fingerprint examiner, Constable Elton John Swartz, was told to return with his team in the morning. Superintendent Kock from the Forensic Science Laboratory was called in to look for traces of genetic material that might have been left by the killer.

Later that night, Bartholomew says, he helped remove Inge's body from the flat, sealing her hands in a pair of envelopes to preserve any blood or skin cells that might be found under her fingernails. Then, the next morning, he returned to the flat to supervise Constable Swartz and his two colleagues' search for fingerprints, as well as to help with the spraying of ninhydrin on the walls. Before that, he had gone to the morgue to search for fingerprints on Inge's body, a process that involved sealing her remains in an airtight bag and exposing her body to the vaporised fumes of superglue in the hope these would adhere to areas that her killer may have touched.

The following day, 18 March, Bartholomew returned to the morgue to witness the autopsy, bringing his digital camera along so that he could take photos of Inge's many wounds, the size and shape of which might later be compared against any weapons that might be found. Then, having heard the pathologist's suggestion that some of the wounds might have been caused by a hammer, he returned once more to Inge's flat to look for one. There he recovered an ordinary carpenter's hammer and stopped to photograph a palmprint that had been revealed by the ninhydrin he'd sprayed the day before.

From the point of view of proving Fred's guilt, these efforts produced no usable evidence: there were no biological samples under Inge's fingers and no prints were found on her body; no blood was found on the carpenter's hammer, which was, in any event, too large to have created the wounds to Inge's head and neck; the palmprint on the wall remains unidentified to this day. The presentation of all of this to the judge, though, is not really about Fred; it's about Bartholomew, and is intended to show that his approach to the investigation was as disinterested and as methodologically sound as that of a Nobel Prize-winning physicist. It is only in this way that it bears any relevance to the core of Bartholomew's testimony: the match he says he found between a bloody mark on the bathroom floor and the sole of Fred's right squash shoe.

*   *   *

Shortly after having kicked the unwanted hordes out of Inge's flat, Bartholomew broke out his dust-lifter.

The essentials of dust-lifting are that dust and other dry residues are either disturbed or deposited wherever you walk, and if these disturbances are transferred onto a surface whose colour contrasts with those residues, it may be possible to produce an image of the sole of the shoe that did the disturbing. The dust-lifter achieves this effect using conductive film and electrostatic forces of attraction identical to those that lift the hairs of your arm if you brush against the screens of some analogue televisions. Depending on the vagaries of the kinds of residues carried on the shoe and those already on the floor, together with the nature of the underlying surface and various atmospheric conditions, a dust-lifter might produce an image clear enough to be used later to match or to exclude particular shoes.

As Bartholomew describes the workings of this device, it sounds to the layperson – and, if the questions he poses are any guide, to the judge, too – that his dust-lifter was the very acme of modern forensic investigation. In fact, as I would discover when I read a textbook on the subject some months later, it is a technique whose first crude instruments were developed by Japanese police officers as far back as the mid-1960s.

Bartholomew used his dust-lifter in the two rooms in Inge's flat in which he knew the killer must have been: the lounge in which Inge was found, and the bathroom in which the killer appeared to have cleaned himself up. As Bartholomew tells the court about this, he refers to a plan of the flat on which various items have been carefully marked, and describes his actions with a precision that borders on the obsessive. 'I laid the film down from point T to point TK,' he says of his work in the bathroom. 'Plus or minus.'

Bartholomew says that he found numerous footprints in the lounge and another one in the bathroom, but he also says he knew that a number of police officers and paramedics had tramped through the scene before he'd arrived. In order to check whether any or all of the impressions he'd found could be matched to his colleagues' shoes, he asked them to line up outside the flat and lift their feet. 'What I discovered,' he says when asked about the results of this, 'is that these police officers had been terribly curious.'

Between the officers on the scene and one of the paramedics, Bartholomew could account for almost all the shoeprints he'd found in the flat, including all of those around the couch on which Inge lay. The one exception to this was the impression of a man's sports shoe that Bartholomew had found in the bathroom. This had not been made by any of the cops on the scene, and might, therefore, have been left by the killer.

It was on the basis of this single unidentified dust-lift from the bathroom, Bartholomew says, that he accompanied the group of detectives who searched Fred's flat on 15 April 2005, a month after the murder. The proximate cause of that search was the match that had been made between the fingerprint found on the DVD cover and the exclusion prints taken from Fred on 12 April. Bartholomew had been involved in the making of that match, having been responsible for asking his colleague from the specialised crime scene investigation unit, Captain Jannie Bester, to examine the eleven lifts against the prints taken from Inge's friends. He says that his hope when participating in the search of Fred's flat was that he'd find a shoe that would match the dust-lift from Inge's bathroom.

But he was disappointed.

Asked about whether he found any shoes that might be matched to that dust-lift, he says, 'I looked at them with the naked eye but I could not express an opinion, so I took them with me.' Subsequent examination, he says a moment later, revealed that none of the shoes found in Fred's flat matched his dust-lift from the bathroom floor.

Having disposed of the dust-lift, Teunissen now turns to the bloody mark on the bathroom floor – the mark that Bartholomew says he was able to match to one of the shoes taken from Fred's flat on 15 April. She introduces the subject by asking him to identify the mark in a photograph taken on the night of the murder (*see* PLATE 3).

* * *

Bartholomew tells the court that on 28 April 2005, six weeks after the murder and two weeks after the police had taken possession of Fred's shoes, he and three policemen from Pretoria returned to Inge's flat to conduct further tests. The three – a Superintendent Johannes Koekemoer, a Captain Ziets Alberts and an Inspector Bester, whose first name has been lost to history – had come to Cape Town at Bartholomew's request because, he says, as members of the national team they had superior equipment and expertise. 'I wanted them to use a chemical known as Amido Black,' he says, before explaining that, when applied to a surface, Amido Black reacts with proteins, and will stain even invisible traces of blood.

Bartholomew says that he had no experience with the application of Amido Black, and that he was there just to observe the three men from Pretoria. In fact, he says, for most of the time that Superintendent Koekemoer and Captain Alberts worked in the flat, he was outside on the balcony with Inspector Bester, helping to mix chemical compounds. As a result, he says, he did not see the actual application of the stain. He does know, however, that before they applied the chemical, they had to test that the mark was, in fact, blood, and that they did this by taking a sample of the substance using a bud-like tool called a Multistix, which they swiped across the mark. Satisfied that this was so, Koekemoer sprayed the mark and the surrounding area with Amido Black, turning all the blood, both visible and invisible, a purple-black (see PLATE 4). Bartholomew says that the newly treated mark was clearer and showed a good deal more detail than had been visible in the original: 'You could see inside the mark.'

According to Bartholomew, about two months after Bartholomew and Koekemoer and Alberts and Bester were in Inge's flat, he compared a photo of the chemically enhanced stain with the shoes he had taken from Fred's flat and found that the stain matched the right heel of Fred's Hi-Tec shoes.

Having made this claim on the stand, Carien Teunissen hands Bartholomew a copy of the statement he swore out on 22 August 2005. It is a statement in which the operative paragraph consists of a sentence that I have already quoted: 'Concerning the type, size, place, position and relationship of the unique characteristics to one another, the class of the shoeprints agree with the right shoe belonging to one Fredrick Barend van der Vyver.'

The statement having been read into the record, Teunissen has Bartholomew describe a court chart he'd prepared about six weeks earlier (*see* PLATE 5). 'If we look at the court chart,' he says, 'Point One indicates an area on the tread of a shoe and the bloody mark on the floor. Point Two indicates the curve of an intershape. Within this curve, four white spots are visible.'

These four marks are the subject of a second court chart, composed of one photo of the bloody mark and another of the shoe's sole, both of which are enlarged to twice life-size. On it, the white spots in the enhanced mark are indicated by four numbered arrows. Four arrows on the image of the shoe's sole indicate the four grains of sand that Bartholomew says correspond with the four white spots. Teunissen continues:

> Q: Now Superintendent Bartholomew, we know that with fingerprints one must have seven points of correspondence to make a positive identification. Could you possibly inform the Court what the process is in relation to shoe identifications? How does the process work for an expert to make a positive identification? What do you look at?
>
> A: International standards determine that, in some circumstances where it has sufficient value, you only need to point out one unique characteristic. In this case, I've identified four.
>
> Q: What do you look for first? Before you look at any characteristics?
>
> A: The whole process of comparison begins with looking for the class, the corresponding class.

Q: In this comparison what would you say are the class
characteristics that you compared?

In response to this question Bartholomew proposes two features of the
mark as corresponding with class characteristics of the shoe, as suggested in PLATE 6. The first is the V-shaped form lying above the grouting
line between the two tiles. This, he says, matches the white shape running through the middle of the shoe, something he demonstrates using a transparency of the picture of the mark laid over an image of the
underside of the shoe. The second is the curved section of the mark that
lies below the grouting, which he again lays over an image of the shoe.
This, too, is demonstrated with the help of a transparent overlay. It is
a process, however, that generates some confusion because it turns out
that is not possible to line up both the curve in the bloody mark with the
corresponding oval shape in the heel while at the same time aligning the
V-shaped mark with the longer shape running through the middle of the
sole. The judge asks the obvious question: 'Why don't they line up?'

A: M'Lord, my conclusion is that there was a second step.
There were two footprints left.

JUDGE: What does that mean?

A: With other words, there was a step on the heel portion.

JUDGE: Yes?

A: The black line in the middle is the end of one tile and
the beginning of the next one.

JUDGE: Yes?

A: And then there was a turn ... a turning in the second
step.

JUDGE: If you talk about 'stepping', you mean stepping with the shoe?

A: That is correct, M'Lord.

JUDGE: So do we understand you correctly that you are saying
that there were two steps made with the shoe?

A: That is correct, M'Lord.

> JUDGE: So the marks are not the result of one footfall, but actu-
> ally two?
>   A: That is correct.

To the irritation of the judge, Teunissen immediately covers some of the same ground again, so he interrupts with a question about a short, squarish nodule that protrudes from the bottom of the curve of the bloody mark, but which he notes does not quite fit into the groove of the shoe that runs north-to-south from the oval intershape to the outer heel of the shoe. This, Bartholomew explains, is because the mark was not made by the shoe, but by Superintendent Koekemoer's swabbing of the bloody stain before the application of the Amido Black. The answer generates some discussion between the judge and Fred's lawyer, who points out that Bartholomew had said he was not in the room when Koekemoer tested the mark or applied the chemical. This proves of little interest to the judge, who allows Teunissen to continue. She, in turn, ignores the issue of the nodule altogether and turns her attention to the four white spots and their relationship to the sand stuck in the grooves of Fred's shoe.

Bartholomew says that he placed the shoe and the picture of the mark in a comparison microscope in order to test their correspondence, noted the four points and asked a certain Captain Frans Maritz – a captain in the ballistics section of the police laboratories – to help measure them with electronic precision.

'And you were satisfied,' Teunissen asks, 'after the measurement of the two that these were precisely the same?'

'They correspond,' he says, 'one hundred percent.'

23

A couple of hours into his testimony, Bruce Bartholomew seemed the very embodiment of the ideal policeman. He seemed a man who combined the hard-edged temperament of the street with the recondite knowledge of the laboratory. He seemed a man who could intimidate the unpredictable crowds drawn preternaturally to crime scenes in Cape Town's ganglands, but one who possessed also the rigorous attention to detail and the forensic know-how needed to transform a cold body found in a wrecked room into a text, a document whose author would be revealed through a close and careful reading.

This was my first impression, sustained, for a time, by the account he gave of the efforts he'd made to find evidence in Inge's flat and by the work he put in later. By the end of the three days of cross-examination to which he was subjected, three days in which he'd given a masterclass in the formulation of answers that never quite addressed themselves to the questions that had been asked, my idea of Bartholomew was much diminished. By then, I felt that I was watching a badly shot animal die slowly and I wondered if he was sufficiently self-aware to recognise how much he had lost, how much, to put it bluntly, had been taken from him.

* * *

De Bruyn's assault on Bartholomew's testimony was along such a broad front, and was composed of so many varying strands, that it is no simple matter to convey the extent of the damage done by any single attack. Some of the doubts the lawyer raised, it is true, appeared less important than others. Thus, it turned out that the four arrows pointing to the grains of sand in the photo of the underside of Fred's shoe could not be made to line up precisely with the four arrows pointing to white spots found in the picture of the chemically enhanced bloody mark. As a result, it proved impossible to put a transparency of the one image over the image of the other and to line up more than two arrows at a time. Bartholomew insisted that this had something to do with way the arrows had been printed, rather than with any deficit in the correspondence between the white spots and the grains of sand. It was not an unreasonable thing to say. Still, it must have been humiliating to be asked to demonstrate to the judge the failure of all the arrows to align, as the defence insisted Bartholomew do.

Other problems with the white spots were less easily explained.

One of these was that in a letter written to a fellow shoeprint expert on 30 January 2006, Bartholomew had described the match he'd made between the bloody mark and Fred's shoe. In that letter, he wrote of three white marks as being the basis of the match, rather than the four to which he pointed on the stand. 'The heel of the right shoe has sand grains which was stuck in the groove,' he wrote with the uncertain grammar of one using his second language. 'The blood mark was investigated and three small round marks are visible. Both the sole and the blood mark were enlarged. The sand grains and the round marks were electronically measured. The sand grains, according to me, made the three marks in the blood mark.'

Whether one were looking at three or four spots would seem an important question when conducting a microscopic measurement of the distances between them and of the angles created by the intersection of the resulting vectors. De Bruyn doesn't quite put it this way to Bartholomew, but that may have been because, when he asked questions about the precise number of spots that had been identified, he had yet to be provided with any documentation about this aspect of the investigation. That is despite the fact that it was by then a week into Bartholomew's testimony and nineteen months after Bartholomew had actually done this work.

In the absence of these seemingly important details, De Bruyn asks Bartholomew about the procedure that had been followed when the measurements were taken and how it happened that the four spots were found to align with the grains of sand.

Bartholomew explains that a transparency of the bloody mark had been placed over the sole of the shoe and that this resulted in the identification of a number of white spots in the Amido Black that seemed to correspond with the grains of sand. Having noted these, he says, he asked his colleague, Captain Frans Maritz, to measure them electronically. Initially, he says, there were three marks that they looked at, but then Maritz drew his attention to a fourth that was also in correspondence with a grain of sand. By the time he left Maritz's laboratory, Bartholomew says, he was personally satisfied that all four were in correspondence.

How is it, then, De Bruyn asks, that in the letter Bartholomew wrote six months later he made reference to only three marks? 'How,' he asks, 'do you explain that? Why not four?'

> A: I was not 100 percent certain about the last one,
> M'Lord.

Q: When did you become certain of it? Or are you still uncertain?

A: I am sure. That is why I marked it on the court chart, M'Lord.

Q: When did you become certain?

A: When I did my final preparation of the court chart, that is when I became convinced.

Q: What changed with the court chart? What did you have on the court chart that you did not have access to before that convinced you about this mark?

A: Just the electronic measurement, again.

Q: But that happened in July or August 2005?

A: That's right, M'Lord.

Q: So you always had that. What else happened that you became convinced about the fourth point?

A: Captain Maritz and I spoke about this, and we decided on it together.

Q: Oh, you consulted with Captain Maritz.

A; Yes.

Q: When was that consultation?

A: Last week, Tuesday. Monday, M'Lord. Monday.

*   *   *

Perhaps you noticed in the last exchange that De Bruyn had dated the electronic measurement of the marks no more accurately than to 'July or August 2005'. The reason he'd been so imprecise was a result of another uncertainty that had arisen about the chronology of the investigation.

In his statement, sworn to on 8 September 2005, Bartholomew had said that Maritz had measured the shoe and the white spots under the microscope on 22 July. There was other evidence, however, that showed that this would have been impossible: the shoe had been in a sealed evidence bag until the end of July, when it was opened by another official; she only returned it to Bartholomew in early August. So no electronic measurement could have been done before then.

Presented with this, Bartholomew had had to concede that the date in his statement, as well as the repeated references he'd made to that date in his testimony when Teunissen had led him through his evidence-in-chief, must be wrong. He could offer no explanation of how the mistake could have happened.

Another curious detail about which Bartholomew can offer no explanation is that the stain in the bathroom seemed to be the only evidence that the killer's shoe had acquired blood during the crime. This is a problem because Bartholomew accepts that the mark is what experts call a 'transfer stain', which means that the blood was not deposited directly on the floor (as it might do if it dripped from a shoe or a weapon or a wound), but was pressed onto it by some other object that had acquired the blood at some point before it made contact with the floor. In this case, that means that there must have been blood on the sole of Fred's shoe before the shoe made contact with the bathroom floor. The trouble was that if the blood was acquired in the lounge, there ought to have been bloody footprints from the lounge to the bathroom. There ought to have been, but there weren't. This was not easy to explain. Nor was it easy to explain why none of the bloodstains in the lounge appeared to have been stepped in. And, because the direction the bloodied shoe would have been facing, if and when it made the mark, was towards the window of the bathroom, the absence of any sign of footprints leading out of the bathroom was another detail about which an inquiring mind might have cause to wonder. It is as if the killer stepped in blood in the lounge (without leaving evidence of this), hopped into the bathroom, put his foot down (twice, since the mark, if it was made by Fred's shoe, required two separate strikes) and then took the shoe off. It is an extremely odd sequence, and all Bartholomew can do is insist that the mark was made by the shoe, even as he agrees that the absence of any other bloodied shoeprints is peculiar and inexplicable.

There is more that Bartholomew cannot explain.

He cannot explain, for example, why the herringbone patterns that frame both the oval and V-shaped devices on the sole managed to avoid leaving any trace of their presence in the bathroom, even though these are by far the most prominent features of the sole of the shoe, projecting a long way above the grains of sand that he claimed did make contact with the floor (*see* PLATE 7).

Bartholomew also cannot explain how it is that Fred's shoe managed to make contact with the ground twice, with each contact leaving evidence of only one small portion of the bloodied sole of his right shoe. He cannot explain, in other words, how it was that the first contact with the floor left blood from the oval intershape at the heel of the shoe but no blood from the V-shaped device in the centre of the shoe, while the second contact left blood from the V-shaped device but no blood from the oval. Nor, when it comes to it, can Bartholomew explain why there was no evidence that the second strike had smudged or disturbed or in any other way changed the mark that had been deposited by the first contact between shoe and floor. Given the proximity of the two devices to each other and the inflexibility of the middle of the sole, it seemed important to be able to offer some account of the mechanics of how this might have happened. Bartholomew could offer none.

Another issue that begged for more explanation than Bartholomew seemed able to offer is the question of how it was that the grains of sand were in the groove of Fred's shoe at all.

One version of this complaint is that Bartholomew admitted that no special measures were taken to preserve the grains of sand in the grooves of the right sole when the shoes were seized on 15 April 2005. It was, therefore, extremely fortuitous that they were still in the shoe in late July or early August when Maritz put them under his microscope. Since the sand was there at that point and was still there during the trial, however, that complaint is beside the point. More pertinent, though, is that if it were true that the shoe had had blood on it on 16 March, when Inge was murdered, Fred would have had to have given it a thorough scrubbing between then and 15 April, when the police took possession of it. We know this because forensic tests of the shoe conducted between 25 July and 2 August 2005 revealed no evidence of blood. Since the porous rubber of the shoe's sole would usually be expected to have retained traces of blood, Fred would have had to have cleaned the shoe particularly conscientiously to explain that negative result. If he did so, how was it possible, De Bruyn asks the judge to wonder, that the sand would not have been removed?

24

Although it is never framed in these terms, much of what transpires at Fred's trial is about how objects and artefacts and documents are to be read. The stakes raised by the reading of the artefacts – Folien One and the bloody stain, in particular – are higher than those raised by the reading of the documents. But documents, too, need careful attention and raise interesting questions: if there is a gap between what a document says and what its author says he intended it to say, which meaning should prevail? Should a judge or a lawyer or a witness – or, for that matter, a writer – forgive an author for his infelicities of expression, and take him at his word when he says that he intended to say something different from what he in fact conveyed when he put pen to paper? Or, on the other hand, should someone who swears out an affidavit whose literal contents later prove inconvenient be held to what he had, in fact, said?

It is the classic question of literary criticism – who determines the meaning of a text, its author or its reader? – and it arose with a great many witnesses. Constable Swartz had sworn out a statement that said that he'd used a single folien on the DVD cover, but later testified that he'd used two, one of which no longer existed. Captain Matheus swore he'd fulfilled a range of administrative obligations in relation to the fingerprint in time frames that more or less conformed with established procedure, but which were not supported by the dates he and others had entered into the registers intended to record those activities. Superintendent Koekemoer, who we will meet in a moment, signed a statement saying that he asked some unidentified person to take the swab of the bloody stain, but testifies that he took it himself, accounting for the difference between his statement and his testimony by a too-liberal use of his computer's cut-and-paste functions. There was also Superintendent Bartholomew, whose statement said he found the fingerprint team in Inge's flat on 17 March, but who testified that he'd broken the seals on the front door, and whose statement also said that he and Captain Maritz had examined the sole of Fred's shoe under a microscope on 22 July 2005, a date that could not have been correct since the shoe was in an evidence bag until 25 July.

Then there was Marius Botha, who was called to testify about what transpired at Mrs Lotz's home after the murder, events that, according to Mrs Lotz's testimony – if not her statements – included Fred's telling her that Inge had been murdered, an event he could time-date as having occurred that afternoon, as well as a curious offer to become the child in Mrs Lotz's home. These were incriminating acts, but they had not appeared in either of Mrs Lotz's sworn statements, and Marius's testimony was offered in support of her evidence. Oddly enough, however, Marius's own sworn statements also fail to mention Fred's offer to replace Inge. More peculiarly still, far from corroborating Mrs Lotz's account of Fred's words to her – '*Tannie*, Inge was murdered in her flat this afternoon' – Marius's statement said that it was he, rather than Fred, who conveyed the news of Inge's death to Mrs Lotz.

*   *   *

Marius Botha, Fred's flatmate at the time of the murder, had known Inge longer than Fred had. He is a handsome young man, his handsomeness marred only by the fact that his good looks are, if anything, too conventional. He is slim and athletic, a distance runner with a distance-runner litheness, and hair so dark as to shine. There is intelligence in his face. And charm, too. In a smart jacket and tie, he has the presence and self-assurance of a young executive, upwardly mobile, comfortable with himself, at ease in his world.

But it is not easy to be comfortable in court. And it is not easy to convey testimony as heartbreaking as one's memories of the moment at which one broke the news to a mother that her only child was dead, testimony that is heartbreaking precisely because it relates to the precise moment when a life was irretrievably split into a distinct 'before' and an equally distinct 'after'; testimony that relates to a moment at which every previously imagined future was erased forever to be recalled later only with unending bitterness and regret. The poignancy of that awareness fills the court as Marius speaks, his cool, confident voice growing so strained that, in a moment, it will break into wracking sobs that will lead to a brief postponement and that will be recorded in the transcript, almost like a stage direction, as 'witness emotional'.

'I parked in the driveway in front of *Tannie* Juanita's home,' Marius says. 'Fred's bakkie was in the side street. As I went past it, I saw that Fred was sitting in it. I got out of my car and Fred got out of his car and came towards me over the grass. We met at the wooden gate at the entrance to *Tannie* Juanita's home. I told him that I did not have good news, that Christo had called me back and that Inge was dead. Fred said nothing. I told him that I was sorry and that I wasn't sure precisely what had happened, that Christo had said it looked like it could be murder or suicide.'

Q: Do you know where Mrs Lotz was at that point?

A: No.

Q: What was Mr Van der Vyver's reaction to the news?

A: He just stood there speechless and looked at me with disbelief. I tried to support him by giving him a hug. Tears came to his eyes, and, at that point, *Tannie* Juanita came to stand nearby. I don't know where she had been before. *Tannie* Juanita said, 'Fred, what's going on? Where is my child?' Fred stepped towards her and said, '*Tannie*, Inge was murdered this afternoon.'

Q: Anything else?

A: *Tannie* Juanita also said in disbelief that that could not be. Fred tried to support her and said, '*Toemaar, tannie.* Everything will be okay. I will be the child in the house.'

(WITNESS EMOTIONAL)

JUDGE: 'Everything will be okay. I will be the child in the house.'

A: Yes.

JUDGE: You can sit for a moment if you like, Mr Botha.

A: Don't worry. It's alright. *Tannie* Juanita ran into the house. She screamed. She just said, 'It can't be. Not my child.' Fred and I basically ran after her, and, if I remember correctly, one of the first things that *Tannie* Juanita did was to call Jan to tell him what had happened.

Q: That is Mr Lotz.

A: Yes. Inge's father.

(WITNESS EMOTIONAL)

So there you have it: according to Marius's testimony from the stand, Fred *did* offer to become the child in the house and he *did* convey the news to Mrs Lotz.

It is curious, however, that neither statement made its way into any of Marius's numerous affidavits. But it is not as curious as the comparison between what he says on the stand – '*Tannie* Juanita said, "Fred, what's going on? Where is my child?" Fred stepped towards her and said, "*Tannie*, Inge was murdered this afternoon."' – and what his statement actually says: 'While Fred and I stood outside the front door, I gave him the news. As I spoke to him, he leaned against the wall. I could see he was very emotional. I thought he might collapse and I supported him physically. Fred said nothing and began to cry. While I spoke with him, *Tannie* Juanita came outside. I could see that she expected the worst and I shared the news with her. *Tannie* Juanita was very badly upset and ran into the house.'

In the context of what had gone before, the difference between whether he told Mrs Lotz that Inge was murdered or whether Fred did is significant, and, when he is asked by De Bruyn to explain it, Marius offers an explanation in which one is asked to expect that a sworn statement need not convey accurately what it is said to convey. 'My statement was just a summary of events,' he says, 'During questioning by Director Attie Trollip, when we went through these events, I told him what had happened. He told me that the statements were just a summary, but later he did ask me to think more carefully about the details of what precisely had happened. I was not aware that this particular conversation was relevant to the investigation, but I did tell him during questioning that it was Fred who conveyed the message. My statement does in fact say that I conveyed the news, but that was in reference to the entire process of me bringing the news to the house. The detail about that specific portion is not in the statement, although I had already told the investigators.'

It might be easier to accept that Marius's statement was a summary of what happened if its language were less categorical than he told Mrs Lotz that Inge was dead, if it said, for example, 'Mrs Lotz was told the news' or '*We* told her the news.' But the interpretive difficulties created by the gap between what Marius says on the stand and what his statements say is much less significant than a similar problem that arises from perhaps the most important sentence of Bartholomew's two sworn statements, the one that I have quoted twice and which reads, 'Concerning the type, size, place, position and relationship of the unique characteristics to one another, the class of the shoeprint agrees with the right shoe belonging to one Fredrick Barend van der Vyver.' It is a sentence that, had it been accepted by the judge, would have sent Fred to prison for the rest of his life. By the standards of the processes set out in the textbooks in which the protocols for conducting shoeprint impression examinations are set out, however, it is also a sentence whose meaning is not exactly crystalline, for it seems to say that various 'unique characteristics' of the mark mean that the 'class of the shoeprint' matches Fred's right shoe.

* * *

Bartholomew's sentence about the match he made presents its reader with all sorts of problems of interpretation. Not the least of these is that there is literally no indication of what the 'unique characteristics' are or how their size and place and position can say anything about the class of the shoeprint. More important though, is that embedded in this sentence is a serious category mistake: 'class characteristics' are defined in the textbooks of shoeprint impression evidence – to which Batholomew himself made reference – as being the macro-features of the shoe, such as its make and size, factors that could easily belong to thousands of shoes of the same kind or 'class' when they leave the factory gate. 'Unique characteristics', on the other hand, are defined in those textbooks as imperfections that result from the use made of a particular shoe, and which will differentiate it from every other shoe of the same class. There is, therefore, no way that any number of unique characteristics can add up to a single class characteristic because they refer to completely different elements of the shoe and the impression it leaves.

Perhaps the most bewildering aspect of Bartholomew's sentence, though, is that the phrase 'the class of', which is the source of much of the difficulty of interpretation, was not part of the original type-written statement at all. At some point after the statement was typed up, Bartholomew had gone back to it and added this phrase in by hand, doing so, he explains, because it had been accidentally omitted by the typist. Bizarrely, without that phrase the sentence actually succeeds in stating something quite precise – that the unique characteristics in the shoeprint agree with those of the shoe. With the addition of the phrase 'the class of', a phrase consciously and deliberately added later, that lucidity is lost. Of course, what that alteration does do is introduce the word 'class', something that was altogether missing from the original. Since the textbooks demand that a match be pronounced only if there is some correspondence of both class and unique characteristics, that omission would have left a reasonable-doubt-sized hole in Bartholomew's evidence.

It is not obvious why Bartholomew's statement is so unclear on this point and why it makes him appear so uncertain about the key concepts of the shoeprint examiner's art. It is possible that this reflects the thinness of Bartholomew's grasp of matters. It is also possible that he simply has no way with words: a practical man, he might be the kind of cop who resists paperwork with such determination that he cannot bring himself to make sure his own statements read clearly.

And yet, even if his language skills were not what they might be, the words Bartholomew used or failed to use in his statements must matter. Perhaps the most important of the words he used and failed to use were those relating to the nodule that he testified had been cre-ated when Superintendent Koekemoer took a swab from the bloody mark. It was a nodule about which there was absolutely no explicit ref-erence in his sworn statements (two) or his court charts (three), but to which he may have referred in an email he sent to a fellow expert on 30 January 2006.

* * *

During the trial, the nodule (*see* PLATE 8) was variously called the 'appendage' or the 'tongue' or the 'thumb' or the 'nipple', or, on two occasions, the '*piepie*'. It was small and squarish, each side running to a little less than six millimetres, and it is doubtful that so small a bloody mark has ever raised as many questions in a South African courtroom.

When Bartholomew testifies about this, it is primarily in an attempt to draw attention away from it: he says that it had been created when his Pretoria-based colleague, Superintendent Koekemoer, ran a swab through the mark on the floor in order to satisfy himself that what he was looking at was blood, and that the nodule played no role in the subsequent matching of the stain to Fred's shoe.

De Bruyn is not entirely satisfied with Bartholomew's account of the source of the tongue, and for many reasons. One of these is that he insists that, having altered the mark by taking a swab, the police were not then entitled to claim to have matched the same mark to Fred's shoe. In support of this, he points out that Superintendent Kock, who had looked for trace DNA evidence in Inge's flat on the night of the murder, had testified that he had deliberately refrained from taking a sample from that mark precisely because he wanted to avoid disturbing what might become crucial evidence. Swabbing the mark, De Bruyn says at one point, violated a 'golden rule' of forensic work that one ought never to disturb a transfer stain since that would immediately raise questions about any subsequent match that might be made.

In reply to these complaints, Bartholomew insists that, while the addition of the tongue did alter some of the macro-characteristics of the mark, the match he had made did not rely on any of these changes. He says that is why he was not bothered by the fact that Koekemoer's procedures had altered the mark. A swab, he keeps saying, had to be taken from somewhere ...

Bartholomew's is an argument against which De Bruyn can make little headway, but then the lawyer raises another problem, which, if he's right, has enormous implications for how one understands what happened during the investigation of Inge's murder: Bartholomew, De Bruyn says, had originally wanted to use the nodule to link the stain to the shoe, and had, in fact, deliberately created it for that purpose. The general idea of the investigators, De Bruyn suggests, was to claim that the tongue had originally been invisible, but that it had appeared after the application of Amido Black, and, having become visible, could be matched to the shoe, into the groove of which it fit so neatly. The creation of the nodule, in other words, was less the accidental result of Koekemoer's swab, and more a deliberate attempt to fabricate evidence.

It is an extraordinary allegation, and, while the evidence De Bruyn produces is not quite conclusive, it is also not altogether insubstantial.

*   *   *

To begin with, let us record that in the email of 30 January 2006 to a fellow shoeprint impression evidence expert, in which Bartholomew had written about the three (rather than four) white spots visible in the enhanced mark, he had introduced the matching of the stain to the shoe by writing, 'In the bathroom of the victim's flat, a blood mark was visible on the floor tiles, just beneath the basin. The blood mark was treated with Amido Black and, as a result of the treatment, an additional mark became visible. This was the decisive factor during the identification.'

Note that: '... *an* additional mark became visible.'

Should we read this literally? Or should we accept that Bartholomew, whose first language is not English, intended this phrase to mean the three white spots to which he refers a paragraph later? If this was his intention, as he insisted from the stand, I think we can agree that these were not particularly well-chosen words.

Bartholomew's letter, with its reference to 'an additional mark', was not the only evidence De Bruyn sought to introduce to prove that the mark was not created by Koekemoer's test but had been created in some other fashion. To do this, he pointed to the tongue itself, arguing that there was no way it could have been the result of a single, swipe-like motion. The appendage, he said, is too square, its edges too precise (*see* PLATE 9). In addition, a close examination of the mark before and after the swab was taken suggests that the flow of blood into the appendage from the original mark (which looks like a movement from two o'clock to seven o'clock) was not in the same direction as the appendage itself (which lies on the eleven o'clock to five o'clock axis). He might have added, but didn't, that the appendage is also notably narrower than the area within the original bloody mark that Bartholomew said had been swabbed, something that makes it seem almost to have been created by a second implement of a different size. He also might have said that one would expect that the motion used in taking a swab would leave a feathery trail as the swab was gradually lifted from the tile, rather than the squared-off lower edge of the actual appendage that is visible.

In addition to this, there was, for De Bruyn, the sheer improbability of the coincidence that, when superimposed on Fred's shoe, the appendage that resulted from a random swipe with a bud-like instrument should fit so neatly into the same area as a groove on Fred's shoe would have been when making contact with the floor. In fact, both its location on the curve, as well as its width, mean that the nodule matches all but perfectly the furrow on the shoe.

And then there was something else that raised De Bruyn's suspicions about the true origin of the nodule: Bartholomew, he says, had explicitly told him that the tongue had been made by the shoe.

Bartholomew had done this, De Bruyn says, at a meeting between the defence and the prosecutors on 29 November 2005, a meeting that was also attended by a number of other people. Bartholomew acknowledges being at the meeting and remembers that it was then that the defence had handed the prosecutors a report on Folien One by one of their experts, and at which it was decided that Director Ruben Botha would be approached for an independent report on the arguments about whether the prints had been found on a DVD cover or a drinking glass.

Gratified at this acknowledgement that the meeting had occurred, De Bruyn, who, until Bartholomew took the stand had had no idea that the state would argue anything but that the nodule had developed as a result of the application of Amido Black, continues: 'The meeting was not about the shoeprint, but at the end of it, as people were busy getting up, I referred to the tongue and asked you, "How could the shoe make that mark?" And you made a kind of rolling action with your hand on the table, as if to show someone making a heavy step with the shoe?' As he says this, De Bruyn places his fingers on the table and slowly rolls the heel of his hand onto the counter, as if pressing something into the wood.

At this, the judge asks De Bruyn whether he was planning to testify. De Bruyn, amused, replies that he isn't, but adds that he has 'three other witnesses who are much more credible than I am.' Then, turning back to Bartholomew, he asks if the former policeman remembered this incident. 'I don't,' Bartholomew replies. 'I am sure the prosecutor would have rebuked me had I done such a thing.'

In the end, De Bruyn did not call these witnesses (one of whom has subsequently died), so it is impossible to know whether they would have said what he claimed they'd say. It is worth noting, however, that Alfons had described this exchange between De Bruyn and Bartholomew to me at our very first meeting, some six months before Bartholomew was on the stand, and had used precisely the same hand gesture then as De Bruyn used now. Because Alfons had no way of knowing whether I would convey this information to anyone, it is unlikely that he would have mentioned it to me if he thought it was untrue, since his words to me would have risked exposing De Bruyn as a liar. It is also worth recording that if De Bruyn was lying about what his witnesses would have testified, it would have been a very serious professional lapse, one that would have had equally serious professional consequences.

Having said all that, there were good reasons to think that Bartholomew could not possibly have made the gesture De Bruyn attributed to him. One of those reasons was Bartholomew's denial. More compelling than this was the fact that the police had themselves given the defence the photos that proved the mark had changed shape before the application of Amido Black by the police. If Bartholomew had intended to claim that the mark was revealed by the application of Amido Black – that this was the 'additional mark' that had been developed by Koekemoer's procedures – those photographs would have blown him out of the water. Their handing over those photos, in other words, suggests that Bartholomew and his colleagues were acting in good faith.

Except that De Bruyn did not have those photos in November 2005 when Bartholomew allegedly made the gesture with his hand, and did not receive them until the middle of April 2006. And then, after the defence did receive them, something remarkable happened: within hours of their having been delivered, they were stolen from Fred's car.

'The defence,' De Bruyn says to Bartholomew, 'asked for all the photos pertaining to the case, and, on 13 April 2006, a hard drive containing these was delivered.'

> A: I know something like that was prepared.
> Q: And on that hard drive, the defence saw for the first
>   time – in April 2006 – that the tongue was created
>   before the Amido Black was applied. And then a
>   certain incident occurred which compelled the defence
>   to ask for a copy of the hard drive.
> A: Are you referring to the incident in which the hard
>   drive was stolen or vanished?
> Q: Yes. Stolen. Then we had to ask again for a hard drive.
>   And our supposition is that the hard drive's photos
>   with the red tongue were not intended for us, and that

it was an oversight that this happened.

JUDGE: Excuse me. You are speaking softly. Can you repeat that
question?

Q: Our conclusion was that the hard drive's photos with
the red tongue were not intended for us, and that we
received them by accident.

A: M'Lord, I can't answer that. I didn't prepare the
hard drive. And I must emphasise again that my
identification did not include this tongue.

Almost before Bartholomew has finished his answer, Advocate Teunissen
has risen to her feet: 'M'Lord, I must object at this point. My learned
friend is trying to insinuate that the state tried to withhold certain photos. It was the state itself that put all the photos on the hard drive for the
convenience of the defence. If my learned friend wants to make this kind
of allegation, he must have a reasonable basis for it. The state objects to
this allegation.'

The judge's answer to this is unusually unadorned – 'Yes' – and De Bruyn
takes the matter no further. 'I have said what our allegation is. He says he
doesn't know anything about it. Good. We say that it is from that point that
the tongue vanished as an identifying mark, if it ever was one.' Then he
turned to Bartholomew, 'You say it was never an identifiable mark?'

'Never.'

* * *

One of the ways in which the prosecution seeks to deflect the accumulat-
ing criticism of the handling of the bloody mark is to call Superintendent
Johannes Koekemoer, an officer who was not on the original list of state
witnesses but whose testimony can help establish that the nodule was
created when the stain was swabbed rather than in any other way.

Koekemoer has fuzzy blond hair, wears a blue suit and sports an eye so dead that it creates the impression of an extreme squint. On the stand, he explains in a tumble of words so rapid as to approach complete incomprehensibility that he had to take a swab before applying Amido Black, which, he says, reacts only with blood. He also explains how he did this using a wet Multistix similar to the one GPs use to test urine. Defensively, he adds that he took a photograph of the result because he could see that the original mark had changed shape and because he wanted to record properly that that had happened.

Koekemoer, whom Teunissen calls 'Koekies' when he is not on the stand, testifies that he knew nothing about Fred's shoe, and that Bartholomew had brought only Fred's hammer to the flat. Knowing nothing of the shoe, he thought it likely that the stain might be matched to the hammer, which is why he took the swab at the bottom of the mark, where it would not disturb the V-shaped portion of the stain, since that might have been matched to the hammer's bottle-opener. Knowing nothing of the shoe, he implies, he could not have set out to create an appendage that would have fit into the groove of its sole.

Under cross-examination, Koekemoer's story is unshakable, even when it is pointed out that his statement doesn't say that he took a swab, but that he requested that a swab be taken. This, he says, was a mistake, the result of his cutting and pasting part of his statement from previous statements, a practice that he admits falls short of the ideal. Beyond this, he repeats that he was responsible for the appendage, but can offer no real explanation for what De Bruyn characterises as its 'unnatural' shape. All he can offer on this point is that he may have twisted his wrist in taking the swab, and that since another person – 'a Pogenpoel', for example – might execute this task differently, it is wrong to suggest that there was such a thing as a 'natural' or an 'unnatural' way of doing it. He does admit, however, that he has no independent evidence of his taking a swab, adding that the bloodied Multistix had become a biohazard and was destroyed.

While none of this affected the bulk of De Bruyn's criticisms of the match Bartholomew claimed to have made between the stain and Fred's shoe, Koekemoer's evidence made it seem less plausible that there had been deliberate manipulation of the mark. If the tongue was the result of Koekemoer's techniques, then the mark was not deliberately manipulated. Since only Koekemoer could say what happened, his words couldn't be refuted.

And then they were refuted.

Completely and utterly refuted.

What happened is this: when the prosecutors closed their case, De Bruyn had an opportunity to consult with the private investigators. It was during that consultation that he found in their files the cover letter that Fred had attached to the copy of Inge's letter he'd given them at the end of March 2005. As he was looking through those files, he also found something else: a set of photographs the private investigators had taken of Inge's flat on 1 April 2005. That was a full four weeks before Koekemoer had flown down from Pretoria to treat the bloody mark with Amido Black. And yet, in one of those photographs the bloody mark could be seen complete with the tongue that Koekemoer said he'd created on 28 April.

Recalled to the stand some weeks after he'd finished testifying, Koekemoer was at a complete loss. He knows he took a swab, he kept saying. He also knows he took it at the bottom of the mark. Perhaps, he suggested, the tongue was created in the process of searching for DNA evidence, and perhaps he took his swab over precisely the same spot as the DNA technician had done.

Given the complete absence of any evidence that the mark changed as a result of Koekemoer's second swab, this seems unlikely. Equally unlikely, it seems to me, is the existence of a DNA technician who was never identified either before or after Koekemoer's testimony and whose work is reflected precisely nowhere in the police docket or in all the registers they keep at the forensic science lab. Indeed, Superintendent Kock, whose job it was to search the flat for DNA samples, testified explicitly that he had not taken a swab through this particular stain precisely because he wanted to preserve its shape.

It was a dramatic development, and it reopened De Bruyn's claims that the stain had been deliberately manipulated.

25

I wish I could say that that was the worst of it. But it wasn't.

The email that Bartholomew had written on 30 January 2006, in which he'd spoken – he claimed interchangeably – of 'an additional mark' and of 'three small white marks', had been addressed to William J Bodziak, perhaps the world's leading authority on shoeprint impression evidence. The email was a request to consult with him about the bloody mark found in Inge's bathroom. 'According to me,' it reads, 'I've made a positive identification. My purpose in consulting you is to show my findings to you so you can give your expert opinion on that.' He added, 'It won't be necessary to attend the court case in South Africa.' And he added, 'It would be a lifelong opportunity to meet you in person and maybe to attend one of your workshops to broaden my horizon.'

Although unstated in his email, the reason that Bartholomew was looking for Bodziak's expert opinion was that the usual requirement for a court to accept the evidence of an expert about a match between a shoe and a shoeprint is that the match be verified by at least one other expert. This is an unremarkable safeguard against rogue identifications, so unremarkable, in fact, that it is standard procedure for other forms of impression evidence, including the infinitely more established field of fingerprint identification.

Bartholomew, then, needed his match to be verified. Unfortunately, he had had some trouble in obtaining this from his colleagues in the South African Police Service.

Initially, he had presented the evidence to colleagues in the Western Cape, but none had been able to agree with the match he insisted he'd found. This, Bartholomew would later testify, had less to do with the merits of his match than with the fact that the other experts with whom he'd spoken had had less training and less experience than he. Their inability to verify his work was, he said, a consequence of nothing more than his having more skill at this craft. 'They could not make the identification,' he said on the stand, 'for the simple reason that they were not trained to do so.'

Bartholomew said that the one exception to the rule that other experts in the Police Service were insufficiently trained to verify his work, was a certain Superintendent Louis Kriel, one of the most respected crime scene investigators in the country. And arrangements for Bartholomew to meet Kriel were, in fact, made. That was in September 2005, but when Bartholomew arrived in Pretoria, he discovered that Kriel was busy with final preparations for his move to the United States, where he was to begin working for the FBI. Despite having previously agreed to help, Kriel was unable to meet with Bartholomew, who had to resort, instead, to an informal meeting with a few other officials over coffee at police head office. None of the officers present at that meeting verified his match, however, something that Bartholomew again ascribed to their comparative lack of training and experience.

Unable to get local experts to verify the match (and there were some in the Police Service with whom Bartholomew appears not to have consulted), Bartholomew's boss, Director Trollip, wrote to the Minister for Safety and Security to request permission for Bartholomew to visit Bodziak's home and laboratory in Palm Coast, Florida. In that letter, Trollip wrote that Bartholomew had conducted his analysis of the shoeprint on the basis of Bodziak's theories. He wrote that Bodziak had worked for the FBI in this field for 25 years and had published seven books on the subject, including the leading textbook in the field. He also wrote that Bodziak was 'internationally regarded as the leading expert in the examination of footwear and tyre tread impression evidence' and that a consultation was necessary because 'the defence team will do everything in its power to create reasonable doubt by discrediting the identifications made by the South African Police experts.' He wrote that 'it is necessary to consider the involvement of the best possible assistance with the authentication of the matching of the shoeprint in question.' Trollip wrote that all indications were that Bodziak, with whom both Bartholomew and Advocate Teunissen had been in contact, would 'be prepared to evaluate the work done by Captain Bartholomew and supply a corroborating report.' The consultation with Bodziak, Trollip concluded, 'is essential for the successful investigation of the case.'

Permission to visit Bodziak was duly granted. Bodziak's fee was negotiated and money was transferred to his account. Bartholomew left for Florida at the end of June 2006.

*   *   *

When I worked in the Ministry for Safety and Security in the late 1990s, it was a standard requirement that a report be written after every official overseas visit that had been authorised by the Minister. In the case of Bruce Bartholomew's visit to Florida, however, the defence was told that this did not occur. That may have been because, three weeks after his return, Bartholomew left the police and began a new life working in the private sector. It is possible, in other words, that he simply neglected to complete the standard paperwork. Whether or not this was the reason, there was no official report about what Bodziak had said and what Bartholomew had achieved in the United States.

Or so the police and the prosecutors insisted between July 2006, when Bartholomew returned from the United States, and 8 March 2007, when he was being cross-examined by Fred's lawyer. So committed had the police and prosecutors been to the position that no report existed that it had been on this point, and on this point alone, that the prosecutors had objected after the reading-in of Fred's plea explanation on the first morning of the trial. 'The impression has been created,' Christénus van der Vijver had said then, 'that there is certain information about Mr Bartholomew's visit to the USA that the state is withholding. We wish to place on record – and these are our instructions – that there is no report of this kind.'

Well, less than a month after Van der Vijver's categorical statement, Bartholomew produced just such a report, one that had been signed by Director Trollip, a man – the point bears repeating – who had been sitting less than a metre from the prosecutors when Van der Vijver rose to assure the judge that no report existed.

This is what Director Trollip's report said about the Bartholomew–Bodziak consultation.

It said that authority for Bartholomew to travel to the United States was granted on 7 June 2006.

It said that Bartholomew travelled to the United States and that he met with William J Bodziak on 30 June 2006.

It said that 'Mr Bodziak confirmed the identification of the murder scene shoeprint.'

It said that Mr Bodziak advised Superintendent Bartholomew that 'the identification must primarily be based on the three design marks visible on the shoe. These marks are unique to the exhibit (shoe) and will not be duplicated by any other shoe.'

It said that Mr Bodziak advised Superintendent Bartholomew that 'the sand granules which are visible should be used as additional points of identification.'

It said that Mr Bodziak advised Superintendent Bartholomew that 'a test print would be of no value as the crime scene prints can never be repeated. (Basically the same as in the case of fingerprints.)'

It said that Mr Bodziak felt that 'Superintendent Bartholomew would be the most suited person to give evidence in court due to his presence at the crime scene and his in-depth background knowledge of footwear impressions.'

It said that Mr Bodziak told Superintendent Bartholomew that the analysis of the provisional court chart completed by defence experts was 'typical of someone who is unaware of the basic principles of footwear comparisons and who does not understand the process of shoeprint identification.'

Then, under the heading, ELUCIDATION BY DIR. TROLLIP, it said that 'it was never the intention to use Mr Bodziak as a witness in this case' but that 'the consultation enables Superintendent Bartholomew to testify with more confidence.'

Under the same heading, it said that 'it is clear from Superintendent Bartholomew's feedback that Mr Bodziak was impressed with the quality of work performed by local crime scene investigators.'

It said that 'Advocate C Teunissen was briefed regarding the consultation and she expressed her appreciation for compliance with the Director of Public Prosecution's request.'

All of which raises an interesting question: why is it that when Carien Teunissen led Bruce Bartholomew through his evidence-in-chief, she had asked no questions about his visit to the United States and his consultation with William J Bodziak, a consultation she had requested and for which she had apparently expressed her appreciation? Why would a consultation with the world's leading authority on shoeprint impression evidence that produced so ringing an endorsement of the work of the prosecution's star witness have generated not a single question from the prosecution itself?

One possible answer is that the report shows a certain illiteracy in the handling of shoeprint impression evidence. In writing that the design marks were unique to Fred's shoe and that they would never be duplicated in another, for example, the report gets matters exactly backwards: design marks, by definition, are never unique to a shoe and are always duplicated in others.

Another possible reason Teunissen hadn't asked Bartholomew to talk about the report was that it had been written by Director Trollip after Bartholomew returned from the United States. It was, in other words, not in Bodziak's name, and Bodziak had made it clear that he would not travel to South Africa to testify. In effect, the contents of Trollip's report were now third-hand hearsay – Trollip's account of what Bartholomew told him about what Bodziak had said. If Bodziak refused to travel, that meant the report would be of no evidentiary value. Failing to introduce the report might, therefore, be seen as a manifestation of scrupulous lawyering: the report, the prosecutors may have said to themselves, is of no evidentiary value, so let's not waste the court's time.

That's one possible answer, but, as we shall see, there are reasons to doubt it is a complete one. More likely, it seems to me, is that the prosecutors didn't ask Bartholomew about the report because not even they believed its contents.

* * *

Because Bartholomew handed in a copy of the report Director Trollip had signed about the visit to the United States, and because Bodziak was not on the list of state's witnesses, the defence was within its rights to approach the American expert for his reaction to it. This they did, scanning it into a computer and emailing it to him on Friday 9 March. They received a reply the next day, and it was its opening line, so packed with astonishment that it lost its grammar, that made the headlines: 'Dear Mr De Bruyn,' Bodziak wrote, 'I am both shocked and amazed of how many lies are contained in that report.'

What kind of lies did Bodziak find in Trollip's report?

He wrote that he had not confirmed the match, because the photos of the bloody stain were 'not suitable for a proper examination.'

He wrote that, based on his own examination of the shoe, he felt that sand grains 'were not even in the same location as Supt Bartholomew was surmising.' More importantly, he was convinced that the sand was far too deep in the groove of the shoe to have left an impression on a two-dimensional surface.

He wrote that he did not tell Bartholomew that 'a test print would be of no value as the crime scene prints can never be repeated.' He added, 'This is the opposite of what I said. I advised that a test impression must be made.' Bartholomew, he wrote, was unwilling to allow a test impression to be made of the shoe 'because he was afraid it would damage the condition of the shoes and change the features, namely the three grains of sand he believed were important.' Absent a test impression from the shoe thought to have made the mark – something Bodziak's textbook makes clear is standard practice in this kind of work – he asked Bartholomew do a test impression with the other shoe. He did this in order 'to prove that material in the groove could not be part of the impression left on a hard surface. Bartholomew, he wrote, complied with his request, conducted the experiment and, when he saw the result, concurred with Bodziak's conclusion that the sand could not have affected the stain. Bartholomew, Bodziak wrote, 'did not appear happy with the results.'

Bodziak wrote that he had not been presented with a report written by experts for the defence so he could not have said that it was 'typical of someone who is unaware of the basic principles of footwear comparisons and who does not understand the process of shoeprint identification.' He also wrote that he and Bartholomew had never discussed who would be best suited to giving evidence in court, though Bodziak had emphasised that he would not be prepared to travel to South Africa to do so.

* * *

The high praise that Trollip had lavished on William J Bodziak's expertise in shoeprint impression evidence, when he'd applied for permission to send Bartholomew to visit him, was justified: Bodziak is, in fact, one of the world's leading exponents of that corner of forensic science. He has more than thirty-five years of experience in the field. He is the author of the standard textbook on the subject. And, to the extent that laypeople have any notion about the subject at all, it is probably because he spent a large portion of the mid-1990s testifying against OJ Simpson.

That was when he was based at the FBI's headquarters in Washington, DC. Bodziak's contribution to the (unsuccessful) prosecution of Simpson for murder and the (more successful) civil claim lodged by the families of Nicole Brown-Simpson and Ron Goldman was his demonstration that a set of bloodied shoeprints left at the crime scene (including on Nicole's back), had been made by an expensive model of size 12 shoes produced by Bruno Magli. He was also able to establish that these shoes had been worn by someone whose stride pattern suggested would have been a little more than six feet tall.

During the criminal investigation, the police never found the shoes in question and could not prove whether OJ had ever owned a pair. By the time the civil trial rolled around, photos had emerged of OJ – who happened to wear size 12 shoes and who was six foot two inches tall – wearing a pair of Bruno Maglis of the appropriate model. Because fewer than three hundred pairs of size 12s had ever been sold in the United States, and because OJ had denied ever owning such a pair, by simply identifying the class of the shoe worn by the murderer, Bodziak helped to persuade a jury to award $33 million in damages to the victims' families. It was a virtuoso performance, and it accounts for his status as one of the discipline's superstars.

That Bodziak was a superstar who was reluctant to travel to South Africa to testify in Fred's trial was no secret. Courtroom rumour had it that this reluctance had at least as much to do with a fear of travelling to Africa to testify against the authorities as it had with the reasons he actually gave for refusing to do international work: that he was concerned about disrupting his schedule and that it was not always easy to secure payment from clients based outside the United States. So afraid was he of Africa, or so the rumours had it, that one of his requests, during the negotiations that eventually secured his attendance at the trial, was that an official from the US embassy should meet him at the airport.

I have some doubts about this story, but I relate it because, until almost the very end of the trial, Bodziak had in fact insisted again and again that he would never be persuaded to come to Cape Town. Six months into the trial, however, he changed his mind and made himself available to the defence. This was partly because they were prepared to meet a hefty fee for his time – $20,000 and a first-class ticket from Florida. It also had to do, as he told me later, with the fear that damage might be done to his own reputation if Bartholomew's account of what had transpired during their consultation was allowed to go unchallenged.

Whatever his reasons, Bodziak did come to Cape Town at the end of August 2007. And he did testify. And what he said, in a quiet, almost extravagantly fastidious way, was devastating to Bartholomew's evidence.

He agreed that he met Bartholomew in Florida in June 2006, but he denied that he had offered any support whatsoever to the policeman's view that the bloody stain had been caused by Fred's right shoe. The fact was, he said, that Bartholomew had presented him with almost nothing on which to base an opinion because all but one of the images on a CD full of photos that Bartholomew had brought with him refused to open. But even with only that image, together with hard copies of some crime scene photographs and the actual shoes (which the policeman had brought with him), he was persuaded that Bartholomew's identification was spurious. There was, he said, no way that the sand grains could ever make contact with a two-dimensional surface such as a ceramic tile: the rubber was far too hard and the sand was far too deep in the groove.

He said he thought he'd persuaded Bartholomew of this when he had the South African put on the left shoe and stamp on a piece of equipment custom-made for the purpose of testing what impressions the sole of a shoe would leave. He said that the resulting image (*see* PLATE 10) showed that the area in which the sand grains were lodged on the right shoe could not be made to touch the floor and could not, therefore, be responsible for the four white spots.

Bodziak went on. Having now had the opportunity to study all the available evidence, he said that he was completely convinced that 'this shoe could not have made that mark.'

Not only were the grains of sand not able to touch the tile, he said, but the whole exercise of matching the white spots to the sand was flawed. There were, he said, a great many grains of sand in the groove of the shoe (*see* PLATE 11), so it was no surprise that four of them could be made to line up with four white spots found in the chemically enhanced bloodstain. It was, he said, particularly unsurprising that sand could be made to line up with the spots because, in the absence of any corresponding class characteristics between shoe and stain that might anchor a transparent overlay placed on the sole of the shoe, it was possible to keep adjusting that overlay until the examiner found the matches he was looking for.

Another reason Bodziak offered for thinking that the match was illegitimate was that the white spots were present only in the chemically-enhanced stain and could not be seen in the original mark. He said he thought it very likely that the spots were caused by the wiping away of excess Amido Black – an essential step in the application procedure. He said that because the tile had tiny bumps and imperfections, and because it was difficult to fix relatively thick blood sufficiently securely to the floor before applying Amido Black, it was likely that the spots were simply the result of excess fluid being wiped off tiny 'peaks' in the grain of the tile (*see* PLATE 12).

Apart from the illegitimacy of trying to line up spots and sand, Bodziak's most frequently repeated concern was the complete absence of any sign in the stain – whether enhanced or unenhanced – of any of the obvious class characteristics of the outsole of Fred's shoe. That meant that Bartholomew could not prove that the stain had been left by a Hi-Tec shoe. Or, indeed, by any shoe at all.

*   *   *

When it was her turn to cross-examine Bodziak, Teunissen made little headway. She began by noting that she'd spoken to Bartholomew, who had told her that he would stick to his version of what happened in Florida. She then tried to challenge Bodziak on the merits of his examination by offering a series of hypothetical suggestions about what might have occurred: perhaps the blood had not been acquired by the shoe in the lounge, but while Fred cleaned up in the bathroom and that this explained why there were no bloody stains between the lounge and the bathroom; perhaps there was no evidence of some of the obvious design elements in the shoe because the blood had begun to congeal before it came into contact with the shoe; perhaps the fluid used to conduct the test impression with the left shoe was thinner than blood and did not, therefore, attach itself to the shoe in the same way.

Bodziak conceded nothing to her speculations and hypotheticals – one of which she introduced with the self-defeating phrase, 'I'm just asking, but …' A more or less typical reply to these questions would begin, 'This doesn't correspond at all in any respect, so I disagree with your theory', or 'Oh, that's even further off', or 'Well, I disagree that it was made by a shoe to begin with, but under the hypothesis that you're giving …'

It was not pretty. But Teunissen can console herself, at least, with the thought that she is not the first to find herself struggling to unpick Bodziak's testimony. During the OJ Simpson trial, that job fell to F Lee Bailey, one of America's most prominent and controversial defence lawyers and a member of OJ's all-star legal team. So poorly did Bailey fare, however, that Johnnie Cochran, the leader of OJ's defence, instructed him to rein himself in. 'You're trying to show how smart you are,' he scolded, 'and all you're doing is showing how smart *he* is.'

*　*　*

Bodziak's testimony about the shoeprint was compelling stuff, but the most astounding testimony he offered had nothing to do with the stain or the shoe or Bartholomew's account of what happened during their consultation in June 2006. More astounding than all of that was his evidence that on 15 January 2007 – a month before the start of the trial – he had had a telephone conference with Advocate Christénus van der Vijver, Advocate Carien Teunissen and a number of other people, not all of whom he could identify, and that during that teleconference he told them that he had disagreed with Bartholomew. He also testified that after the call, he had faxed all his notes about Bartholomew's visit to Advocate van der Vijver, notes now read into the record that set out all the difficulties he'd had with Bartholomew's work when they'd discussed it in June 2006.

The prosecutors knew, in other words, that Bodziak disagreed with what Bartholomew's testimony about the consultation would be, and that Bodziak would say that the contents of the report signed by Director Trollip were almost exactly the opposite of what had actually happened. Rather than any fastidiously ethical lawyering, I think this is the real reason that they asked no questions about the consultation in Florida and the resulting report.

In the interests of fairness, one must be careful about precisely what is at stake here. Christénus van der Vijver, for example, took great offence at media reports about Bodziak's testimony, which, he said, had done him a great injustice. Asking the judge for permission to address him at the start of the following court day, he noted that a report in that morning's *Die Burger* had 'created the impression that the state in general, and me in particular, withheld information from the defence.' This simply wasn't true, he said. The defence, he said, had had access to Bodziak throughout 2006 and had, in fact, emailed him about the case. The defence also knew that Bodziak and the prosecutors were to hold a telephone conference on 15 January 2007. To prove this, he read out portions of a number of letters he'd received from Fred's lawyers in which their knowledge of this phone call was made clear. To say, then, that he or his colleague had withheld information, 'is not in accordance with the facts' and that the claim that Bodziak's differences with Bartholomew had first became known to the defence only when Bodziak set foot in South Africa was also 'devoid of all truth.'

Concluding with what some might see as a touch of self-righteousness, Van der Vijver said that his integrity had been impugned. 'How,' he asked the court reporters to consider, 'would my grey-haired mother feel if she read this story this morning?'

Well, in the interests of avoiding any further upset to Mrs van der Vijver snr, let it be recorded that it is, indeed, true that the defence was aware that Bodziak's account of the consultation with Bartholomew differed from the policeman's well before Bodziak arrived in South Africa. Mrs van der Vijver snr can also rest easy in the knowledge that her son and his colleague, Advocate Teunissen, did not lead Bartholomew through the evidence about his trip to Florida in the knowledge that Bodziak would dispute almost every word of it. In fact, they didn't raise it at all: the whole question of Bartholomew's travels arose only when De Bruyn brought it up during cross-examination. Mrs van der Vijver snr, then, can rest easy that neither her son nor Advocate Teunissen led a witness through testimony they might have had good reason to think would be untrue.

Unfortunately, however, that doesn't completely exhaust all the questions Mrs van der Vijver snr might want to think about. She might, in particular, want to think about this: since the prosecutors knew that the email that began 'I am both shocked and amazed of how many lies' accurately reflected what Bodziak would say if he were to testify, and since they believed, at the time that De Bruyn confronted Bartholomew with it, that Bodziak was not going to testify, Mrs van der Vijver snr might want to ask whether it was right that the prosecutors' first instinct was to try to persuade the judge that Bodziak's email was inadmissible hearsay. Mrs van der Vijver snr might want to know why it was that, even after the judge had said that he would provisionally allow Bodziak's email to be read into the record, Advocate Teunissen said that, in the absence of Bodziak's *viva voce* testimony, the judge and the defence would have to accept whatever response Bartholomew offered, and that the text of the email would then have to be struck from the record.

Since they knew from having spoken to him that the email accurately reflected the testimony Bodziak would offer if he were in court, and since a young man's liberty was at stake, Mrs van der Vijver snr might want to ask herself whether these efforts to keep the email out of the record were in the interests of justice.

Finally, Mrs van der Vijver snr might also want to ask herself why, when Carien Teunissen made this point about the likely need to strike the email from the record, standing as she always did right next to Mr van der Vijver jnr, she also felt it necessary to say that, 'when the state was still in a position to contact Mr Bodziak – when Mr Bartholomew was sent there – he gave a clear indication that, as a result of his busy schedule, he would not travel to South Africa'?

Wouldn't it have been fairer – to say nothing of its being more accurate – to point out that the last time the state had been in contact with Bodziak was not in June 2006, when Bartholomew visited Florida, but in January 2007, and that she and Advocate van der Vijver had been part of that conversation?

Of course, if she had said that, the judge, whose interventions and questions were not always easy to anticipate, might have asked something about the content of that conversation and whether they had not considered calling the American themselves. Even if that question had come in the privacy of his chambers, it would not have been an easy one for the prosecutors to answer.

26

As a child, I attended the same synagogue as Percy Yutar, the chief prosecutor during the Rivonia Trial, in which Nelson Mandela and nine others were charged with, and eventually convicted of, high treason. For liberal Jews, Yutar was something of an embarrassment. He was a man, I was given to understand, who had come to the conclusion that Jews in the Diaspora had to be seen as dependable friends of power, and who, in giving expression to this view by becoming a prosecutor for the apartheid state, had abandoned essential elements of Jewish morality. It was a Faustian bargain that was understood to verge on the wicked, yet for many Jews in the second half of the twentieth century the logic of choice was also not without its attractions.

The Yutar I saw greeting his friends in *shul* as a child, then, was a figure of some complexity and ambivalence: a religious man, and therefore (so

I thought) a moral one, he had committed his professional life to ensuring that the apartheid government would not turn on Jews in the same way it had turned on almost everyone else. In the process, he had chosen to sacrifice some of his soul for the greater good of his people. It was only later, when I read the thoroughly absorbing account of the Rivonia Trial by Joel Joffe – another Jewish lawyer, but this one who worked for Mandela's defence – that I realised that the Yutar of my youthful imagination had almost nothing to do with the Yutar who appeared in the Pretoria High Court in 1964. That Yutar, the empirical Yutar, was a small-minded, ill-prepared and irredeemably stupid prosecutor who was quite happy to parade a series of unimpressive, sometimes woefully dishonest, witnesses before the judge. That Mandela and his comrades had been convicted, it turned out, owed nothing to Yutar's marshalling of the evidence and everything to the fact that the accused admitted the essential charges – they were, indeed, working to overthrow the apartheid state.

It would be unfair to say that old habits die hard, or that all of the witnesses the prosecutors presented in Fred's trial were as unimpressive as Yutar's, but, in truth, that's almost exactly what happened.

* * *

By the time he testified in Fred's trial, Frans Maritz, formerly a captain working in the ballistics section of the Forensic Science Laboratory in Cape Town, was plying his trade for the state police in South Dakota. And he must have been doing well there, because, as he happily told the judge, just the day before he took the stand, he'd received a call from his employers telling him he was to be promoted to assistant director of the laboratory.

Maritz was a thin man with long, slender hands and a skin so pale as to be translucent. His hair was dark and framed a face whose most memorable characteristic were the sunken hollows out of which his eyes peered at the world with something approaching vulnerability. It was a face that had not seen the sun as much as it should have, and, perhaps because his frame did not quite fill his suit and his ears stood proudly from the sides of his head, the image that came to mind was of a scurry-clawed creature newly extracted from its warren.

It was an unfortunate image, and it was belied, in part, by the peculiar grace with which Maritz wielded Fred's hammer as he testified about the similarities he'd found between its shape and size and those of the injuries Inge had sustained. A gawky, unathletic man, Maritz's handling of the hammer was precise and sure, possessed of an elegance that was almost balletic. There was something almost reverential about his gestures, as if he were a member of some obscure religious order and had been trained to view the precise handling of objects such as this as a kind of sacrament. His dexterity lent a nonverbal credibility to his evidence, conferring on it an unspoken guarantee of expertise.

More a novelty item than woodworking tool, Fred's hammer had a bottle-opener where a carpenter would expect to find a claw-grip with which to remove nails. The hammer was 28cm long and weighed only 330g but, because it was top-heavy, it felt heavier and more lethal than its weight alone would suggest (*see* PLATE 13). It had been a Christmas gift from Inge's family, who had had the legend FRED 2004 engraved on the shaft, and Fred had claimed to have forgotten all about it after he put it under his car seat more than two months before the murder.

However beautiful his handling of the hammer, that Maritz was testifying about it at all spoke to a gap in the state's case against Fred that, depending on whom one asks, may or may not be thought to be important. This was that, despite the pathologist's suggestion to the police who attended the autopsy that they look for a hammer, and despite their finding the hammer in Fred's car, the police had had some trouble tying it to the crime. In the twenty-first century, that kind of connection would normally be made by finding traces of blood or other genetic material on the hammer and then showing that those came from the victim. This the police had been unable to do.

It is true that Sergeant Peta Davidtz, a forensic examiner at the police laboratories, had testified to having found invisible traces of blood on the hammer when she sprayed the hammer with Luminol, a chemical compound that produces a cold, bluish light when it comes into contact with the iron in haemoglobin. One of the difficulties with a Luminol test, however, is that it reacts with a reasonably wide range of substances, including bleach, paint and some furniture polishes. For this reason, it is not used as a definitive test for blood. Still, Davidtz had testified that the colour, duration and intensity of the light she'd seen in her darkened laboratory were of the kind she would associate with a reaction with blood rather than with any other substance, and that she was reasonably confident the reaction she'd seen had been caused by blood.

The problem that confronted the police and the prosecutors with this evidence is that, having found traces of something that might have been blood, Davidtz sent the hammer to another scientist elsewhere in the laboratory to see if she could extract enough DNA to prove that the blood – if it was blood – was Inge's. And, indeed, that scientist – Dr Sharlene Otto – did find DNA. Unfortunately, it was male DNA, and, although it wasn't profiled thoroughly, the one segment of the chromosome that was tested proved to be identical to Fred's. Whether or not the DNA was Fred's, simply because it came from a man, it could not have been Inge's.

In the absence of a genetic match with which to link the hammer to the crime scene, Bartholomew had approached Maritz, whose career as a ballistics expert had included training in the individualisation of tools and toolmarks. The forensic application of this skill-test is premised on the observation that if a surface is struck by an object that is harder than itself, it is sometimes possible to use the resulting mark to identify the object that left it. Maritz's job, then, was to test whether the hammer could be matched to the wounds on Inge's head and face through a close examination of the shape and dimensions of the wounds themselves.

* * *

Maritz testified that he received Fred's hammer on 17 May 2005, a little more than a month after it had been found, and a week after the unsuccessful test for Inge's DNA. Two days later, on 19 May 2005, he and some colleagues went to an abattoir to try to produce a set of test impressions of the kinds of marks that the hammer might leave if either its round striking surface or its bottle-opener were slammed into a human head. They did this by using the hammer in a series of assaults on the decapitated heads of recently slaughtered pigs and sheep. Maritz also testified that he repeated these tests on 2 June, this time using only sheep heads. Between 19 May and 2 June, he had also tested the hammer on a lead plate (curved to reproduce the shape of the skull) and on a clay model of a human ear.

Depending on one's point of view, the testing of the hammer by smashing it into animal carcasses might seem either farcical or grotesque, but the logic, as Maritz explained it, seemed reasonable enough. 'To reproduce a toolmark,' he told the judge, 'one must use a material as close as possible to the material in question, and the flesh of sheep and pigs is closest to human flesh.'

Whether using the animals, the lead plate or the potter's clay, however, the basic purpose was the same: to identify the characteristics – in particular, their size and shape – of the marks left by the striking surface of the hammer and the bottle-opener. In this Maritz claimed some success: allowing some tolerance for the vagaries of the amount of force used and the angle at which contact was made between hammer and head, the impressions left on the animals' heads by Fred's hammer were similar to those Maritz saw in the pictures Bartholomew had taken of Inge's body during the autopsy. This meant that he could conclude his report by saying that 'the most prominent blows to the back of the head, the right side of the head, the left side of the head, as well as behind the ear, are compatible with the dimensions and profile of both usable sides of the hammer, as well as with the class characteristics of the toolmarks left by the hammer on various other test media.'

These were the broad outlines of Maritz's findings, and, in order to convince the judge of them, he took the court through a process of comparing some of the individual wounds on Inge's head and face to the marks Fred's hammer had made on the animal heads. Referring to a bean-shaped wound to Inge's head, for instance, he showed a wound of a similar shape photographed on one of the sheep heads. He did the same with many of Inge's other wounds: whether it was circular or semicircular, linear or curvilinear, each seemed similar to a mark he'd made on one or other of the carcasses.

There were, he admitted, some injuries that Maritz could not attribute conclusively to one or other end of the hammer. One of those was on Inge's forehead. This, he said, may have been created by two separate blows, one with each side of the hammer. Another was a wound behind Inge's ear. About this one, Maritz acknowledged a mistake in his report where, thinking that two photos depicted two different wounds when in fact they were of the same wound, he'd mistakenly attributed it first to the striking surface of the hammer and later to the bottle-opener. He asked the judge to ignore that second opinion.

One wound about which Maritz was certain, however, was perhaps the most devastating of the blows that had rained down on Inge as she lay on the couch. It is a broad, deep wound to her forehead, the force of which was so great as to crush the bone and penetrate into the brain. In describing how the hammer might have caused this wound, Maritz produced a series of photographs of a sheep's skull so badly crushed by blows from the hammer that brain matter is revealed. So gruesome was Inge's injury that one of these images shows the bottle-opener end of the hammer buried almost to the shaft into the sheep's skull. It was the result, he said, of a single blow.

Having completed the comparison of photographs of Inge's injuries to photographs of the damage done to the carcasses, Maritz moved on to a more direct comparison of the hammer and Inge's injuries.

Asking the judge to overlay a transparency of the hammer on a set of

1:1 pictures of Inge's wounds, he tried to demonstrate how close a fit he'd found between Inge's wounds, on the one hand, and the size and shape of one or other end of the hammer, on the other. In pretty much every case, the dimensions of that part of the hammer Maritz said had caused the injury were not exactly the same as those of the wound. Maritz insisted, however, that the lack of precise correspondence was not that surprising: with blunt-force injuries, he said, the wound will often be slightly larger than the implement used because it will have struck the flesh at an angle, causing the skin to stretch around the underlying bones. In other cases, however, the elasticity of the skin could mean that it will stretch, tear and then return to its original position, making the resulting wound look smaller than the object that had caused it. This, he said, was something that often happens with bullet wounds. The small differences in size between the wounds as depicted in the photos Bartholomew took at the autopsy and the head or bottle-opener of the hammer were, Maritz insisted, much less important than the similarities of size in shape.

Maritz's bottom line, then, was that the class characteristics of both sides of the hammer's head were reproducible on more that one test medium (lead, clay and carcass), and, more importantly, that the appearance of these test impressions, in shape and dimension, was very similar to the actual injuries Inge had sustained. In his report, he put it this way: '[Fred's hammer] or one like it appears to have caused the head wounds.'

* * *

By now the pattern of the trial will be familiar, with Maritz taking his turn to embrace the role of the hapless witness defending the indefensible as his evidence crumbles around his feet. And, as with other witnesses, the deficiencies that emerge with Maritz's testimony are not just a question of the substance of his evidence; they reflect also on the honesty and competence with which he approached his task. One example of this arises almost immediately that De Bruyn begins.

After reminding Maritz of his mistaken attribution of a single wound, first to the striking surface of the hammer and second to the bottle-opener, a mistake Maritz had acknowledged on the stand, De Bruyn points out that the problem is that the photos Maritz had used for his examination were not taken with a great deal of care.

Maritz kicks this question for touch, claiming that because he didn't take the photos himself, he cannot answer questions about their quality. De Bruyn then asks Maritz to confirm that a particular injury to Inge's head was, in his opinion, caused by the round striking surface of the hammer. Then, noting that that surface is 21.7mm across, he asks Maritz to measure the wound as it appears in the photo that he'd used to attribute it to the hammer. Maritz hums and hahs a little, but eventually measures the wound at just over 17mm across. Even adding the bruising that extends beyond the open wound, the wound still appears to be only 21mm across, slightly smaller than the hammerhead.

> Q: Would you say that that is the correct measurement to compare with the hammer?
>
> A: In my opinion, it is comparable. Taking into account the elasticity of the flesh and its natural tendency to return to its original position.
>
> Q: Here's the problem: the photo was taken at an angle, not so?
>
> A: M'Lord, it would appear as if there is a reasonable angle to the photo. But, as I said, I cannot comment on this because I did not take it.
>
> Q: But, sir, you don't have to be an expert to see that that photo was taken at an angle. Something closer to 45 degrees rather than 90 degrees.
>
> A: I can't express …
>
> Q: You *don't want* to express.
>
> A: It would appear as if there is a reasonable angle.

Q: It's not just that there is a 'reasonable angle'. We can take Dr Adendorff's measurements, which she took of the wounds at the autopsy. You said that you used that measurement, not so?

A: That is correct.

Q: Okay, good. Dr Adendorff's measurement for that wound is 30mm.

A: That is correct. That is how it is recorded in the autopsy report. But I am not aware of what instrument Dr Adendorff used to make these measurements.

Q: But you consulted with Dr Adendorff?

A: That is correct.

Q: All I am saying to you is that, compared to Dr Adendorff's measurements, the photograph is completely unsatisfactory.

A: Not if Dr Adendorff took her measurements incorrectly. I can't comment about that.

Q: The doctor might have taken the measurements incorrectly?

A: It's a possibility. I can't testify about that.

Q: And if her measurements are correct? Then your exercise is not correct?

A: M'Lord, if we look at the photos, you can see an ordinary ruler. That is not a precise instrument.

Q: No, no, no. Answer my question. If Dr Adendorff – who we heard is a doctor with a lot of experience – if her measurements are correct, do you concede that the whole exercise with the photos and the transparencies is not scientific?

A: No. I do not concede that.

Q: You don't concede?

A: It was identifiable.

Q: No, no, no. M'Lord, I don't know … We have
   measurements in the autopsy report that this witness
   says he used and they disagree with the distances on his
   photos by fifty to sixty percent. You don't concede that?

A: I don't concede.

Q: It's not possible that the measurements that you're
   working with are from a photo taken at an angle and
   are not the same size as the wound.

A: The information I received was that the photos were
   life-size.

Q: Sir, life-size is not the point here. You know that as a
   scientist. It is the angle that is misleading. You cannot
   see the correct size on these photos from this angle.

A: The angle could be misleading. As I said, I can't express
   myself about the photos.

It's an eye-rolling exchange, and it is repeated moments later when De
Bruyn takes Maritz through the differences between his measurements
of the wound in another photograph (which are 19mm and 27mm, depending on whether the bruising is included) and the 35mm measured
by Dr Adendorff. Once again, Maritz refuses to concede that his approach is flawed. This time, however, he offers a different answer about
how the hammerhead, which is 21mm, might have created a wound that
measures 35mm, saying that all the textbooks he consulted said that the
wound could be bigger than the surface of the weapon.

De Bruyn presses Maritz on the evident mismatch in size between Inge's
wounds and the alleged weapon. 'A line must be drawn somewhere,' he
says. 'Some tolerance must be allowed. But it stops somewhere, not so?'

'Nowhere have I seen any reference to a specific tolerance,' Maritz
says.

It's an awful answer, because, as De Bruyn quickly points out, in one
of the peer-reviewed journal articles Maritz had himself submitted the

previous day in support of his contention that forensic science was able to identify weapons from the marks left on the bodies of victims, the defence had found the following statement: 'a match was made [between abrasions and the weapon that caused them] with projections lining up with the abraded area to a 1mm tolerance.'

'M'Lord,' Maritz says, 'I didn't write this article myself. I was in no way involved in that investigation and testing. I can't say that that is an acceptable tolerance, that that is generally accepted in the scientific community.'

This is how it proceeds for the best part of two days, and, perhaps because Maritz proves so unwilling to concede even the obvious – to refuse, almost, to *see* the obvious – De Bruyn humiliates him towards the end of his third day on the stand. Asking Maritz to take out his digital callipers, the lawyer presents him with the photographs Bartholomew had taken of Inge's wounds and over which Maritz had laid his transparencies of the hammer to show the judge how well it fit Inge's injuries. In each of these photos, Bartholomew had placed a short, black and white ruler in order to show they were life-size. Because the photos were taken at all sorts of angles, however, there is rather more foreshortening and distortion than there should have been.

> Q: As I understand it, to establish if a photograph is one-to-one, one must take the ruler and measure it with callipers to see if you get the distances that you are supposed to get. Is that correct?
>
> A: That is correct.
>
> Q: Thank you. If you look at that photo and use your callipers to measure the distance between 200mm and 250mm on the ruler, instead of getting 50mm, we get 48mm.
>
> A: 48.3, M'Lord.
>
> Q: Thank you. Staying with that photo, if you measure the ruler between 250mm and 300mm, we get 45mm instead of 50mm.

A: 45.39, M'Lord.

Q: Yes. In other words, that portion of the photo is not one-to-one.

A: That is correct. I have already conceded that the photos don't appear correct.

Q: Thank you, Mr Maritz, that makes it easier and saves time.

*   *   *

Maritz was a man desperate to project himself as a detached, disinterested and unsentimental scientist. There was his insistence on referring to Inge's injuries as 'toolmarks' rather than 'wounds', a technical word that called a certain amount of attention to itself. There was the quiet pleasure he took in measuring weights and distances to two decimal points. There was the extravagant way in which he corrected his own written statement, which, having been written before he attended courses offered by the more pedantic bureaucracies for which he now works in the United States, made the mistake of referring to 'digital photographs'. The phrase he should have used, he testifies, was 'digital images'. There was the rather gratuitous use of the word 'trigonometrical' in his description of the much more mechanical task of measuring the grains of sand in Fred's shoe, a process that requires absolutely no trigonometry. His claims to being detached and disinterested and unsentimental were dealt a cruel blow by a photograph he'd included in his sworn statement, however. Making matters worse, it was a photograph that he had taken himself, and about which he could not claim to have been misled by Bartholomew's assurances as to its being life-sized. The image in question was the one of a sheep's head into which the hammer's head had been buried, bottle-opener first, almost to the shaft (*see* PLATE 14). Such was the violence and the cruelty of the assault on Inge that that image was intended to show that Fred's hammer was capable of smashing through Inge's forehead and into her brain, as indeed some object had been.

The photo was taken during the second set of tests on animal carcasses on 2 June 2005, tests that, Maritz's statement says, were conducted using a 'Bar hammer with the inscription FRED 2004 on the shaft.'

On the stand he confirms this. 'Your statement,' De Bruyn says, 'refers to marks made by the bottle-opener side and that it was tested on the skull of a sheep.'

A: That is correct.

Q: A photo of one of those tests referred to is shown in your statement. It shows the bottle-opener driven into the sheep's skull. Correct?

A: That is correct, M'Lord. The photo is to illustrate that the bottle-opener part is capable of being driven through the skin and skull.

Q: And that is Exhibit Two? The hammer before this court?

A: That is correct.

That is, in fact, not correct.

In fact, Maritz had used another hammer during the second set of tests on 2 June.

In fact, the first hammer – Fred's hammer – bent and almost broke when the bottle-opener end had been struck against a pig's skull.

We know this not because Maritz volunteers the information in his statement or during his testimony, as a more detached and disinterested and unsentimental scientist might have been expected to do, but because a video taken of the tests on 19 May shows that when the bottle-opener was slammed into the forehead of a pig for the first time, it had bent and almost broken. On the video, Captain Bester's long 'ooooh' of disappointment can be heard. Simultaneously, the hands holding the pig's ears to lock the head in position, hands that belonged to Captain Maritz, sag visibly.

Showing the video in court (which the prosecution, unsurprisingly, had failed to do), De Bruyn echoes Bester's 'ooooh' with the perfect timing of a comedian. Then, in mock puzzlement, he says, 'And now this dangerous weapon bends with the first blow.'

'That is correct, M'Lord,' Maritz replies, unfazed and unflustered.

Maritz, as was his custom, refused to concede immediately that the hammer buried in the sheep's head was not Fred's, as he'd insisted it was in his statement and on the stand. Instead, he tells a long tale about the efforts to which he'd gone to find a second hammer. Then, claiming that both hammers had been used during the second set of tests on 2 June, he says that he simply can't remember which had been used in this particular picture.

It may have been easier to believe that Maritz had used Fred's hammer during the second set of experiments on 2 June, risking breaking it, if that hammer appeared in any of the photos taken that day. It would also have been easier to believe if the picture that Maritz had included in his report had not been cropped in such a way as to make it impossible to see the portion of the shaft on which FRED 2004 would have appeared had that really been his hammer that was used.

But if detached-and-disinterested Maritz didn't volunteer that the original hammer bent, how did the defence find out that it had? Well, they'd seen it on the video. And, like the tell-tale photos of the nodule before the application of Amido Black, that video had been handed to them only in April 2006, when it had been saved on the hard drive given to the defence. The same hard drive that managed to get itself stolen only a few hours later.

Until that point, no-one had even suggested that such a video existed, much less that the hammer had bent under testing.

PART SEVEN

27

For many of those who followed Fred's trial, its real interest didn't lie in the intricacies of the conflicting testimony about shoeprints and DVD boxes and ornamental hammers, but in a series of questions which, they would complain, went unasked. Writing about the trial in the women's monthly, *Marie Claire*, five months after Fred's acquittal, for example, one of the country's most experienced journalists would complain that 'much of the evidence was varnished with a layer of respectability,' and that, 'issues of sex, repression, guilt and jealousy were never fully examined.' This complaint, offered under the headline WHO KILLED INGE LOTZ?, would be followed by an example of the kind of detail whose omission from the trial the journalist, Lin Sampson, regarded as most indicative of this exaggerated sensitivity to questions of respectability. 'It was never made clear,' she wrote, 'whether Inge was a virgin or not.'

Nor was it only after the trial that this complaint, of details having been withheld, would be aired in public. Writing in the middle of the trial in an English-language Sunday paper whose readers would not have been as familiar with the case as were readers of the Afrikaans press, Janet Smith would compare Fred's trial with two other recent *causes célèbres*. 'Like the other cases,' Smith wrote in August 2007, 'his has become extraordinary for its grotesque but intoxicating combination of attractive characters, sexual mystery and, as happened with Rodrigues, a main protagonist who will not testify.' Since the 'Rodrigues' in question was Dina Rodrigues, a woman who'd just been convicted of hiring killers to stab to death the baby daughter of the man with whom she'd been having an affair, Smith's reference to her lent a certain piquancy to her comment that Fred's trial was playing out 'under the shadow of unrequited love'.

This interest in questions that went unasked, and the underlying conviction that there was more to Fred's story than met the eye, is interesting in a number of ways. Not the least of these points of interest is the apparent eagerness with which some embraced a construction of Fred's case as being about issues of love and fidelity, of sex and violence, issues that seemed a good deal more vaporous than the technical questions raised by the application of the forensic sciences. Vaporous though these issues were, they had framed coverage of the investigation from the very start, when the common wisdom had quickly condensed that this was a crime committed by someone close to Inge.

Nor were issues of sex and fidelity the only vaporous questions that seemed to matter to the coverage of the trial, with questions of culture and religion also managing to find their way into Sampson's article in *Marie Claire*. Both Fred and Inge, she wrote, came from 'close, religious families and Afrikaans backgrounds where a veneer of respectability counted.' The murder, she wrote, had been committed in the 'cosseted Afrikaans community of Stellenbosch.' Fred's father, she wrote, was 'dominating and indomitable', adding that the best word to use to describe Fred's family was 'control'.

It was hard not to read these stories and think that there was a template here, a pre-existing, predetermined story-line which Sampson and Smith seemed to feel would have made for a more interesting trial. Inge, so this story-line seemed to insist, had been killed by someone who had loved her and who may or may not have been her brilliant boyfriend, a boyfriend whose psyche may or may not have been fractured by an overly severe father.

This is the story that developed in the months after the murder, and it was a story that had been reinforced by evidence that emerged throughout the trial, some of it in a kind of code.

There had been, for example, the evidence of a police forensic psychologist, Dr Gerard Labuschagne, who testified that the fact that nothing had been stolen and that Inge had not been not raped, together with the ghastliness of the crime itself, meant that this was a murder he would classify as 'psychologically motivated'. The extent of the violence deployed by Inge's killer (he called it 'overkill') and the 'depersonalising' assault to her face suggested to him that she had been killed by someone who felt a rage that was directed at Inge herself.

Labuschagne had also conducted a 'psychological content analysis' of Inge's letter in order to try to understand her state of mind when she wrote it. The letter, he testified, suggested that Inge was seeking to placate Fred after a serious fight. That fight, he said, could have had something to do with Fred's suspicions about her faithfulness, since Inge had addressed this explicitly. Fred's suspicions, he implied, might have been justified because Inge may have crossed out the promise not to betray Fred precisely because she had wanted to avoid seeming hypocritical. For Labuschagne, then, it was possible that Fred's doubts about Inge's fidelity were a possible motive for the crime.

If the sense that Inge had been murdered by someone who loved her could draw some of its strength from an interpretation of the crime scene and the letter, there was also evidence that the social set within which Fred and Inge moved was shaped by dynamics that might strike the casual observer as a little close and overheated.

There was evidence, for example, that Inge inspired interest in many of the men with whom she and Fred were friends. Her best friend, Wimpie Boschoff, testified that Marius Botha, who was Fred's flatmate, had been so in love with Inge when they first met at university that he had, on occasion, written her poems. Wimpie also said that Jean Minnaar, to whose flat Fred had delivered the cupboard on the evening of the murder, had been in love with Inge. Finally, he also testified that Jean's flatmate, Braam Kruger, had dated Inge.

There was evidence, too, that issues of sex and sexuality had been treated with peculiar, almost neurotic, circumspection in Inge's relationship with Fred. Superintendent de Beer, for example, had testified that when he interviewed Fred on the morning after the murder, Fred had cried only when the policeman had refused to say whether Inge had been raped. De Beer had also testified that when he asked Fred if he and Inge had had 'relations' the night before she died, Fred had said they hadn't and that, to the best of his knowledge, she had never had relations with any man.

How the issue of whether or not Fred and Inge had sex related to the overheated dynamics of their social circle was a question raised by another intriguing fragment, this one coming from a sworn statement made by Marius Botha. In it, he related how he had come home unexpectedly on a Saturday night a few weeks before Inge's death, and that when he entered the flat he found Fred and Inge under a duvet watching TV. Realising that they wanted some privacy, he'd left to visit Jean Minnaar before coming home some time later. Inge, he wrote in his statement, spent the night with Fred, and, after her departure the following morning, he'd asked Fred about the relationship. Fred told him that all was well. The next sentence in Marius's statement strikes an odd note however: 'I asked him if he and Inge were still pure in their relationship. He confirmed they were.'

If the reference to sex as a matter of one's purity would seem curious to many, equally curious was Marius's presumption that this was the kind of question he could ask, as well as Fred's apparent willingness to answer it. It was not hard to think that all of this could be explained by a set of shared religious beliefs, since Marius was also a member of His People Church.

It was also possible to read Marius's questioning of Fred in another way: as a marker of an interest in matters of an exquisitely personal nature that might verge on the unhealthy. And that reading, in turn, seemed to be reinforced by Marius's acknowledgement in the same affidavit that it was in notes that he had written in which had been found the request for God's forgiveness for a 'curse' that had been uttered about Fred and Inge's relationship. It was from those notes, whose author had been left un-named at the time, that *Rapport* had quoted six weeks after the murder, under the headline MURDERED STUDENT WAS 'CURSED': POLICE TARGET LOTZ'S FRIENDS, and which had gone on to relate how the notes spoke about their author's insecurities and his fear that his family was cursed.

On the stand, Marius had gone some way to defuse the interpretation that *Rapport* had offered, saying that the 'curse' for which he had asked God's forgiveness related less to a 'direct' curse than to the sin of gossip. It was a sin he had spent some time considering during the early weeks of 2005 at a weekend church seminar that was, he said, 'focused on physical and emotional healing for Christians.' His notes, he said, were 'a confession before God and a plea for forgiveness. It was in no way a direct curse on Fred and Inge.'

Fragmentary though all of this was, the fragments did not seem to ad-mit of a neutral interpretation. Instead they seemed to hint at a broader pattern, not quite visible, out of which might be created a story whose plausibility was premised on its familiarity: an excessively religious up-bringing in a conservative community, an oppressive father, a tendency to violence. That the familiarity of this story owed more to its mirroring of the back story of a substantial number of the homicidal maniacs de-picted in popular fiction since Alfred Hitchcock's *Psycho*, did not seem fundamentally to affect its perceived credibility.

A startling example of the power of that template to shape how one saw and understood what was going on in court was on display towards the end of the trial, on the second morning of Fred's testimony.

That day, I was sitting next to a radio journalist whose first day in court had been the day before. At the first break in the proceedings that morning, as the court rose to bow to the judge, I asked about her impressions of Fred. 'He seems really clever,' she said. 'But he comes across a bit cold and unemotional.'

I was a bit surprised at this because Fred had broken down not too long before, crying in the witness stand as he was led through evidence about the series of SMSs he and Inge had exchanged on the morning and afternoon of her death. 'Except when he cried,' I suggested.

'Oh,' the journalist replied. 'Did he cry?'

'Yes,' I assured her. 'The judge told him he should have a drink of water.'

'Is that what happened?' she said, voice rising in surprise. 'I hadn't noticed.'

28

Part of the art of the trial lawyer is to construct a plausible story from the slivers and fragments of evidence presented in court. If you are the prosecutor in a criminal trial, the story you are expected to construct must be so compelling that the judge must have no reasonable doubt that it is the truth. If you are a defence attorney, by contrast, all you need show is that your client's protestations of innocence are reasonably possibly true. It is an asymmetrical conflict, and the asymmetry is intended to protect the innocent from false charges laid by institutions whose resources far outweigh those available to any individual.

The story that the prosecution had sought to construct in Fred's trial was that he had been enraged by something Inge had done or something he suspected she had done, and that he had bludgeoned her to death on the afternoon of 16 March using an ornamental hammer given to him as a Christmas present by her parents. They had no eyewitnesses to the crime, but they had a slew of circumstantial evidence. There was evidence of a lovers' quarrel in the placatory language of Inge's letter, combined with the evidence from Mrs Lotz that Inge may have been having second thoughts about His People Church, to which she had accompanied Fred. This was presented as evidence of his motive for the crime.

Then there was the evidence of Fred's incriminating behaviour on the night of the murder – the worry he expressed but which Mrs Lotz suggested was exaggerated, his apparent knowledge that there had been a murder and that it had been during the afternoon, the offer to become the child in Mrs Lotz's home. There was also the all-too-ready alibi he offered to Superintendent de Beer the next morning along with insincere tears, and his attempts – hinted at only – to influence his colleagues' recollection of his presence or otherwise at the meeting on 16 March. Most importantly, there was the forensic evidence that was said to place him at the scene – the fingerprint on the DVD cover and the shoeprint in the bathroom – as well as the evidence that his hammer could well have caused Inge's injuries.

For the defence, the most significant links in the narrative chain were the shoeprint and the fingerprint. They alone could establish Fred's presence in the flat at the time of the murder, and, no matter how serious one thought the fight between Fred and Inge, if you couldn't place Fred at the crime scene, you couldn't convict him. The hammer, by comparison, was important but not crucial because not even Captain Maritz and his decapitated sheep heads had been able to say more than that the hammer could not be excluded as the murder weapon. Obviously, being unable to exclude the implement was quite a long way short of proving that it had actually been used to kill Inge.

So, in response to the web of evidentiary threads laid by the prosecutors in the hope of entangling their client, when it was their turn, Fred's lawyers approached their task by narrowing all the critical questions down to just one: was there any credible evidence that Fred had been in Inge's flat on the afternoon of 16 March or, indeed, that he had so much as left the office?

And, having already rent large holes in the fabric of the prosecutors' case, the defence called just seven witnesses of their own, none of whom would provide any evidence at all about the more vaporous issues around which much of the coverage of the trial had been shaped – the issues of sex and sin, of religion and fidelity.

* * *

Of the seven witnesses called by De Bruyn, two were alibi witnesses. The first was Stefanus de Wet van der Spuy, who testified that Fred had been at his desk at about 17:10 and who had also testified that Director Trollip pressed him to change his statement about this. The second was Mkuseni Mbomvu, Fred's boss and a fellow attendee of the workshop on 16 March, who said that Fred had sat next to him that day from late morning until late afternoon, but whose cross-examination might be read as revealing some confusion about whether he was remembering the Wednesday of the murder or the Tuesday before that.

The other five witnesses were all forensic experts, some of them the leading exponents of their craft in the world, called to undercut the prosecution's claims about the fingerprint, the shoeprint and the hammer.

Among these was William Bodziak, the author of the leading textbook on shoeprint impression evidence, and who testified that the mark on the bathroom floor had not been made by Fred's shoe, that Bartholomew was lying when he claimed that the consultation in Florida had resulted in Bodziak's agreeing with the match, and that he had told the prosecutors as much before the trial began.

Of the remaining four witnesses, one – Paul Francis Ryder – also gave evidence regarding the stain that Superintendent Bartholomew deemed a shoeprint.

* * *

Paul Ryder was a chemist, employed by the organisation that has provided crime scene and forensic expertise to the British police for almost

20 years, who specialised in the location, recovery and enhancement of marks found at crime scenes. He was a quiet, self-effacing man whose testimony suggested an expert who was, if anything, even more convinced than Bodziak that the stain on the bathroom floor could not have been made by Fred's shoe.

Ryder testified that he found 'no scientific evidence' to support Bartholomew's conclusion about the match, saying that he could not find so much as a single component of the mark which properly matched any of the characteristics of the shoe. In the absence of that, he said it was impossible to argue that the stain had been made by a Hi-Tec sports shoe, much less that it had been made by Fred's Hi-Tec sports shoe. In fact, he went further: because there were no bloody tracks from the lounge to the bathroom, he said that he thought it 'extremely unlikely' that the mark had been made by a shoe at all. Much more likely, he said, was that it had been made when the killer put his murder weapon on the floor while cleaning himself up.

About the grains of sand in the groove of the sole, Ryder believed, as Bodziak did, that they were too high to have made contact with the floor and could not have affected the stain. He also said that it was impossible for the sand to have made contact with the blood and then to test negative for blood cells when Luminol was sprayed on the shoe. Luminol, he said, was an extremely sensitive chemical, and if any sand in the shoe had made contact with blood, then there would have been a reaction. It was a conclusion that made it impossible to argue that any sand that was still in Fred's shoe could have been responsible for Bartholomew's four white spots.

* * *

As was the case when it was Bodziak's turn, Teunissen's cross-examination of Ryder was a parade of hypothetical scenarios, some of them mutually exclusive: if the blood got onto the sole of the shoe only when Fred washed up in the bathroom, there might be no tracks from the lounge; if the shoe had been washed, the sand grains might have been pushed further up into the groove than they'd been at the time of the crime; if the blood had been coagulating when the shoe struck the tiles, then the various design features that Ryder had said he would have expected to find in the stain might not have been there.

Ryder made no concessions to Teunissen's hypotheticals, excluding all of them as possibilities. In fact, his evidence was so uncompromising that Teunissen would propose during final arguments that this should count against his credibility as a witness. She would complain, for instance, that Ryder had not been prepared to concede that it might be possible for the sand to have remained in the shoe even if the shoe had been washed sufficiently rigorously for all the blood to have been removed before it was seized by the police and later sprayed with Luminol.

On some levels, this complaint was a cunning one, playing as it did on a judge's inclination to distrust overly categorical conclusions offered by experts. It is a distrust that has its roots in the sense that strong conclusions reflect badly on an expert's objectivity, while also suggesting an unhealthy desire on the part of that expert to supplant the judge as the 'trier of fact'. Teunissen's complaint was cunning also because it echoed a complaint the judge had himself made about this part of Ryder's testimony when he'd demanded how Ryder could come to that conclusion without having done any tests on the shoe and the sand. 'I have difficulty with that evidence, Mr Ryder,' the judge had said then. 'You're an expert on shoeprints. Now you're professing to have expertise in whether sand particles ingrained in the sole of a shoe might be removed by a washing process. Is that part and parcel of your expertise?'

But if these were good reasons for Teunissen to raise Ryder's unwillingness to make this particular concession during her final arguments, there was one very good reason she should not have done so: Ryder's answer to the judge's question about his expertise on the question of whether the washing of the shoe would have removed the grains of sand.

'Yes, M'Lord,' Ryder had replied.

> JUDGE: How?
>> A: I am also an expert in the transfer persistence of particle material.
> JUDGE: Yes?
>> A: Yes.
> JUDGE: Well, on what basis would you be able to say this unless you've done the tests on something similar, if not these shoes?
>> A: From the studies that have been done on the persistence of materials. If you were to put them in a washing machine …
> JUDGE: Well, it probably depends on what kind of washing machine. Wouldn't there be quite a few variables?
>> A: It does, M'Lord. But if those sand particles have been in contact with blood – which they must have been if they had contributed to the mark – and if the process of washing the shoes had removed all traces of blood, it must have been sufficiently vigorous to get in between all the sand particles. I would, therefore, have expected it to remove the sand particles as well.

* * *

Ryder and Bodziak, the two experts called to testify about the shoeprint, were preceded by the defence's fingerprint experts, the first of whom was Pat Wertheim, whose report on Folien One had so seduced me when I'd read it ten months earlier.

On the stand, Wertheim took the judge through the contents of that report, emphasising the many individual components of the lift which he thought were inconsistent with the claim that it had come from a DVD cover, each of which he also said was much more consistent with a lift from a drinking glass: the curved, parallel lines; the lack of back-ground noise; the shape and orientation of the fingerprints; the smudge he thought might be a lip print. To these, he added another element that he had not recognised when he had written his report, but which he had noticed subsequently after having what he described as a moment 'when you just thought, "Ah," and say, "Why did I miss this the first time?"'

So help me, as he said this, he slapped his forehead like Homer Simpson.

Using a laser pointer to indicate a series of irregular black marks on a test lift he had done using a folien, he said, 'In every lift I've taken from a DVD cover in the past year, I've found these bubbles.' Their existence, he said, could be explained by the fact that the fingerprint examiner can-not ensure that the folien he uses when lifting a print from a soft plastic box is in complete contact with the surface. 'If I'm putting the folien or piece of tape on a hard surface, such as a piece of flat metal or piece of flat glass,' he said, 'I can roll it down in such a manner that I avoid bubbles forming under the surface. However the plastic of a DVD cover is flexible and when you try to roll the tape or the folien onto it, you're going to end up with disconformities in the plastic where the tape doesn't make com-plete contact. It's completely unavoidable. To the best of my knowledge there is no way to use tape or folien to make a lift absent these bubbles.'

If Wertheim's first conclusion was that the lift had come from a glass rather than a DVD cover, his second was that he believed that the police had not made an innocent mistake when they'd labelled Folien One as having come off a DVD cover. He offered three interconnected reasons for this. The first was that it is so indisputable that the lift could not have come off a DVD cover that any claims to believing the contrary were in-herently suspicious. The second was that, because none of the lifts among the eleven taken from Inge's flat looked as if it came off a DVD cover, it was impossible to believe that two lifts had been accidentally switched. The third reason for concluding that this was not an honest mistake was Director Botha's report. Ostensibly written as an objective evaluation of the contending claims made by the officers who'd lifted the print and those made by the first expert the defence consulted, Daan Bekker, Wertheim said repeatedly that Botha's reasoning was 'flawed' and his conclusions 'preposterous'. So preposterous, in fact, that Wertheim smelt a cover-up: the weaknesses of that report, he said, 'convinced me that it was not an honest mistake, because you wouldn't defend an honest mistake.'

*　*　*

Wertheim was cross-examined by Christénus van der Vijver, whose approach to the American's analysis of Folien One was to try to show that even if each of the elements Wertheim had spoken of were more consistent with a lift from a glass than from a DVD cover, it could, nevertheless, also be associated with a lift from the latter. He did not present Wertheim with any element of Folien One about which he could say something like, 'Look at this: unlike all the other elements, this one is more consistent with a lift from a DVD cover than from a glass.' Instead, he contented himself with offering a range of hypothetical scenarios under which Wertheim would have to acknowledge a particular element might be associated with a lift from a DVD box.

There was something quixotic about this quest for concessions from Wertheim because the American had not maintained that any one of the elements he'd identified in his analysis by itself proved that the lift came from a glass. His argument was that, if Folien One really came from where the police said it had come, then it was vanishingly unlikely that there'd have been so many features more consistent with a glass than a DVD cover and none that were more consistent with a DVD cover than a glass. It was, therefore, relatively costless for Wertheim to make the concessions Van der Vijver tried so hard to wrench from him. The result was that Van der Vijver seemed always to be on the point of celebrating a victory he had not quite won.

Still, the prosecutor was not without his successes. He showed, for example, that the bubbles that Wertheim had said were an 'unavoidable' feature of folien lifts from DVD covers were not present in one of the lifts Wertheim had himself made from a DVD cover. Confronted with this, Wertheim, who appeared to have conveniently forgotten the strength with which he'd made the original statement, said that his argument was only that 'bubbles are a common characteristic of a DVD cover, and uncommon on a glass.'

There was more along the same line of argument, though not all of it was as successful at eliciting agreement from Wertheim that the element in question could have come from something other than a glass. Van der Vijver, for example, sought to show that the lower of the two parallel lines was not curved and that it might not, therefore, relate to the bottom edge of a drinking glass. This was something that Wertheim refused to accept, pointing out that the prosecutor was looking at a very short portion of the line when making the claim that it was straight. Van der Vijver appeared to accept this answer because a few minutes later he suggested that the curvature of the lower line might be explained by the fact that the folien Constable Swartz had used to effect the first lift – the folien, in other words, which no longer existed and about which no records were kept – had been cut by hand. That, Van der Vijver said, explained why it was not geometrically straight.

And so it went with element after element, with the largest proportion of Van der Vijver's energies consumed by the smudge in the top left corner of Folien One that Wertheim had said might have been left by a lip (*see* PLATE 15).

Whether Van der Vijver chose to focus so much attention on this mark because he thought it was the key element he needed to exclude from the judge's mind as being indicative of the lift's having been taken from a glass, or because he felt he had Wertheim on the back foot, I cannot tell. What I can tell is that fully a quarter of the pages filled by Van der Vijver's cross-examination of Wertheim relate to this mark.

About this smudge, Van der Vijver made a number of points. With the assistance of the judge, who had initially pointed out that it was possible to hold a DVD cover in one's mouth and other parts of one's body (including one's chin), he suggested that there were other kinds of contact with the DVD cover that might have been responsible for it. As a result, Van der Vijver had Wertheim acknowledge that he could not definitively exclude the possibility that the mark had been made by something other than a lip.

Picking up on a comment that the judge had made when Director Botha had been on the stand a few months earlier, Van der Vijver also had Wertheim acknowledge that the 'lip print' did not run parallel to what Wertheim supposed was the rim of the glass. This, he said, was something that 'bothered' the prosecution about Wertheim's testimony because it suggested that the mouth that made it 'wasn't in the normal way when it touched the glass'. It was, he joked, something that might occur only very late at night.

Finally, Van der Vijver offered his own theory of what happened: that the mark had been left by a careless policeman. Perhaps, he suggested, it was the result of the fingerprint examiner's holding the DVD cover, scissors-like, between two fingers while wearing slightly damp latex gloves. To prove the possibility, he showed Wertheim a folien with just such a mark that, he said, had been produced the previous day by one of the police officers with whom he'd planned his cross-examination. Wertheim, while pointing out that that mark was a good deal larger than the mark on Folien One, conceded that there were also some similarities between the new mark and the smudge on Folien One.

Van der Vijver seemed pleased with this.

* * *

One of the more disconcerting aspects of Wertheim's evidence was that the judge, to whom each witness is expected to address his answers, kept nodding off. The room, usually over-air-conditioned, was hot, and the trial had been a long one. Still, given that Wertheim was the first witness called by the defence, it was a little worrisome that the judge might have to catch up with his testimony from the transcript. Since Wertheim was obviously a man who attached some value to the very American show-manship he brought to the witness stand, his inability to keep the judge awake was an obvious subject about which to tease him. 'It didn't bother me at all,' he told me when I asked about it. 'Jurors fall asleep all the time. Usually it's because you've made them think too hard and they're tired.'

I confess that I'm not sure whether Wertheim believed what he said or was pulling my leg. I do know that there were times when he looked uncomfortable in the face of Van der Vijver's questions, especially some of those relating to the supposed lip print. When I asked about that, he demurred: '"Uncomfortable"? I was practically having an orgasm in my pants.'

It was an unexpected response, so I asked why it was that those ques-tions had brought him so much pleasure. 'Because,' he replied, 'I knew that Arie was going to deal with all Van der Vijver's objections.'

The 'Arie' to whom Wertheim referred was Arie Jacob Zeelenberg, the most senior fingerprint expert in the Dutch National Police Force, and a man whose style and tenor was in every way the opposite of Wertheim's brashness. In his late fifties, Zeelenberg had the manner and manners of a certain class of European bureaucrat – understated, grey-suited, multi-lingual and professional – and, having begun his career in crime scene investigation in the early 1970s, he all but destroyed the prosecutors' case just by reading out his cv.

'I was,' he said, 'a crime scene investigation officer in Utrecht from 1971 to 1982.'

'I was,' he said, 'head of the National Fingerprint Department in the Netherlands from 1982 to 2005.'

'I am,' he said, 'a permanent forensic expert assigned to the High Court of Amsterdam presenting and reviewing evidence as a second opinion on whatever matters arise.'

'I was,' he said, 'chairman of the Interpol European Expert Group on Fingerprint Identification and co-author of the final report dealing with standards for fingerprint identification and best practices, officially endorsed by Interpol in 2000.'

'I was,' he said, 'a member of the follow-up to the Interpol European Expert Group on Fingerprint Identification, and the sole author of the second report on fingerprint procedures and standards that was issued by Interpol in 2004.'

'I am,' he said, 'chairman of the Interpol Fingerprint Monitoring Expert Group, a global group dealing with all fingerprint matters established in 2005.'

'I am,' he said, 'an associate member of the European Network of Forensic Science Institutes, and a member of the Fingerprint Working Group dealing with standards and best practices. At present, I'm reviewing the new manual.'

'I am,' he said, 'an invited co-author for the *Encyclopaedia of Biometric Recognition*, an edition from Springer Scientific Publishers, which is the second largest publisher in the world on scientific issues.'

'Just last week,' he concluded, 'I was invited by the International Association for Identification to be a member of a panel revising standards for fingerprint identification.'

The kicker?

'I would like to emphasise,' he said, 'that I'm here on official duty with the permission of my employer. Of course, my employer wanted the defence to pay for my expenses, but I receive no fee from the defence. In that respect, I am completely independent.'

The reading into the record of Zeelenberg's CV was followed by the projection of the 210-slide PowerPoint presentation he'd prepared about Folien One. It was a presentation composed of the most spectacular high-resolution, high-magnification photographs of every grain of powder that had adhered to the folien, photographs that explored every puff and shadow on that surface. It was a presentation that concluded with two distinguishable findings: first, that Zeelenberg felt he could completely exclude the possibility that Folien One came from a DVD cover, and, second, that it was, in his opinion, overwhelmingly probable that Folien One had been lifted from a drinking glass.

There were a number of similarities between Zeelenberg's reasoning and Wertheim's, with both noting the curved, parallel lines, the lack of background noise, and so on. But the Dutch policeman offered a slew of additional evidence.

Citing a scientific publication of the British Home Office that is widely regarded as the fingerprint examiner's bible, he showed that international best practice was to use foliens on drinking glasses, and not on lifts from plastic surfaces. This, he said, was because it was simply impossible to avoid intolerably high levels of background noise when foliens were used on the latter.

Zeelenberg also showed that a print lying next to the print of Fred's thumb was almost certainly also a thumbprint. He was happy to acknowledge that there was insufficient detail discernible to be certain that it was Fred's, but he also said that it was important that the two thumbprints lay next to each other because a small glass presents its users with only a limited number of comfortable positions in which to place one's thumb. The same is not true of a DVD cover, so finding the only two thumbprints on the folien to be adjacent to each other was not without significance.

Zeelenberg showed that it was indisputable that the parallel lines were curved.

He showed that it was impossible to produce a curved line from a straight substrate even with extreme pressure, and that, in any event, the brittle plastic of a DVD box would not survive that kind of pressure. This, he said, refuted Director Botha's suggestion that the curvature was the result of excess pressure Constable Swartz may have applied.

He showed that, at high magnifications, it was possible to detect tiny imperfections and black spots – he called them 'artefacts' – in the top parallel line, and showed that these could be associated with tiny chips and imperfections in the smoothness of the rim of a drinking glass. He said that they were so clear that they might one day be used to prove which glass was powdered and which could be excluded.

He showed that at high magnifications, a thin shadow in which no powder had adhered to the folien could be seen just beneath the higher of the two parallel lines, and that this could be associated with the presence of the tiny rim at the top of machine-made drinking glasses.

He showed that there was no way that the lower of the parallel lines could have been produced by a first lift without that lift also leaving a number of other tell-tale signs of its existence, and that none of those tell-tale signs were, in fact, present in Folien One.

He showed that there was evidence that at least five droplets of some or other fluid had dried on the substrate of Folien One before Fred's prints had been deposited on it. He showed that the dried droplets were of more or less the same size, and that this was something that would be expected only if they were the result of condensation forming on a more or less vertical surface. He showed that it was all but impossible to produce condensation on a DVD box. He showed that the marks left by the dried condensation tended to the oval along the horizontal axis, something that would result from the interaction of the surface tension of the water and the convex surface of the glass. He showed that the droplets of dried condensation had existed before the object was handled, refuting Director Botha's suggestion that the reason there were wet marks on Folien One might have been that the DVD cover may have been placed on a wet surface after handling, possibly even by one of the fingerprint examiners. On their own, Zeelenberg said, the droplets of dried condensation were reason enough to reject the claim that the fingerprint was lifted from a DVD cover.

In relation to the lip print, the element to which Van der Vijver had devoted a quarter of his cross-examination of Wertheim, Zeelenberg showed that portions of the mark itself were composed of spots of water produced by condensation, and that this was something common for lip prints on drinking glasses. He showed that it was natural and normal that a lip print be angled towards the root of the thumb because the lifting of a glass to one's mouth necessitated a series of mechanical movements by arm, hand and thumb, the results of which were not perfect. As a consequence, the weight of the glass would often pull towards the root of the thumb and result in an apparently skewed lip print. This, he showed, is exactly the angle which Van der Vijver had identified as being at odds with the notion that the mark had been made by a lip, and that Van der Vijver was wrong about this.

*　*　*

Mbomvu and Van der Spuy had testified about Fred's whereabouts on the day of the murder. Ryder and Bodziak had testified about the shoeprint. Wertheim and Zeelenberg had testified about the fingerprint. That left only the hammer, and the testimony of Professor Gert Saayman, the head of the Department of Forensic Medicine at the University of Pretoria, a man with nearly thirty years' experience as a pathologist, during which time he'd conducted or overseen upwards of 20 000 autopsies.

The point of Saayman's testimony was to refute the prosecution's contention that Inge's injuries could have been caused by Fred's hammer. To make that point necessitated the use of a series of photographs, some of Inge's injuries and some taken from the pages of the leading textbooks on forensic medicine, so raw and vivid they became almost too unreal, too cartoonish, to horrify.

Almost.

The idea that a hammer had been used by the killer, it will be recalled, had arisen first during the autopsy when the pathologist had noted that many of Inge's injuries were of a similar size and shape. Because these injuries tended to the circular or semicircular, she'd told the detectives that it was possible they had been inflicted by a monkey wrench or a hammer. That suggestion had been made two days after the murder, and when the police searched Fred's car a month later they had found an ornamental hammer/bottle-opener lying beneath his seat. If Fred were to be believed, the hammer had been there since Christmas, when he'd received it as a gift from Inge's parents.

Subjected to a Luminol test by Sergeant Peta Davidtz on 18 April, traces of what the forensic technician said was likely to have been blood had been found. The link between the hammer and the murder had been weakened, however, when Dr Sharlene Otto had sought to profile any genetic material on the hammer, but had found only male DNA. The police had, however, been able to link the hammer to the murder – or so they claimed – when Captain Maritz had proved that the dimensions of marks left on a series of animal heads on which the hammer had been tested matched those of Inge's wounds. It was a conclusion he'd supported by asking the judge to lay transparencies onto which the image of the hammer had been copied over photos of Inge's wounds, an exercise intended to show how closely these matched each other in size and shape.

There had been much to criticise in Maritz's evidence, but Saayman went further still, suggesting that the whole premise of Maritz's work was false, and that the pathologist had been wrong to think that Inge's injuries could have been caused by a hammer.

Saayman said it was wrong to think that, just because the lacerations of the skin on Inge's head were semicircular, the implement that caused the injury must also have been circular or semicircular. The skull, he said, is curved, so when a rigid, rod-like implement strikes it, only a few centimetres of the weapon actually make contact with the head. Demonstrating the basis of his conclusion with a series of horrendous photographs from the world's leading textbooks of forensic medicine – 'I know Professor Whitwell personally,' he said. 'She has been a guest in my house.' – he pointed out that the shape of the lacerations caused by a rod-like weapon would be determined by the underlying curvature of the skull. He said that the topical effect of the blow from a hammer would tend to look like a starburst. In any event, he said, the curvilinear lacerations Maritz had identified as matching the shape of the hammer were almost fifty percent too large to have been caused by it.

Saayman went further. He said that there was ample professional and academic literature documenting the underlying damage done to the bones of the skull when it is struck with a hammer. Hammer blows, he said, would result in well-defined, highly localised, depressed fractures, and these would tend to be of the same size and shape as the striking surface of the hammer. The principal injuries to Inge's skull, he said, were not at all like that. Using images of the bones broken during the assault to her head (after the flesh had been stripped away), Saayman showed that the fractures to Inge's skull were much larger than the head of the hammer. They were also not localised. Instead, a great many fault lines radiated away from the point of impact. So generalised was the damage, he said, that Adendorff's report noted that one of the bones in the base of the skull had fractured. It was not clear from her report precisely where that fracture was, but he said that it was unlikely that a hammer could cause the kind of shock waves needed to crack as heavily fortified a structure as the base of the skull. Certainly, he said, it was extremely unlikely that Fred's hammer – with its 21mm diameter striking surface and its 330g of mass – could have done so.

So what had caused Inge's blunt-force injuries? Saayman's assessment was that it was something long and rigid and heavy: a steel bar or a heavy torch or the barrel of a largish gun.

29

Fred was not among the seven witnesses who'd testified by the time his lawyers closed their case on 11 September 2007. MK had testified that day, but, for some reason that may or may not have had something to do with the prosecution's ability to attack her evidence, Shahana Toefy had not. The final act of the defence case was the handing-in of a statement drafted by Henry Kevin Olsen, a police forensic investigator who'd conducted an electrostatic examination of a writing block found in Inge's flat. He'd been asked by Director Trollip to determine if the short note that Fred claimed had been part of – and the conclusion to – Inge's letter had been written while still attached to the pad, and whether a close examination of the remaining sheets would determine if any dates could be identified. He had written his statement in November 2005, and his conclusion was that Inge's note had been written while the sheet was attached to the notepad and that nothing was written on the pad after that.

In all, the defence's case had lasted less than a month, and for many people, despite the involvement of some of the world's leading names in forensic science, its most notable aspect was that Fred had not taken the stand.

'He's got something to hide,' I was told more than once. 'He's afraid to testify because he knows that the prosecutors will tear him apart.'

It was a natural reaction, and it was premised on the same assumptions about human nature that frame the legislation governing the testimony of an accused in a criminal trial. This is legislation whose most important provision is that the accused has every right to remain silent. It is a right that has its historical roots in the desire to avoid putting someone in a position of having to choose between telling the truth and risking earthly punishment and the eternal damnation that might flow from lying under oath, but which is justified today by the conviction that the state must prove its case, and that no-one can be forced to incriminate himself.

But if the right to silence is an aspect of a right not to incriminate oneself, then choosing to remain silent is easily interpreted as a kind of acknowledgement of fault; as proof, at the very least, that the accused has something to hide. Nor is this attitude just a matter of the weak grasp a layperson might have of the intricacies of the law. The law itself affirms it by providing that when an accused does refuse to testify, a judge is entitled 'to draw such inferences from the accused's conduct as may be reasonable in the circumstances.' Since it is hard to see how a judge could be asked to infer from an accused's silence anything that would be in his favour, choosing to remain silent is not without its risks.

The right to silence, then, is qualified. And yet it remains controversial, being seen by some as an example of the many ways in which the structure of a criminal case favours the accused (though more often than not, those who make this complaint will say that the structure of the trial favours the 'criminal', a view that more or less completely prejudges the critical questions that the process is designed to answer). Another aspect of this more general complaint about the structure of the process is that the requirement that prosecutors prove their case 'beyond all reasonable doubt' has had the effect of creating a class of defence lawyers and expert witnesses who will say and do anything to get their client off. Another version of that more general complaint is that it leads to perverse outcomes. The exclusionary rule, for example, states that any evidence that the police acquire unlawfully – usually because they did not get a warrant – must be excluded from the trial, even if it proves that the accused did what the prosecutors say he did. In the American system, evidence acquired in this way is sometimes called 'the fruit of a poisoned tree', and, while the current Supreme Court looks set to soften some of the restrictions on prosecutors' use of this kind of evidence, on the whole the general drift of Western jurisprudence over the past century has been to tighten these provisions, to make it harder for police officers and prosecutors to use evidence acquired improperly.

The odd thing is that, far from being excessively tilted in the defence's favour, my impression of Fred's case was that, if anything, the judge's general attitude made it much more difficult for the defence to make its case than it should have been. There were, for example, the many occasions on which the judge sought to persuade the defence not to allege that the police had fabricated evidence, and to assert and reassert his position that he would not allow such allegations to be lightly made. It was a point he made repeatedly, often enough doing so before the defence had been able to present the argument at all.

The most obvious example of this was when it had been the judge, rather than the prosecutors, who had first objected to De Bruyn's reading into the record the letter Bodziak had emailed to the defence expressing his shock and amazement at the lies in the police report about his consultation with Bartholomew. Bodziak's emailed response, the judge said, was something that he was not interested in, and he expressed some

FRUIT OF A POISONED TREE

surprise that De Bruyn would even presume to test him in this way.

Surprised or not, it quickly became obvious that the judge's initial objection was legally untenable because if the defence were prevented from confronting Bartholomew with Bodziak's claims, then Bodziak would not be able to testify about these if he were persuaded to come to Cape Town. This point emerged during an angry exchange between De Bruyn and the judge, and as the judge saw he was mistaken, his anger fixed on De Bruyn's assistant, Advocate Terry Price.

A large, gregarious man with curly hair and more chins than most, Price is a former policeman who was once a bodyguard for apartheid's last foreign minister, and he has the kind of temperament that would not serve him well at poker. From the moment the judge began questioning De Bruyn's right to place Bodziak's email before the court, Price had been shaking his head in apparent disbelief at the judge's words. It was something that gave the judge an opportunity to vent. 'We are in the middle of a trial,' he almost shouted. 'And now there are reactions. Please do not shake your head when I am talking to Mr de Bruyn. Understand? I do not expect that kind of reaction from advocates who appear before me. Do we understand each other? In a case like this, your body language must always remain neutral.'

Another example of this kind occurred during Pat Wertheim's cross-examination by the prosecutor, Christénus van der Vijver. The first signs of trouble came early on when the prosecutor tried to show that Wertheim's approach to Folien One had been skewed because he had been 'fed' misinformation by the defence. It was, Van der Vijver said, for this reason that Wertheim had developed a mistaken impression about the quality of the police investigation as a whole. It was this misinformation, the prosecutor also suggested, that had led to some of Wertheim's more general criticisms of the investigation: that too little time had been spent in Inge's flat; that too few prints had been found; that too little attention had been paid to the marking-up of evidence; that the crime scene had been handed back to Inge's family too hastily; and that the returning of the DVD cover to the DVD store was so poor a decision as to be 'inconceivable'.

Noting all of these criticisms, Van der Vijver tried to show that some of Wertheim's conclusions were wrong because the information he had about the investigation was inaccurate. And, in fact, he made some real progress: he showed Wertheim a photograph of Inge's bathroom, for example, in which a great many surfaces had clearly been dusted, and which went some way to undermining Wertheim's critical assessment about the rigour of the fingerprinting effort in Inge's flat.

In the midst of this, however, Van der Vijver said, 'The question I want to ask you on this particular score, Mr Wertheim, is why did you deem it necessary to put it in your report? How could that impact on what you were asked to do? To compare a drinking glass with the DVD cover and to give your expert opinion on that? Why was it necessary to put this material in your report?'

Now, it should be said immediately that Wertheim is qualified as a crime scene analyst, has worked in the field for some decades, has trained police officers in crime scene investigation and is recognised as an expert on the subject by American courts. It should also be noted that when De Bruyn had originally approached Wertheim, the lawyer had included in his brief the request that Wertheim address his report to any other aspects of the investigation which might be relevant. Before all of this emerged, however, the judge added his views on Wertheim's efforts: 'This is not an inquiry into the nature of the investigation,' he said, growing quite cross. 'Do you realise we are busy with a criminal matter and that your personal opinions about whether the investigation was properly done or not are totally irrelevant for purposes of a South African court? I'm not sure whether it's relevant for an American court. I'd be most surprised to hear that they were. But to make comments as you have as to it being "inconceivable" in a murder investigation that a critical piece of evidence disappears – you weren't called upon to give that kind of comment. Why do you do that? That's what counsel is asking you. Why do you deem it necessary for the purpose of your scientific evidence, to comment on the nature of the investigation?'

On any reading, it is a breathtaking thing for a judge to say: how, one wants to plead, can the question of whether an investigation was properly conducted be irrelevant to a criminal trial? Surely some of the most important questions a judge has to ask revolve around nothing except the quality of the investigation? And why, when it comes to it, should the defence alone be responsible for asking these questions? Is that not also the role of prosecutors and judges? It is, after all, they who will have to look themselves in the mirror after an accused is sent to prison, and the judge's apparent preference to suppress these questions was troubling.

Nor was this the only time I was troubled by the judge's attitude to the evidence that Wertheim was offering about the conduct of the police investigation. There was, for example, his tendency to fall asleep when these matters arose, something a psychologist might ascribe less to tiredness (as Wertheim suggested to me) and more to the listener's unconscious resistance to what is being said. Then there was this comment, offered a few moments before the surprising assertion that questions about the quality of the investigation were not relevant during a criminal trial, and which was made after Wertheim had explained the care he might have taken at the crime scene: 'That's what happens in an ideal world,' the judge agreed. 'But I can promise you it doesn't happen in South Africa. I've been involved with crime for many, many years, and in ninety percent of the cases there has been some kind of lapse or lacuna in the investigation. Despite that, eventually we still have to find our way through and try to establish the truth. But it's quite correct, that would be the ideal situation, but it doesn't always happen like that.'

In relation to a judge's capacity to discern the truth despite any missteps of the police, it is an oddly hubristic attitude, and it should be read along with a comment he would make a few days later when Arie Zeelenberg was on the stand. Then, when Zeelenberg would be dealing with one of the last of his 210 slides, and would be offering yet another reason to doubt that Constable Swartz had complied with the provisions of police standing orders, the judge would say, 'Isn't this just a little pedantic? Does it really make any difference?'

The common thread in all of this was an apparent willingness to forgive the police their missteps. Given the depth and breadth of the public conviction that the courts bend over backwards to protect the rights of the accused (or 'criminals'), it was surprising to observe how far out of his way the judge would go to protect the police from criticism.

These were some of the many difficult moments for the defence, and they would result eventually in Christénus van der Vijver making a daring gamble during closing argument when he would seek to show the judge that His Lordship had to choose between two options – convicting Fred or finding that as many as six police officers had lied. I will return to that below. For the moment, let it be recorded that the hardest time the judge gave the defence came late during those closing arguments. And it led to one of the most dramatic sequences of the trial.

The prosecutors began their final arguments at 10:20 on 1 October. De Bruyn took over just before 15:00. At 15:20, he asked for permission to continue his argument the next day. Permission was granted, and the court reconvened at 10:16 on 2 October. De Bruyn proceeded with his arguments until tea at 11:16. Then, when everyone returned from tea, De Bruyn asked for another break, without explaining why. By the time court reconvened at 14:29, Fred's father had hired a new lawyer, who promptly applied for a two-week postponement so that arguments could be put together so that the defence could apply to reopen their case and have Fred testify in his own defence.

It was an extraordinary sequence, one that is unprecedented in South African courts. To understand what happened, one has to return to the question of why Fred had chosen not to testify in the first place.

* * *

Fred's original decision not to testify was a risky one. Both in the court itself and in the court of public opinion it was a decision that was easily interpreted as a signal that he had something to hide. Nor was this an unreasonable interpretation: most of those who refuse to testify in their own trials do so because there are questions that they don't want to answer or which they cannot answer truthfully without incriminating themselves.

Now, it may be that this was why Fred chose not to testify, in which case his cross-examination, when it eventually came, would prove to be immensely interesting. On the other hand, there might have been another reason Fred's lawyers didn't put their client on the stand: they didn't think he had anything to contribute to his case.

From a legal point of view, the absolute prerequisite for convicting Fred was tying him to the crime scene. It doesn't matter how strange his behaviour after the murder might be made to seem; if the prosecutors couldn't show that he'd left his office, much less that he was in Inge's flat at some point on the afternoon of 16 March, there was simply no way the judge could convict him. It was for that reason that five of the seven witnesses they called had focused on the three pieces of forensic evidence that might conceivably place him at the crime: the fingerprint, the shoeprint and the hammer. The only other witnesses presented were Mkuseni Mbomvu and Stefanus de Wet van der Spuy, while a mistake by Christénus van der Vijver had allowed them to enter into the record Shahana Toefy's statement to the effect that Fred had been sitting next to her between 11:00 and 17:00 on the day of the murder. Had her statement not been entered into evidence, it is likely that she would have been the eighth and last witness.

In addition to all of this, there was other evidence that had been presented to the court. A sworn statement setting out Fred's alibi had been entered as a plea explanation on the first morning of the trial. Another of Fred's affidavits, sworn to on 12 April 2005, had also been entered into the record when Inspector de Villiers was on the stand, while Superintendent de Beer had testified about what Fred had told him on the morning of

17 March 2005. In each of these, Fred's alibi was offered to the judge. Finally, there had been the evidence of Herman Louw, the security official at Old Mutual, who'd been unable to find any evidence of Fred's leaving the building, as well as of various police witnesses, who'd testified about Fred's phone calls and computer records, all of which seemed to place him far from Inge's flat.

Given all of this, Fred's lawyers might have been convinced that it was unnecessary to call Fred. He could say nothing about the forensic evidence since he had no expertise in this area. And, given that the only evidence led by the prosecution that might prove Fred had so much as left the office was the unsupported testimony of the furniture store clerk, while a great deal of evidence suggested that Fred had not left the building, his lawyers might have believed that it was unnecessary for Fred to testify about this either.

So what changed? Why did Fred's father go to the extraordinary lengths of hiring a new lawyer to argue for the reopening of the case precisely so Fred could testify? In a word: the judge.

*   *   *

There were two distinguishable sets of comments that the judge made during closing arguments which upset the defence's original calculations about the need for Fred to testify. One set of comments had to do with how he might approach the task of weighing all the evidence.

Discussing this, the judge said to De Bruyn, 'Remember that when a judge assesses an alibi, he doesn't look in isolation at the fingerprint, the shoeprint, *et cetera*. It is very clear that the law requires that he must take account of all the evidence, seen holistically.' A moment later, he added this: 'You will remember that the behaviour of the accused was an aspect that was raised by the state. I've said it before: there were strange aspects to this behaviour. It would have been much easier if he had come here to explain that. He is not obliged to. He is not obliged to take the stand.

But it would have made the case much easier if we could have obtained some clarity from him. I mention this because you can't look at these issues individually. At the end, we must look at the whole picture. Only then, when we are convinced that the alibi is reasonably possibly true, will there be an acquittal. Only then.'

Responding to this, De Bruyn offered that 'You cannot say that the accused's alibi is untrue as a result of any possible "strange behaviour".'

'No,' the judge replied. 'Strange behaviour is just one part of the evidence that has been put before us and that must be taken into account when looking holistically at the evidence as a whole. That's all that I'm saying to you.'

Of course, all of this is true: a judge must evaluate all of the evidence, and it is hard to think that a criminal justice system would become fairer and more just if judges could pick and choose between which kinds of evidence they would take seriously and which they would not. But the commitment to evaluate the evidence *holistically* was not just a commitment to evaluate all of the evidence, and it drew on other ideas that shape judges' thinking about cases in which the evidence against an accused is circumstantial. If the judge's comments were anything to go by, they were ideas that in this case might mean that evidence about Fred's 'strange behaviour' might influence the interpretation of the forensic evidence. There was something fishy about this, and the best explanation I can give for why the judge suggested it at all is the power of metaphors to shape thinking.

*　*　*

In the popular mind, the term 'circumstantial evidence' is sometimes taken to be a synonym for 'weak evidence' or 'unreliable evidence'. 'Oh,' one might hear about the evidence against a particular shady politician, 'the evidence that he took a bribe is only circumstantial.'

In a trial at law, by contrast, evidence is defined as circumstantial not by its strength or weakness, but by its difference from 'direct evidence'.

The latter is evidence that, if accepted, proves the truth of some or other claim directly, and, in a criminal trial it might take the form of a statement such as, 'I saw the accused stab the deceased.' Direct evidence, in other words, is evidence that a witness offers that helps to prove some element of the crime without the judge's having to fill in any gaps in the chain of reasoning. If Matthew saw Mark stab John, then the judge can convict Mark of murder if he is sure that Matthew is neither making a mistake nor lying (and that Mark was not defending himself).

Circumstantial evidence, by contrast, is evidence offered by a witness that, while not directly establishing guilt, suggests that the accused committed the crime. Because it is only suggestive it requires the judge to join the dots himself. Sometimes this kind of evidence is relatively nebulous. A witness might say she knew that the deceased was afraid of the accused or that she'd heard them fight in the hours preceding the murder. Neither statement proves guilt, but, with other evidence, might help convict an abusive husband. By the same token, circumstantial evidence can also be extremely compelling: a witness might say that she heard screams coming from the deceased's room, and that when she went to investigate she saw the accused climbing out of a window with a knife between his teeth and blood on his hands. Few people would require much more proof of the accused's guilt, yet the evidence against him would still be entirely circumstantial, since no-one had actually seen the blows being struck. Instead, the judge would have to infer from the fact that the accused was climbing out the window, had a knife with him and had blood on his hands, that it had been he who had slit the deceased's throat.

Whether nebulous or compelling, circumstantial evidence is 'circumstantial' because it requires the judge to draw inferences between what the evidence literally shows and what the prosecution is trying to prove. And this means that it has a peculiar characteristic that distinguishes it from direct evidence: in addition to worrying about whether the witness is mistaken or lying, the judge must also worry about whether the inferences he is asked to draw are sufficiently compelling as to be the only reasonable inferences that could possibly be drawn.

That is the fundamental difference between direct and circumstantial evidence. In Fred's case, all the evidence was circumstantial: forensic evidence is by its nature circumstantial, as was the evidence about Fred's motive and the evidence about his suspicious behaviour. And, because the evidence was circumstantial, it triggered a particular set of ideas about the holistic character of judicial reasoning, ideas that have been shaped by two sets of images. The first dates back to an English judgment delivered in 1910, and which encourages a judge to regard circumstantial evidence as a web or 'a network of facts around the accused man', one that may be 'as insubstantial as the air itself' but which might also be 'so close, so stringent, so coherent' that 'no efforts on the part of the accused can break through.'

If the first image that a judge is encouraged to hold in his head as he contemplates a case composed of circumstantial evidence is of a web, the second is that of a mosaic.

'The breaking down of a body of evidence into its component parts is obviously a useful aid to a proper understanding and evaluation of it,' the judges of South Africa's Supreme Court of Appeal said in 1998. 'But, in doing so, one must guard against a tendency to focus too intently upon the separate and individual part of what is, after all, a mosaic of proof. Doubts about one aspect of the evidence led in a trial may arise when that aspect is viewed in isolation. Those doubts may be set at rest when it is evaluated again together with all the other available evidence ... There is no substitute for a detailed and critical examination of each and every component in a body of evidence. But, once that has been done, it is necessary to step back a pace and consider the mosaic as a whole. If that is not done, one may fail to see the wood for the trees.'

* * *

Trees and woods. A network of facts. A mosaic of proof.

These were the words, and the ideas to which they alluded, that the prosecution had used in summing up the case against Fred during their closing arguments. Even if there were some weaknesses in some of the evidence, they'd argued, the whole of their case was greater than the sum of its individual parts, and nothing but Fred's guilt could explain all the individual facts that they'd presented. The defence was convinced that none of the individual elements of the state's case bore any scrutiny, but the judge's comments suggested that he took a different view. He would not 'look in isolation at the fingerprint, the shoeprint, *et cetera*' because the law requires that he 'take account of all the evidence, seen holistically.' It was a requirement, he suggested, that demanded that he look at least as closely at evidence of Fred's 'strange behaviour', which would have to be 'taken into account when looking holistically at the evidence as a whole.'

If the judge deemed the evidence of Fred's strange behaviour to be sufficiently compelling, in other words, it might be used to offset some of the weaknesses in the forensic evidence. They were comments that seemed to suggest that, in evaluating the evidence holistically, a horse, as the Russian proverb has it, might be conjured out of fifty rabbits. For Fred's lawyers, the prospect was deeply disturbing.

And then there was something else the judge said during closing arguments which also affected the balance of the defence's calculations.

In failing to take the stand and testify, the judge said, Fred had failed to offer any evidence for his alibi. There was, according to this view, no basis for the judge to say that Fred had been at work, since the claim that he'd been there had not been formally entered into evidence. It was an odd view given all the evidence that had been led about what Fred claimed about that day: evidence that included Superintendent de Beer's account of his interview with Fred on the morning after the murder, as well as Fred's sworn statement from April 2005, Fred's sworn plea explanation from day one of the trial, the evidence from his cellphone and computer records, the (absence of) evidence from the security system, MK's testimony and Toefy's sworn statement. All of this seemed to suggest that there was plenty of testimony and documentary evidence supporting Fred's claim to having been at work, but the judge's complaint was more technical: because Fred had not taken the stand, no-one had formally entered his claimed alibi into evidence.

This was a point the judge made more than once on the second morning of closing argument, and it was one he had made earlier in the trial too. One passage is instructive of his thinking, and it begins with him saying, 'The prosecution doesn't have to prove that he left the building. He is relying on an alibi.' Then, in reference to the forensic evidence and its relationship to Fred's claimed alibi, he went on to say, 'Evidence that may refute his alibi has been presented. It is, then, the accused who must present evidence for his alibi.'

    DB: But the evidence for the alibi is before you.

    JUDGE: It is not evidence, Mr de Bruyn.

    DB: What is not evidence?

    JUDGE: All that we have before us is a broad plea explanation. But it is not evidence; it is just a plea explanation. Only when an accused himself says where he was at every moment of that day, does it become evidence. A plea explanation is an accommodating document. It is not submitted to cross-examination. There are a great many questions that arise from this plea explanation, which could have been asked if it were presented by means of testimony. So the question is, 'What is the evidence that we have for the alibi?' We have evidence that refutes it, but do we have evidence about an alibi from about 15:30 that afternoon to 17:10? That is the evidence that must be tested under cross-examination and that is what bothers us about the whole alibi.

    DB: M'Lord, with the greatest respect, it shouldn't

bother you because there is more than just the
plea explanation. But even if there were just the
plea explanation, if the account set out in that plea
explanation is reasonably possibly true, then the
accused must get the benefit of that. But there is also a
sworn statement from him that has been entered and
that says that he was at Old Mutual the whole day. That
is evidence.

JUDGE: But is not evidence yet. It is not evidence until he comes
to the stand and says that that is indeed what happened.
He attests to the contents of the statement. A statement
is not evidence. It has not been tested through cross-
examination. That is the whole idea behind cross-
examination – to test his account.

I am not best qualified to say whether or not this position was or was not
correct. I can say that when Fred's new lawyer, the exceptionally experienced Henry Viljoen SC, presented an application to reopen the case two
weeks later, he made the rather unsubtle point that it was cold comfort
for him to know that if Fred were convicted, the judge's decision would
be overturned on appeal solely on the basis of this passage of the transcript. I can also say that, in response to Viljoen's application, the judge
allowed the defence to reopen its case.

Fred's testimony began two hours later.

30

Henry Viljoen, now the more senior of Fred's senior counsel and, for that reason, the man who would lead him through his evidence, is a tall man in his seventies. He has white hair and deep wrinkles. His skin is pale and his neck is long. Combined with his black robes, the overall effect is of nothing so much as a vulture. It is an immediate impression, but it is one that would be reinforced during Teunissen's cross-examination of Fred when Viljoen would frequently rise to his feet to object to some or other line of questioning, doing so with the aggressive relish of a scavenger pulling a morsel from a ripening corpse.

Long as Viljoen's career might have been – the judge commented that Viljoen was a senior advocate in Bloemfontein when he himself was starting out – he would have seldom appeared in a court as packed as the one in which he appeared that Monday.

Fred's friends and relations had come from across the country. The Lotzes, too, were well supported, as were the police officers, some of whose bosses had turned out. But the most notable thing about court that day was how the prospect of Fred's testifying had electrified the press corps and the public they served. The result was that the room was full to overflowing. So full, in fact, that because I was a little late coming in from the airport, I could not get my usual seat on the bench beneath the judge and beside the other journalists. I stood, instead, at the back of the room for the first hour or so. After a short break, during which the judge prepared his decision about whether Fred would be allowed to testify or not, however, I was able to squeeze into my accustomed spot where I found myself sitting next to two women who were not journalists.

That two ordinary members of the public should have such prized seats plainly annoyed some of the other reporters, whose numbers had swelled considerably. Two approached the women to ask them to give way. Before the women could move, however, the court orderly pulled himself away from his tabloid and shuffled over to offer the portentous news that the judge had specifically requested that space be kept for these two women. The journalists fell back to the walls in some alarm.

Later in the morning, there was another break after the judge gave his decision to allow Fred to testify, and, when everyone returned, the two women were once again beside me. Once again, two journalists approached them to move and, once again, the orderly intervened. This time, however, Carien Teunissen, overhearing the conversation, interposed herself on the journalists' side. These were seats reserved for journalists, she said, and the women must move. Cowed by her manner, the two women departed.

When the judge entered the court a few minutes later, and having settled into his seat and surveyed the room, however, the first thing he noticed was the absence of the two women from the bench at the front.

'Where,' he asked, leaning forward and looking about, 'are the members of my family?'

* * *

By the time Viljoen led Fred through his account of the day of the murder, his account of the sequence of events was familiar. There was Fred sleeping over at Inge's the night before, and his attending a lecture the next morning. There was Inge's delivery of a letter to him. There was the visit to the furniture store. There was the drive to Pinelands and the meeting at which he'd spent the best part of the previous ten days and to which he had made a presentation the day before. There was the discussion of that presentation for the rest of the day, the sending of two emails from his desk afterwards, and the conversation with Stefanus de Wet van der Spuy. There was the departure for his flat just after six, the cooking and eating of his dinner with Marius, and their delivery of the cupboard to Jean's flat. There was the growing anxiety about Inge's silence. There were the unanswered smss and phone calls. There were the calls to Mrs Lotz and the decision to go to Stellenbosch. There was Marius's offer to call Christo. There was the collection of keys from Mrs Lotz. There were the calls from Marius telling him that he had bad news and asking him to meet him at the Lotzes' home. There was Marius's telling first Fred and then Mrs Lotz that Inge had been murdered.

But, if the broad sequence was familiar, the emotional content was not. We learn, for example, of some of the details of the smss that passed between Fred and Inge that day.

INGE: Hi! The class wasn't so bad after all :-) Even the girl who verbally abused me was there!! Love you, *skat* and have a good day. xx

FRED: Hi, I'm glad class was good and hope you had a good time with Wimpie? I read your letter quickly over lunch. Thank you. I'll look at it more carefully tonight.

> I appreciate it. Hope you have a good afternoon. Love
> you, *skat*, F. xx
>
> INGE: I had a good time with W! The tiles are already laid!
> Miss you already … xx
>
> FRED: Hi my *skat* … I'll call you a bit later tonight just to hear
> your voice. I love you – F.
>
> FRED: Hi *skat*, are you OK? Give me a missed call when you
> get this sms and I'll call you back … Love F. x

That last sms was sent at 21:35, and, just before, Fred had sat down at his computer to compose an email in which he would set out his response to the letter Inge had given him that morning. He wrote only a sentence and a half, however, before getting up to call Mrs Lotz to find out if she'd heard from her daughter. 'Hello, my *skat*,' the aborted email reads. 'Thank you for your letter. I really appreciate it, and, because I know you so well, I can see that it's very sincere, honest and comes from the bottom of your heart. As I have often said to you …'

Dealing with this incomplete email, Viljoen refers to the technical printout that accompanied the forensic analysis of Fred's computer. 'There is an indication here,' he says, 'that reads: "Created: 16 March, 21:38:47. Modified: 21:38:48. Accessed: 21:38:48." Did you write that letter in two seconds?'

> A: No, M'Lord.
>
> Q: Explain it to us.
>
> A: I don't understand precisely how it works, but what
> I believe is that a computer will automatically save a
> document every once in a while. As I understand it,
> when I broke off from writing this letter in order to
> send Inge an sms this is what the computer did.
>
> Q: Maybe I can just finish off with what happened to that
> letter later, when that letter once again came to your
> attention and you saw it on the screen again.

A: Yes, M'Lord. What happened is that I broke off to send Inge the sms, and I didn't finish the letter that night. Then I left, and I recall that when my parents brought me the computer on the Friday so that I could begin work on the notice for the funeral, this thing came up on the screen with a message that it had been recovered and did I want to save it. I clicked 'No' because it was no longer needed.

It is an answer Fred can barely complete before sobs wrack his frame.

*   *   *

Along with the raw emotional content, new details also emerge. Some reflect important differences between his testimony and that offered by other witnesses. Of the latter, the most important are Fred's denials that the strange and suspicious conduct that had been attributed to him by Mrs Lotz and by Marius had ever occurred.

He says that he did not tell Mrs Lotz that Inge had been murdered in her flat, much less that he said it had happened in the afternoon. He insists that Marius told Mrs Lotz about Inge's murder, though he cannot say if Marius used the phrase 'this afternoon'.

He flatly denies offering to become the child in Mrs Lotz's house.

He does not deny that he chose initially to withhold the long letter from Mrs Lotz, but he says that he did so in order to spare her and Professor Lotz the pain of reading the paragraph relating to Professor Lotz's drinking. He also says that Inge had asked him to treat the letter as private. He says that, in any event, when the issue of the letter had arisen with the private detectives, he had given them a copy of it.

Of the new details that emerge, though, by far the most significant relate to the fight he and Inge had had before she died, the only previous access to which had been through Inge's letter.

The trouble began, he says, when he phoned his brother, Dawie, to congratulate him on his wife's pregnancy. At the time, there was still some simmering tension between the two of them because of an argument Fred had had with Alfons at Dawie's wedding the previous December. It was a fight, Fred says, that began when he told Alfons off for being unnecessarily 'rowdy'. He says that he and his brothers had not talked through the tension that arose that night, and the consequence was that Dawie was 'cool' to him when they spoke on the phone. 'It bothered me,' he says. 'It upset me. And because Inge knew me so well, she picked it up immediately. She asked what was wrong, but I was tired and really didn't want to talk about it. I just said, "It's nothing." Later, she asked again, and I said that my relationship with my brothers wasn't as good as it should be.'

He says that soon after that exchange, he took a shower and went to bed – on the sleeper couch in the lounge. It was, he says, unusually early and admits that he was much quieter that evening than normal.

Perhaps because he'd gone to bed early, he woke early the next morning, went to Inge's room and got into bed with her. He thinks they slept for another hour or so, until the alarm went off. Then, as he was getting up to go to the shower, Inge asked him again what was wrong. He says that he told her that nothing was wrong, and went to shower.

It became clear over breakfast that Inge was upset with him because he'd been so silent and uncommunicative. It was clear, too, that she had taken it to heart: 'She questioned my love for her; she wanted to know if I was sure about the relationship. I told her that I loved her a great deal, that I was absolutely sure about the relationship and that that was not what was bothering me. But she went on, and I asked her how it could be that she could immediately assume that she had done something wrong. I told her it was unnecessary and that she shouldn't do such things. As we spoke, she became very sad and began to cry. At that point, I began to think that maybe there were other things on her mind, so I asked her, "But what's bothering *you*?" and "Are *you* sure about the relationship?" She told me that she was certain she loved me.

'We really had very little time,' he says. 'I had to go to class. I stood up and gave her a kiss and a hug. But she was still upset when I left. It bothered me that we were parting like that, without me knowing what was wrong, so I went back to the flat. I found her in her bedroom. I gave her another hug and tried to comfort her. I told her I loved her and tried to find out what had upset her. But I really had to go to class, so I asked her to send me an email about it. I thought, whatever it was, it needn't worry her so much. She could tell me what it is and we could talk about it when I saw her again. She agreed, and I left. I held her again and gave her a kiss and told her I loved her. Then I left.'

31

Of the two prosecutors, it was just Carien Teunissen who had been involved in Fred's case since the beginning, with Christénus van der Vijver having been brought in only when it became clear how long and complex the trial would be.

It was said of Teunissen that she was one of the province's more successful prosecutors; that she had lost, as one newspaper would report after Fred's acquittal, only one previous case in more than a decade on the job. But a win–loss record is a less fruitful measure of a prosecutor's skills than the ability to cross-examine a self-possessed, highly intelligent witness. In this, her colleague, Christénus van der Vijver, seemed the more able. One example of this was that he'd been able to create some doubts about the reliability of Mkuseni Mbomvu's testimony about Fred's presence at the meeting during the afternoon of 16 March, while at the same time managing to treat the witness with some civility. Teunissen, by contrast, had done nothing to weaken the evidence of Stefanus de Wet van der Spuy that Fred had been at his desk at about 17:10 or that Director Trollip might have been over-aggressive in seeking to get him to change his original statement. And, in failing to dent Van der Spuy's evidence, she had also managed to conduct herself with what seemed an unnecessary degree of sourness and suspicion. That sourness and suspicion seemed particularly unnecessary since police evidence corroborated what Van der Spuy had said: somebody with access to Fred's password had logged onto his computer at 17:13 and had sent two emails from it.

Perhaps this is an unfair comparison, but when one of the other journalists spoke to the police investigators, they apparently made it clear to her that they'd have preferred Van der Vijver to have cross-examined Fred. The only reason this did not happen, my colleague was told, was that the advice of the police psychologist, Dr Labuschagne, had been that it might be more strategic for a woman to confront Fred to test his reaction to that experience.

If it were given – and Labuschagne was, in fact, in court for those days – it was advice that seems premised on an approach to forensic psychology that drew more on the traditions of Hollywood than anything else. And it was advice that led to an important strategic mistake. The extent of this mistake can be measured by a single metric: that after a cross-examination that lasted three days, producing a transcript of more than 300 pages, when Fred's lawyers were given the opportunity to re-examine their client in order to shore up any of his evidence that might have been weakened during his cross-examination, they would ask no questions at all. In three days, Teunissen had produced not a single challenge to Fred's evidence that his lawyers thought sufficiently serious as to warrant asking a follow-up question. Not one.

* * *

It is difficult to describe the organising principles of Teunissen's cross-examination of Fred. At a minimum, she needed to show him to be an unreliable witness, to show that his story was too riddled with contradiction and inconsistency and implausibility to be taken seriously. But she seemed to want to do more than this: she seemed to want to show that the fight with Inge had been serious enough to induce a murderous rage. And she seemed to want to show that Fred was sufficiently strange that he might be capable of bludgeoning a woman to death. She wanted, in effect, to prove that the psychodrama, whose contours had become so fixed in the public mind, was right; to show that Inge's tragedy had been to fall in love with a super-intelligent but deeply troubled young man.

Teunissen's dilemma is obvious in retrospect. In order to attack the credibility of Fred's evidence, as she needed to do, she needed to question him closely on all the details so as to extract inconsistencies and contradictions. This, however, takes time, time in which Fred might become less and less obviously the psychopath of popular imagination, and become, instead, more and more ordinary and familiar and unthreatening.

If that was the essence of Teunissen's dilemma, its resolution was relatively straightforward: because a judge is expected to accept evidence given under oath unless there are compelling reasons not to, Teunissen had to keep Fred on the stand long enough to find contradictions in his own evidence, as well as inconsistencies between what he said and what other witnesses had said.

This was Teunissen's overriding objective. But, as the decision of Fred's lawyers to ask no follow-up questions of their client after three days of cross-examination would show, it was beyond her. Mostly, this was because she could find no real weaknesses in Fred's story. But it also had something to do with another kind of problem altogether: her own lack of facility with the management of the details of the case.

Nor was this lack of facility a complete surprise to anyone who'd followed the case closely, having emerged in its starkest form at the end of the prosecution's case, some weeks before any of Fred's witnesses testified and some months before he himself took the stand.

* * *

As was their right, Fred's lawyers applied at the close of the state's case to have the charges against him dismissed on the grounds that the cross-examination of the prosecution's witnesses had already shown that there was no case to answer. Legally and procedurally, the argument they made was something of a stretch, and it would have required a very expansive reading of the relevant provisions of the law for the judge to have granted their application. Less important than the defence's legal chance-taking, however, was the fact that, in answering the application, the prosecutors had had to put together an account of what they believed their witnesses' evidence had proved. In the course of this, they suggested that what had probably happened on 16 March 2005 was that Fred had gone to visit Inge at some point in the afternoon in order to try to straighten out the fight that had happened that morning. When he left work, they suggested, he had not intended to kill Inge, and that, precisely because he did not intend to kill Inge, he had had no fear of showing himself again at Merriman Furniture in order to pick up the cupboard. Something happened in the course of his conversation with Inge, however, to provoke him to murder.

By this telling, the murder was spontaneous and unplanned, and it was not for that reason alone implausible. But to accept this account – to offer it, in fact – demanded that one overlook details that some might have thought were important to the prosecution's case. For example: if Fred had not intended to kill Inge, surely whomever it was he was supposed to have been with at Merriman Furniture would not have been an accomplice and would, therefore, have come forward by now. For example: if Fred had not left Old Mutual intending to kill Inge, he probably would have used his card to get out the building, making it difficult to explain how he'd left no trace of this. For example: if Fred had not intended killing Inge when he left Old Mutual, he would have been in his work clothes rather than his Hi-Tec squash shoes when they spoke. For example: if Fred had not intended killing Inge when he arrived at her flat, he would not have been carrying his hammer.

To offer these challenges is not to quibble over minor details, but to go to the heart of the state's case, and the fact that the prosecutors could have constructed an account of what happened that was open to challenges of this sort suggested that they were not particularly good at relating the individual details of their case to the story they wanted to tell. The result was an account that made no sense, that was contradicted by the evidence needed to prove it to be true, and which, as a result, collapsed under the merest whiff of scepticism.

It was gaps of this disconcerting kind between the literal content of the state's case and the account of the crime they wished to prove that would emerge again and again during Fred's cross-examination.

Consider, for example, Teunissen's questioning of Fred in relation to the letter Inge had written, and recall that there had been much debate about whether the short, undated note on blue letter paper was part of the same letter as the dated foolscap sheet of lined paper. Fred had said that the short letter followed from, and concluded, the long one, while it was the prosecutors who'd insisted that the short letter had been given to Fred at some time before the murder, that it was unrelated to the long letter, and that Fred's attempt to pass it off as the letter Inge had given him that day was suspicious and incriminating. Given that that was their case, one might wonder why Teunissen would challenge Fred's account of the letter by pointing out that, in both his plea explanation offered at the start of the trial and in his sworn statement of 12 April 2005, he'd referred only to 'a letter', in the singular. Why, she demanded, hadn't he spoken of two letters?

It was hard to make sense of this question because it was hard to imagine any circumstances – irrespective of whether Fred was guilty or innocent – under which he would have spoken of 'letters', in the plural. He would not have done so if he were guilty and had tried, as the prosecution alleged, to pass off the short note as the whole letter. Nor would he have done so if he were innocent, irrespective of whether or not the short letter had accompanied the long one. In both circumstances, he'd have done exactly what he did: speak of only one letter. The question made no sense, and the result was that Fred's answer to it served only to reinforce the point that his evidence on this question had been consistent from the beginning: 'M'Lord,' he said, 'I saw them as one letter.'

If Teunissen's tactics here were obscure to the point of incomprehensible, consider another example of the same kind of problem she had with relating the details of the case to the story she was trying to tell. This time, the example relates to the claim made repeatedly by the prosecution that Fred's worry on the night of the murder was unjustified and was, therefore, suspiciously overwrought and indicative of a guilty conscience. Quoting from Marius's testimony, Teunissen notes that it recorded the recollection that Fred had told Marius before he left the flat that Mrs Lotz was worried about her daughter. 'Did you say that?' she asks.

A: That is correct.

Q: But, sir, that cannot be correct because Mrs Lotz testified that she was not worried. On the contrary, she invited you to go look in on Inge for yourself and she didn't even go along. She was not worried. She said she'd talk to Inge again later that night. Why did you tell Marius that she was worried?

A: M'Lord, as I testified, I understood that Mrs Lotz had also tried to get hold of Inge and that she was worried. If I can refer to the exhibit: my conversation with Marius was between 22:18 and 22:22, between those two calls to Mrs Lotz. That is when I told him I was going. If you look, by that point Mrs Lotz had already made one, two, three, four, five, six calls to Inge in six minutes. The only thing I can think is that, during that

349

call, Mrs Lotz told me that she had also tried to get
hold of Inge.

Q: Yes. But she wasn't worried.

JUDGE: Well, I think if she made six calls in six minutes, it does
sound like she was worried.

Q: But, M'Lord, there was testimony from Mrs Lotz that
she wasn't really worried because she knew Inge had
her phone on silent. Now you see that there were a
number of calls. But did you know that before you left
or did Mrs Lotz tell you she had made those calls and
Inge hadn't answered?

A: I hoped to make that clear. Obviously I only saw this
after the state made it available to us. But my memory
of that conversation with Mrs Lotz was that she had
also tried to get hold of Inge and was worried. And it
accords with this.

JUDGE: Well, I see that she made ten calls between 22:14 and
22:48.

So, in raising the question of Mrs Lotz's state of mind, Teunissen had
allowed Fred to introduce details, previously unaired, that conveyed the
message that, whatever Mrs Lotz had said in court, the evidence from
her cellphone records suggested that she must have been worried about
Inge. This had been one of the issues on which Teunissen had spent some
time during her first set of closing arguments; it was a question for which
Fred had obviously prepared, and, in giving his answer, one might say
that he'd displayed a certain degree of ruthlessness. Still, it was now also
obvious that to say that Fred had presented suspiciously more worry
than Inge's mother (who had professed herself to have been calm) was
no longer as tenable as it had been before Teunissen asked the question.

* * *

In cross-examining Fred, Teunissen's strongest card is the letter Inge wrote on the morning of her death. It is a letter, it will be recalled, in which Inge expresses her love for Fred and speaks of being 'absolutely committed' to the relationship. But, as will also be recalled, there was more to the letter than that: there were the references to her poor self-image and to various 'problems' (some unspecified); there was her stated fear that she might sometimes disappoint Fred by failing to be perfect; there were her promises to remain faithful.

It was a letter that might be read as placatory, something that raised the critical question: why did she feel she needed to placate Fred?

These were questions that were reinforced by Teunissen's other trump card – the testimony of Inge's best friend, Wimpie Boschoff, with whom she'd had lunch on the afternoon of the murder.

Wimpie had testified that he and Inge talked about her relationship with Fred being at an end that day, and that she had told him that they had had a 'helluva fight'. 'Those were her precise words,' he'd emphasised before saying that she'd said 'everything was over' between herself and Fred.

All of which helped explain why the prosecutors had their doubts about whether the short letter, the tone of which was much more unambiguously upbeat, followed on and concluded the longer one. 'I also just want to say how much I appreciate you and how special you are,' it read. 'Thank you for your love and that you are ALWAYS prepared to listen to my little problem! I love you VERY, VERY, VERY much. All the best for your day and week. I know Jesus will be with you every moment.'

If these were Inge's last thoughts before she finished the letter, they would tend to close off some of the interpretive possibilities left open by the longer letter, with all its uncertainties and ambiguities, uncertainties and ambiguities that had been greatly reinforced by Wimpie's evidence.

But it wasn't as if Wimpie's evidence was without uncertainties and ambiguities of its own. He had testified, for example, that he hadn't taken Inge all that seriously when she'd announced that her relationship with

Fred was over. This, he'd said, was something she had said about other boyfriends, and that nothing much had happened then. Besides, he'd testified also that Inge had been happy that day, that she'd spoken of the trip she and Fred were planning for the Easter weekend, and that she'd also spoken of her desire to get engaged to him at the end of the year. These were not the kinds of things that one might expect a young woman to say if she genuinely believed that her relationship with her boyfriend was irretrievably broken, and it opened the possibility that she'd spoken of the fight partly out of the pleasures of self-dramatisation.

What, then, was the truth about the letter? Why had Inge written it on the day she died, and what did it signify?

When Teunissen confronts him about it, Fred's approach is to cast Inge's letter against the background of their interactions over the course of the previous evening and into that morning. Inge, he suggests, had been upset by his distance and inaccessibility, something he describes as having been provoked by the coolness of the conversation he'd had with his brother. This, he says, had resulted in a tearful breakfast and parting and Inge's accusation that he didn't love her anymore. Inge's letter, he says, should be read as an explanation of, and an apology for, actions she described in the letter's first paragraph as 'unreasonable'. All she wanted to do was explain what was on her mind and why.

There is, of course, no way of knowing if this is really what Inge intended. Certainly, there is much in the letter that supports this reading, but there are also many threads that cannot be made to fit so neatly into this fabric. The most important of these are the promises Inge made at the end of the letter to remain faithful.

Asked by Teunissen how he understands these words, Fred offers no really satisfying answer. Initially he says that perhaps it was 'something that two people might say to each other if they love each other and are serious about the future.' This is hardly convincing, however, and he quickly retreats from it to a position of professed ignorance at Inge's intentions. It's perhaps the most vulnerable moment of his cross-examination, but

Teunissen lacks the tools to break through his defence because she has no evidence that either he or Inge had fought about infidelity, much less that either had actually been unfaithful.

From one point of view this is unimportant because the absence of evidence does not mean that Fred had had no suspicions about Inge. From another point of view, however, the absence of evidence is significant in the same way that it seemed significant that no-one at the Old Mutual workshop recalled Fred's having been out of the room for any length of time, and in the same way that Sherlock Holmes realised the significance of the failure of the hound of the Baskervilles to bark: as soon as one thinks about it, one feels drawn to the inescapable conclusion that if there was someone with whom Inge was being unfaithful, he would surely have come forward by now.

There are only two reasons I can think of why this might not have happened: either the person didn't exist or he didn't want to reveal himself in case it brought unwanted investigative attention to bear on him.

*   *   *

Almost all of Teunissen's questions to Fred related to issues of his motive and to the behaviour that the judge had characterised as 'strange', issues that could tend to the psychological and which were, for that reason, vaporous. The one exception to this rule was the extensive questioning to which she subjected Fred about a detail that was so precise and so particular, but at the same time so obscure, that the attention devoted to it seemed to imply that it must signify intrigues and mysteries that had yet to be properly aired. The detail in question? The the precise colour of the pants Fred was wearing when he left Inge's flat on the morning of the murder.

That this should be an issue at all was the result of the notes Superintendent de Beer had taken during his interview with Fred on the morning of 17 March. Testifying about what he learnt during that interview, he repeated what Fred had told him about his movements of that day. It was an account that included this: 'He dressed in the bathroom. The type of clothes were black jeans and a blue shirt.'

Those 'black jeans' were not, however, the pants Fred appeared to be wearing in the CCTV footage that recorded his arrival at work just after 11:00. That footage is black-and-white, but in it, he appears to be wearing pants that are grey rather than black.

During Teunissen's first set of closing arguments, offered two weeks before Fred testified, she'd made much of this apparent contradiction. 'It raises,' she said, 'the question as to why he changed clothes before he arrived at Mutual Park.'

Precisely what question was raised by the possibility that Fred had changed his clothes somewhere between five and nine hours *before* the murder was not immediately apparent, and the obscurity of the issue was to increase a moment later. Relating the testimony of Marius Botha, Teunissen said then that his evidence had been that when Fred got home that night, he'd been wearing grey work pants. Marius had also testified, she said, that that night Fred broke his usual habit of changing out of work clothes even though he knew he still had the cupboard to deliver. 'One would expect,' Teunissen offered, 'that a person would try to spare his smarter clothes, so the question must be asked: did he know then that he would be going out later?'

This argument had been made before Fred testified, and, having heard it, he tried to explain what he thought had happened. When De Beer interviewed him, he testified, he was still wearing the clothes that he'd put on in Inge's flat twenty-four hours earlier: a blue office-wear shirt and grey corduroy pants cut like a pair of jeans. He said that what he suspects happened is that when De Beer asked him about the clothes he'd worn the day before, he simply indicated that they were the ones he was in. De Beer, he said, must have written the words 'black jeans and blue shirt' in his notes. He did not, he says, tell De Beer that his jeans were black.

The suspicions Teunissen had about Fred's changing clothes between leaving Inge's flat and getting to work, then, might have had their roots in an understandable misreading of De Beer's testimony and the cryptic notes on which that was based, in neither of which is it clear how De Beer came by the particular details about Fred's outfit that day. But since grey pants are what can be seen in the CCTV footage, and since Marius had said Fred was wearing grey pants when he got home, and since Marius had also said that Fred did not change before he left for Inge's flat, and since there is no evidence anywhere of Fred's changing his pants at the Lotzes', it is not implausible that Fred really was wearing the same grey pants when De Beer interviewed him as he'd been wearing when he got to work the previous morning.

If De Beer had referred to them as black jeans, that may have been a mistake born of indifference to this seemingly minor detail or because the precise character of the pants was uncertain: perhaps the grey was a dark one, or, as is sometimes the case with corduroy, perhaps the black had a faded, washed-out quality so that they might appear grey on black-and-white CCTV footage and in Marius's memory. De Beer's notes might, in other words, have simply reflected the fact, widely established in empirical work on eyewitness testimony, that different people register and record details of the same event in sometimes surprisingly incompatible ways.

So, not only had Teunissen offered no reason to think that if Fred really had been wearing black jeans at 8:00, his changing into grey pants by 11:00 would be suspicious, it now also seemed that there was an entirely plausible explanation for how the uncertainty about their colour had arisen. Teunissen could easily have let the matter go. But a suspicion of this kind can sometimes exert a powerful hold, so when she questioned Fred about his pants she adopted a new but equally puzzling argument.

Having first asked Fred to repeat his claim that De Beer must have written the word 'black jeans' after Fred had indicated that the pants he was wearing then were the some ones he'd put on in Inge's flat, she asks, 'But why were you wearing the same clothes? You had a tog bag with clothes that you'd taken because you would have stayed over at Inge's had there been nothing wrong.'

    A: M'Lord, I did have a tog bag and clothes with me to stay over at Inge's that night. But I didn't stay over. After we got the news that night, everything was just chaos. I never thought about changing my clothes.

    Q: But you had clothes to change into?

    A: That's correct. I had a bag with clothes.

    Q: But surely if you had gone to work the next day you would not have worn what you were wearing the day before.

    A: No, M'Lord, I wouldn't have. I would have put on other clothes.

    Q: It wasn't because the police caught you unexpectedly or that they arrived at the Lotzes' unexpectedly, and you didn't have time to change. That wasn't the reason you were still in the same clothes?

    A: No, M'Lord.

Again, these were questions that made no sense. But at least they appeared to be premised on an acceptance that Fred was still in the grey pants Marius had testified he'd been wearing after work. Two weeks later, however, when she had the opportunity to supplement her original closing arguments on the basis of having now heard Fred's testimony, Teunissen's take on the question of Fred's pants would go in the exact opposite direction. Arguing that Superintendent de Beer's evidence about Fred wearing black jeans when he left Inge's flat had never been disputed, she would say, 'With respect, M'Lord, grey pants and black jeans are two different things. There has been an attempt to adjust the testimony around this by referring to the fact that the pants had a jeans cut. But that doesn't take matters any further.'

And that is all she would say: she would offer the judge no thoughts on whether the gap between Fred's 'grey pants' and De Beer's 'black jeans' arose because Fred had been wearing black jeans when he left Inge's flat and had changed before he got to work, or arose, alternatively, because Fred had been wearing black jeans when he was interviewed by De Beer, and must, therefore, have changed out of the grey pants he'd been wearing when he arrived at work and when he and Marius had had supper together. It seemed that the fact of the inconsistency between Fred's evidence and De Beer's was all that interested Teunissen. Something suspicious, she was insisting, had been found, but precisely what it was and why it was suspicious was a question that was cryptic to the point of inscrutability.

* * *

Teunissen's lack of facility with the management of detail became more and more apparent over the four days of cross-examination, during which she persisted with questions about details that could never help her prove that Fred killed Inge. Where had Fred parked when he visited the furniture store after his class? What route had he taken to get there? How many U-turns had he made? How many speed cameras were on the main road between Stellenbosch and Pinelands? What alternative roads could he have taken? Had he ever taken those roads? How many speed cameras were posted on these? It was painful stuff, and it sometimes seemed possible that it was intended to test Fred's ability to control the rage she must have assumed he was concealing in his heart.

Another of her tactics was the surprise question, thrown in from left field in an attempt to wrong-foot Fred. Thus, on the morning of Tuesday 23 October, Teunissen's first question of Fred's fifth day on the stand, asked without so much as a 'good morning' to either Fred or the judge, was: 'Mr van der Vyver, the decision not to begin a serious relationship immediately, to wait, instead, so that you could get to know each other better, did it have anything to do with the teachings of His People Church?'

A: No, M'Lord. It had nothing to do with that.

Q: Were there any prescriptions or teachings or principles of the church that were part of your relationship?

A: M'Lord, I'd say that Inge and I tried to apply everything that is taught in the Bible as far as we could. The Church's position was based on the Bible, so you could see it that way. That is correct.

Q: Yes, but we know that both of you grew up in the Dutch Reformed Church, and that His People Church doesn't necessarily interpret the Bible in the same way, not so? They could have different approaches to certain things?

A: M'Lord, I believe their views were based on the Bible. It is quite hard to give a general answer to that question.

Q: Was there a principle that when one of the parties to a new relationship had been involved in prior relationships, he or she must first end those relationships and make a confession about them?

Now, you might think that after an opening like that, Teunissen would have something specific in mind. You might think she'd have had evidence that His People Church would involve itself intrusively in any relationships that began to bud between members of its flock. You might think that she'd have a document setting out bizarre rituals of confession and cleansing and enforced sexual abstinence with which to confront Fred, a document that might prove he was a weirdo and a liar. In fact, her actual follow-up, after Fred's protestation of ignorance about what she was getting at, is this: 'Did you and Inge ever talk about her previous relationships?'

A: That's correct. We did talk about them from time to time.

Q: And what was your attitude to her previous relationships?

A: M'Lord, I can't say that I had a specific attitude. They
had happened. I mean, everyone at university has had
relationships. There was nothing specific … Really, I
don't know how to answer that question.

JUDGE: I think that the question is just about how you felt about
her having had previous relationships.

A: M'Lord, I didn't have a problem with that.

It was cross-examination that recalled Denis Healey's phrase, now pro-
verbial in the British House of Commons: like being savaged by a dead
sheep.

* * *

Teunissen devotes the last few hours of her cross-examination of Fred to
the contradictions between his account of events at Mrs Lotz's home and
the account offered first by Mrs Lotz and then by Marius when they had
testified. And there were, indeed, a number differences: Fred said that he
and Mrs Lotz went indoors after she found him in his car where, he said,
he'd been waiting for Marius; Mrs Lotz, by contrast, had said that Marius
arrived before she and Fred had had a chance to speak. Mrs Lotz and
then Marius both said that Fred told Mrs Lotz that Inge had been murdered that afternoon; Fred, by contrast, said Marius conveyed the news
of the murder first to him and then to Mrs Lotz. Mrs Lotz and Marius
said Fred proposed becoming the child in the house; Fred denied saying
anything of the sort.

Confronting Fred with these differences, Teunissen asks, 'So, you are
saying that both Marius and Mrs Lotz are telling lies about this?'

It is a trap, of course: for Fred to call Mrs Lotz a liar would make him
seem cold and calculating. He doesn't fall for it.

A: M'Lord, the account Mrs Lotz gave in court is not how
it happened. I can't explain why that is. I understand

that she might have been confused. All that I can do is tell you what really happened. That is also how Marius described it in his detailed statement, and it is the truth.

Q: Marius didn't testify that you and Mrs Lotz were in the house. On the contrary, he denied it. Are you saying he's wrong or that he is lying when he said you were outside in the bakkie?

A: Yes, M'Lord. Marius is wrong if he says I was in my bakkie. I was in the house. I opened the gate for him from inside. I met him at the gate.

Q: You say that Mrs Lotz may have been in shock, but Marius seems to have remained calm that night. That's why he decided that he should bring the message to you and Mrs Lotz. He supported you. He was worried about your car. Why would he deny your account?

A: M'Lord, I can't explain why Marius departed from his statement when he testified in court. All I can say is that what is in his statement supports my account and is the truth about what happened that night.

Confronted with this explicit questioning of her own witness's credibility and consistency, Teunissen has this to say: 'M'Lord, I'll leave it there.'

PART EIGHT

32

You could write a history of civilisation as a history of the evolution of judging.

Such a history would be a history of law and, therefore, of the state and its authority. It would be a history of reason and its relationship both to passion and to superstition. It would be a history of god and religion, from which most societies derive their ideas of right and wrong, and a history of the role of mortal man in the pursuit of divine plans. It would be a history of the idea of truth, a history of the idea of crime, and a history of that most unstable of all ideas – justice.

It would not be a history of uninterrupted moral progress, one in which the ideas that dominate one generation's thinking, and the practices to which they give birth, are always and everywhere better than the ideas and practices of previous generations. Sometimes new ideas betray older commitments, as has happened to the Americans in Guantanamo Bay. Sometimes new ideas turn out to be no more than silly fads that make no lasting impression, as some kinds of modern sentencing strategies will one day seem. And yet, for the most part, a history of judging would be a history in which new thinking has usually been an improvement on old, a history about which it might legitimately be said that institutions in much of the world have tended to become fairer and more rational from one century to the next, from one generation to the next.

And, at the heart of this history is the judge, and, as importantly, the idea of the judge, whose various incarnations over the millennia include the tribal elder, the religious mystic, the feudal lord, the papal inquisitors of Spain, the witch-hunters of New England, the frontier magistrates of the New World, the political committees of revolutionary Russia, and the war crimes jurists of the second half of the twentieth century. It is a freighted, contradictory history, and it is one that helps to shape the thoughts and ideas (and even the dress) of modern judges in liberal-democratic orders, whose most important distinctions from their predecessors are their training and experience, the transparency of their proceedings, their legal and institutional independence from the rest of the state, and the consequent insistence that they apply the law without fear, favour or prejudice.

And yet, despite the progress towards greater rationality and fairness, judges remain real human beings, with human fallibility and human blind spots, with human prejudices and human affiliations to people and ideas and institutions. All of which shapes their thoughts in ways they may not be aware of.

This is an issue that arises again and again when judges are appointed to their countries' highest courts, when it is often suggested that different life experiences would lead to new interpretations of the law. It is an inescapable reality that is condemned by some, in thrall to the idea of the neutral, disinterested application of the law. Judges, they say, must transcend their experience and apply the law as it is written. For others, this is impossible, and it means that judges with different experiences will interpret the law in incompatible ways. This is one reason (among others) why the demand for the transformation of the judiciary in South Africa has such political and social traction, and it is the reason also why Sonia Sotomayor, the first Hispanic appointment to the US Supreme Court, once said, unwisely perhaps, that she would hope that 'a wise Latina woman with the richness of her experiences would more often than not reach a better conclusion than a white male who hasn't lived that life.'

For the most part, discussions about how a judge's background affects his or her decision-making relate to how that background might affect the way he or she interprets the law. Is a black judge from a poor family more or less likely than a white judge from a rich family to view the rights of tenants more sympathetically than the rights of landlords? Would a woman judge interpret the rights to equality and to dignity more expansively than a man? Would a gay judge be more sympathetic to the marginal and the excluded than a straight one?

For most people, I think, it is impossible to believe that, however hard a judge tries to transcend his own values and commitments and tries to decide the case strictly in terms of the law, there will be times when a judge's background is a factor – sometimes an important factor – in his interpretation of the law. But the interpretation of the law is not something that judges – apart from those who serve on the highest courts – are required to do all that often. For the most part, a judge decides cases on the basis of established law, which he applies to the facts. It is a process to which a judge's background and personality and values might be thought to be irrelevant: the facts are the facts, the law is the law; the decision is determined by the application of the one to the other.

But there is a problem with this model, too: facts don't arrive at court washed and chopped and ready to be used in the presiding officer's soup. They are delivered, instead, in the testimony of witnesses, testimony that, as often as not, will conflict with the testimony of other witnesses. And, as a result, choosing between conflicting testimony about the same facts is itself a process of interpretation. Sometimes that will be easy because one witness might be so entangled in his own lies that he will lose all credibility. But at other times, deciding who is lying and who is not will be less straightforward. And when that happens, a judge's existing prejudices and commitments might help shape his views about the credibility of the individual witnesses.

An instructive example of this is the view taken by Judge Deon van Zyl that MK's evidence, to the effect that Fred was sitting next to him on 16 March, was unreliable, something he stated explicitly during the course of closing arguments. That's fair enough, of course, and there was at least some confusion in MK's testimony. Harder to understand, however, was that the judge repeated this assessment of MK's evidence in his judgment even after he'd concluded that Fred had not killed Inge and that he could not have done so because he was at work. MK's evidence, in other words, was judged to be unreliable even though it was also judged to be true. For the evidence of a witness to be both true and unreliable would seem to be something of a contradiction. Unless, of course, the question of a witness's reliability was not exclusively a question of his perceived honesty.

This question of how judges interpret the evidence of different witnesses is also a question that Christénus van der Vijver raised when he cross-examined Pat Wertheim. With his very first questions, the prosecutor had suggested that the advantage of having a judge rather than a jury hear a case is that it is far harder for a wily lawyer to throw dust in the eyes of an experienced judge. Juries, Van der Vijver said, lack the knowledge to apply properly the concepts of probability and improbability. It is a prejudice common to many who work in South Africa's courts, and, as much as anything, it draws its strength from the coverage of the OJ Simpson trial in the mid-1990s. Only a jury, so the thinking goes, could have so wilfully ignored the evidence of Simpson's guilt; a judge, with his superior knowledge, his impartiality and his intellectual discipline, would have had no trouble convicting the former sports star.

Whatever the prejudices, the question of whether juries are more susceptible than judges to lawyers' tricks is ultimately an empirical one, and it can be explored by comparing the decisions judges and juries would come to if asked to assess precisely the same cases, presented by precisely the same lawyers. That sounds hard to do properly, but a number of American studies have asked judges to record their own assessment of the correct decision in cases that are decided by juries. And the outcomes of these studies are extremely consistent: in about eighty percent of cases, judges and juries come to precisely the same conclusion, while in the remaining cases, judges are between four and six times more likely to convict than are juries.

These are studies that should temper Van der Vijver's prejudice against juries (they come to the same conclusion as judges in eighty percent of cases), while at the same time confirming it (when judges and juries disagree, it is usually the jury that would acquit). It is possible, then, that defence lawyers really are sometimes able to confuse juries into wrongful acquittals.

And yet, matters are not quite so simple. Consider the arresting finding of one study, in which, in addition to recording their assessment of whether or not the accused should be convicted, judges were also asked to evaluate the strength of the prosecution's case. Asked to do this, it emerged that judges would have convicted the accused in about half the cases in which they themselves deemed the prosecution's case to be weak. The numbers were not large, but it meant that in about five percent of all cases, judges said they would convict an accused even though their own assessment of the evidence against him was that it was weak. This result, along with some others, leads the seven authors of the study to conclude that, compared to juries, judges have a lower evidentiary threshold for a conviction.

Why is this? Why are judges willing to convict on evidence that they themselves deem 'weak'? The studies I've seen don't answer this question particularly convincingly. They can tell us that the more educated a juror, the more likely he or she is to acquit. They can tell us that men are more likely to convict than women, and that black jurors appear more willing to acquit than white. But it seems to me that the focus on the jury misses the critical question of why it is that judges tend to be more willing to convict than jurors. One possibility – the one I suspect Van der Vijver would endorse – is that jurors are more easily confused than judges. Another, though, is that judges tend to be more willing to believe the prosecution's witnesses than are jurors. And, since many prosecution witnesses are police officers, it may well mean that American judges are more willing to take police officers at their word than juries are.

That, of course, is speculation. What is not speculation is that when Christénus van der Vijver offered his closing arguments in Fred's case, he seemed to assume that Judge van Zyl would be so unwilling to call the police liars that he would have no alternative but to send Fred to prison.

* * *

On the morning of 1 October, Carien Teunissen had risen in her pew to begin making what would turn out to be only the first set of closing arguments for the state, arguments to which she would add her reflections on Fred's testimony some four weeks later. She began by setting out aspects of the law she regarded as critical to the case she was making: the evidence against Fred was all circumstantial, she acknowledged, but it all fit together to create a mosaic from which the only reasonable inference that could be drawn was that Fred was guilty.

The most important circumstantial evidence was forensic, but, before she got to that, Teunissen focused the judge's attention on various examples of Fred's suspicious behaviour: his exaggerated worry on the night of the murder; the peculiar encouragement he gave Marius when his flatmate suggested that Christo Pretorius be asked to check up on Inge, even though he was himself going to Stellenbosch; his failure to answer Mrs Lotz's call when he was sitting in his car outside her house;

his incriminating knowledge that Inge had been murdered and that she had been murdered in the afternoon; his offer to become the child in Mrs Lotz's house; his actually moving into the house and into Inge's room; the volume of his clothes Inge's uncle had found in the room a week later; the withholding of the long letter from Mrs Lotz; the presentation of a short letter that may have been written at some earlier date, and his 'instructions' to the private investigators not to show it to Inge's mother after he made it available to them; his failure ever to mention to anyone that he and Inge had argued on the morning of the murder; his claim to have been wearing 'black jeans' when the CCTV footage of his arrival at work shows him in grey pants; and the readiness of the alibi he offered to Superintendent de Beer on the morning after the murder (a point she made twice).

Regarding Fred's alibi, Teunissen pointed to the evidence of Jakobus Nicolaas Swart, the clerk at Merriman Furniture who had testified that Fred had come into the store twice on 16 March; that the first visit was in the morning when he looked at the cupboard and that the second was after lunch, and that Fred had been accompanied by a second person. She argued that the fact that Fred drew R500 during his lecture in the morning didn't prove he'd bought the cupboard on his first visit, and that because there were only two transactions recorded in the store's books that day, it was likely that Swart would have remembered Fred. She said that Janine von Stein, the facilitator of the workshop at Old Mutual, did not think Fred's presence at the meeting on 16 March was crucial and said she would not have missed him if he left. She said that the evidence given by Mkuseni Mbomvu was confused and that the judge ought to draw negative inferences from the fact that the defence did not call Shahana Toefy despite her presence in court. She said that the real reason Stefanus de Wet van der Spuy was called was not to prove that Fred was at work at 17:10 and that he appeared calm and collected, but to give the police another slap in the face. She said the fact that Fred's phone registered at Mutual Park during the day did not mean that he was at Mutual Park, and that there was no evidence that he alone had access to his phone. She said that the security system at Mutual Park had so many deficiencies that it was possible for Fred to slip out and return without his movements being recorded.

It was a long litany of issues, accounting for two thirds of her argument, none of which came close to establishing that Fred was anywhere near Inge's flat when she was killed. For that, she needed the judge to accept the police account of the forensic evidence.

Teunissen said that it was never the state's case that one could see with the naked eye that the bloody mark had been made by Fred's shoe; she said that it could be linked to the shoe through the four white spots which matched grains of sand embedded in the sole. She said that it was no surprise to her that no blood had been found on Fred's shoe because he had the shoe in his possession between 16 March and 15 April, and there was testimony from Marius suggesting that the shoe looked as if it had been cleaned. She said that one could only speculate about why there were no tracks leading from the lounge to the bedroom, and that blood may have landed on the sole of the shoe only when Fred was already in the bathroom. She said the square appendage that Koekemoer had added to the stain was not used in the match with the shoe. She said that the tests Bodziak had done with the other shoe in order to test whether the grains of sand could have made contact with the floor were not relevant because they were done with a thin fluid that was not as sticky as blood. She said that the defence witnesses were not credible. Ryder, she complained, made no concessions to her hypotheticals. About Bodziak, she said it was impossible to establish who was telling the truth about Bartholomew's visit to Florida, and that she doubted that Bodziak had made the notes on which his evidence relied at the time of the consultation since he had no intention of coming to South Africa then. She said that neither Ryder nor Bodziak could explain how it happened that the four white spots matched four grains of sand in Fred's shoe.

Teunissen said that it had been proved by the Luminol tests that there were traces of blood on the hammer, and that the DNA test that had failed to find genetic material that matched Inge's was less sensitive than Luminol because it required the presence of comparatively rare white blood cells. She said that Captain Maritz's work showed that the hammer (as well as its replacement) could cause the injuries that were found on Inge's head and face, and that the first hammer may have bent because of 'metal fatigue'. She said that the differences between the dimensions of the wounds as measured by Dr Adendorff and their size as they appeared in the photos that Maritz used were 'minimal'. She said that Maritz's testimony was more reliable than that of Professor Saayman, who, in any event, had not categorically excluded the hammer as the murder weapon.

There was much that was troubling about these arguments. There had never, for example, been any evidence presented that metal fatigue might explain why the hammer bent. There had never been any evidence presented that said Luminol was more sensitive to the presence of blood than was a DNA test, although there had been plenty of evidence to the effect that Luminol often reacted with substances other than blood. There was no evidence that Bodziak's notes were not made at the time of the consultation with Bartholomew, and Teunissen had not even raised the possibility when Bodziak was on the stand. She also complained that Bodziak had never seen fit to tell the police (who had paid his fee, she noted) about his shock and amazement at the report prepared about the consultation in Florida, in the process apparently forgetting that that report had not been presented to anyone until Bartholomew testified in March. That, it will be recalled, was eight weeks after Bodziak had told the police and the prosecutors in a teleconference that he had not supported Bartholomew's conclusions.

Nor was it strictly true to say that neither Ryder or Bodziak had explained why the four white spots had matched four grains of sand: in fact, both had said that there were a lot of white spots and a lot of grains of sand, so finding a match between any four of one and any four of the other was not all that surprising. Both had also provided a compelling explanation of how the white spots had come into existence.

But if these arguments tended to the audacious, it was as nothing compared to what was to come when Teunissen's colleague, Christénus van der Vijver, summed up the fingerprint evidence in a way that amounted, finally, to the throwing down of a gauntlet before the judge: since there was no room for Folien One to have been switched with a lift that looked more like it had been taken from a DVD cover, Van der Vijver would argue, to find that it was not lifted from a DVD cover meant that the judge would also have to find that a whole group of officers must have deliberately lied.

At the outset, Van der Vijver made a gesture to the fact that, at the beginning of the trial he had told the judge that the fingerprint evidence, which he now said had 'grown in stature', would be presented only to show the *bone fides* of the officers involved, and to refute suggestions of deliberate fabrication. That assurance, made in February, had been backed up by a letter from the chief prosecutor of the province who had written the previous November to say that 'the state no longer intends to proceed with the evidence concerning your client's alleged fingerprints on the DVD cover.' It was also a letter to which had been attached the reports of Superintendents Rance and Dixon, both of whom were serving police officers and each of whom had come to the conclusion that Folien One was not consistent with a lift from a DVD cover.

That was in February. By August, Van der Vijver had argued that 'after hearing all the evidence, after hearing the evidence of Botha and Swartz even on questions about the powder that was used, the state is no longer convinced that a mistake crept in here.' Now he would go further still, pointing out all the police evidence that the judge would have to reject as untrue if he were to decide that Folien One did not come off a DVD cover.

There was, he said, no evidence that a glass of the appropriate size had been dusted for prints in Inge's flat. Nor were any of the other ten lifts taken from the crime scene consistent with a lift from a DVD cover. Coming to the same conclusion as Wertheim had, he said that these facts meant that there was no prospect that Folien One could have been taken off a glass and then been mistakenly identified as having come off a DVD cover. There was no evidence that a mistake could have been made, he said, but there was plenty of evidence that a lift had been taken from a DVD cover.

There was, first and foremost, the statement of Constable Swartz, the only person who could definitively say where Folien One came from. His evidence was supported by Bartholomew, who saw Folien One in the flat, and by the two other fingerprint examiners, who both said they were aware that the DVD cover had been dusted, even if neither saw the resulting lift. Van der Vijver said that, to find that the lift had come from anything other than a DVD cover, the judge would have to find that the statement Constable Swartz signed on 14 April 2005 was false. He said that there is no other word to describe the finding the judge would have to come to.

But the judge would have to go further, Van der Vijver said. He would also have to reject the testimony of Captain Matheus, who had said that he had conducted a twenty-four-hour inspection of Swartz's work on 18 March 2005, and that he was satisfied with the results. The judge would have to reject Captain Bester's evidence to the effect that, when he was asked on 12 April 2005 to compare the exclusion prints taken from Fred and a few others against the prints lifted from Inge's flat, Bartholomew's request had indicated that he should focus on Marius Botha's prints. This was evidence that Van der Vijver described as having 'the ring of truth' but which undermined the idea that there was a conspiracy against Fred. Given that they were the investigating officers, Van der Vijver said, if there had been a conspiracy to fabricate evidence, it would also have had to have involved Director Trollip and Inspector de Villiers. The evidence of both would also have to be rejected.

Van der Vijver acknowledged that there were problems with the evidence in the registers and statements, but he sought – judo style – to turn what seemed to be one of the strengths of the defence's case to his own advantage. The police, he said, would have had to have been extremely clumsy if they constructed a conspiracy and then left so many inconsistencies in the record. Those inconsistencies, he said, should be seen as evidence that there was no conspiracy.

In every sense of the word, Van der Vijver's argument was daring, and it ran the risk of disaster: by taking the possibility of a mistake off the table, he was, in effect, challenging the judge either to rule in his favour or declare a whole swathe of officers to be perjurers committed to sending an innocent man to jail.

33

Judgment Day was on 29 November 2007, a Thursday.

I had spent the previous evening listening to Christmas carols in a Johannesburg park, and had watched a pristine dawn from a window seat of a plane filled with the salespeople and middle managers and consultants whose jobs dictate a regular commute between South Africa's two largest cities. Having by now graduated to the status of a preferred customer at the car rental company, I'd slipped out of the airport ahead of the unpreferred masses and wound my way through the traffic to central Cape Town. I'd parked, as I usually did, at an open-air lot a few blocks from the court and trudged through the rising heat to the coffee shop I liked, with its red-and-black decor and its pretty waitresses.

I'd dawdled to court, resisting, I suppose, the idea that this was the end.

By now, we were in a larger, grander courtroom, the move a consequence of the huge media interest in the case. Instead of sitting in front
of the judge with my back to Fred and the lawyers and the families, here
I had an elevated seat on the side of the room from which I could see all
the role-players and watch their reactions. There must have been twenty
journalists in court. There were two television cameras and a pack of
photographers. Fred's family had come in from all parts. So had the family and friends of the Lotzes.

It was impossible to be unaware of the conflicting hopes and pas-
sions in the room in the moments before the judge entered. Fred looked
composed but drawn, his brothers standing beside him, talking to him
quietly. His father's jaw was set, his eyes hard; he spoke to no-one. Fred's
mother looked as if she had not slept in the three weeks since the second set of closing arguments had been delivered; she looked exhausted,
near despair and without resources. The Lotzes, too, looked drawn, and
must have been weary of the court and the lawyers and the journalists.
They stood with family and friends, Marius Botha among them. They
spoke with the prosecutors and with Director Trollip and Inspector de
Villiers.

Given the stakes and the irreconcilable commitments of the people in
the room, everyone was painfully polite, studiously avoiding eye contact
with anyone whose hopes diverged from his own, much less engaging
more intimate interactions and transactions: this was not a soccer match
where the opposing captains might tease each other or wish each other
the best of luck before the kick-off.

It was a relief when, just after 10:00, the judge entered and everyone
could fall silent.

* * *

Unlike a jury trial, a judge in a South African court is expected to explain
his reasoning, so by the time Judge van Zyl formally acquitted Fred, about

an hour and a half after he began to speak, and after having reviewed all the evidence the state had presented, the decision surprised no-one.

The prosecution's argument that Fred had left work, travelled to Stellenbosch, murdered Inge and then returned to the office in something less than two hours, without leaving any trace of his exit from the office park or his return, while managing all the time to act normally, was, the judge said, 'highly improbable, if not impossible.' It was his opinion, he said, that 'even with the most careful planning, this would simply not have been practically possible,' and that if Fred had planned matters as carefully as that, the murder would not have had the appearance of a spontaneous expression of uncontrolled rage.

He went further.

He said that he understood that the community and the victim's family would demand justice in a case such as this, but he said that the community and the family must also understand that a court cannot convict in the absence of sufficient evidence, and that he doubted whether there had ever been sufficient evidence even to bring this case to court.

His finding, in other words, was not just that the state had failed to prove beyond a reasonable doubt that Fred had killed Inge, but that the defence had shown that there was no evidence at all that Fred was a murderer, and that, purely as a practical matter, he could not have killed Inge.

The decision was all that Fred could have hoped for, and when the judge finished, moments after reading this passage, a great yell of victory came up from some of his family sitting in the gallery. For his part, Fred – who'd lost a quarter of his body weight and whose appendix had burst during the trial and who had crunched through a gum guard while sleeping one night – dropped his head into his hands in tearful prayer. His father and mother embraced and wept. De Bruyn, meanwhile, was clambering over the pews to get to Fred, like a Wimbledon champion climbing into the crowd to kiss his girlfriend.

But not everyone was happy: throughout the reading of the judgment,

I'd been watching the prosecutors and the police, and they were not pleased. About halfway through, Teunissen had put her hand to her forehead, shielding her eyes from the judge and from everyone else in the room. You could almost hear the frozen horror. Trollip, by contrast, had stared hard at the judge, his wizened face tight and angry, his eyes saying something like, 'I hope you never need the police in an emergency.'

And yet the police and prosecutors got off quite lightly.

Accepting Bodziak and Ryder's evidence that the bloody stain could not be matched to Fred's shoe, the judge said that Bruce Bartholomew, who was no longer a serving member of the police, made a 'poor impression' as a witness. His evidence, the judge said, was 'unreliable' and had been 'tainted by the seriously misleading account about what happened during his visit with Mr Bodziak.' Bartholomew, the judge said, also failed to 'play open cards' with his superiors when he reported back on this visit.

Noting that Professor Saayman's testimony about the character of wounds one would ordinarily expect if a hammer were used in an assault to someone's head was compelling, the judge said that the tests done by Frans Maritz, who was also no longer a member of the SAPS, were 'unscientific' and 'altogether unreliable'. It was his view, the judge said, that Maritz's failure to mention that the original hammer had bent and had been replaced 'borders on the unprofessional'. It was something, he said, that tainted the rest of Maritz's testimony.

Of the serving police officers who testified, only the testimony of Constable Swartz and his immediate superior, Captain Matheus, were criticised by the judge. Swartz, whom the judge pointed out had less than two years' experience when he stood in Inge's flat, had acknowledged violating various provisions of existing policy, but had been able to offer no reasonable account for why he'd done so. There were also, the judge said, material contradictions between his testimony and his sworn statement, and, as a witness, he too made a poor impression. He was, the judge said, inclined to evasiveness and could not be regarded as reliable.

Matheus, too, was unimpressive as a witness and evasive, offering only 'extremely unsatisfactory explanations' for his conduct.

But that was as far as the judge would go.

While four police officers or former police officers were described variously as 'evasive' or 'unimpressive' or 'unprofessional' or 'unreliable', none was described as a liar and none was said to have deliberately fabricated evidence.

The judge said, for example, that he was persuaded by Wertheim and Zeelenberg (whom he described as possessing extensive expertise and wide experience that had deservedly brought them international acclaim) that it was overwhelmingly probable that Folien One came from a glass. Still but he declined to accept Christénus van der Vijver's challenge to conclude that that must mean that the police had conspired to fabricate evidence. He said that it was true that that was the view of both Wertheim and Zeelenberg, but said that he could not exclude the possibility that the true story was one of 'negligence' or 'utter incompetence'.

About the complaint that the bloody stain had been manipulated to make it seem more like a shoeprint and that this evidence was also fabricated, the judge offered the dubious view that the allegation had become 'diluted' over time, and that he therefore had no reason to express an opinion.

Although the judge did not expressly exclude the possibility that evidence had been deliberately fabricated, his final word on the investigation was this: 'As reluctant as I am to question the functioning of the police, it appears that there was some ineffective and even clumsy investigative work at the outset of this case. Unfortunately, that might be ascribed largely to inadequate training and a lack of experience.'

We will return in a moment to this somewhat surprising statement about an investigation run by some of the province's most senior officers. But before we do so we need to record that, even as the judge devoted two thirds of his judgment to recounting how none of the evidence suggested that Fred killed Inge, he did seem to accept one central premise of the state's case: that she had been killed by someone close to her.

That the judge understood Inge's murder to have been the work of someone she trusted was obvious from the start of his judgment when he described the crime scene, from which, he noted, nothing had been stolen and which showed no signs of forced entry. 'It would appear,' he said, 'that Inge opened the outside gate and the security gate for her attacker, whom it would appear was known to her. It would seem that she returned to the couch to watch her DVD and read her magazine while she waited for her visitor.' Being security-conscious, the judge said, Inge was unlikely to have done this for a stranger. It appears, he continued, that the visitor attacked her from behind without any warning while she was reclining on the couch. 'The nature of her injuries,' he said, 'suggest a ferocious and uncontrolled attack that must have been entirely unexpected and against which she could offer no resistance. The violence of the attack is testament to an indescribable viciousness directed at a young woman.'

This is not an unreasonable reading of the evidence, and the judge echoed and endorsed the conclusion of the police psychologist, Dr Labuschagne, whose opinion it was that the murder was 'psychologically motivated', that the motive was 'personal' and that 'the offender must have been well known to the victim and motivated by anger.'

All of which might help to explain why the judge spent a fair amount of time recounting the evidence he'd heard about the overheated social dynamics of Fred and Inge's circle, something that was not, strictly speaking necessary, in the context of his finding that Fred's alibi had not been damaged by any of the evidence presented by the prosecution. It was, in other words, unnecessary for him to recount the evidence that Fred's flatmate, Marius Botha, had been in love with Inge at some point, that he had sent her a poem and that he had asked God's forgiveness for having 'cursed' their relationship. Unnecessary though they were, these details found their way into his judgment.

Having decided that Fred could not have killed Inge, it was also, strictly speaking, unnecessary for the judge to offer an explanation for how it may have happened that Marius had been able to tell both Fred and Mrs Lotz that Inge had been murdered when Christo had been convinced that she had committed suicide. It is possible, he said, that Marius misheard Christo because it was possible that Christo might have used a strange expression when he told him of Inge's apparent suicide. Citing the testimony of the man who'd opened the complex gate for Christo and to whom Christo had run after he found Inge's body, the judge noted that that man had described Christo as telling him that Inge had 'murdered herself'. It is an odd expression in both English and in the Afrikaans in which the conversation would have happened. If Christo had used a similar expression when he spoke to Marius that night, the judge suggested, it might explain Marius's misapprehension and his telling Fred and Mrs Lotz that Inge had been murdered.

It is a solution to a puzzle that might have pleased Dan Brown, and it seems to have allayed some of the concerns the judge had repeatedly expressed about the potentially incriminating manner in which the news of Inge's death was presented to Mrs Lotz. Yet he remained convinced that the crime scene and the manner of Inge's death suggested that the killer must have been known to her. It is a conviction that might have been weakened had the judge been presented with a fuller account of the entire investigation. If that had happened, he might have permitted himself to doubt even that so apparently obvious a premise.

34

My favourite writer is Joan Didion, the American narrative journalist. One of her books – *Salvador* – is about the fantasies that drove Ronald Reagan's policies in El Salvador, and it begins with the observation that to fly into that country during the civil war of the 1980s was to 'plunge directly into a state in which no ground is solid, no depth of field reliable, no perception so definite that it might not dissolve into its reverse.' It is a sentence of a master craftsman, and it describes perfectly a part of the story of Fred's trial that I have yet to mention: that someone else confessed to Inge's murder, that he later recanted that confession, that he recanted that recantation, and, finally, that he then recanted the recantation of the recantation.

It is a murky, confusing story in which muddied waters rise so fast they threaten to drown the unwary, so it is well to begin at the beginning.

On 28 March 2005, twelve days after Inge's murder and three weeks before the matching of Fred's fingerprints to a lift supposedly taken from a DVD cover in Inge's flat, police officers based in Stellenbosch, who were unconnected to the investigation Inspector de Villiers was running, interviewed two local men, Willmore Adams and Jaco Swanepoel. The latter, at least, was well known to the local constabulary, and it appears that what may have happened is that the local cops hauled in 'the usual suspects' to ask them about the gruesome murder then dominating the daily papers.

The resulting statements say that on 24 March, the two men were at the home of a certain Werner Carolus, who showed them a large bunch of keys, used apparently in the housebreakings he committed, and who said to them that he was involved in the murder of the student. He showed them bite and scratch marks, and told them that he had used women's clothes and a wig (which Jaco Swanepoel also said he'd seen Carolus buy) when he committed the crime. He told them, the statements said, that he had subsequently burnt these. Finally, the statements say that Carolus told the two men that he had stolen nothing from the flat because he was afraid that the police might catch him with something that could link him to the crime.

These were statements made on 28 March 2005. Three weeks later, on 18 April, a week after the supposed matching of Fred's fingerprints to Folien One and three days after Fred's car and office had been searched, Werner Carolus was arrested in the small town of Springbok in the Northern Cape, about five hundred kilometres from Stellenbosch. The ostensible reason for the arrest was the suspicion that he was in possession of a stolen cellphone. But this seems a little implausible. More likely, the police in Stellenbosch had traced Carolus's family ties to Springbok and had asked their colleagues there to look for him. At any rate, there is evidence in the notes taken by the detective who interviewed Carolus on 19 April that he had been told by his father that the police were looking for him in connection with murder, and that another person – described deliciously in the detective's notes only as 'Eddie (another drug dealer)' – had told him that Jaco Swanepoel knew who had committed the murder.

The interrogation of Carolus in Springbok produced two documents. One was a set of handwritten notes made by the detective to whom he spoke. The other was a formal confession before a magistrate, sworn out that afternoon. The two documents agree on the main points, not all of which are consistent with the murder and the resulting crime scene.

Carolus's confession says that events began on Saturday night, when he and four others (Jaco Swanepoel, two people identified only as 'Mervin' and 'Eleanor', and someone whose name Carolus claims not to know) were selling drugs at a pub in Stellenbosch. They were also, the confession says, smoking tik, the local name for crystal meth.

At some point, the statements say, they went from the pub to the student centre on the university campus. There, Jaco pointed to a young woman and said, 'There is the white girl from that night.' He also said, '*My broer*, in that girl's flat is a laptop, a cellphone and money' and '*My broer*, she is all alone.' The confession makes no reference to the time that this is all supposed to have happened, but the notes from the interview with the detective read '+/- 22:00'.

The girl, the detective's notes say, was 1.76m tall and had green eyes and blonde hair. Jaco, the notes say, had his .38 calibre firearm with him.

The confession says that when they arrived at Welgevonden Estate, the gang climbed over the 'spike-fence' into a 'yard'. He and Eleanor went to look in the window of the flat into which the girl they were following had gone. The flat, the confession says, was open-plan, with a kitchen and lounge in one. They saw the woman scratch around in her handbag and go through a door they thought must lead to a bathroom. They came down the stairs and told Jaco, Mervin and the third man what they had seen. The three men went up the stairs and climbed into the flat through a window. The confession says Carolus told Jaco that he wanted to go into the flat too, but that he was told to stand guard.

After about five minutes, Carolus says he heard two screams, and that as he and Eleanor walked towards the flat, Jaco jumped out of the window and the two other men ran out of the door. He says that he asked them what was going on, and that Jaco said, '*My broer*, we have to get away from here.'

The confession says nothing about why he decided not to run away immediately, choosing instead to return to the flat. In the detective's notes, however, Carolus is recorded as saying that he told Eleanor that he wanted to go up to the flat to get some 'stuff'. In any event, Carolus's confession says that he lifted up the flat's window and poked his head through it, and that when he did so, he saw the girl lying on the couch. The description of how the body lay is none too clear: her head is said to have been on the seat, her upper body on the couch and her legs lying off the couch. Blood, he says, was running down her arm. At that point, he turned to Eleanor and told her that they had to get out of there.

He says that he and Eleanor ran to Jaco's house, and that when he got there, he heard Jaco ask Mervin what he had done with the knife. He says he went to Jaco's room, where he passed out. He says that the next morning – then adds that he is not sure that it was the next morning – he asked Eleanor about the knife, which she said was hidden by the river. He and Eleanor went to retrieve the knife, he says, and hid it in front of Jaco's house. He says that it eventually wound up in Jaco's knife drawer.

From the detective's notes written before the confession to the magistrate, other, sometimes arresting, details emerge. Jaco, for example, is described as 'a white man who speaks the language of prison like a Coloured.' He is also said to become 'stupid' when he is drugged and that he had his .38 calibre firearm with him during these events. And, while the confession ends with the knife finding its way into the drawer, the notes continue. They say that Jaco told him to keep his mouth shut. They say that he left town to stay with someone on a farm in Helderberg for a night, but that he came back to town to collect money from Jaco, owed to him for his efforts selling drugs. Jaco asked him where he'd been, and, disbelieving the claim to having been in Helderberg, accused him of consorting with the members of another gang (the 'Atchas'). All turned out well enough, however, and he, Jaco and Jaco's girl spent the day smoking tik. Later that night, however, a certain 'Kiaam' (for whom Jaco was said by Carolus to be a runner) arrived and began to beat him, hitting him over the head with a gun and 'pricking' him with a knife. He was then told by Kiaam to find another of his runners, rendered in the notes sometimes as 'Logmaan' and sometimes 'Logaan', whom Kiaam wanted to kill. He went to find Logmaan/Logaan and warned him that Kiaam wanted to kill him. Logmaan/Logaan, who was high, took the news in his stride, however, saying that it was 'all right' and that he knew Kiaam wouldn't do it.

It is a surreal, dream-like tale which ends – confusingly and inexplicably – with Carolus sitting alone on a lawn outside a friend's house.

* * *

After the interview and confession on 19 April, the police in Springbok called their colleagues in Stellenbosch to tell them what had transpired. Those colleagues called Director Trollip, who had been appointed the 'overall coordinator' of the investigation a week earlier. He made arrangements for Carolus to be brought to Stellenbosch so that inquiries could continue.

Those inquiries took the form of a pointing-out. This is an investigative procedure which is the practical equivalent to a confession, and involves a suspect taking detectives to places that might be of interest to their investigation: the crime scene itself, the location of a hidden weapon or, in some cases, a hidden grave. Properly done, a pointing-out is preceded by a great deal of careful checking that a suspect understands his rights, and is conducted by a detective who is not personally involved in the case so that he cannot unduly influence the suspect. All of which appears to have been done in this case, with Carolus's being handed over to a Superintendent Koen from the Detective Academy on the morning of 21 April.

Superintendent Koen supervised a pointing-out later that day. It was not a complete success, however, with Carolus able to take the policeman only to Inge's complex, not to the flat itself. The significance of this failure was the subject of some debate in court, but here is what Koen recorded in the standardised report that officers fill in on occasions such as this. Next to the word APPEARANCE, he wrote, 'Stressed. Began to cry and tremble at Welgevonden Estate. Very stressed.' Next to the word ATTITUDE, he wrote, 'No longer as relaxed as when we began.' Next to the word OTHER, he wrote, 'The pointing-out was stopped as a result of the suspect's stressed appearance.'

Apart from these notes, there is no official record of Koen's experience with Carolus. This is peculiar because pointings-out in serious cases are usually done in front of a video camera, and, in fact, in Koen's notes there is a reference to his having filled in these forms in front of a video camera, with the cameraman's name duly recorded for posterity. The video tape itself appears to have been lost to history.

According to a statement by the commanding officer of the Stellenbosch detective unit, Carolus asked to do a second pointing-out the next day. This time another disinterested officer was charged with managing the process. And, as Koen had done the previous day, the officer – Captain Niklaas Paulse – took Carolus through the lengthy questionnaire about whether he understood that he was not obliged to do the pointing-out, that anything he did or said would be recorded and might be used against him in court, and that he was entitled to legal assistance at the state's expense. Paulse's questions also tested whether anyone had assaulted Carolus, whether anyone had threatened him and whether anyone had made any offers to induce his cooperation.

To all the questions, Carolus gave answers that indicated that his pointing-out was voluntary. And this time the video record of the interview and the pointing-out has survived.

The video runs for a little more than thirty-six minutes, with the first and longest scene taking place in the office of Captain Paulse, a large man in a black leather jacket, a blue shirt and a dark tie. He goes through a long list of questions, speaking in a tone one might use with a skittish horse: calm and deep and unthreatening. Carolus appears. He looks young, and he tells Paulse that he is just seventeen years old. His hair is peroxide white, cut short and frames a boyish face. He is dressed in calf-length white pants and a grey sweater. In a moment, Paulse will ask him to strip down so he can show the camera that there are no signs of assault. At that point, the policeman will find two old scars: a non-descript one to the shoulder and a large dog bite to the knee. When Carolus raises his arms in a crucifix and turns in front of the camera, we will see that he is wearing black boxers with white trim. When we first see him, though, his right foot, crossed over his left knee, shakes nervously as he looks at the wall on which hang a couple of WANTED posters.

The visible signs of his nervousness will only increase as the video proceeds.

Next to Carolus is his aunt and guardian, Joyce, present at the pointing-out to look after her minor charge. She co-signs the forms and gives the detective her cellphone number. She appears truculent: silent, resigned and unwilling.

Flash-cut and we are in the police station's parking area, where the time and the reading on the vehicle to be used during the pointing-out are dutifully recorded. This is so that it might never be said that Carolus was taken to some desolate corner of town and beaten into confession.

Flash-cut and we are at a house in Stellenbosch, at which Carolus tells Paulse he and some friends once plotted a break-in. Precisely when this is said to have happened is unclear. What is clear is that they did not complete the crime: the alarm went off and they ran away.

The time and kilometre readings are noted once again.

Flash-cut to the parking area of Inge's complex. A collection of grey-and-white two-storey buildings line the edges of the lot. In one direction, the surrounding security wall is two and a half metres of grey-painted brick. In another it is green, spike-topped palisades. It is a few minutes after the arrival at the previous location, and Carolus has begun to tell Paulse what happened. The sound is poor, and the cameraman, caught off-guard, has missed the start of the conversation. As we join, though, Carolus is saying that he was with Jaco Swanepoel, someone called Phillip and Kiaam. He adds Mervin's name as an afterthought.

'Why were you here?' Paulse asks.

'I told you already.'

'But you must tell me again. That is the purpose of the pointing-out. What happened?'

Carolus's answer is urgent: 'I wasn't in there.' Then he says that Jaco, Kiaam and Mervin went into the flat. He says that he, a girl who was with them and Phillip did not go into the flat. He is not sure if everyone else went into the flat. He says that he saw them run out of the flat a few minutes later, and that he heard screams. He points at the main gates and says that Jaco, Phillip and Mervin ran that way, but that he is not sure which way Kiaam ran.

A helicopter flies overhead, and Carolus looks up. There is increasing distress in his bearing; the silences between Paulse's questions, during which the policeman makes notes of Carolus's answers, seem excruciating.

'Did you also run away?'

'Eleanor and I went that way,' he says, pointing at the palisades, to which he takes the police officer so he can indicate a supporting wall he says he scaled before pulling Eleanor after him.

He wipes his face. He chews a nail. He is unable to make eye contact with anyone. Tension floods from every pore.

'How do you know a murder happened?'

'I went up there, after they ran out. I saw the girl lying there. I was high. I can't remember exactly where it was. I heard the screams. She was lying on a couch. Her body was upright. He lower body was on the couch. There was blood on her arm, dripping onto the floor.'

Then it is over and, flash-cut, we are back in the police parking lot. We have been gone for forty-eight minutes and have travelled eleven kilometres.

* * *

The second pointing-out was done on 22 April 2005, and, by that point, Carolus had given three versions of events. Within these, there are a number of statements that are completely consistent with Inge's murder: there is his identification of the location of the murder at Welgevonden Estate; there is the open-plan living area to which he'd referred; there is his mention of a handbag visible from the kitchen window; there is the position of her body on the couch.

There are also a lot of problems with these accounts: there are inconsistencies about the number and names of the people who were at the flat; there is the statement that the crime had occurred on a Saturday; there is the suggestion that Inge might have been known to Carolus's friend and that they had followed her at 22:00; there is the claim, physically impossible given the presence of security bars, that people had climbed through Inge's windows.

These are troubling issues to which we will return, but first we must complete the Wagnerian cycle of confession and recantation, renewed confession and reaffirmed recantation.

* * *

Asked about Carolus and his pointings-out when they are on the stand, the investigating officer, Inspector Deon de Villiers, and the 'overall coordinator' of the investigation, Director Attie Trollip, both say that on 25 April, the Monday after the second pointing-out, they interviewed Carolus in the holding cells of the Stellenbosch magistrate's court. Carolus, they say, recanted his admissions and apologised for the trouble he had caused.

When he hears this the first time, the judge asks, 'Why would a man lie about a thing like this?' To which De Villiers replies, 'M'Lord, we established later that he sold drugs for someone else and that he had run away with those drugs to Springbok. Those people had assaulted him and he wanted to get back at them. That was his answer to us.'

Carolus's recantation, De Villiers says, was captured in a statement on 20 June during an interview in Pollsmoor Prison where, he says, Carolus was serving an eleven-year sentence for burglary.

It is an account that Trollip confirms when he testifies and is asked a similar question by the judge about Carolus's motivation for lying. 'M'Lord,' Trollip says, 'at the time I interviewed him he told me that it was to get back at a person named Kiaam and some others to whom he owed money and drugs, and who had assaulted him because of that. This was how he was going to get them back.' Later, he adds that in the statement Carolus signed in Pollsmoor, he went further. 'He talks about the debt and then says that he thought this was a way of staying out of jail.'

There are a number of curious features about the statement Carolus signed and about the representation of its contents offered by De Villiers and Trollip. For one thing, Carolus's name is misspelled throughout, rendered on every page as 'Carolous'. For another, it wasn't signed on 20 June 2005, as De Villiers had implied, but on 20 June *2006*, or fourteen months after the initial interview.

More importantly, in addition to speaking of a drug debt and of a desire to stay out of jail as his motivations for confessing to a crime he did not commit, Carolus's statement of 20 June 2006 seems to suggest that the Stellenbosch police went well beyond the call of duty in pursuit of his evidence. It says that before he embarked on the pointings-out, 'The members told me that I was in big trouble and wanted to know if I knew what I was doing. They asked me if I wanted to testify about the case or if I would identify the other people. The police also told me about the witness protection programme and of what it consists. I believed that this was an opportunity to stay out of jail and that I would be paid. I then lied again and made another statement in which I implicated other people.'

Later in the statement, it says that Carolus invented his story about being upset during the first pointing-out, and that the reason he needed to do so was that he could not identify Inge's flat. He says that before they left the police station the next day for the second pointing-out, he became involved in a conversation with some officers. 'I heard the members talking to each other about how the flat could be seen from the road,' he says. 'Someone also said that there were workmen near the flat. On the basis of this, I was able to establish where the flat was.'

He says that it was on the basis of this new information, as well as the presence of police tape in Inge's window that he was able to identify the flat during the second pointing-out. He also says that when he returned to the police station after the pointing-out, he could see that 'the members were satisfied' and that he thought that he would be placed in the witness protection programme.

It is hard to escape the conclusion, then, that if Carolus's statement is true, a number of officers conspired to persuade him that he would be treated particularly well if he implicated his friends in the crime. It is not clear, of course, if this is a trick designed to entice him into implicating himself or to implicate other habitual criminals and drug dealers, but Trollip's account, offered on the stand, reinforces the sense of irregularity that is not quite as deliberate and blameworthy. The Stellenbosch police officers, Trollip suggests at one point, asked leading questions of Carolus, and allowed him to learn more and more about the murder as their interrogation of him progressed.

Perhaps. But the problem with that thesis is that if the police really wanted to get Carolus to implicate himself and his friends, they probably would have done more to correct some of the obvious mistakes in his original confession, most significantly the dating of the crime to a Saturday night. There is, however, no evidence of an attempt to do that. Instead of becoming progressively more consistent with the facts of the murder, the notes from the second pointing-out actually add new mistakes. Thus, while the notes of the first pointing-out record Carolus as saying that he can't remember the date of the murder, but does remember that it was at dusk, the notes of the second pointing-out say the crime was on a Saturday night in March 2005.

There is, then, little evidence of deliberate coaching there.

Another troubling aspect of the recantation statement signed on 20 June 2006 is that it says that when he met Trollip and De Villiers in the court cells of Stellenbosch, they told him they were investigating Inge's murder and that they knew he was lying. It says that they told him that his cellphone had not registered anywhere near Welgevonden at the time of the murder.

This is a point made by both De Villiers and Trollip when they are on the stand: they knew Carolus was lying, they say, because they had his cellphone plotting and that put his phone in Springbok during March 2005.

There are two important problems with this. The first is that although the officers say that they applied for a warrant in terms of section 205 of the Criminal Procedure Act to get the details of the calls made to and from Carolus's phone, and that it was on the basis of this that they knew it to have been in Springbok, it is not possible for them to have received that information in the time available. Generally it takes weeks, even months, to get cellphone plotting data. So even if Carolus's cellphone number was obtained in Springbok when he was arrested on 18 April (and there is no explicit record that this happened), there would not have been enough time to get that data before the interview in the cells on 25 April. In fact, based on the evidence presented at the trial, it took a number of weeks to obtain Inge's cellphone records after a warrant was applied for on 22 March. Indeed, it is even possible that the police didn't have her records when they claimed already to have had Carolus's.

But there is a bigger problem: the number for which the cellphone data were obtained – the only number that appears in any of the documents relating to this leg of the Carolus investigation – was not given to the police by Carolus himself. Instead, it came from the mouth of his aunt, with whom he appears in the video, and she provides it in answer to a question Captain Paulse asks immediately after asking about the address of *her* home in Springbok: 'Do you have a phone number there?'

It seems, then, that the cellphone plotting that places Carolus in Springbok during March 2005 is for a phone that belongs to his aunt, who lives there. No other plotting appears to have been done.

* * *

In December 2007, two weeks after the end of Fred's trial, eighteen months after he signed his recantation statement and thirty-two months after his interview with Trollip and De Villiers in the holding cells, Carolus was approached by Daryl Els, a private investigator working for Fred's lawyers. Carolus was still in prison at the time, and Els approached him because he suspected that the recantation statement was not kosher. In the presence of his lawyer, and after discussion with Els, Carolus signed a new statement. In it he recanted his recantation.

Describing his encounter with Trollip and De Villiers, Carolus says that he was taken to an office and was forced to sit on the floor. Trollip, he says, sat on the edge of a desk, while De Villiers remained standing. Trollip asked him about the car theft charge he was facing. Then he said that he had read through the statement Carolus had given to the magistrate in Springbok and had watched the video of the pointing-out. Trollip, Carolus says, said that both of them knew that the contents of all of this were 'shit'.

He says that De Villiers told him that if he continued to claim knowledge of, or involvement in, Inge's murder, he would go to jail for a long time. Trollip, he says, came off the desk, squatted next to him and said, 'I want you to deny that you were ever involved in the murder of that girl, and that everything you told the magistrate in Springbok is false.'

De Villiers, he says, then said that if he did not change his story, his life would become 'very hard'.

In the statement of December 2007, Carolus says that Trollip and De Villiers told him that if he cooperated with them, his trial for car theft would end that day. It says that as a matter of fact the charge was withdrawn later that day. 'Because I was afraid of going to jail,' his statement reads, 'and also feared what would happen if they were to "make life hard for me", I agreed to change my statement.'

The statement's final paragraph reads, 'After I made the statement before the magistrate in Springbok, I made a drawing of Inge Lotz's flat before Mr Nel of the police in Stellenbosch. I left the drawing in the possession of Mr Nel.'

No such drawing appears anywhere in the docket.

* * *

It is a disturbing statement, one that suggests that senior police officers intimidated someone who might be characterised either as a witness to Inge's murder or as a participant in it. It is also, of course, a statement whose contents cannot be verified, and, as we shall see, one whose contents Carolus has subsequently recanted. Finally, it is a statement whose contents could not be put to either Inspector de Villiers or Director Trollip when they were on the stand because it was taken after the trial concluded. It is, however, perfectly obvious that they would have denied the allegations Carolus made because it is completely inconsistent with what they said about their meeting with Carolus and with their overall assessment of the value of his evidence.

This is Trollip's account of his reaction to the news on 19 April that a confession had been made to a magistrate in Springbok: 'I instructed Captain Talmakkies and others to go ahead with their investigation of Carolus. I spoke with one person from Springbok on the phone – Inspector Carel du Toit. I got as much information about Carolus as I

could through interviews. At that time, I had no doubt about the direction I had taken in the investigation to that point. I continued to take
statements that would take the investigation against Fred van der Vyver
forward, and I asked other people to report on the progress of the investigation into Carolus. It was as a result of that progress that I had my own
interview with him. In fact, when I was called and told that he could not
identify the flat during the first pointing-out but was prepared to try to
do so again the next day, I supported that and said they must go ahead. It
was Superintendent de Wee who then made the arrangements. But even
after he made the pointing-out at the Shiraz flats, I still did not believe he
was telling the truth. So at no time did I regard him as a suspect in this
case, M'Lord. I just made sure that everything he conveyed to the police
was followed up. Later, during the investigation – obviously, this couldn't
all happen on one day – I established that his fingerprints were not found
on the scene, that his shoes were examined, as were his clothes, and that
none could be linked to the Shiraz flat.'

It is perhaps the longest answer to any question in the trial, and it
would have continued if De Bruyn had not intervened to make a modest objection. 'M'Lord,' he said, 'with the greatest of respect, this is now
hearsay evidence. And this issue of the shoes: I'm under correction, but
there is nothing about this in the file, so I must object to this evidence.'

The judge, treating the objection lightly, asks Trollip to take into account what De Bruyn has said, and Trollip says that he is not depending
exclusively on what was written in the statements and in the docket.

'Did you give instruction that this should be done?' the judge asks.

'That's correct, M'Lord.'

It is the briefest of interruptions to his flow, and Trollip continues with
his account, explaining what it was in Carolus's various statements that
did not accord with the facts of the murder. 'M'Lord,' he says, 'there were
serious contradictions, if I can describe them like that. There were issues
that were initially not said but which were said later, which made it quite
clear to me that this was someone who was fabricating information,

whose knowledge of the circumstances was building as he was being questioned. Basically, that is what convinced me that he was fabricating his whole account.'

At this point, the judge asks why he would do that, and Trollip says that there were two reasons: he wanted to get back at some drug dealers from whom he had stolen drugs and money and who had beaten him up, and because he thought he'd get better treatment from the police. By way of example, he says that some of the cases that were open against Carolus at the time were withdrawn.

Van der Vijver, leading Trollip, points out that Carolus describes the murder as happening on a Saturday, and then asks if there were other issues that did not conform with the facts of the case. In response, Trollip says that it would have been impossible for anyone to climb through Inge's windows, as Carolus claimed.

That is the bulk of Trollip's evidence about why he thought Carolus's claims were implausible, but there were two other issues that arose elsewhere and which must be recorded. One was Trollip's assessment of the reason why the notes taken during the first, abortive pointing-out suggested that Carolus had become too emotional to continue. Asked by De Bruyn about this, he says, 'That's what the notes say, M'Lord. But I want to add that where he did the pointing-out that day was nowhere near the crime scene. I assume that he became stressed because he could not point out anything more.'

> Q: You're speculating now, I think, really.
> A: I'm not speculating, M'Lord. If you look where the photos were taken and their relationship to the crime scene, you can see that this person must have become stressed. He's nowhere …
> JUDGE: His lies were catching up to him?
> A: That's right. He just couldn't do any more, M'Lord. And I think, as I read it now, that he must have been in an emotional condition. That emotion is because of the

> fact that he cannot point anything more out. He had
> become confused in his pointing-out, and he couldn't
> go on.
>
> Q: Excuse me, but you weren't there, and this evidence
> you're giving, I'm going to ask that it be treated as
> worthless. It's an opinion you're expressing about
> something about which you know nothing.

If this is Trollip's account of Carolus's failure to complete the first pointing-out and the detective's notes about his state of mind at the time, another issue that Trollip raises is that Carolus's statements suggest that Inge was known to the gang, and that he implied that she was a drug user. Cross-examining the detective, De Bruyn says, 'Is it correct that there are no notes or statements anywhere in that dossier to the effect that the lady who was murdered was someone who bought drugs from them?'

'No, M'Lord,' Trollip says, 'that is not in the dossier. But one of the statements – that of Carel du Toit – says that the lady came out of the pub. He also says that Jaco said, 'That is the girl from that night.' I remember that I asked about that because it creates the impression that they knew her, and I remember that that question led to the allegation that they knew her because they had sold her drugs. Also, if you read the statements in totality, you will see that Jaco says that they knew where she comes from, suggesting that Jaco had been to the lady's house.'

There is literally no way of knowing whether it is true that someone told Trollip that the words attributed to Jaco in Carolus's statement before the magistrate in Springbok – 'There is the girl from that night' – were properly interpreted to mean that the whomever it was the gang supposedly followed home was known to them as a drug user. There is no corroborating evidence anywhere in the docket of the question being asked or of the answer that was supplied, and Trollip doesn't even say who it was that he asked about the meaning of those words. Still, the words are there: along with all the other anomalies in Carolus's statements, there is, indeed, the suggestion that Jaco Swanepoel, a low-life, a drug dealer and, according to Carolus, a murderer, claimed to know Inge.

But there is an alternative interpretation of the anomalies, one I offer on the basis of the expertise of a group of middle-aged, middle-class recovering addicts I happen to know.

* * *

One of the first things we learn about Carolus is that he is a drug dealer and user. 'It was on a Saturday night,' he tells the magistrate in Springbok. 'I sold drugs to a drug dealer. We sold drugs in front of the pub and I also smoked. It was tik.' Elsewhere in the statement, he says that after the incident he ran to Jaco's house, where he passed out from the drugs. He says in that statement that he woke the next morning, but he is not sure that it was the next morning. In the notes taken by the detective in Springbok, Carolus's waking is followed by his taking more drugs and then by the dream sequence of encounters with Jaco and Kiaam and Logmaan/Logaan and his winding up alone on a lawn in the night.

I tell this story to my addict friends and ask about their perception of time and space when they're high using crystal meth.

'Tik is a terrifying drug,' says the schoolteacher. 'One of the things about it is how cheap it is. It means you get kids taking it while their brains are developing. Who knows what it's doing to their minds.'

'Tik is the only drug I am afraid of,' the journalist says. 'It's cheap and it's very easy to get. And, once you're on it, coming down is so painful, it's almost impossible not to buy more just to take the pain away. You end up going for days. You don't sleep. You can't sleep. I mean, you can imagine what it's like, what's happening in your head. By that point, nothing really makes sense.'

'It takes four strong men to arrest a tik-*kop*,' says the policeman. 'You can't believe the strength and the violence they have in them.'

'I saw a movie once,' the advertising guy says, 'that gave a pretty good impression of what it's like to binge on crystal meth. I forget what the film is called, but there's a scene where a man meets a girl in a club. They hook up and go home. He ties her to the bed – a kinky-sex thing. But then he gets a phone call and it distracts him; he forgets what he's doing; he starts to leave. She's screaming for him to come back and untie her. Screaming. But he's on the phone, distracted. He comes back two days later; she's still tied up. That's exactly what it's like: you lose your sense of time, your perception of it. Everything's warped. Everything's fucked. Minutes seem like hours. Hours seem like minutes. Afterwards, it's hard to put it all back together, to know for sure what happened and when and with who.'

Here's the point: perhaps the problem is not that there are contradictions and anomalies in Carolus's statement; perhaps the problem is the expectation that someone who may have been on a four-day tik binge would be able to offer a sequential account of events nearly six weeks later. It may be, in other words, that Carolus really did know more about the murder than he should have done, and that some of the anomalies about the time at which it happened and the people he was with and precisely what they did, might be explained by his drugged-up state.

That, at least, is what I thought for a long time: I didn't know whether Carolus killed Inge himself or whether he was merely present at the murder but did not himself strike any of the blows. If anything, I favoured the former because it seemed better able to explain the tidiness of the scene and the fact that nothing was stolen than would an account that suggested three or four people were in Inge's flat when she died. Against that, there was the fact that a number of weapons had been used in the assault on Inge, and which suggested there had been more than one killer as Carolus had said. It was also an intuition that was confirmed by something a seasoned investigator told me might account for some of Inge's post-mortem injuries: between a pair of killers, he said, a dominant personality might kill the victim but then insist that the subordinate personality strike some blows of his own in order to be part of the murder.

Still, I was agnostic about whether Carolus did it or whether his friends did or whether they all did it, but, having watched the video and read the statements, I was pretty sure that Carolus knew more than he ought to have done. Trollip's suggestion, made more than once during his testimony, that perhaps Carolus had picked up these details from press reports, seemed to assume too much about the newspaper-reading habits of seventeen-year-olds of his social, economic and narcotic-using profile. The only other possibility was that he'd been spoon-fed the details by over-eager investigators, but since his original confession was made to a cop working five hundred kilometres from the crime scene, and that in it he had named Inge's complex and reported both the open-plan nature of her flat and the position of her body, that didn't seem all that likely either. No, I thought, Carolus knows more than he ought because he was there, and between Trollip and De Villiers, they had gone out of their way to persuade him to withdraw his confession. The only explanation I could give of why they might have done that had nothing to do with the cellphone plotting, and everything to do with Folien One: Carolus came to their attention on 18 or 19 April, a week after Bester and Bartholomew had matched Fred's prints to the lift from the DVD cover. If Trollip and De Villiers did not know that there were problems with that match, they would have assumed that they had their man, and they would have approached their interview with Carolus determined not to allow him to divert the course of justice.

It seemed a neat explanation because it also helped explain why it was that the police in general, and Bartholomew in particular, worked so hard to produce further forensic evidence against Fred even after they had the fingerprint. If they knew the fingerprint might not stand up to scrutiny, and if they knew that Trollip and De Villiers, acting under the conviction that Fred was their man, had secured a recantation from Carolus using dubious means, they might have felt compelled to produce further evidence of Fred's guilt.

And then something happened that, if not quite persuading me that I was wrong, certainly queered the conclusion: Carolus recanted the recantation of his recantation of his confession. And, because he now offered a completely new version of events, his statement, in effect, says that not only did he lie when he confessed and lied when he recanted, but also that he lied when he reinstituted his original confession. In effect, one could say that nothing he had said before was true, that no thought or supposition that was grounded on his statements was solid, that no depth of field was reliable, that every perception had, in fact, dissolved into its reverse.

*   *   *

The new statement, attested to in June 2009, was taken down by the same private investigator who'd recorded the sworn recantation of the recantation in December 2007. That was the statement in which Carolus had accused Trollip and De Villiers of intimidating him into his original recantation, and it had led to the laying of charges against the two policemen for obstructing justice. In the new statement, Carolus makes no mention of that experience. Instead, acting on the advice of his lawyer, he returns to the original murder and says that he didn't have anything to do with it. His new version of events is that he was an eyewitness to Inge's murder and that the real killer was not someone he knew.

In his latest statement Carolus says that he was in Inge's complex on the day of the murder and that he was planning to break into one or other of the flats. 'I heard a scream,' he says, 'and went to investigate. When I looked in the kitchen window of Inge Lotz's flat, I saw her murderer.' About the murderer, all he can say is that he was a white man, and that he would be able to recognise him again if asked to do so.

If the idea that someone snooping around a building looking to break into it would run *towards* a scream seems surprising, it is not as surprising as those portions of the statement that explain why Carolus implicated himself and his friends in the crime. These sections are short – running to no more than two hundred words – but they are three times as long as the paragraph dealing with what Carolus actually saw. In them, he offers three reasons for his earlier account of the murder. The first is that he was under the misapprehension that because he saw the murder but did not prevent it, he was himself guilty of murder. He has, he says, now been disabused of this notion.

The second reason he offers for implicating Kiaam, Jaco, Phillip and Eleanor and the rest is that he was afraid of the real murderer. He was afraid, he says, that he would wind up in prison with that killer because, he says, the man is 'vicious'. He is not, he says, similarly afraid of Jaco Swanepoel and the others.

Finally, almost as an afterthought, he adds a third reason for his earlier statements: 'Jaco Swanepoel,' he says, 'is responsible for the fact that I am currently serving a prison sentence.'

That, then, is Carolus's third version of what happened: the first was that he and his friends were involved; the second was that he falsely implicated his friends because he owed them money and drugs; the third was that he saw the real killer and he falsely implicated himself and his friends because he felt responsible for Inge's death, he was less afraid of his friends than of the real killer and, in any event, he was angry with one of his friends for getting him into prison.

Add to that the tale of being intimidated by the police into recanting his first confession, and we have a veritable smorgasbord of stories, the existence of each of which makes the others that much harder to believe. So, even if the muddying of the investigative waters was not the purpose of Carolus's last statement, that is its effect.

Still, it's worth asking a question or two about this latest statement and the plausibility of the self-portrait that emerges. The Carolus of the last statement is a man who understands – or understood – that the law is so structured that it treats as culpable anyone who witnesses a murder but who fails to intervene to prevent it. It is a view of the law in which its underlying moral premise is that we are all our brothers' keepers. Carolus regarded himself as potentially guilty of murder, the statement suggests, because he failed in these fraternal duties.

This version of Carolus, then, is a man with a certain moral depth. It is an image that stands in some contradiction to the tik-smoking burglar serving an eleven-year sentence who emerged from his previous statements. It also stands in some contradiction to the claim made in this statement that he knowingly implicated four people in Inge's murder whom he knew to be innocent of the crime.

How does he square this circle? Not through moral courage, certainly: he says that he felt he had to implicate them since he was afraid of the real killer, with whom he feared he might wind up in prison.

Perhaps this is true. But if it is, it is a surprising truth given what is known about some of the people he did name. Take Kiaam, for example. He is a man whose surname is never given, though he is described repeatedly as a drug dealer and, in the first statement given in Springbok, as the man for whom Jaco Swanepoel was a runner. Kiaam is also a man who, in that first statement, beats Carolus with a gun and 'pricks' him with a knife.

Now, it turns out that police officers and journalists in Stellenbosch know of a Kiaam who is also, as it happens, an associate of Jaco Swanepoel. He is the same Kiaam Majal described in a May 2009 edition of the local paper as one of Stellenbosch's pre-eminent drug dealers. He is the same Kiaam Majal whose bail conditions included the bizarre provision that he not set foot in town except for the purposes of attending his trial on a charge of possessing a stolen car.

Kiaam Majal, I was told by journalists who work that beat, is a leader of the local subsidiary of the Americans gang, and is, for that reason, among the most feared men in town. It is a gang whose deputy leader, according to local press reports, was a certain Jacobus 'Boet' Philander. Boet, I read, had been charged with twenty-four serious crimes between 1992 and 2007, including ten of murder or attempted murder, four of assault, one of rape, and three of possession of an illegal firearm. He was also the man who, in 2007, was charged with burning to death his twenty-year-old girlfriend, Laverne Damons, during a tik-induced psychotic episode in which he became convinced there were snakes in her belly. It was a circumstance that led him to douse her in turpentine and then set her on fire. He is a man who, shortly after this incident, threatened to beat his own father to death with a hammer.

These are the kind of people amongst whom Carolus appears to have moved. It is people from this world from whom he acquired his moral depth. And it is people from this world whom he preferred to implicate in Inge's murder in order to avoid winding up in the same prison as the real killer: the lone white man whose brutality had so frightened him.

35

What are we to make of Carolus? What are we to make of Trollip's claim, made under oath, that 'at no time did I ever regard him as a suspect in this case'?

To begin with, it is important to say that the varied and contradictory accounts Carolus has given of his involvement or otherwise in Inge's murder make it impossible and inappropriate to guess which, if any, is true. About the only thing that one can say with any confidence is that Carolus is someone who is happy to tell any story he believes the person sitting in front of him wants to hear. Perhaps that was why he may or may not have told Jaco Swanepoel and Wilmore Adams at the end of March 2005 that he was directly involved in the murder then dominating the newspapers, and that he had the scars to prove it. Perhaps that was also why he named names in Springbok on 19 April and again during his pointings-out on 21 and 22 April 2005. Perhaps that was why he agreed to recant that story when Trollip and De Villiers interviewed him in the cells of the magistrate's court in Stellenbosch on 25 April and when he signed a statement to that effect fourteen months later. Perhaps that was why he was prepared to reinstate his confession and to accuse the police of intimidation in December 2007. Perhaps that is why he is now prepared to implicate the unidentified white man that his most recent statement places in Inge's flat.

Perhaps in each case Carolus said only what he thought would impress and please and placate the person to whom he was speaking. An excess of suggestibility is not an uncommon phenomenon, and has been reported in a great many miscarriages of justice. It is possible, in other words, that Carolus knows nothing about the murder and that Trollip was right to dismiss him as a suspect.

But even if he does know something, one thing is indisputable: no-one will ever be convicted of a crime on the basis of Carolus's uncorroborated testimony. Not the four or five or six people he first claimed as having been with him at Inge's complex when she died, some of whom he claimed killed her. Not the police he once accused of intimidating him. Not the white man he now claims to have seen in Inge's flat. Not even Carolus himself, whose confessions and retractions now cover too much ground for a prosecutor to use only the former successfully.

This is something that can be said with confidence now, with the benefit of hindsight. But it raises an important question: why were Director Trollip and Inspector de Villiers so quick to dismiss Carolus's claims when they first heard them? Why was it that – by their own account – they walked into the first conversation they had with him, barely a week after he first came to their attention, already disbelieving his claims?

Trollip's answer to this question is that there were too many things about Carolus's original statements that didn't jibe with what he knew about the crime scene: the suggestion that the murder was on a Saturday night, for example, and the claim that someone had climbed through a window, for another. These anomalies, Trollip testified, meant that Carolus was never a suspect in the investigation, not at any time.

It is possible that this is true. It is possible that, before conducting any further investigations, Trollip's reading of the statement made to the magistrate in Springbok and of the notes taken by the detective who arrested Carolus, had persuaded him that this man did not know as much about the crime scene as he ought to have. He may have concluded then that Carolus's mistakes were so material as to overwhelm those parts of the statement that were either actually true or that rang true: that the crime was committed in Welgevonden Estate, that the flat was open-plan, that the victim had green eyes and blonde hair, that she was lying on a couch.

If it is true that Carolus's mistakes led Trollip to conclude that no further investigation was needed, it suggests that he treated Carolus's words with a literalness so strict as to verge on the scriptural. It suggests also an attitude to Carolus's mistakes that was a great deal less forgiving than the stance Trollip and the prosecutors would later take to mistakes made by experienced police officers whose statements were not supposed to record events that took place six weeks earlier while under the influence of tik.

That is a possibility, and if it is what happened, Trollip must have approached Carolus's statements with a puritanical lack of imagination and curiosity. There is, however, another possibility: that Trollip rejected Carolus's admissions with such confidence not because of their errors and inconsistencies, but because the policeman was already convinced that he had his man. Carolus's admissions, after all, came to Trollip's attention in the fourth week of April 2005, barely a week after the matching of Fred's prints to a lift that had supposedly come off the DVD cover, and less than a week after the search of Fred's office, flat and car had uncovered the ornamental hammer and the letter from Inge.

Whether Trollip knew or suspected at that point that Folien One had not come off a DVD cover is impossible to say. But even if he had doubts about Folien One, it's quite possible he would still have been convinced that Fred had killed Inge. The crime scene, after all, screamed that the killer was an acquaintance or intimate of Inge's. Add that to the letter and the hammer, and it's easy to see how the policeman might have persuaded himself that Carolus must be lying.

Of course, if Trollip was convinced that Carolus was lying – 'At no time did I ever regard him as a suspect in this case, M'Lord.' – then he would not have approached the interview in the courthouse cells with anything like an open mind. He would, instead, have been looking to achieve what was in fact achieved – a recantation of Carolus's admissions.

All this is speculation, but to complete the tale, let me offer another thought: that having elicited a recantation from Carolus, the pressure on the investigating officers to prove that Fred had in fact killed Inge would have doubled and redoubled. Not only did they now have a high-profile case, but they had a high-profile case in which the recantation of a freely offered confession had been actively (and perhaps embarrassingly) pursued.

No wonder, then, that further forensic evidence to buttress, corroborate and reinforce the implications of Folien One was so assiduously sought. No wonder that Bartholomew went back to the flat at the end of April to examine the bloody stain and that he worked so hard to match it to Fred's shoe. No wonder that Bartholomew and Maritz went to such lengths during May and June to show that the hammer, on which none of Inge's genetic material could be found, could be linked to the crime in some other way. No wonder that Director Botha's report purporting to demonstrate the possibility that Folien One might have been lifted from a DVD cover was treated by the investigating officers as more definitive than all the other reports – including two from police forensic specialists based in Pretoria – that had concluded the opposite.

If this is what happened, if the efforts to see Fred convicted were doubled and redoubled in part because Carolus had been persuaded to recant his original confession, it is a textbook example of what is variously called, in the academic literature about miscarriages of justice, 'premature closure' or 'investigative tunnel vision'.

In accounts of this phenomenon, academics and reformers tend to focus on the unwillingness of the investigators involved in a case to re-examine their assumptions and conclusions in the light of new evidence. They are accounts that typically lead to proposals that would seek to involve officials otherwise unconnected to an investigation in the periodic review of its progress and to apply fresh minds and eyes to the evidence. But the unwillingness to re-examine assumptions and conclusions is, I think, only part of the dynamic that can emerge, and another was pointed to with great insight by Imre Kertész, the Nobel Prize-winning writer, in his novella, *Detective Story*.

Set in an unnamed South American country, Kertész's story is of a security policeman implicated in the torture and eventual death of a young man whom the police had mistakenly believed to be a member of the illegal opposition to the ruling junta. Framed as the policeman's account to a truth commission of the events that led to the man's death, the cop reflects on how it was that, even as he and his colleagues became convinced that the man they had in custody was a deluded boy rather than a dangerous revolutionary, they became more and more aggressive in their pursuit of evidence that would justify their previous beliefs and actions. 'Our line of work is hazardous,' the policeman says more than once. 'Sometimes the only way back is to keep going straight ahead.'

* * *

The idea that there are circumstances in which it is all but impossible to admit that one has made a mistake and to retrace one's steps is one to which anyone can relate. Whether it's with a lover or an employer or a client or a friend, there are times when the admission of a previous mistake seems more costly than allowing the story premised on that error to unfold. Another common experience is that dynamics of this kind tend to consume ever-increasing energies as we try to redeem the beliefs we had and the actions we took.

It was, I think, a dynamic such as this that drove the increasing urgency with which evidence was sought to prove that Fred had killed Inge. And it is the growing desperation for something – anything! – with which to prove Fred's guilt and vindicate all the actions previously taken by the police that explains the lengths to which they went to persuade themselves, the prosecutors and the judge that they really had their man.

If I am right about this, then there is a profound but very human irony here, for it means that the principal forces that propelled Trollip and the other cops into the sticky, dangerous territory from which they could not extract themselves, were the twin imperatives of self-preservation and self-justification. Their troubles mounted precisely because they were trying to protect themselves.

It is an explanation of what happened to Fred that accounts, I think, for much of what transpired. But it is an account that cannot completely explain why it was that neither the police officers themselves nor the institutionally-independent prosecutors failed to take any of the innumerable opportunities to rethink the case they were building. Why didn't they rethink it when the defence reports on Folien One began rolling in? Why didn't they rethink it when they could find no evidence that Fred had left his office on the day of the murder? Why didn't they rethink it when none of Inge's DNA was found on the hammer, or when the hammer bent on striking the head of a pig? Why didn't they rethink it when the supposed match between the bloody stain and Fred's shoe was rejected by Bodziak?

Between them, the police and prosecutors never missed an opportunity to press ahead with the case even as all the evidence melted away. Far from it: every time a piece of evidence appeared to be shaky, they doubled down and produced new and increasingly implausible tales: a suggestion that Fred was conspiring with his colleagues to influence their statements about his presence at work; the implausible report about Bartholomew's visit to Bodziak; the mutually exclusive accounts Swartz gave of the lifting of Folien One; Director Botha's far-fetched analysis of Folien One; Maritz's failure to mention the bending of the hammer; Koekemoer's claim to having produced the square nodule. The list is long and painful, and it begs for an explanation a little stronger than the instinct for self-preservation, an instinct which, in any event, should have led at least some of the officers to retreat from the investigation, if only because they could see that it would end in disaster.

And yet they didn't retreat or regroup even as the dangers mounted. Why not?

The only answer I can give is that they really, really, really believed that Fred killed Inge. But, in the absence of any evidence proving that, why did they think that?

It is not a thesis I can prove conclusively, but I suspect that a lot of it had to do with the story line that, aided and abetted by the police, had wound itself into the coverage of Inge's murder from the beginning: the idea that the root cause of Inge's death lay in Fred's membership of a strange, cultish church, whose practices and doctrine were alien to everything good Afrikaans boys and girls ought to believe. It was an idea that had bubbled below the surface of the explicit and the literal, but it was one whose occasional eruption into the trial or coverage in the press had the flavour of an unhealthy fixation.

The most arresting example of the way this issue surfaced came right at the end of the trial, during Fred's cross-examination by Carien Teunissen. Like the question of the colour of Fred's pants, the issue Teunissen raised then had its roots in the notes Superintendent de Beer took of his interview with Fred on the morning after the murder. This time, however, what was at stake was the account Fred gave to the policeman of Inge's faith and religious practices. 'He told me that she was religious,' de Beer had said when he was on the stand. 'He told me that she was involved in

His People Church in Stellenbosch.'

It is an extract that Teunissen approaches obliquely when cross-examining Fred: 'You told Superintendent De Beer that Inge was a religious person?'

A: That was in answer to a specific question. He asked if Inge was religious, and I said, 'Yes.'

Q: Good. She was a member of the Dutch Reformed Church in Welgemoed, correct?

A: She went there with her mother, yes. I'm not sure if she was a member of that specific church. I don't know. But, yes, she went there with her mother.

Q: Why did you find it necessary to mention that she was involved in His People Church if she only went with you a couple of times to that church. She wasn't a member of His People Church was she?

A: No, M'Lord. She never became a member of His People Church, no.

Q: So it is not completely correct to link her religiousness to His People Church. In reality, she was a member of the Dutch Reformed Church. Why then did you mention His People Church and not the Dutch Reformed Church?

A: All I said was in answer to his questions: Inge was involved with His People Church in Stellenbosch. She went there with me, not just in 2005, but in 2004. She had joined a cell group. I can't see that there is anything wrong with what I said.

Q: No-one is suggesting that you did something wrong, Mr van der Vyver. The question is why you did not make mention of the Dutch Reformed Church in Welgemoed since it was part of Inge's background.

A: M'Lord, if he asked me about whether Inge went to

the Dutch Reformed Church in Welgemoed, I would
have said, 'Yes.' I can't remember precisely how the
conversation went.

JUDGE: I think the question that Advocate Teunissen is asking you is why it is that you referred specifically to His
People Church in Stellenbosch but made no mention of
the Dutch Reformed Church in Welgemoed. It looks to
me that the deceased was very involved there – that she
sang there regularly, that she sang solo and also in the
choir. She was very involved in that church.

A: That's correct.

JUDGE: The question is just why you did not mention also that
she was involved in that church, in that congregation.

A: M'Lord, I really can't answer. What I remember is
that Superintendent de Beer was trying to get some
background about Inge's social world, and I know she
had friends in the His People Church cell group. I just
mentioned that. I can't tell you why I didn't say she was
involved in the Dutch Reformed Church.

JUDGE: Mrs Lotz testified that Inge came home almost every
week she was at the university. Do you remember that?

A: I remember.

JUDGE: Do you have any problem with that testimony?

A: No, M'Lord.

JUDGE: And that she sang solo or in a duet in that church at
least once a month.

A: That's correct. I testified already that she sang in a duet
on the Sunday morning before her death.

JUDGE: But it was a regular event. She was involved every
Sunday, and sometimes she sang there. Do you remember that Mrs Lotz testified to this?

A: No, M'Lord. I don't remember that she specifically said

that Inge was involved every Sunday or that she went to
church in Welgemoed every Sunday.

JUDGE: I understood that she came home every weekend. I
don't remember her saying that she went to church
every Sunday, but I supposed that she would probably
have gone to church if she was home.

A: M'Lord, I remember that two weekends before her
death, Inge did not go to that church on the Sunday
morning. She slept at my place that night, and we
went through to her parents' house only later that
morning. That's just an example. She didn't go to the
Dutch Reformed Church in Welgemoed every Sunday
morning.

It is an intriguing exchange, one that bears extended quotation. Here we
have the explicit statement that the Dutch Reformed Church was part of
Inge's background, together with the not quite explicit suggestion, implied by the drift of Teunissen's questions, that Fred's linking of Inge's
faith to her sometime attendance of services at His People Church was a
revealing slip. Explicitly, Teunissen says that no-one is accusing Fred of
doing anything wrong when he mentioned His People Church but failed
to mention Inge's family's church, but the tone of the exchange suggests
that this is not quite true. In fact, there is a suggestion of wrongdoing; it
is just that it is made in a pitch just beyond the range of normal hearing.

So what, precisely, is Fred supposed to have done wrong?

The essence seems to be that he had shown a disrespect for history and
tradition, for family and community, and failed to locate Inge within the
social bonds to which Mrs Lotz and Carien Teunissen and even the judge
seem to insist that Inge was committed. Fred had failed to acknowledge
her commitment to her church – her mother's church! – and had had the
gall to suggest that Inge herself would have ascribed some importance to
her membership of His People Church. Framed in this way, Fred's inten-

tions in relation to Inge were made to seem less than entirely innocent: by claiming Inge for his church, he was denying Inge's 'true' identity and claiming her loyalty – one is tempted to say 'her soul' – for something else.

And not only was he laying claim to her, he was claiming her for an entity believed to be intent on separating members of its flock from their families. It is an intention that, if not exactly well documented, is a matter of conventional wisdom.

If that is what is implicit in Teunissen's questions, it is a theme that was rendered explicit by Inge's mother when she was on the stand eight months earlier. One way in which Mrs Lotz suggested her concern that Fred might have been attempting to come between Inge and her family came when she described Inge's parting from Fred on the last Sunday before her death. As Inge said farewell, Mrs Lotz testified, Fred had asked her if he should collect her for church that evening. Inge, she said, had refused. Then she'd said, 'In fact, I am not going to that church again.'

Message: Fred wanted Inge to do something she was uncomfortable with, and she was resisting.

Another, more arresting, indication of Mrs Lotz's sense of Fred's intentions in relation to Inge and the church emerges from her reaction to Inge's letter and, in particular, her reaction to the paragraph which Fred had asked the private investigators to try to keep from the Lotzes and which the Lotzes had themselves asked the court to keep out of the public domain. It was the paragraph in which Inge had expressed the fear that Fred might break up with her after he saw her father with a few drinks in him. 'I don't want to lose you because of that,' she had written, 'and I don't want you to see that side of our family.'

It is a sentiment no father would want to see in a letter drafted by his daughter on the morning on which she died, and it must have caused Professor Lotz great pain to think that this was one of her thoughts that day.

It would have caused pain. But it also would have caused anger. 'Who,'

Inge's parents must have asked themselves, 'does this young man think he is? By what right does he insinuate himself into our daughter's life and then turn her against her own parents?'

How do I know that this is what Inge's parents thought? Because it is almost exactly what Mrs Lotz testified immediately after telling Fred's lawyer that she believed the reason Fred tried to withhold the letter from her was that he did not want her to know that he and Inge had fought shortly before her death. 'And is it your testimony,' De Bruyn asked, 'that that is the reason why the letter was not shown to you?'

A: I can't think of any other reason.

Q: I must say that I am a little stunned by your answer. I'm not going to read it out, Madam, and I am sorry that I have to raise it at all, but can I put the letter before you?

A: I have it.

Q: If you can look at the first page, the fifth paragraph from the top. Read it to yourself. I don't want it read out.

A: No. I have read it many times.

Q: You've read it many times?

A: Yes.

Q: You don't think that that is enough reason for the accused to keep the letter from you and your husband?

A: No.

Q: Are you serious about that?

A: I am serious. It is an abnormal paragraph. It was not in her nature.

*   *   *

It is 'an abnormal paragraph'. The sentiments it expresses were 'not in her nature'.

Those are Mrs Lotz's words about the paragraph, and they suggest that her impression of Fred was of a young man intent on turning Inge away from her parents. It is precisely what members of churches like His People Church are reputed to do. More subtly, it is also precisely how one might interpret the social and political significance of these churches – as threats to the cultural integrity and coherence of Afrikanerdom.

It is possible that I am over-reading all of this. It is possible that Fred's affiliation to His People Church was of no significance to the path of the investigation. It is also possible, however, that Afrikanerdom's loss of power – a process that has nowhere in history produced unambiguous joy among the newly disenfranchised – has exploded a set of social and cultural and political institutions that were deeply rooted in popular and nationalist mythology. For some, this must be experienced as a liberation. For others, though, it must seem an all but existential threat.

If that is true, is it not possible that part of the reason for the fixity of the conviction that Fred was a killer, a fixity common to cops and to members of the public, had something to do with an unconscious, unarticulated sense that he represented something strange, that he was a product of the extent to which a cultural world had been knocked off its axis? Isn't it possible that they saw in Fred a manifestation of the unwinding of tradition and established institutions that has followed in the wake of the loss of power and which has been understood by many as akin to an eruption of madness?

And if Fred was a product and a manifestation of that madness, doesn't that mean that he must also *be* mad?

36

Obviously, I cannot be sure that Fred's religious affiliations played a role in what happened to him. To the extent that I was not in the room when Inge was bludgeoned to death, I also cannot know with absolute certainty that Fred was not there. I can say, however, that if Fred did kill Inge the fact that he was on trial for her death was a staggering coincidence. If the police got the right man, then they had solved the perfect crime. And if they solved the perfect crime, they did it on the basis of a perfect hunch – one that was without any evidentiary foundation at all.

In fact, even that understates the police's achievement, for not only had they solved the perfect crime with the perfect hunch, in doing so they achieved an almost Zen-like state of perfection themselves in that nothing that they claimed turned out to be true.

An achievement of this magnitude is not the work of a day. And it raises a question to which at least a gesture must be made: what does it all mean?

* * *

A system of criminal justice – *any* system of criminal justice – is built on two pillars. One is the structure and substance of a society's profoundest fears: of the violent criminal, of the dangerous underclasses, of those who reject the established social order. The other pillar is composed of society's hopes and aspirations: its desire to be fair, its devotion to reason, its pretensions to civilisation.

Often enough, the fears trump the aspirations. Think about Guantanamo Bay and Abu Ghraib. Think about the eager embrace of politicians who speak of shooting to kill. In each case, it is society's fears that shape what leaders think and say and do.

The problem with being ruled by one's fears is not that this is somehow spiritually bad for a society, but that fear can blind one to two basic problems with which a system of justice must grapple: ignorance and fallibility. The police don't know who the bad guys are. And they make mistakes, sometimes catastrophic ones.

These are the fundamental reasons why the tempering of a justice system by rules of fairness and reason and civilisation is so important. It isn't because these aspirations are spiritually good for us, but because they are an essential corrective to the blind hubris of ignorant, fallible fear.

Decent justice systems, then, are constructed to deal with society's fears, but are premised also on the need to give flesh to its aspirations to be just, aspirations that are rooted in a prior recognition that the system can never completely overcome the ignorance and fallibility of its agents.

Apartheid's legal order and the system by which it was enforced was a more or less untempered expression of the fears of those who erected it. For the country's rulers, there were greater dangers associated with

tempering the system than with allowing it to function with as few con-
straints as possible. According to the foundation myth of the new South
Africa, all that was supposed to have ended after 1994, when a raft of
new legislation – from the Constitution down – incorporated into South
African law almost every due-process protection ever imagined.

And yet, if Fred's case teaches any single lesson it is that, in practice,
the process of transforming the existing legal order has been less a process of turning a page and starting afresh than one in which some dead
skin has been sloughed off, leaving much of the rest of the system un-
changed. If Fred's case teaches anything, in other words, it teaches us
that to construct a decent legal order demands something more than the
passage of laws full of good ideas with pretty names.

One example of what I mean relates to the much celebrated claim that
the move away from apartheid's legal order can be measured, in part,
by the distance we have come from a system that relied on confessions
(many of which had been extracted in dubious circumstances) to one
that relies on evidence.

That may be true, but if we recall Captain Bester's testimony to the
effect that some of his colleagues in the fingerprint department had fabricated evidence in order to meet monthly quotas, and if we tot up all
the very many inadequacies and dishonesties in the evidence presented
against Fred, perhaps we need to qualify our assessment of the value of
the changing place of confessions in our courts. It is true that these can
be obtained in dubious and deeply problematic ways. But at least the
risks involved are known and understood by all parties, and techniques
could be devised (and have been devised) to minimise the chances of
someone being convicted on the basis of a confession extracted under
duress. By contrast, our prosecutors, judges and defence lawyers may be
much less well equipped to assess the quality and honesty of the forensic evidence presented by the police, and it might be correspondingly
harder to guard against abuses.

I recall telling a friend of mine about Fred's case. He was a man who

had been a prosecutor and a member of the Scorpions and who still dab-
bled a little in the world of law enforcement, and, as I told him what
I thought and what I believed, he laughed at me. He was unsurprised
about some of the things I told him, suggesting more than once that
I was naïve to think that things worked any other way. 'The Scorpions
sometimes write their witnesses' statements,' he said, by way of example.
'It's not good practice, but it happens.'

My friend drew the line, however, at the idea that anyone might risk
lying about fingerprint evidence.

Well, it was a long, late lunch on a Pretoria pavement, and I had my
computer with me. I hauled it out and found Captain Bester's testimony
to show it to my friend. Then I opened an image of Folien One and explained how contested the evidence was. When I finished, he was much
less sure of himself. 'I prosecuted cash-in-transit cases,' he told me.
'Often the *only* evidence against the accused was a fingerprint found at
the scene.'

So, one of the things Fred's trial means is that there may be no point
in celebrating the move from a confession-based system to an evidence-
based system unless something is also done to ensure a greater commitment to truth-telling. In this regard, I confess myself to be not much
encouraged by Director Trollip, who spent most of his career before the
inauguration of democracy in the hated security police, but who responded to the allegation that evidence might have been fabricated with
the assurance that he had 'spent thirty-seven years fighting dishonesty.'
There are, I am afraid, very few who would accept that that was what
many cops of the old order did, especially those who, like Trollip, spent
significant proportions of their careers in the Security Branch.

That's one of the meanings of Fred's case: it disrupts the comforting
story sometimes told of a crude, often violent, organisation evolving
since 1994 into something smarter and more refined.

The second meaning runs in the opposite direction, disrupting the
other tale that is often told about post-apartheid policing, the tale in

which the moral and spiritual trajectory of the organisation is relent-lessly downward because of the overly aggressive pursuit of affirmative action. By this account of what has happened over the past 16 years, the criminal justice system has been eviscerated by misguided human re-sources policies that have focused on demographic representivity rather than merit. The performance of the police officers and prosecutors in Fred's case, who formed what is probably the most experienced and – let us say it – the whitest team assembled to investigate a single mur-der since 1994, undercuts that story. If anything, the whiteness of the team and its experience might have made its thinking more rigid: for its members, the admission of mistakes of the magnitude made here might have risked undermining the carefully constructed narrative of how their competence and professionalism have been under-appreciated and under-rewarded in the new South Africa.

These are depressing conclusions.

Together they suggest that building a decent criminal justice system, using as raw material the personnel and institutions of more authoritar-ian times, requires a species of organisational renewal that is as much spiritual as anything else. This would be complicated enough at the best of times, but it is hard to see how it might be achieved during a crime wave as severe as any in the history of the modern world. Certainly, it is hard to see how it might happen at a time when the country's political class is stressing the strategic and tactical merits of the increased use of lethal force over organisational introspection.

*　*　*

These are the grand, abstract lessons to draw from Fred's trial. But to see only these is to miss the human scale of the tragedy. At the heart of that tragedy is Inge: a beautiful, talented and intelligent young woman, bludgeoned to death in her living room. Hers is a life unlived, a unique combination of memories and feelings, of experiences and thoughts, that has been snuffed out forever. What happened to her should revolt us. We should not be able to sleep at night.

Beyond Inge are her friends and family. Above all, there are her parents: robbed of a daughter, an only child born ten years after their marriage, and compelled to sit through a lengthy trial of a man who, in other circumstances, might very well have become the father of their grandchildren. Grandchildren they will now never have.

To their more obvious cause for suffering must added two others: that they have been let down by the police and the prosecutors, and that it is now all but certain that whomever killed Inge will go unpunished.

Fred's parents, on the other hand, have had to live through three years of newspaper headlines screaming the accusation that their youngest was a killer. They spent years fighting to keep Fred out of prison, eventually having literally to sell the family farm to do so.

And then there is Fred. Accused of murder, widely believed to be a psychopath, deprived of his reputation by the capaciousness and longevity of Google's memory, Inge's murder and his trial will be the pivot around which his life will forever turn. Nor is it just the trauma of being falsely accused with which he must live. He must live also with the loss of a woman he loved and who loved him in return, a woman with whom his final communication was through a series of SMSS, preserved forever in the records of his trial.

> INGE: Please let me know when your class is over. I want to give you something. All my love. x
>
> FRED: I must go at about 10:15 because I must be at the office by 11. I'll give you a missed call when I'm out. Love F.
>
> FRED: Looks like we'll finish early. Could we meet at 10, or is that too early for you? Love F.
>
> INGE: Hi! The class wasn't so bad after all :-) Even the girl who verbally abused me was there!! Love you, *skat* and have a good day. xx
>
> FRED: Hi, I'm glad class was good and hope you had a good

time with Wimpie? I read your letter quickly over
lunch. Thank you. I'll look at it more carefully tonight.
I appreciate it. Hope you have a good afternoon. Love
you, *skat*, F. xx

INGE: I had a good time with W! The tiles are already laid!
Miss you already … xx

FRED: Hi my *skat* … I'll call you a bit later tonight just to hear
your voice. I love you – F.

FRED: Hi *skat*, are you OK? Give me a missed call when you
get this SMS. and I'll call you back … Love F. x

AUTHOR'S NOTE

I had no way of knowing how all-consuming this project would become when I arrived in Cape Town on 12 February 2007 for the first day of Fred's trial. Had I known, I might have slept in, missed my flight and devoted the next three years to earning a more substantial living. Perhaps I would have taken a job. Perhaps I would have tried my hand at fiction. Perhaps I would have avoided becoming one of those dinner-party bores with only one self-involved topic of conversation.

It was not to be.

Becoming a monomaniacal dinner-party bore (especially when one's wife makes repeated reference to it) is not a good thing, but it does present a writer with one important advantage: he learns to anticipate the kinds of responses that his story will elicit. In my case, the most common was disbelief. 'Of course he did it,' pretty much everyone would say when I told them that I was writing a book about Fred's trial. 'He got away with murder.'

It was a reaction I got in Johannesburg and Cape Town, in Stellenbosch and Stanford. Just about anyone who'd heard of the case was convinced that Fred was a murderer.

Most of the people who offered this view justified it – if they justified it at all – on the basis that Inge's parents, refusing to accept the judgment of the court, had lodged an R8 million civil claim against Fred for the pain and suffering he'd caused them when he murdered their daughter. It was a development that was often reported in the press along with reference to the discovery of some new but otherwise unspecified evidence which would prove that Fred had killed Inge.

The idea that there was some new evidence that proved Fred's guilt took something of a beating however in after a request made by his lawyers for more particulars about the nature of the Lotzes' claim. Responding to this, their lawyers said that their case was based on the same facts as the criminal trial had been, and that there were no new material facts that would be presented. Even in the absence of any new evidence, however, the fact that Inge's parents were sufficiently convinced of Fred's guilt to go down this road exerted a certain moral pressure on good people who would have felt uncomfortable about entering a dispute of this kind with a pair of grieving parents. 'If they're convinced about this,' people thought, 'there must be something there.'

The Lotzes eventually withdrew their suit in May 2009, some fifteen months after instituting it. During that time, I poked and probed and tried to find anyone who could tell me what the new evidence was supposed to be. I heard nothing from anyone who was remotely authoritative, but there were two rumours that had gained some currency. The first was that a careful assessment of the contents of the hard drive of the computer confiscated from Fred on 15 April 2005 had revealed evidence that he had been trawling the internet for information about how to commit the perfect crime. The second, which stood in some contradiction to the first because it implied that Fred already knew how to commit the perfect crime, was that he had gotten away with it before, having murdered a previous girlfriend in Bloemfontein some nine months before killing Inge.

About the first rumour, there was little I could do to establish its veracity. But I have to confess to some immediate scepticism. One reason for this was that Fred's computer had been subjected to forensic examination by a police expert who'd found nothing. He may have been incompetent, of course, but given the rather dubious life histories of the other evidence against Fred, any 'newly discovered' evidence, especially when the object in question had already been investigated, would have to meet some stringent chain-of-evidence standards before I'd take it seriously. Besides, it was hard to see how damning one's internet search records could really be. What, I wondered, could his records reveal that would persuade a judge to overlook the complete absence of any other evidence of his guilt?

Most importantly, I thought that if it were true that Fred had trawled the internet for ideas about how to commit the perfect crime, and if it were true that he'd found sufficient information in order to get away with murdering Inge (as he must have done), wasn't it likely that one of the titbits he would have found would have been that a prospective murderer really ought not to leave a cyber-trail? Wouldn't one of the first pieces of advice have been to use an internet café?

So the cyber-forensics sounded implausible. What of the claim that Fred had murdered a previous girlfriend in Bloemfontein in July 2004? Again, I didn't follow this trail very far. Far enough only to establish three things. One, that there was no evidence that Fred had been in Bloemfontein that July. Two, that the dead girl was not a previous girl-friend. And three, that, in all probability, she hadn't been murdered. Or so, at least, was the conclusion of both the magistrate who ran the inquest into the unfortunate young woman's death and the chief prosecutor, who declined to have a murder docket opened.

This was not, I decided, a fruitful line of inquiry.

More fruitful, it seems to me, was the inquiry into why it is that so many people were so sure that Fred is a murderer. The coverage of the case, and the consequent construction of a certain idea about Fred, is part of the answer, and there have already been two postgraduate disser-tations on the subject written by students in the journalism department at the University of Stellenbosch. But I have come to think that it was not the coverage alone that was to blame for the pervasiveness of this attitude. As important, I think, was the fact that the idea of Fred's getting away with murder fit so neatly into a pre-existing set of ideas about the nature of justice, and the apparent ease with which the wealthy and the well-connected get away with their crimes. This is a conviction common to a great many jurisdictions, but in a country in which the headlines are dominated by Jacob Zuma and Julius Malema and the many others whose dirty laundry has been aired in public without much apparent consequence, few now believe that justice is blind. That Fred – or, more precisely, his father – had the resources to mount a R10 million defence is, in this world, something that could be held against him.

Still, the supposed existence of some new evidence raised an important question: was there anything I might learn that would induce me to change my mind about Fred's innocence? This would have been an especially interesting question for my old lecturers, who insisted that no theory ought to be admissible if it does not contain within it some means by which it might ultimately be disproved. So let me make this as simple as possible. If you wish to persuade me that Fred is a murderer, you do not have to produce a witness to the killing. You do not have to show that he was in Stellenbosch on the afternoon of the crime. You do not have to produce the weapon. You do not have to produce any forensic link between him and the crime scene. All you would have to do is show that he left work sometime between 11:00 and 18:00 on 16 March 2005.

In a court of law, this wouldn't be enough to convict him of murder. But I'm not a judge, so I'm prepared to say that if it turned out that Fred was lying about his presence at work from the very beginning, then that would be so devastating to his credibility (and, let us face it, to mine), that I would be prepared to think him a murderer.

Most people, I think, would concede that showing that Fred left the office is not a particularly demanding standard to set. But, as the numerous failed efforts of the police demonstrate, it is not completely straightforward either. Nor would it be enough to show that Fred *could* have left the office or even that Shahana Toefy *did* leave the office. You would have to show that he really did leave it. And the evidence that you produced would have to be compelling and credible and objective and verifiable. Still, if such evidence were produced (and it has never been produced), I would be prepared to rewrite this book as an account of how a well-meaning writer was duped by a vicious psychopath and his well-paid lawyers.

Good luck.

*   *   *

Obviously, I don't think I've been duped. And, in seeking to avoid that embarrassment, my most important source material has been the transcripts of Fred's trial and the many sworn statements which were entered into the record. While I have sought to use these scrupulously, two important features of the transcript are worth pointing out.

The first is that, like any verbatim record of what people say, trial transcripts are filled with hesitations and grammatical mistakes and numerous other infelicities. This is inevitable because, as anyone who has ever read verbatim notes will know, few people's speech conforms with the standard rules of the language. In reproducing the questions asked and answers given, I have taken the liberty of tidying this up. This was not something I originally intended to do, but reading *Standard Operating Procedure: A war story*, an immensely interesting account of interviews conducted with the US soldiers who'd been stationed at Abu Ghraib prison at the time that the Iraqi prisoners were mistreated, I encountered this arresting thought: that writers will automatically extend to themselves the privilege of editing their own words to make them as sensible and coherent as possible, and should, therefore, not subject their interviewees to the cruelties of exact transcription. That book, by the way, is by Philip Gourevitch and Errol Morris, and was published by Picador in 2008. Like Gourevitch and Morris, in tidying up the transcripts of the trial I have sought to remain faithful to the unmistakable meaning of the speaker, whether it is a lawyer or a prosecutor, a witness or a judge.

Seeking to remain faithful to the unmistakable intention of the speaker was not always easy, however, and was made more complex by the second important feature of the transcripts: they were largely in Afrikaans, a language that is not my first and which, like other languages, sometimes offers its interpreters a variety of words with which to translate a given phrase. One example of this that nearly affected the outcome of the trial is that the word '*getuienis*' means both 'evidence' and 'testimony', a fact that created some difficulties in translating those sections of the trial in which the judge questioned whether Fred's alibi had been properly entered into evidence. Was he saying that there was no evidence of an alibi? Or was he saying that there was no testimony about Fred's alibi? The distinction seemed to be the essence of the dispute, and I couldn't help thinking that matters might have been more easily resolved if the disputants had chosen to debate the issue in English. They didn't, making more complicated the difficulties of rendering the opposing sides of this debate.

There were other problems of this sort, and I have no doubt that others might have chosen different words in the same circumstances. All I can say is that I have tried always to convey what I took to be the intention of the speaker, using a literal translation except when doing so might mislead a reader. An example of this is the manner in which Inge signed off the short, undated letter to Fred: '*Sterkte met jou dag en week.*' Translated literally, that means, 'Strength with your day and week', but the tone of that phrase in English is more formal than the more standard meaning of the Afrikaans, which is closer to 'Good luck for your day and week'. By the same token, however, 'good luck' seemed a too-distant rendering of what Inge was probably intending to say, something one might say to an acquaintance rather than to one's boyfriend. Hence my final choice – 'All the best for your day and week.'

Did I get this right? There's literally no way to know.

If the transcript is the principal source for the book, there were a great many other books and articles which I read and which influenced my thinking. In the interests of brevity, and with only a few exceptions, I will cite only those that I quoted directly or indirectly.

On page 44, the account of the incident in which Hendrik Biebouw first used the term 'Afrikaner' comes from Hermann Giliomee's book on the 'coloured' community of Stellenbosch, *Nog Altyd Hier Gewees: Die storie van 'n Stellenbosse gemeenskap*. It was published by Tafelberg in 2007.

On page 49, the quote about how before God there is neither Jew nor Greek, slave nor free man, is from Lamin Sanneh, a Gambian mission theorist, and is quoted in 'Christianity in South African history' by Richard Elphick. The essay is the introduction to a collection of essays edited by Elphick and Rodney Davenport called *Christianity in South Africa: A political, social and cultural history*, which was published in 1997 by David Philip.

In an act of gratuitous self-plagiarism, some of the paragraphs in the opening section of Chapter seven come from an essay of mine that will be published in a collection being edited by Catherine Jenkins and Max du Plessis entitled, *Law, Nation-building and Transformation*.

On page 107, the quotes from Janet Malcolm are from her book *The Crime of Sheila McGough*, published by Vintage Books in 1999. The American judge quoted on page 123 was quoted first by VS Naipaul in *A Turn in the South*, published by Picador in 1989.

The discussion of the weaknesses of the scientific case for fingerprint identification on page 129 and onwards draws on Simon Cole's *Suspect identities: A history of fingerprinting and criminal identification*, published in 2001 by Harvard University Press. The most authoritative account of the travails of Brandon Mayfield, referred to on pages 130–131, comes from *A Review of the FBI's Handling of the Brandon Mayfield Case*, published in 2006 by the Inspector-General of the US Department of Justice. The case of Herman Wiggins is described by Pat Wertheim in an article, 'Detection of forged and fabricated latent prints: Historical review and ethical implications of the falsification of latent fingerprint evidence', published in the *Journal of Forensic Identification* in 1994.

Dominick Dunne's essays, from which I drew the points made on page 230 are collected in *Justice: Crimes, Trials and Punishments*, published by Time Warner Paperbacks in 2001.

Repeated reference was also made to William Bodziak's textbook, including on page 239, where it is the source of the comment that dust-lifting was invented by police officers in Japan in the 1960s. The full title of his work is *Footwear Impression Evidence: Detection, recovery and examination* (second edition), and it was published by CRC Press in 2000. Jeffery Toobin's account of the OJ Simpson trial, referred to on pages 278–79, is *The Run of His Life: The People v OJ Simpson*, published by Random House in 1996.

On page 283 reference is made to Joel Joffe's account of the Rivonia Trial. It was published in 2007 by Oneworld Publications and is called *The State v Nelson Mandela: The trial that changed South Africa.*

The studies comparing the decisions of judges and juries, referred to on pages 366–67 include 'Judge–jury agreement in criminal cases: A partial replication of Kalven & Zeisel's *The American Jury*'. It was written by Theodore Eisenberg, Paula L Hannaford-Agor, Valerie P Hans, Nicole L Mott, G Thomas Munsterman, Stewart J Schwab and Martin T Wells, and published by the Cornell Law School. A similar study, by Bruce Spencer, is entitled 'On measuring the balance between wrongful convictions and wrongful acquittals in criminal trials', and was presented to a conference at New York University's School of Law in 2007.

On page 382, the quote from Joan Didion is from the first page of *Salvador*, published by Granta in 2006, while Imre Kertész's *Detective Story*, from which I quote on page 410, was published in 2009 by Vintage Books.

The two master's theses referred to on page 429 are by J Le Roux and A van der Spuy. Both were written in 2009 and are available in the library of the University of Stellenbosch.

Finally, there are three works that played a more significant role in shaping this book than many of the others I read. Two of them helped shape my understanding of Afrikanerdom and its history. The first is Hermann Giliomee's magisterial *The Afrikaners: Biography of a people*, published by Tafelberg in 2003. The second is an older book by T Dunbar Moodie, *The Rise of Afrikanerdom: Power, apartheid and the Afrikaner civil religion*, published by the University of California Press in 1975. The quotes on pages 193 and 194 were taken from these books.

Finally, I read many books and articles on investigative techniques and forensic science (enough, I suspect, to persuade a forensic analyst who might examine my computer's hard drive that I was seeking out information on how to commit the perfect crime), but the most useful and influential was a 2007 collection, edited by Newburn, Williamson and Wright, called *Handbook of Criminal Investigation* and published by Willan Publishing.

The credit for the pictures is as follows. The pictures on plates 1, 3, 4, 5, 13 and 14 were taken by various members of the SAPS in the course of their duties. Plates 2 and 15 are photos taken by Arie Zeelenberg. The remaining photos were all taken by William Bodziak and Mike Grimm. All of the images were entered into the record of the trial at some point.

ACKNOWLEDGEMENTS

Acknowledgement sections are never easy. In the case of this book, however, my first and most difficult acknowledgement must go to the Lotzes, who, for entirely understandable reasons, preferred not to make themselves available for on-the-record interviews. Merely by picking through the trial and bringing it, once again, to public attention, my work will likely cause them pain. It is something that distresses me and which I wish could be avoided.

At first glance it seems as understandable that the Van der Vyvers, Fred in particular, should have made themselves available to me as it was for the Lotzes to refuse to do so. In reality, their choice was filled with risk. This was a painful time for them, and, as an immensely proud family, opening themselves to a stranger would not have been easy. That they would do this while accepting unconditionally my decision not to show them drafts of the manuscript, reflected more their confidence in their case than their confidence in me. It was, nevertheless, flattering.

If the Van der Vyvers' decision to trust me was important, equally important was the not unrelated decision of Fred's lawyers to do the same. Dup de Bruyn and Terry Price were indefatigable in defence of their client, consistently honourable and frequently amusing.

There are others to whom I owe debts of gratitude. There is Fiona, who made her spare bedroom available to me and who humoured me by listening to daily updates from the courtroom.

There are also the many people who read portions of the developing text, and who offered their comments and advice. Some were the members of a writing group based at Wits University who offered comments on extracts from an earlier draft: Ashlee, Chris, Craig, Elsie, Gerrit, Gillian, Graeme, Jill, Jo-Anne, Karen, Karl, Kay, Kevin, Leon, Michelle, Pat, Pier, Rohan and Vuyo (I hope that's everyone!). Ivan Vladislavić also provided me with extensive comments on that draft, comments that helped persuade me to rethink the whole thing (thanks, Ivan!). There were others who also read and criticised: Debra was characteristically frank, as was Jo. My father was kinder, but he is my father. The lovely Jackie May didn't read that draft, but criticised it nonetheless. By way of contrast, Michael Titlestad has been unfailingly supportive and helpful throughout the project.

Finally, my editor, Alfred LeMaitre, has proved to be watchful and smart, hard-working and happy to discuss the proper grammar of the gerund. Valda Strauss who proofread the final manuscript has been just as careful and rigorous, and I thank her too.

*   *   *

The costs of my research were partly covered by a grant made by the Taco Kuiper Fund for Investigative Journalism based at the University of the Witwatersrand, whose contribution is greatly appreciated.

I also benefited from a month-long residency at the Stellenbosch Institute for Advanced Study. I owe its leadership – Hendrik Geyer, Paul Cilliers and Jannie Hofmeyr – a debt of thanks for the space to work, the stimulating conversation and the great lunches.